ENGL
551

D0796765

Literary Pluralities

Literary Pluralities

EDITED BY CHRISTL VERDUYN

broadview press / *Journal of Canadian Studies*

Copyright © 1998 Broadview Press Ltd., and
Journal of Canadian Studies/Revue d'études canadiennes

All rights reserved. The use of any part of this publication reproduced, transmitted
in any form or by any means, electronic, mechanical, photocopying, recording, or
otherwise, or stored in a retrieval system, without prior written consent of the publisher –
or in the case of photocopying, a licence from CANCOPY (Canadian Copyright Licensing
Agency) 6 Adelaide Street East, Suite 900, Toronto, Ontario M5C 1H6 – is an
infringement of the copyright law.

Canadian Cataloguing in Publication Data

Main entry under title:
Literary pluralities

Includes bibliographical references
ISBN 1-55111-203-5

1. Literature and society – Canada. 2. Canadian literature – History
and criticism. I. Verduyn, Christl, 1953-   .

PS8027.L57 1998 C810.9 C98-933032-X
PR9185.2L57 1998

Broadview Press Ltd., is an independent, international publishing house,
incorporated in 1985.

North America:
Post Office Box 1243, Peterborough, Ontario, Canada K9J 7H5
3576 California Road, Orchard Park, NY 14127
Tel: (705) 743-8990; Fax: (705) 743-8353; e-mail:
75322.44@compuserve.com

United Kingdom:
Turpin Distribution Services Ltd., Blackhorse Rd., Letchworth,
Hertfordshire SG6 1HN
Tel: (1462) 672555; Fax: (1462) 480947; e-mail: turpin@rsc.org

Australia:
St. Clair Press, P.O. Box 287, Rozelle, NSW 2039
Tel: (02) 818-1942; Fax: (02) 418-1923

www.broadviewpress.com

Broadview Press gratefully acknowledges the financial support of the Book Publishing
Industry Development Program, Ministry of Canadian Heritage, Government of Canada.

PRINTED IN CANADA

Acknowledgements

The creation of a book involves the diverse talents and energies of a myriad of individuals other than those whose names appear on the title page. This is especially the case with respect to this volume, which comprises the work of 22 authors. In the first instance, then, I would like to express my thanks to the contributors to this collection. They gave generously to the enterprise, graciously enduring the imposition of deadlines and various other publication requirements. Individually and collectively, they were a pleasure to work with and I gained much from their insights and collaboration. Their work and the inspiration it generates form the foundation of this volume.

This book is a joint publication of two esteemed Canadian institutions, the *Journal of Canadian Studies* and Broadview Press. I would like to thank Don LePan for his ongoing commitment to publishing critical studies in the humanities, as well as for his personal support of the project. The staff at Broadview Press was most helpful and co-operative in bringing the text to publication.

I am especially grateful to Kerry Cannon, Managing Editor *extraordinaire* of the *Journal of Canadian Studies*. This book could not have been completed without her superb technical and editorial expertise. Her tireless efforts were matched by her good humour, and it was a joy to work with her. Joëlle Favreau and Joanne Ward rounded out an exceptional production ensemble.

The idea for this collection grew out of research projects on Canadian and Quebec writing supported by the Social Sciences and Humanities Research Council and Canadian Heritage – Multiculturalism, whose funding I am pleased to acknowledge.

Finally, I would like to thank my family for ensuring pluralities in my life throughout this and other scholarly projects.

Table of Contents

CHRISTL VERDUYN

Introduction

The essays in this volume offer an overview of significant developments and debates in Canadian and Québécois literary and cultural criticism at the end of the 1990s.[1]

During the last decade of the century, intellectuals and artists have brought increasing critical attention to bear on the importance of race and ethnicity in discussions about the country and its cultural expressions. The essays assembled here explore a nexus of key related issues, including the dynamics between race, ethnicity, class, gender, and generation; Canadian multiculturalism, and its meaning within Native and Quebec communities; the politics of language; the new field of life writing; and the international dimensions of the deliberations. The essays vary in argument, conclusions, and style, from the full-length academic study to the shorter reflection piece. Together they present a valuable picture of Canadian and Québécois cultural and literary criticism at century's end. The purpose of this introductory essay is to provide a synopsis of the insights and challenges presented by the authors who have contributed to the volume, against a backdrop of some of the themes and issues prominent in the developing literature.

In the 1970s and 1980s, critical attention focussed on the evolving categories of class and gender. This focus generated extensive conceptual reflection, debate, and writing about the appropriate use of such categories. This powerful, well-articulated, and now familiar project has been highly productive and helpful in drawing attention to other, equally vital categories of analysis.

In the 1990s, race and ethnicity emerged from the previous project as critical criteria in the study of Canadian and Québécois society. The shift in focus resulted from a combination of factors, as outlined in essays by Enoch Padolsky ("Ethnicity and Race: Canadian Minority Writing at a Crossroads"), Lucie Lequin ("Paroles transgressives et métissage culturel au féminin"), and Tamara Palmer Seiler ("Multi-Vocality and National Literature: Towards a Post-Colonial and Multicultural Aesthetic"). Demographic change, the impact of postmodern and post-colonial theory, an ongoing critique of Canada's multiculturalism policy, public debate about representation and cultural appropriation, and increased media attention to issues of race relations, all contributed to a developing discourse of race and ethnicity. On the eve of the decade, Vision 21 – a multi-disciplinary group against racism, sexism and economic disparity in the arts in Ontario – leafletted a PEN International meeting held in Toronto with a view to educating the public about issues of representation. A brief exchange between June Callwood and Nourbese Philip fuelled public commentary for months in newspaper and magazine opinion columns.[2] Public controversy continued with the 1994 "Writing Thru Race" conference with regards to the organizers' decision to limit daytime discussions and events to First Nations writers and writers of colour. In the same year, Neil Bissoondath's equally controversial book *Selling Illusions: The Cult of Multiculturalism in Canada* was published and was widely discussed on television and radio as well as in newspapers and magazines.

By the mid 1990s, it seemed possible to talk about a new Canadian consciousness of race and ethnicity, or at least a heightened awareness of racism within some segments of Canadian society and within some critical currents where previously such awareness was not particularly notable. "As old as Canadian history," Enoch Padolsky observes in his essay, "racism in Canada ha[d] now moved from being a 'quiet' and ignored topic[3] (except of course for Canadian minorities who have never had the luxury of ignoring it), to a mainstream issue."

Once serious investigation developed on questions of race and racism within Canada and Canadian history, it was necessary to reflect on and critique the terminology employed in pursuing these questions. Like class and gender, race and ethnicity are categories that require interrogation and analysis. This task has been a crucial component of recent cultural and literary criticism, and is a central feature of the essays in this collection. In his "Essai de théorisation d'un problème ancien aux contours nouveaux," Jean Jonassaint critically reviews various terms that have come into circulation through the discussions. Essays by Aritha van Herk ("The Ethnic Gasp / the Disenchanted Eye Unstoried"), Nadine Ltaif ("Ecrire pour vivre l'échange entre les langues") and Kateri Akiwenzie-Damm ("We Belong to This Land: A View of 'Cultural Difference'") illustrate the insufficiencies of labels and terminology by touching on some of the complexities and contradictions that exist within the categories they identify.

Jonassaint's analysis has particular relevance for the designation "racial and ethnic minority writing," the body of work addressed by the majority of essays in this volume. Is this a useful distinction or construct to be used within Canadian and Québécois literatures? It appeared to be a viable one in 1990, when Linda Hutcheon and Marion Richmond's *Other Solitudes: Canadian Multicultural Fictions* struck a timely chord with readers. Editors Hutcheon and Richmond present fiction excerpts by, and interviews with, writers described as "immigrants or the children of immigrants" (Preface). *Other Solitudes* was the first in a series of books and studies on racial and ethnic minority writing that appeared throughout the 1990s.[4] While differing in the material that they select, these publications share the objective of presenting writing by Canadians and Québécois of racial and ethnic minority identifications. As the 1990s draw to a close, the question arises as to whether this delineation retains its earlier resonance. The essays that follow offer varying answers.

In addition to scrutinizing terminology, writers and researchers have also been obliged to question central social and political constructs, such as Canadian multiculturalism. Four essays in this volume pay particular attention to this important subject. Janice Kulyk Keefer and Myrna Kostash revisit the original rationale and ideals of Canadian multicultural policy, seeking to valorize what might be a common purpose today when "coca-colonization" poses ever greater threats of dominance. Eva Karpinski and Himani Bannerji turn a critical eye to some of the outcomes and products of multiculturalism.

In "Imagination, Representation, and Culture," Myrna Kostash outlines what she calls a "politics of resemblance." This is a concept she has constructed from her experiences both as a writer and as chair of The Writers' Union of Canada at the time of the "Writing Thru Race" conference. Kostash recalls multiculturalism's roots as a positive public policy against the concept of an "official culture." It offered a vision and a possibility of socio-economic justice for minorities who had consistently been under-represented in the governing elites. Notwithstanding its birth pains and problematics, Kostash suggests that from multiculturalism a possible commonality may be found that is beyond "the usual contradictions of majority and minority, centre and margin, self and other, ethnic and universal." She perceives positive potential stemming from a new cultural "politics of resemblance."

Janice Kulyk Keefer envisions similar achievements for multiculturalism, and expresses them via the image of a bridge in her essay "'The Sacredness of Bridges': Writing Immigrant Experience." This is not, she insists, "to call upon conventional pieties or duplicitous nostrums urging us all to just get along together, to 'just do it' as the Nike ad urges." Rather, she explains, "we live in a world where the bridges we desperately need to enable us to connect, in spite of profound differences, are under threat of demolition or else disintegration through neglect, deliberate or inadvertent." Keefer conceives of a "continuum of immigrant experience." This continuum recognizes the "world of difference between [specific] experiences," but at the same time proposes that some measure of common experience can balance specific instances of experience as mitigated by realities of race, class, gender, and generation.

Keefer's focus is on a possible commonality – as opposed to universality – of experience. Her "bridge" is made up of "an amalgam of paper and ink, canvas and pigments, celluloid, the wood and metal of sculpture and musical instruments, the boom and whisper of the human voice and body." Viewed in this light, multiculturalism "keeps struggling to open doors and borders, to create possibilities of change and exchange." In her work, Nadine Ltaif envisions a similar bridge of exchange. "Je cherche … à établir des ponts, des dialogues entre les peuples et les cultures," the poet writes. "Je suis pour l'échange, le partage, pour sortir de l'isolement des deux communautés."

But multiculturalism in Canada is by no means accepted as a benign notion or as a "gift" by all. In "Multicultural 'Gift(s)': Immigrant Women's Life Writing and the Politics of Anthologizing Difference," Eva Karpinski conducts a critique of multiculturalism by examining some of the publications that have appeared under its auspices, in particular collections of life writing produced by immigrant women. Karpinski's focus is strategic, as it allows her to locate and scrutinize the intersections of ethnicity, race, gender, and class. She maintains that these primary categories have all too often been ignored in the public discourse surrounding multiculturalism. In the process, she suggests, multiculturalism comprises strategies of containment and diffuses divisive issues.

Karpinski's critical framework may be extended from discussions of literary anthologies to collections of critical essays such as this. The process of constructing multicultural content can, as Karpinski warns, generate a form of containment. The challenge is to assemble material that is guided by the twofold awareness of the multiple forms of oppression, and the many levels on which it may be experienced simultaneously.

Himani Bannerji has long insisted on the kind of multilayered, multi-faceted analysis and presentation of Canadian experience and cultural expression that Karpinski calls for. "Thinking in terms of culture alone, in terms of a single community, a single issue, or a single oppression will not do," Bannerji asserts in "On the Dark Side of the Nation: Politics of Multiculturalism and the State of 'Canada.'" The issue at stake is more than cultural. "It is about power – this power can only come through the actual possession of a geographical territory and the economy of a nation-state." Bannerji calls for "creating counter-hegemonic interpretive and organizational frameworks that reach down into the real histories and relations of our social life." In this, writing – particularly ethnic and racial minority writing – presents enormous rich potential, as Enoch Padolsky explains in his contribution to the volume:

> Canadian minority writing ... [offers] a primary cultural site for the discussion of plural, cross-boundary and intersecting concerns. Literature does not of course directly determine social outcomes, but its experiential base does provide it with considerable analytic power. As such, Canadian minority writing may very well provide some insights into the ways and means by which "plural" conceptions can function in the area of race and ethnicity.

Joseph Pivato has emphasized the experiential dimension of minority writing. "Ethnic minority works are grounded in the real experience of the writer, his or her family and cultural background," he states.[5] In this, Pivato sees the valorization, not a diminishment or reduction of the work to conventional realism over more freely imaginative work.[6] Reading "minority" writing leads Pivato to question quintessential literary axioms. For example, he challenges the notion that works of literature are primarily – or preferably – the products of other works of literature. Reading "minority" writing suggests that writing may be a reflection of life experience.[7] In his essay for this volume, "Representation of Ethnicity as Problem: Essence or Construction," Pivato makes the case for literary realism. Its conventions, he argues, lend themselves to the storytelling of many minority groups.

Arun Mukherjee sees merit in writing that reflects life experience as well. In 1993, she edited *Sharing Our Experiences*, a collection of letters about "real pains and pleasures, by women who were writing out of their day-to-day experiences of surviving in a racist, sexist, classist, and heterosexist world." In her introduction to the collection, Mukherjee writes of the profound effect the letters had on her. "As a person who makes her living by teaching literature to university students," she states, "I felt that the letters' 'aura' of authenticity was not just textual effect." Well aware that the letters are not devoid of literary device, Mukherjee emphasizes that "they are about the writer's own life" and they have led her as a reader and a critic to question received understandings of "capital L" literature.

In her contribution to this volume, Mukherjee goes even further and questions established critical method. She introduces the possibility of a new hermeneutics, based on the premise that knowledge to decode (language in) texts is readily available in the social environments that readers inhabit. This knowledge may be acquired through communication with friends, neighbours, and colleagues. "Such a hermeneutic," Mukherjee proposes, "is far more democratic than the expert-dominated literary criticism of the past." Mukherjee's point of departure is language – in particular "foreign" words in the text. A single one can make all the difference, as Mukherjee demonstrates through examples taken from her experience teaching "minority" writing.

Language also locates the debate surrounding multiculturalism at the level of words themselves. This introduces new questions and concerns into the discussion. The very term "multiculturalism" has limited linguistic currency in Quebec. The phrase *communautés culturelles* (in translation "cultural communities") is preferred to the word multiculturalism, which some associate with the federal government and its policies. At the same time, expressions commonly used in Quebec do not fare so well in English Canada. *Ecriture migrante* and *métissage culturel* are two examples. Their literal translations – migrant writing and cultural interbreeding or cross-breeding – do not evoke the same positive notions of movement and change ascribed to the French phrasing. Essays by Lucie Lequin and Maïr Verthuy demonstrate the positive potential of migrancy and *métissage*. At the same time, Lequin and Verthuy acknowledge the real social and practical difficulties endured by "minority" characters in the Quebec literary works they examine. In "Pan Bouyoucas: le principe des vases communicants ou de la nécessité de 'sortir de l'ethnicité,'" Verthuy investigates the work of Pan Bouyoucas, a Québécois writer born of Greek parents in Lebanon. She comments that "le portrait que nous brosse Bouyoucas de la vie immigrante à Montréal, pour ne pas être entièrement catastrophique, n'est pas particulièrement positif. Les deux solitudes paraissent insurmontables; séparées par une espèce de *no man's land*."

This assessment corroborates my own findings, outlined in "Perspectives critiques dans des productions littéraires migrantes au féminin, au Québec et au Canada." In many cases, language itself is the critical part of the problem. In other instances, as George Elliott Clarke shows in "Liberalism and Its Discontents: Reading Black and White in Contemporary Québécois Texts," the tensions are ideologically rooted. Clarke explores how two subjectivities – Black and Québécois – have been linked by Québécois writers, as in Michèle Lalonde's "Speak White" (1968) and Pierre Vallière's *White Niggers of America* (1971). By uncoupling the subjectivities, Clarke not only exposes a longstanding rivalry between liberal and nationalist ideologies in Quebec, but also "disturbingly perverse racial constructions" in some of its literature.

Nation and Native Languages
Language issues in Canada are not limited to the French-English question. Critical work in the 1990s has validated the importance of nation language in the cultural and literary expression of Canada. Nation language is often referred to as Caribbean dialect, vernacular or demotic.[8] It has been used by writers such as Austin Clarke, Dionne Brand, and Nourbese Philip.[9] But only recently have major publishers taken the "leap" to publish works written at length in nation language. In this regard, the publication of Dionne Brand's first novel *Somewhere Else Not Here* by Knopf in 1996 marked a turning point.

The breakthrough of nation language underscores the widespread absence of mainstream attention to Native language expression in the not-so-distant past. The oral tradition of Native culture is no excuse for this oversight, particularly as critical attention to race and ethnicity has accrued. Jean Jonassaint drives this point home when he writes in his essay that "le nouveau discours (néo-colonialiste) canadien (tant anglophone que francophone) est encore incapable de penser le fait amérindien, occultant systématiquement (avec naïveté ou cynisme) le fait colonial canadien (l'actuelle colonisation interne dont l'expression la plus manifeste est le concept des deux peuples fondateurs, et son corollaire 'the two solitudes')."[10] Canadian preoccupation with the "two solitudes" has had the effect of marginalizing the importance of First Nations of Canada. In particular, Native cultural production has frequently been ignored, misunderstood or dismissed as simplistic. In "We Belong to This Land," Kateri Akiwenzie-Damm points out that the literary establishment has often categorized traditional and sacred Native stories as "children's literature." She concurs with Paula Gunn Allen's characterization of this phenomenon as "aesthetic colonization." This has been the fate of writers like Pauline Johnson, Armand Ruffo observes in his essay "Out of the Silence." Ruffo introduces readers to the work of the Mohawk poet Dawendine (Bernice Loft Winslow) who was profoundly influenced by Pauline Johnson. Dawendine's work is evidence that Native culture continued to sustain itself through traumas such as the residential school period and the disinterest of the critical establishment. Indeed, in theatre arts, Native production has flourished. One of its foremost practitioners, Drew Hayden Taylor, recounts the remarkable growth and successes of Native theatre in recent years. As Taylor explains in "Alive and Well: Native Theatre in Canada," Native storytelling tradition is a key to the distinctive nature and vigour of Native theatre.

International Backdrops

As outlined above, there have been significant developments in Canadian and Québécois cultural and literary discourse related to the work of writers of racial and ethnic minority identifications. This growth has occurred in concert with international and comparative discussions. In the introduction to his 1991 collection *Contrasts: Comparative Essays on Italian-Canadian Writing,* Joseph Pivato signalled the "internationalist" nature of ethnic writing, and suggested that "future scholarship should look to ethnic writing as a way of taking Canadian writing into a truly international context of comparative study and exchange" (29-30). Canadian ethnic studies, Enoch Padolsky has noted, have "continually engaged these international discussions in ways that have Canadianized theoretical issues and integrated and adapted them within extensive studies of Canadian society."[11] Padolsky points out that Canadian ethnic studies "had its links to international discussions of the so-called 'ethnic revival' and to international theories of ethnicity that changed and developed over time."[12] At the same time Padolsky, Pivato, and other scholars in the field have cautioned against merely importing theory.[13] Padolsky explains:

> Post-colonial theorists wishing to apply their international comparative models to Canadian writing need to examine not just how the theory fits the writing, but also how the "new" contexts of writing challenge the validity of the theory itself. Theoretical concepts from elsewhere which do not adequately engage non-mainstream Canadian reality will encounter fundamental problems in claiming relevance to the contexts Canadian "pluri-ethnicity."[14]

Smaro Kamboureli's essay "Staging Cultural Criticism" is an excellent illustration of Canadian critics' fluency with creative and critical developments on the international scene. Kamboureli focusses on two books, Michael Ignatieff's *Blood and Belonging* (1993) and Myrna Kostash's *Bloodlines* (1993). Both explore the same European territory – the Ukraine – but in strikingly different ways. Kamboureli is interested in the authors' differing cultural criticism and how their respective narratives say as much about the complexity of otherness as they do about the narrators' methodological practices.

Canadian and Québécois critical discourse is not only conversant with international theoretical work, it is also making original contributions to the discussions. Sneja Gunew's essay "Operatic Karaoke and the Pitfalls of Identity Politics" rises to the challenge set by Peter Stummer and Christopher Balme, the editors of *Fusion of Cultures?* (1996). In their introduction, Stummer and Balme exhort critics to "transgress the received wisdom of recently established post-colonial orthodoxy with its emphasis on difference and alterity, on subversion and counter-discourse" (1). This would allow analysts to reconsider the possibilities of syncretism, cross-fertilization, creolization, and comparative studies (*Ibid.*). Gunew enjoins readers to step outside the limits of "traditional" narratives of race, grounded in the visible and the corporeal, to explore possible alternative lines of analysis. These strategic possibilities include voice and listening, and Gunew offers the intriguing example of opera.[15]

In opera, what is seen (a corpulent soprano) is not what is imagined (the nubile heroine or hero). The disjunction between the visible, the audible, and the imagined reality, or the reality of the imagination, is further illustrated by the off-beat examples of karaoke, and ventriloquism. In all cases, voice exceeds the confines of the body and, in confounding expectations of identity, creates new possibilities of representation. Gunew proposes that the work of the writer Evelyn Lau functions in ways similar to opera, karaoke and ventriloquism, and suggests that Lau's work should be read *listening for textual voice*. Voice crosses the boundaries of the visible and raced authorial body, and in so doing exceeds "the claustrophobic paradigms of identity politics."

Hiromi Goto derives similar insights from another popular phenomenon, the fascination with extraterrestrial aliens. The familiar figure of E.T. is an example *par excellence*. In "Alien Texts, Alien Seductions: The Context of Colour Full Writing," Goto asks unsettling questions about society's simultaneous "repulsion/attraction" response to the unknown or foreign "other." She draws disconcerting parallels between the way extraterrestrial aliens are constructed in modern societies, and the way in which Canadian society views "foreigners." By inverting the stereotypical image of the extraterrestrial, Goto comments critically on stereotypes projected onto all those who arrive from outside the territory.

These examples – opera, karaoke, extraterrestrials – indicate another significant development in recent critical analysis and theory: the search for new models and concepts. The essays in this collection offer some of the most interesting suggestions and compelling writing and thinking about Canadian and Québécois literary and cultural discourse during the last decade of the century. In highlighting work by researchers and writers in the 1990s, I am not seeking to heighten the millennium fever that threatens to engulf us. Work in the field of "minority writing" extends well back before the 1990s, as Padolsky and Lequin show, and will continue towards and beyond the year 2000. In the volume's final essay, "Taming our Tomorrows," Nourbese Philip articulates the need to think carefully about "our tomorrows." As records of significant accomplishments in Canadian and Québécois cultural and literary criticism during the 1990s, the essays presented here constitute a firm foundation on which to build tomorrow's critical frameworks.

NOTES

1. Of the 22 essays, 11 date from the first half of the decade and were read at a gathering of writers and critics at its mid-point. I organized the August 1995 Windy Pine Colloquium as an opportunity for sustained, in-depth exchange among some of the contributors to a field that might broadly be described as racial and ethnic minority writing in Canada and Quebec. Conference proceedings were published in the *Journal of Canadian Studies / Revue d'études canadiennes* 31.3 (Fall 1996).

2. See Adele Freedman, "White Woman's Burden," *Saturday Night* 108.3 (April 1993): 40-44, for one account of this event. It was also rehearsed in the Writers' Union newsletter, available to Union members. See also "PEN Rebuts Charges of Racism: Vision 21'made its point at our expense,' says Callwood," *Globe and Mail* [Metro Edition] 29 December 1989: C8 and "Is the Canadian PEN Centre Racist?" [Letters to the Editor], *Books In Canada* 19.3 (April 1990): 7-10.

3. "It wasn't that we had never talked about [issues of racism]," Myrna Kostash recalls in her essay for this volume, "it's that we had subsumed them within the familiar categories of 'otherness,' 'assimilation,' 'community,' and of course 'ethnicity.'"

4. See articles in this volume, as well as the bibliography for further suggestions. These publications included books as well as theme issues of scholarly journals. Among the latter, Diana Brydon, guest ed., "Testing the Limits: Postcolonial Theories on Canadian Literature," *Essays on Canadian Writing* 56 (Fall 1995); Winfried Siemerling, guest ed., "Writing Ethnicity," *Essays on Canadian Writing* 57 (Winter 1995); "Postcolonial Identities," *Canadian Literature* 149 (Summer 1996); "Idols of Otherness: The Rhetoric and Reality of Multiculturalism," *Mosaic* 29.3 (September 1996); and Joseph Pivato, guest ed., "Literary Theory and Ethnic Minority Writing," *Canadian Ethnic Studies* XXVIII.3 (1996). For books, see: J.W. Berry and J.A. Laponce eds., *Ethnicity and Culture in Canada: The Research Landscape* (Toronto: University of Toronto Press, 1994); Carol Camper ed., *Miscegenation Blues: Voices of Mixed Race Women* (Toronto: Sister Vision, 1994); Arun Mukherjee, *Oppositional Aesthetics: Readings from a Hyphenated Space* (Toronto: TSAR, 1994); Himani Bannerji, *Thinking Through: Essays on Feminism, Marxism, and Anti-Racism* (Toronto: Women's Press, 1995); Makeda Silvera ed., *The Other Woman: Women of Colour in Contemporary Canadian Literature* (Toronto: Sister Vision, 1995); Eva Karpinski ed., *Pens of Many Colours*, 2nd ed. (Toronto: Harcourt Brace Jovanovich, 1996); Lucie Lequin and Maïr Verthuy eds., *Multi-culture, multi-écriture : La voix migrante au féminin en France et au Canada* (Paris: L'Harmattan, 1996); Smaro Kamboureli ed., *Making a Difference: Canadian Multicultural Literature* (Toronto: Oxford University Press, 1996); Danielle Schaub, Janice Kulyk Keefer, Richard E. Sherwin eds., *Precarious Present / Promising Future? Ethnicity and Identities in Canadian Literature* (Jerusalem: The Magnes Press, 1996); Marino Tuzi, *The Power of Allegiances: Identity, Culture, and Representational Strategies* (Toronto: Guernica, 1997); Daisy L. Neijmann ed., *The Icelandic Voice in Canadian Letters* (Ottawa: Carleton University Press, 1997); Bénédicte Mauguière ed., *Cultural Identities in Canadian Literature* (New York: Peter Lang, 1998) among others.

5. "Shirt of the Happy Man: Theory and Politics of Ethnic Minority Writing," *Canadian Ethnic Studies* 28.3 (1996): 27-28.

6. *Ibid.* 33-34.

7. *Ibid.*

8. I share Teresa Zackodnik's preference for the expression nation language:

"Designations such as 'demotic,' 'dialect,' and 'vernacular' impart the notion that this is somehow not a language but a bastardization or degeneration of standard English" (Zackodnik 209). The important implication of the expression nation language is that it is a distinct language. For more on nation language see Brathwaite.

9. See Kaup for the use and significance of nation language in the work of these writers.

10. Himani Bannerji makes a similar point in her essay for this volume. "The Anglo-French rivalry ... needs to be read through the lens of colonialism. Canada, with its two solitudes and their survival anxieties and aggression against 'native others.'"

11. "'Olga in Wonderland': Canadian Ethnic Minority Writing and Post-Colonial Theory," *Canadian Ethnic Studies* 28.3 (1996): 19.

12. *Ibid.* 18-19.

13. For more on the relationship of theory and "minority" writing, see *Canadian Ethnic Studies* 28.3 1996. Guest edited by Joseph Pivato, this collection of essays originated as papers for an Association of Canadian and Quebec Literatures panel discussion on the subject of theory and minority writing at the 1994 Learned Societies' Conference in Calgary.

14. Ibid. 18.

15. Opera is mentioned in Lucie Lequin's essay as well. The art of the "va et vient entre la voix solo et les voix de choeurs, entre la singularité et collectivité" is introduced in her discussion of the writing of Monique Bosco, one of a handful of women writers whose work Lequin locates in a "mouvement de mutation encore trop actuel pour pouvoir bien le cerner."

ENOCH PADOLSKY

Ethnicity and Race: Canadian Minority Writing at a Crossroads

Canada is at a crossroads in the management of its racial and ethnic agenda (Elliott and Fleras 313).

* * *

People talk race this ethnic that. It's easy to be theoretical if the words are coming from a face that has little or no pigmentation (Goto 89-90).

If you are writing for your community, and by that I don't mean India, but people who are not white, people who, for instance, have suffered from racism and fascism, you would say things and present experiences that would not be universally acceptable in this society (Bannerji, "The Other Family" 150).

... and then there are the perennial warnings in the daily press about Canada losing its "English" and "French" character to masses of "immigrants." These terms are euphemisms for white and Black, light and dark (Brand, *Bread out of Stone* 161).

The terms of reference in the latter three of the above quotations – "pigmentation," "not white," "white and Black, light and dark" – signal the increasing racialization of the Canadian social and literary discourse over the last few years. Race has of course always to some extent been a factor in Canadian social discourse, but its emergence (or rather re-emergence) as a prominent factor is a fairly recent event. "Canadian writers who are not white," Dionne Brand notes, are in the process of becoming "the new wave of Canadian writing" ("Interview with Dagmar Novak" 277). As the number of writers "of colour" has increased, the issues of "colour" and "race" have, not surprisingly, also grown in salience. There have been high profile debates by Canadian literary figures on multiculturalism and appropriation, on representation in PEN Canada, and on the "Writing Thru Race" conference. At the same time, numerous books, journals, and magazines highlighting race and colour as organizing principles provide further evidence of this trend.

The reasons for this new racial awareness are complex and multi-origined. Contributing factors no doubt include changes to Canadian demography due to post-war non-European immigration; the discursive impact of the highly racialized society of the United States; the growing influence in Canadian intellectual circles of international post-colonial theory and "Third World" perspectives; and increasing media attention in Canada to race relations.

The new Canadian consciousness of race has brought along with it a growing attention to racism. As old as Canadian history, racism in Canada has now moved from being a "quiet" and ignored topic (except of course for Canadian minorities who have never had the luxury of ignoring it) to a mainstream issue. Recent years have seen increased attention to manifestations of racism in the justice system, the military (the Somalia "affair"), government, schools and universities, the housing and job markets, and the media. As racism has become a more overt public topic, public reaction to it has also become more evident. Older "red-necked" versions of racism by extremist groups – anti-immigrant, white supremacist, anti-Semitic – have by no means disappeared, yet to some extent have fallen out of favour and been displaced by underlying systemic versions, including the so-called "new racism" (see Elliott and Fleras 57 ff.). These continue to flourish, especially within the newly "coloured" constructions of race, and particularly with reference to Black Canadians and Aboriginal peoples. Furthermore, as in the United States, mainstream political parties and politicians are being elected who use the current economic climate to call into question a range of social policies and programmes of central interest to Canadian minorities (as well as to women and the poor): immigration policies, affirmative action programmes, land claim agreements with Aboriginal peoples, anti-discrimination and anti-racist policies, multiculturalism, and social welfare programmes of all sorts. Furthermore, in such a climate of uncertainty, attempts to combat racism, sexism, or other forms of injustice are often tarred with the brush of extremist "political correctness."

The question I would like to raise concerns where this racialization of the Canadian literary and social discourse is likely to go from here. In conceptualizing this problem, I would like for argument's sake to examine two alternative scenarios. Admittedly speculative and somewhat reductive, these alternatives of course do not exhaust all the possibilities. It may even be that in some ways they also overlap or occur simultaneously. Nevertheless, it is useful to distinguish these two alternatives for analytic purposes in that they represent two different directions in the conceptualization of race and ethnicity.

The first alternative, which some may associate with the United States, entails an historical and decisive parting of the ways *between* race and ethnicity. In this definitively "racial" scenario, the end result is an "irreducible and fundamental constitution of the ... social order in racial terms" (Sanjek, "Intermarriage" 109). If this is the scenario of the future in Canada, then a number of consequences might be anticipated. Canadian social groups who now consider ethnic or national allegiances to be as important as (or even more important than) racial allegiances would slowly gravitate to a reduced number of "race-oriented" categories. A similar re-orientation to "race" would likely occur around related categories (class, gender, sexual orientation, and so on) as racial issues begin to determine the negotiation of other facets of individual and group identities. "Race" in this outcome would thus become the determining factor of analysis and social interaction. Note that this scenario is equally likely to apply to both "white" and "non-white" groups. Individuals and groups not fitting these categories in comfortable ways (for example, those of mixed race or from source nations with different racialized systems) would nevertheless be under pressure to choose allegiances. Taken to its logical conclusion, this scenario could result in a final binary racial division between "white" and "non-white," but as Sanjek notes in the American context, and Kymlicka in the Canadian ("The Impact of Race" 17-18), a "Black"/"non-Black" outcome is also a possibility. In some respects, the Canadian discourse of race and ethnicity could be interpreted as already moving along the general lines of this "racial" scenario.

There is, however, a second scenario, that points Canadian society in a somewhat different direction. In this scenario, which I might label the "pluralist" outcome, the process of racialization that is currently underway would stabilize at some point and develop an equilibrium with a continuing salience of ethnicity within a Canadian framework of pluralism. Inter-racial and inter-ethnic relations, whether co-operative or contentious, would be carried on in complex combinations *across* intersecting boundaries of varying kinds (racial, ethnic, gender, class, etc.). Cultural and instrumental issues of identity, representation, and economic opportunity and of political, cultural, and social empowerment would all be framed within these wider terms of reference rather than strictly or primarily within racial terms. In this scenario, internal ethnic group allegiances (of whatever "racial" category) would continue to be strong. European ethnic minority groups, for example, would not, as in the United States, feel obliged or willing to trade "linguistic extinction" and "cultural loss" for "the privilege of white racial status" (Sanjek, "Enduring Inequalities" 9). Similarly, ethnic identities within other racializing categories (Asian, Black, etc.) would continue to be recognized and valued. This outcome would not necessarily be less problematic than the first scenario, but it would likely be more plural, since multiplicity itself would be the central ideological basis of inter-group and individual negotiations on various social, cultural, and political issues.

These two scenarios, even as crudely drawn as they are here, suggest different emphases and different outcomes for race and ethnic relations in Canadian society: one in which race provides the primary "irreducible and fundamental constitution" of the social order, and one in which a plurality of elements, including race and ethnicity, provide such a basis. As such, they can perhaps be described, as my title indicates, as a kind of historical crossroads at which Canadian society, and Canadian ethnic and racial minority groups in particular, now find themselves. If race relations in the United States can be used to indicate one direction a primarily "racial" scenario might take (and this is somewhat unfair since the highly racialized American scene also has its proponents of pluralism, its intersecting categories, its multiple identities, its "rainbow" coalitions, etc.) then the well-known racial difficulties in that country might also indicate some of the disadvantages that such a "racial" scenario might entail.

Given the increasing racialization of the Canadian discourse, then, it may be timely to look at alternatives to this "racial" scenario, and in particular, to examine more closely the second "pluralist" scenario I have outlined above. How viable is this alternative in the light of Canadian ethnic and racial relations historically and in the context of current Canadian constructions of race and ethnicity? In exploring this proposition, I would like to turn to Canadian minority writing as evidence, for if this writing is sometimes a site for the voicing of "narrow" ethnic and racial allegiances, it is also, I would contend, a primary cultural site for the discussion of plural, cross-boundary, and intersecting concerns. Literature does not of course directly determine social outcomes, but its experiential base does provide it with considerable analytic power. As such, Canadian minority writing may very well provide some insights into the ways and means by which "plural" conceptions can function in the area of race and ethnicity. Before moving to these writers, however, I would like to set out briefly some important differences between Canada and the United States on issues of race and ethnicity. These differences suggest one important Canadian context in which Canadian minority writing on these issues is situated.

Canadian-American Differences on "Race" and "Ethnicity"

If a "plural" scenario is still viable in Canada, the explanation may lie partly in a number of differences with the American situation. My opening quotation by Dionne Brand suggests a first difference. In it, she draws attention (albeit negatively) to the competing "bi-national" English-French duality of Canadian "white" dominance against which "immigrants" and racial categories contrast. This bi-national ethnic majority competition historically represents a seminal factor in the development of racial and ethnic relations in Canada. It is this duality which helped to thwart the attempted formation in the last century of a unitary (American-style) pan-Canadian national narrative based on Anglo-conformity. In the process, it has also functioned to retard the formation of a narrative based solely on race. The ongoing salience of ethnicity within majority groups has meant that non-British European immigrants (and even to some extent non-European immigrants) have found in English and French linguistic and cultural competition an alternative discourse to "the privilege of white racial status." In Bharati Mukherjee's story "The World According to Hsu," for example, the main character Ratna feels more at home in Montreal than in Toronto because "In Montreal she was merely 'English,' a grim joke on generations of British segregationists" (41).

Canada's English-French duality has also resulted in a number of ideological and institutional consequences not found in the United States. Among these are a (dual) *Official Languages Act*, official Canadian multiculturalism, and a growing openness to Aboriginal self-government. The first two policies can be traced to a 1960s realignment of French-English relations that opened the door (historically through the Royal Commission on Bilingualism and Biculturalism) to official recognition of other ethnic groups. In a parallel way, the recognition of one national "minority" (i.e., French Canadian) has lately functioned to provide a basis for recognizing other national "minorities" (i.e., Aboriginal "First Nations") within a national framework. As Kymlicka has recently argued, "Canada, with its policy of 'multiculturalism within a bilingual framework' and its recognition of Aboriginal rights to self-government, is one of the few countries which has officially recognized and endorsed both polyethnicity and multinationality" (*Multicultural Citizenship* 22). This is perhaps a somewhat optimistic assessment of Canadian "recognition and endorsement," but it is also to some extent true. Consequently, I would argue, the Canadian discourse of nationhood has tended to accord a higher official recognition to ethnic and racial identities, a higher profile to intersecting factors such as language, and a higher importance to group rights in general than in the United States.[1]

A second major difference between Canada and the United States can be found in the role of Blacks within the discourse of race. In the United States, as a host of commentators have noted, "race" has traditionally meant "Black and white," not only today but from the beginnings of its history as a nation. As Herbert Harris has noted, "racial definitions" in American colonial times were "inextricably tied to the institution of slavery" (7); as for the future, Sanjek argues that this pattern is unlikely to change. Intermarriage, he notes, is increasingly crossing all racial borders in the United States *except* with respect to Blacks. His conclusion is that "in the end ... the critical racial issue will continue to be the place that persons of African descent occupy within the US social order" (Sanjek, "Intermarriage" 122). In similar terms, Naomi Zack's study *Race and Mixed Race*, though it recognizes other racial categories, also insists that the American "racial system" is fundamentally "bi-racial" and with its historical "one-drop rule" for defining "blackness," that it unjustly "does not permit the identification of individuals, in the third person, as mixed race" (4). As for other (racial) groups in the United States, they are constantly under pressure to choose between "Black" and "white." Thus, for example, Angelo Falcón outlines the "politics of racial identity" of Puerto Ricans and their dilemmas in terms of the Black/white racial dichotomy (see also Rodríguez 1994). In a similar vein, Dana Takagi, arguing for the place of Asian-Americans within American racial discourse, feels obliged to attack the "stubborn and persistent frameworks in race relations discussions that construct race, racism, and race relations in terms that are black on the one hand and white on the other" (230).

Whatever the similarities between Canada and the United States in terms of the history of racism against Blacks, it is clear that this American scenario of "race" *as* "Black and white" does not hold true in Canada. For one thing, there are important historical differences between the Canadian and American Black communities. African-Americans, Kymlicka notes, constitute a rather special case anywhere as a very large and long-standing national group that is neither simply a "national minority" (in his sense) nor simply an immigrant ethnic group (*Multicultural Citizenship* 24 ff.). Canadian Blacks also have a long history in Canada, but numerically a much larger percentage of them come from relatively recent immigration from the West Indies, Africa, or elsewhere. Significant exceptions to this should of course be noted – such as the historically important Black communities in Ontario and Nova Scotia (cf. G.E. Clarke's "national" project of "Africadia"). Yet even these older communities (in spite of continuing discrimination and racism) have a different historical relationship to the Canadian state than in the American case, as the phenomenon of "Black Loyalism" (cf. Walker) and the "Underground Railroad" to Ontario illustrate.[2]

Second, the Canadian Black community, unlike that of the United States, has not been large enough historically to determine the broader nature of Canadian race relations. Instead these have been based on shifting "race" lines reflected in the historical changes in Canadian racial ideology, immigration policies, and successive discriminatory practices against a variety of groups: Aboriginals, Southern and Eastern Europeans, Jews, Chinese, Japanese, South Asians, as well as Blacks and others. In nineteenth- and early-twentieth-century Canada, "race" was applied to English and French groups as well as to other minorities in the framework of a racially based national hierarchy of ascribed characteristics (cf. Lord Durham's report, Lionel Groulx's *L'appel de la race*, Ralph Connor's *The Foreigner*, etc.). Later usage (the post-war era of ethnic studies) attacked such categorical ascriptions of "race" as pseudo-scientific "biological trivia" (Anderson and Frideres 17) and moved on to develop a general discourse of "ethnicity" in which "race" was only one sub-category (see Hughes and Kallen 82 ff.). The field of Canadian ethnic studies, which still thrives today, thus historically has been a meeting place of multiple perspectives on "race" and "ethnicity" in Canada, both minority and majority.

The current discourse of "race," on the other hand, is based on the idea that "race," like "ethnicity" and "gender," is a "politically and culturally constructed category which cannot be grounded in a set of fixed transcultural or transcendental racial categories" (Stuart Hall quoted in Alladin 5). Such a definition has some points in common with those of ethnic studies, but it differs in practice by making the concept of "race" itself more central. Yet in the Canadian context even this definition is more general than "Black and white," so that it most frequently is interpreted in broader racial terms such as "colour" or "non-whiteness" (or in governmental terminology as "visible minority"). In sum, Canadian definitions of "race" now and in the past can be seen to be much more multi-ethnic and multi-racial in their orientation than in the United States, where Black and white relations have determined the understanding and contexts of race relations.

The Conjunction of Cultural Identity and Issues of Power

Some commentators on American ethnic and racial issues have tried to divide "race" and "ethnicity" on a distinction between instrumental and cultural domains. "Race" becomes the field in which "repressive, external processes of exclusion" are examined; "ethnicity," the field in which "expressive processes of cultural identification" arise (see Sanjek, "Enduring Inequalities" 8). In Canada a similar division sometimes occurs in discussions of multiculturalism, which is associated with an "ethnic" cultural "song and dance" approach that distracts from issues of racial inequality and power. See for example, the interviews with Himani Bannerji and Dionne Brand in *Other Solitudes* (Hutcheon and Richmond). Elliott and Fleras also note a "difference in emphasis" in the concerns of Canadian "visible and invisible minorities" (249-53): the continuing significance of discriminatory social practices explains the former group's emphasis on racism and equity issues; the decline of "socio-economic disparities among white ethnics" (253) tends to shift the emphasis in the latter case to cultural issues. At the same time, they note, this is not an "either/or situation."

Canadian minority writing, it seems to me, has some useful insights to offer on such questions of culture and power. What this writing suggests, I would argue – at least in the case of a great many minority writers from a variety of backgrounds – is that such a division between political and cultural issues is not made, and if many racial minority writers address cultural and instrumental concerns together, so do many minority writers of "white" European background. Does this shared perception of a conjunction between culture and power provide support for a "pluralist" model of race and ethnic relations in Canada? Let us consider the evidence.

That racial minority writers understand the interconnection of culture and dominance hardly needs proving. A great deal of the theoretical work on "race" (post-structuralist, postmodernist, and post-colonialist) has addressed this point from many angles. My opening quotations can be cited as illustration: Bannerji, Brand, and Goto represent differing and specific ethnocultural origins (South Asian, West Indian, and Japanese) as well as a common "non-white" racial status in Canada, but each in her own way also provides a similar reading of the conjunction between cultural identity and dominant power.

Himani Bannerji's story "The Other Family," for example, portrays a young girl's discovery and affirmation of her racial identity in a "white" world circumscribed by the white teacher's power to define normalcy. The story exemplifies both the girl's discovery of self and her initiation into power politics. The second, "other" family she adds to her drawing thus becomes both a statement of her own identity and a claim about her community's place in Canadian society. Stories by Dionne Brand, in her collection *Sans Souci*, reveal a similar juxtaposition of identity and power both in Canadian society and in the colonial past of the West Indies. In Canadian space Brand's heroines – for example the women in "Train To Montreal," "Blossom," or "At the Lisbon Plate" – affirm their identities within a world deriving from a history of colonialism in the West Indies and racist assumptions and practices in Canada. Located in West Indian space, stories such as "Sans Souci" and "St. Mary's Estate" explore a parallel (colonial) relationship between culture and power.

The same point can be made about Hiromi Goto's novel *Chorus of Mushrooms*. This family saga of three generations of Japanese-Canadians in Alberta focusses on many issues of cultural identity – language, food, displacement, love, family. At the same time, it contextualizes these experiences within a dominant culture that determines difference and normalcy, a power that is symbolized in the novel by the dry wind that blows through southern Alberta. This power is also represented by the assimilative control the English language plays, both in the family and in the writing of the novel, and by the incidents of racism that recur in the story: the children who make racist taunts (Goto 52-53), the "Oriental-type" Valentine's cards (62), the white boyfriend who "squirms in his trousers" (122) when demanding "Oriental sex."

Yet Canadian minority writers not framed within this discourse of "race"– i.e., writers from minority (non-British, non-French) European ethnic backgrounds – can also be found who embody in their writings a conjunction between culture and power. The reasons for this similar conjunction, as I noted earlier, lie in the continuing prominence in Canada of ethnic multiplicity, the history of shifting "race" definitions, and ongoing "Third Force" instrumental issues (cf. Elliott and Fleras 225 ff.). Thus many European-Canadian ethnic minority writers still seem to be conscious of issues of dominance because the bi-national framework to the Canadian national discourse still frames their Canadian minority ethnicity. Furthermore, since ethnicity is still salient, in many cases both pre- and post-immigration experiences of disempowerment continue to reverberate. The same anthology (*Other Solitudes*) that published Bannerji's story can also provide examples of European ethnic minority writers for whom experiences of identity are closely linked with issues of dominant power.

Jewish-Canadian writers are perhaps an obvious group to begin with, since the continuing existence of anti-Semitism and social discrimination against Jews in Canada (cf. Elliott and Fleras 51-52), in spite of advances in cultural and economic spheres, provides an affinity with those groups currently constructed in terms of "race" and racism. Matt Cohen's story "Racial Memories," for example, describes a struggle for identity rooted in Jewish experience of racism in both Europe and Canada. The story's title, and its opening sentence describing the grandfather, serve as reminders that in an earlier Canadian racial terminology, "visible minority" meant dress and appearance and not just pigmentation. His grandfather's beard, Cohen states, "was also a flag announcing to the world that here walked an orthodox Jew" (153). Cohen's story outlines the speaker's "identity crisis" (170) on the one hand in terms of inter-ethnic friendship, intermarriage, and assimilation, and on the other, in terms of racist incidents, anti-Semitism, and police violence. For Cohen, as for Bannerji, Brand, and Goto, cultural and instrumental issues are inseparable.

Janice Kulyk Keefer's story "Mrs Mucharski and the Princess" offers an example of another aspect of ethnic minority experience – the continuing presence of a European past in the link between identity and dominance. In this story, the "mystery" of Mrs Mucharski that in the eyes of her "Canadian" employers sets her apart from the usual "Portuguese or Vietnamese" housekeepers (Kulyk Keefer 279) turns out to be the loss of her children in a European prison camp (289). What Keefer's story indicates is that Canadian ethnic minority identity not only turns within the framework of ethnic and race relations in Canada (which are also apparent in this story) but also can look backward to the power politics of ethnicity and dominance elsewhere. Myrna Kostash, reflecting on her own Ukrainian-Canadian background makes this point even more forcefully in terms of the Canadian politics of race:

> So, if you are going to accuse me of Eurocentricity, you'd better be specific. The centre of *which* Europe, exactly? Are serfdom, famine, and pogroms in Europe? Are the death camps? The gulag? How about the illiteracy of my grandparents, the chattel that were their grandparents, the scattered bones of Galician peasants dead in service to the Viennese emperors? Are all these "European"? ("Eurocentricity" 41-42)

In one sense, this statement forms a commentary on Bannerji's observation cited by way of introduction. What Kostash and Keefer are pointing out is that it is not just "people who are not white" who have "suffered from racism and fascism" (Bannerji); so have many Canadians of European ethnic backgrounds as well. As a result there may be more "acceptance" and understanding "in this society" of the experiences Bannerji refers to than first may be assumed on (current) "racial" grounds alone.

The last example I would like to give is perhaps the most surprising and revealing. W.D. Valgardson is a fifth-generation Canadian of Icelandic background, and his story shows how tenaciously discriminatory Canadian practices of the past are remembered even among the historically more favoured (and more inclined to assimilate) North European immigrant groups. In "The Man from Snaefellsness," Valgardson recounts the linguistic (anti-Icelandic) tyranny meted out to a young boy by a sadistic English teacher. This tyranny continues to rankle into adulthood, and in the story becomes the basis of a rediscovery of ethnic identity and the beginning of a return journey to Iceland. Valgardson too, it would seem, experiences of suffering and oppression continue to be a prominent part of ethnic identity.

The evidence supplied by these writers suggests that to some extent at least there is a shared consciousness on the part of, and not a clear division between, ethnic and racial minorities in Canada concerning the relationship between issues of cultural identity and issues of power. It is difficult to extrapolate from this literary evidence to the larger social discourses, but to the extent that this commonality exists, I would argue, it represents a potentially significant bridge linking race and ethnicity in the Canadian context. From the Canadian ethnic minority (European) side, it shows that the current emphasis on cultural issues does not necessarily represent a clear departure from an understanding of dominant Canadian discourses. And if European ethnic minority writers continue to contextualize their experiences in the power relations of today and of yesterday, if, in other words, they are able to "historicize the present" (Gregory 21), then these experiences represent, at least potentially, an important common basis for understanding the current and past cultural and social situations of Canadian racial minorities. In principle, then, this conjunction should encourage a common agreement among all minorities on the need to struggle against current racist practices.

From the perspective of Canadian racial minorities, this commonality thus provides the ground (again, I would stress only potentially) for alliances on current instrumental issues such as representation and racism. It also provides (to racial minorities) a basis for shared insights in the cultural domain, for if ethnic and racial minorities view cultural experiences as embedded in dominant practices, the cultural issues of identity, family dynamics, language, immigration, and so on, become much more comparable.

If Canadian minority writing does point to a shared common understanding of the conjunction of culture and power in Canadian minority experience, however, this commonality should not be seen in itself as a "solution" to all the problems arising out of race and ethnicity in Canada. A shared consciousness does not in itself change the current situations of Canadian ethnic and racial minorities, nor does it negate the "difference of emphasis" noted earlier between European and non-European minority groups in Canada. Furthermore, common ground may provide a potential basis for common action but it may also be used tactically (and wrongly in my view) to equate, reduce, or downplay the diversity of experiences of Canadian minority groups or to argue for hierarchies of historical victimhood. It is for this reason that I have stressed the *potentiality* of this shared understanding. My argument, then, may be summed up as follows: in the context of a racializing social discourse and in the context of the continuing national salience of ethnic and racial multiplicity, the fact that Canadian ethnic and racial minority writing shares a common understanding of the relationship between cultural identity and issues of power should be seen as having significant potential, if acted upon, for affecting the direction of Canadian race and ethnic relations. Since it provides a basis for mutual understanding and common interest across racial and ethnic boundaries, it also offers one possible support for the viability of a "pluralist" outcome to these relations in the future.

Minority Writing Across Boundaries and Intersections

If the impact of dominant practices on cultural issues forms one support for a scenario of pluralism for Canadian minorities, a second major basis clearly lies in the active exploration by many minority writers of plural intersections within and across racial and ethnic lines. These attempts to build bridges across boundaries also can be linked to the more prominent ideology of pluralism in Canada as implied in bilingualism, multiculturalism, and the multiplicity of ethnicity and race as group categories. In analyzing this intersectionality, I could once again proceed by comparing ethnic and racial minority writers side by side. But since my point is that the intersections in the Canadian "pluralist" scenario link not only race and ethnicity but gender, class, and other categories, a somewhat different approach seems advisable. What I would like to foreground in this section, therefore, are two particularly interesting areas where this pluralism can be seen: 1) feminist discussions of intersectionality, and 2) male writers who exemplify plural strategies in their writing about race.

The Canadian discourse of feminism has to date been one of the most active areas in which intersectionality has been explored. Feminism has historically played a central role in ethnic and racial discourses in Canada. Feminists from minority groups have succeeded in voicing viewpoints that challenge exclusionary structures within both minority and dominant cultures. At the same time, considerable attention has gone into cross-cultural exchanges. These encounters across boundaries have been occurring in two different arenas both relevant to this paper. The first privileges intersections within non-white racial contexts, such as Lee Maracle's dialogue with Sky Lee in "Yin Chin" (Maracle, *Sojourner's Truth*) and the latter's parallel account of the encounter of Chinese-Canadians with Aboriginal history in Lee's *Disappearing Moon Cafe*. These kinds of inter-racial exchanges "of colour" can be seen in a variety of forms in recent publications: collections of essays on racial issues by women writers "of colour" (examples include Bannerji, *Returning the Gaze*; Silvera, *The Other Woman*), collected stories of lesbians "of colour" (Silvera, *Piece of My Heart*), and magazines and journals devoted primarily to "race" and "gender" (for example, *Tiger Lily*). The second arena of exchange foregrounds intersections that cross racial and ethnic boundaries – feminist collections such as *Language in Her Eye, In the Feminine: Women and Words,* and *Telling It: Women and Language Across Cultures* as well as a growing number of general feminist journals (*Canadian Woman Studies, Fireweed,* etc.) devoting special issues to race and ethnicity. Feminist writing in Canada thus seems to be crossing boundaries both within and across current racial categories.

Yet how should this two-pronged feminist effort to compare experiences and build alliances be interpreted in the light of the two scenarios I have been discussing? Is the effort to establish solidarity within non-white racial contexts to be seen as part of the inevitable process towards a "race-oriented" outcome? Or is the evidence of broader forms of interchange and bridge-building (in spite of the cross-cultural difficulties that are equally evident in collections such as *Telling It*) to be seen as part of the second process leading to a "pluralist" outcome?

There is of course no definitive answer to this question, but *both* versions of cross-cultural encounters (within and across "race") can incorporate elements of pluralism or be seen as doing so. Voices arguing for multiplicity can of course be found in venues featuring cross-racial exchanges – this is the very point in setting up such encounters. Joy Kogawa's statement in *Telling It* can perhaps be cited as expressing the underlying motivation behind such attempts: "I don't want to be defined by and limited by any singular identity" (123). The *Telling It* volume is thus one record of how women writers of different backgrounds attempt to move beyond "singular identities" to multiple and plural relations.

At the same time, it is important to note that racial minority women writers speaking out of their individual (racial minority) community experiences or out of a sense of shared inter-racial community with other non-white racial groups – whether in their writings or at "race"-oriented meetings – are not thereby less multiple or inclusive. In the first case, there is no reason, logically, why a loyalty to the "racial" issues of a particular community basis should be seen as limiting. In the second case, it should be remembered that in the Canadian context, the very act of seeing "race" across (non-white) boundaries is itself plural. There would seem to be a common assumption (cf. the media and other reactions to the Vancouver "Writing Thru Race" conference of 1994) that when "non-white" writers discuss "race" as a common interest, their interests are not only racially "sectarian" but also that they are only limited to "race."

The fallacy of assuming that "racial" discourse is a "limited" non-multiple discourse can be illustrated by looking briefly at the writing of two prominent Canadian Black women writers. The case of Maxine Tynes illustrates how a multiple and plural perspective can co-exist with an activist's "racial" community orientation. The writing of Dionne Brand, a well-known activist in "non-white" arenas of racial discourse, can also be seen to address issues of multiplicity and intersectionality within her strong focus on "race."

Tynes, part of the long-established Nova Scotia Black community, has for years documented in her work the contributions and experiences of Nova Scotia Blacks, and especially of Black women, in a context of historical and present day racism. Her most recent work, *The Door of My Heart*, continues this project in poems such as "Head Count: Black Students in My Academic Nest" or "What's Wrong With This Picture?" At the same time, from the opening manifesto "The Poet As Whole-Body Camera," Tynes reaches out to a very broad audience "of those who read, those who follow, we shall go two by two by many, many fold ... Together." This plural theme is pervasive in the collection, in her poems on disability (for example, "We Demand the Right To Pee"), her "embracing all of Dartmouth" ("This Dartmouth At Alderney Gate, 1990"), her cross-racial shared "sister-vision" with Lulu ("I catch fire/ You catch dark"), her love poem to Newfoundland, and so on. Her feminism explicitly addresses intersections of class, ethnicity, language, and disability (as well as "race" and gender) in a "multiple agenda" "that is reaching, reaching for the light" ("Raising the Heart of Women"). Finally, her poem "In This Country" extends this overtly pluralistic vision to the entire country in a "song of Canada" that is "multi-ethnic/multi-language too/ it's young, it's old/ it's Black, it's white/ Aboriginal, immigrant too/ it's disabled and able-bodied/ middle-class, working class/ all of you." In Maxine Tynes's case, it can safely be concluded, a "plural" view of the world has no trouble accompanying a focus on "blackness" and "race."

Dionne Brand, known for her dedicated and effective criticism of "the racist underpinnings of Canadian society" and "the dominant construction of Canada as white" ("Working Paper" 220), may seem at first glance an unlikely writer on whom to build this argument. Brand's rhetoric on issues of "race," seen both in her creative and critical work, is pervasive and uncompromising. Her condemnation of racism against Blacks is far-reaching: repeatedly, in her essays, she shifts back and forth from Canadian racism to slavery, colonialism, and oppression against Blacks in the United States, the West Indies, and elsewhere in the Third World.

Brand's central focus on Black experience, however, makes her an excellent choice for the argument I wish to make, since a close reading of her work reveals not a "narrow" Black racial advocacy but the broadly drawn and multiple context from which she writes. First of all, her perspective on "race" as a solidarity "of colour" ("light and dark" as cited in this article's opening quotation) is, as noted earlier, itself a plural perspective. In this regard, Brand's repeated juxtaposition of Black and Aboriginal commonalities is particularly striking. That Brand links race with gender should also be seen as a form of plural analysis, and if within this feminist perspective, her lesbian "sexual orientation" is added (see, for example, "This Body For Itself" in *Bread out of Stone*), multiple intersections appear here too.

Yet Brand's ideological multiplicity extends beyond race and gender issues. Like Tynes, she too has a central interest in class issues and an openness to alliances with other ethnic minority activists, with other immigrants, and with all those struggling against oppression. Thus Brand's "Working Paper" on Black women in Toronto quite naturally includes class within its title. Her study of gender and race contextualizes the treatment of Black women in a system that normalizes "white middle class women" and marginalizes "working class women – Black, immigrant, white" (Brand, "Working Paper" 230). Brand's championing of "Black and immigrant working class women and white working class women" (226) clearly shows a bridging that crosses racial categories, without of course denying them.

Similar points could be made about many of Brand's essays in *Bread out of Stone*. Along with the attacks on the Canadian system of "whiteness" that permeate the book and which sometimes include "co-opted groups" of European immigrants swallowed into the "white cultural establishment" by an "elasticity of 'whiteness'" (Brand, *Bread Out of Stone* 174-76), can be found repeated references to cross-racial bases of solidarity. Examples include Jewish "sisters" (74) and a shared consciousness of racism and anti-Semitism (68, 161, 179); "white youth ... in solidarity" rioting in Toronto (155); a possibility of finding friends in a "little Italian neighbourhood bakery" (77); and a characterization of Toronto as a "hopeful city" "colourising beautifully" with "all the different people living in it – the Chinese, the Italian, the Portuguese, the South Asians, the East Asians and us" (77). Many more examples could be cited to show the depth of plural sensitivity in Brand's world view. As with Tynes and many other racial minority women writers, Brand's focus on issues of race does not mean that she stops at racial borders. As Brand says, in a very revealing statement of principle, what she aims for is not equality but justice: "Did we want only to be equal to white people or did we want to end exploitation and oppression?" (134).

If this analysis of pluralist perspectives so far has focussed on feminist writings, it is not to be supposed that male writers cannot also be found for whom race, ethnicity, gender, and other intersections form multiple thematic and ideological connections. M.G. Vassanji's *No New Land*, with its cross-racial "rape incident," resolved in the end by a commonality of pragmatic interests between the South Asian and Portuguese immigrant characters, comes to mind as an example. Other writers who might be cited include George Elliott Clarke and Dany Laferrière, two Canadian Black writers from very different backgrounds whose works intersect with the English-French discourse of Canada. In Clarke's case, an ongoing "vision of community" (*Fire on the Water* I: 13) leads to his conceptualization of a Nova Scotia "Africadia" in part as a shared affinity with Maritime Acadians (see his 1992 article "Towards a Conservative Modernity"). Dany Laferrière's novel *Comment faire l'amour avec un Nègre sans se fatiguer* (1985), on the other hand, explores the myths and stereotypes of the "Black-white" racial discourse within both gender and Quebec intersections. His "racial" discourse (written in French of course), deliberately parallels Québécois nationalist discourse (cf. Simon "Language of Difference" 125). His hero's sexual encounters and identity musings are thus carried out primarily in terms of "white" Westmount "imperialist" British-Canadian women. In this way, Laferrière integrates his own "race-oriented" (and gendered) discourse directly into the main narrative of British-Canadian and French-Canadian history.

Two other examples deserve closer attention for the ways they engage racial issues in plural contexts. The first is Lawrence Hill's novel *Some Great Thing*, which provides an encompassing view of pan-Canadian relations seen from the perspective of western Canada. Mahatma Grafton, the young Black hero of this work, not only spends the novel coming to terms with racism, his own identity crisis, his Black roots, his father, and his community history, but he also discovers in the process (and Hill displays for us) the play of class, gender, and ethnic relations in the larger Canadian scene. The novel features a likeable poor British-Canadian hobo (class), a French-speaking Black journalist from Cameroon (Afrocentrism, French linguistic issues), cross-racial love-making with "dominant" women (race and gender), cross-ethnic/racial solidarity (a Black Jewish convert, Mahatma's "South Asian" name) and a plot line that highlights Franco-Manitoban identity problems and French-Canadian linguistic issues (French-English relations). Hill thus succeeds in combining a multiplicity of perspectives as an inclusive (and often comic) context for the exploration of issues of Black identity and racism in Canada.

The last example I would like consider is the story "If The Bough Breaks" (from *There Are No Elders*) by Toronto writer Austin Clarke. This story's plural perspective is especially striking in that it overtly exploits Black racial expectations not only across the boundaries of race and gender but of dominant "whiteness" as well. Featuring a group of Black West Indian women having their hair "fixed" (Clarke, *There Are No Elders* 9) at a hair salon, it opens with a classical "racial" scenario in the Canadian discourse of "race":

It was not an ambulance. There were three police cars. Stopped in the middle of the road, blocking all traffic. The owner of the store who sold high-priced milk came out to meet the policemen. They had left their car doors open. The women could hear the three radios crackling. The six policemen had their guns drawn. In the distance, coming towards them, was another cruiser, flashing in red speed and urgency.

"I bet you," one woman said, "it's some black man in there."

"And not eighteen yet," another said. (11)

The suggestion of police violence in this opening scene picks up a recurring theme in Clarke's fictional works and his essay – *Public Enemies: Police Violence and Black Youth* (on the Toronto riot that followed the acquittal of the Los Angeles police in the Rodney King incident). This time, however, Clarke deals with the theme differently, for when the policemen come out of the store, "Between them was a young white girl. No more than sixteen..." (*Public Enemies* 12). By deliberately setting up a "race" scenario and then twisting it, Clarke opens his text up to a number of very interesting intersections. In one sense Clarke is addressing the limitations of "racial" viewing itself. This point is made when one of the women later indicts the young girl with all the crimes of her race:

A child? She's a white girl. And she is the daughter of the four police in those three cruisers who molested this woman's eight-year old daughter and handcuff her. She is the daughter of that landlord who didn't rent me that musty, stinking basement apartment years ago, in 1961 on Walmer Road. She is the daughter of the woman at the Eaton Centre who had the security guard come up in my face accusing me of shoplifting, a decent person like me. She is the future mother of all the racists we come across in this city. She is just herself. (Clarke, *Public Enemies 20-21*)

Implicit in this accusation is all the experienced racism of Canadian Black history and of Clarke's own literary career spent in documenting it. What Clarke makes clear is that this one incident does not wipe out that history. As one of the other women characters puts it, after "twenty-something years living in Toronto, I have lived to see the day when a police go in a store and don't bring out a black boy or a black girl, but a damn white girl" (*Ibid.* 17).

At the same time, however, the story also makes clear that this attitude will not suffice. The women cannot help but be sympathetic towards the girl. The "given" elements of race and police violence dissolve into less easily answered questions. Perhaps the shopkeeper and even the police have only been trying to help her? When the girl actually arrives in their presence, her helplessness overwhelms them. Tell-tale signs of physical and sexual abuse become visible, and the women are filled with a heart-felt solidarity that crosses racial borders. With telling coding, Clarke notes that the young girl's lips "were thicker than the lips of any of the five women" (*Ibid.* 25). The story ends with the women setting out to call the police themselves.

The point about Clarke's story, then, is that it uses points of intersection, in this case shared female experience ("Why is it always this way with women?" *Ibid.* 28), to cross racial borders. (Clarke's own crossing of gender lines is frequent in his writing; his first novels, for example, dealt extensively with West Indian women domestics in Toronto). And if his story subverts expectations of the usual racism, it also makes certain that racism against Blacks is amply documented along the way. Nevertheless, Clarke's characters are not limited by the effects of racism and are seen to be capable of leaving their own racialized space in order to affirm other parts of their experience, as women, as mothers, as decent human bystanders to another's suffering. The fact that it is a "white" girl, indeed a British-Canadian girl, a potential "daughter of racists" and "future mother of racists" that is the "victim" in this story is also an essential point. It is only in coming to understand the nature of living on the other side of the "racial" fence, in problematizing "whiteness" and dominance too, that these women, like Clarke's readers (presumably), can understand the nature of Canadian society. As in another Clarke police story – "Sometimes, a Motherless Child" (*Nine Men Who Laughed*) – cross-racial solidarity (in that story between an Italian-Canadian and a Black Canadian boy) is suggested as a model for breaking out of racist practices and for putting inter-racial relations on a more positive path.

The Road Ahead
The writers explored in this essay suggest that commonalities and plural perspectives are implicit in a great deal of Canadian ethnic and racial minority writing. I have here pointed to only a few of these, and drawing conclusions from these minority texts on the directions Canadian race and ethnic relations will take should, it goes without saying, be done with care.

Elements of multiplicity, commonality, and intersectionality in Canadian minority writing do not, in any sense, undercut the weight of individual aspects of minority experience. In other words, race, ethnicity, gender, class, and other factors continue to form visceral parts of the experience of Canadian minorities. To point to commonalities or broader contexts should *not* therefore be seen as a way to "retreat from race" (Takagi), or to go "beyond" race and ethnicity. The view held by Neil Bissoondath (and his supporters) that somehow "race" and "ethnicity" are not significant functioning social categories in Canada and that we all can be viewed simply as "Canadians" (*Selling Illusions*), is thus not one that I share. On the contrary, minority writing of all kinds reveals that these categories have been and continue to be at the heart of Canadian social and cultural space. It is for this very reason that cross-cultural exchanges and an ongoing struggle against racism, injustices, and inequalities of all kinds remain priorities in Canada today.

Nor should it be concluded that minority relations in Canada are based only on shared suffering, or only on shared experiences of culture. Other analyses of Canadian minority writing would likely show that other kinds of exchanges and negotiations within and across boundaries are also pertinent: historical injustices between minorities; rivalries for resources under socially limited opportunities; racist, sexist, and stereotypical attitudes ("Yin Chin"); and a host of misunderstandings and misperceptions. These too are a central and visceral part of the Canadian minority discourse of "race" and "ethnicity" and these too need to be included in any evaluation of where Canadian ethnic and racial relations are headed.

What I have tried to argue in this essay, in short, is only one bit of evidence in a case that is as yet not resolved. My point has been that in the context of the current racialization of Canadian social and literary discourse, it is desirable to look more closely at "plural" alternatives to a fundamentally "race-based" society (such as the United States). Some basic features in the Canadian situation, I have argued, tend to favour such a "plural" alternative outcome. I have tried to outline here, without I hope denying and reducing important differences between "race" and "ethnicity," the way in which shared historical, cultural, and instrumental ground is reflected in a comparison of Canadian ethnic and racial minority writers. I have also argued that a close reading of many minority writers, both male and female, reveals the importance in their writing of a plural concern with intersections within and across boundaries of race and ethnicity, gender and class, and even minority and majority status. It is impossible to predict the direction in which Canadian ethnic and race relations will go. What Canadian minority writing does suggest, however, is that at the current crossroads between race and ethnicity, a "pluralist" alternative is still a possibility.

NOTES
1. This can be further illustrated with examples from recent constitutional history: the high profile discussion of Aboriginal concerns in the debate surrounding the proposed Meech Lake and Charlottetown Accords; the overwhelming vote by Aboriginal groups in Quebec to stay in Canada during the 1995 referendum campaign on Quebec sovereignty; the higher percentage of

"Yes" votes among francophone (as opposed to anglophone) racial and ethnic minorities in that referendum; the call by Lucien Bouchard during the referendum for women *"des races blanches"* (note the plural) to produce more babies; the blaming of the defeat of the 1995 referendum on "the ethnic vote" by Jacques Parizeau. None of these "events" resonate, I would argue, in terms of current American race and ethnic relations. They are Canada-specific, indicating the continuing centrality of ethnicity and language in Canadian discourse.

2. Other differences can also be noted. If slavery (of Blacks) was also an institution in Canada, it was a much less defining moment in national terms than, for example, the conquest and enslavement of Canadian First Nations and the ongoing colonization of and discrimination against these peoples over time. Furthermore, Canada did not fight a civil war over the issue of slavery.

LUCIE LEQUIN

Paroles transgressives et métissage culturel au féminin[1]

La turbulence identitaire[2] au Québec que bon nombre de spécialistes en littérature et en sciences sociales situent vers 1980 est sans doute antérieure à cette époque. L'on peut citer à titre d'exemple le caractère métissé de Kathy Macgregor, de Mrs. Macfarlane et du père Joseph-Marie[3] dans *La Petite Poule d'Eau* de Gabrielle Roy; l'hétérogène y est certes en étroit rapport avec l'allégeance religieuse, mais les religions et les cultures s'enchevêtrant inextricablement, les dérives identitaires d'alors passent par la mise en doute à la fois des cultures et des religions. Le métissage culturel – la complicité et l'échange de connaissances que Luzina sait créer entre elle et des personnages d'immigrés, par exemple – irrigue donc l'œuvre régienne et constitue un facteur déterminant de son imaginaire bien avant la problématisation de l'hétérogène des années 1980.

Ce bref détour par Gabrielle Roy pour entrer dans la problématique du métissage culturel veut simplement rappeler que ce mouvement culturel, situé la plupart du temps au début des années 1980 (voir entre autres Simon et Leahy), a commencé à travailler le champ littéraire il y a longtemps déjà, mais de façon lente et parfois invisible, sans trop attirer l'attention. Il faudrait, je crois, revoir à la lumière des préoccupations actuelles autour du métissage culturel, les productions littéraires antérieures aux années 1980. L'exemple de Gabrielle Roy sert donc essentiellement à illustrer mes doutes quant à la pertinence de cette périodisation.

Néanmoins, les années 1980 constituent une balise temporelle pratique, un outil de travail, d'autant plus que l'intérêt pour le métissage culturel s'est accru et est devenu nettement plus visible depuis une quinzaine d'années. L'on parle alors de transculture, de littérature ethnique, de multiculture, de mélange des cultures, etc.; les spécialistes, Simon Harel, Jean Jonassaint, Pierre L'Hérault, Pierre Nepveu et Maïr Verthuy, par exemple, s'intéressent de plus en plus à la production littéraire des auteur-e-s migrant-e-s. Plutôt que de parler de culture monolithique et homogène, l'on parle de culture plurielle et de mouvement de l'hétérogène. L'on s'interroge sur la citoyenneté culturelle, sur l'appartenance à une ou plusieurs cultures, sur l'étranger, sur l'exil.

Depuis les années 1980, l'abondance des publications soit d'œuvres de fiction soit d'études examinant la question d'appartenance culturelle, que j'utilise ici dans un sens très large, ne peut que retenir l'attention. C'est aussi le positionnement du lectorat qui s'est déplacé, à la fois parce que ses propres préoccupations littéraires et sociologiques se sont modifiées, et aussi à cause des transformations plus larges qui ont marqué la pensée occidentale influencée par le postcolonialisme et la postmodernité. Durant les années 1960, par exemple, le lectorat cherchait souvent dans la lecture des œuvres de fiction des certitudes rassurantes, tel que le caractère homogène de la culture québécoise que des penseurs voulaient immuable. C'était l'époque de la quête d'un pays certain et d'une identité précise. À titre d'exemple, il suffit de rappeler la poésie nationaliste des années 1960, traversée par l'idée du pays à construire et d'une culture singulière à créer; l'on cherchait encore à cerner la prégnance des mots Québécois (dans le sens d'appartenance nationale) et la québécité (les éléments constitutifs du pays, de la culture et du fait d'être québécois). Depuis le début de la dernière décennie, le lectorat, sous le signe du changement – la pensée postmoderne[4], la mise en doute de l'hégémonie occidentale, la démographie changeante, entre autres – est plutôt sensible au mouvement, au «hors lieu»; il trouve stimulant l'incertitude, la mobilité et la quête d'un redéploiement identitaire. C'est maintenant le moment du constat de l'hétérogénéité culturelle du Québec. Pierre Nepveu, par exemple, affirme qu'il faut imaginer la «fin» de la littérature québécoise dans une perspective «d'une pluralité de points de référence» (215); Pierre L'Hérault, lui, dit qu'il faut imaginer la littérature québécoise «comme ouverture, la diversité n'y étant plus perçue comme une menace, mais comme le signe du réel inévitablement multiple» (1991, 56); Lequin et Verthuy (1993) parlent de «nouveaux palimpsestes» de la littérature québécoise – et j'en passe.

C'est aussi le moment d'une plus grande conscience de l'interaction entre la réalité sociologique et le champ littéraire: la configuration ethnique des quartiers a changé, celle des écoles aussi; les langues entendues dans les rues de Montréal sont de plus en plus nombreuses (l'arabe, par exemple, est considéré comme la troisième langue, devançant l'italien et le grec). Dans le quartier Notre-Dame-de-Grâces, l'école Saint-Luc, la plus grande polyvalente de la ville, reçoit une clientèle étudiante issue de plus de soixante-dix groupes ethniques. Des villes de banlieue, Verdun par exemple, qui, avant 1980 attiraient peu de familles d'immigrants, en reçoivent maintenant beaucoup. Le «non» au référendum de 1980 a sans doute aussi obligé des Québécois francophones à redéfinir leurs rapports au monde. Cette nouvelle réalité sociologique – je n'ai ici mentionné brièvement que quelques éléments marquants – incite des chercheur-e-s à analyser les croisements de regards culturels qu'elle entraîne.

Dans le domaine littéraire aussi, son influence se fait sentir; par exemple, des auteur-e-s donnent à lire des romans ouverts sur le monde: l'action se passe entièrement ou en partie ailleurs; les personnages sont souvent d'origines culturelles variées, parfois déjà fortement métissés; la défense du territoire ou de la québécité se fait discrète et est souvent tout à fait absente. Certes, les causes de ces nouvelles orientations sont multiples, ainsi que je l'ai montré plus haut, mais elles relèvent aussi du sociologique. La quête du soi dans plusieurs productions littéraires actuelles se pose donc aussi en relation avec la découverte de l'autre et de l'ailleurs. Je pense, par exemple, au roman de Pauline Harvey, *Un homme est une valse*, où l'héroïne, une écrivaine québécoise en cavale à travers l'Europe, veut conserver intact son regard d'étrangère afin d'alimenter son désir d'être étonnée; ou encore à *La pisseuse* d'Anne Élaine Cliche dont l'action se déroule à Montréal, à New York, à Paris et à Prague.

D'une part, bon nombre d'auteur-e-s articulent leur pratique de l'hétérogène en s'ouvrant à la réalité mondiale; ils et elles cultivent le dépaysement, l'extra-territorialité et lancent leurs personnages à la conquête d'un espace autre (les Indes, l'Afrique, la Californie, par exemple) que celui des origines – il faut entendre, ici, le Québec – pour actualiser une réflexion sur l'identitaire. D'autre part, les écrivains et écrivaines migrant-e-s abordent leur questionnement identitaire à l'intérieur même de la dérive, du déplacement. Arrivé-e dans son nouveau pays, l'immigré-e doit se placer, se rétablir. La traversée des frontières (le voyage, si l'on veut), est à peine amorcée. Dans son effort de reterritorialisation, l'auteur-e apprendra à se déplacer dans l'espace intermédiaire entre la (les) culture(s) d'origine et la culture du nouveau pays, donc à apprivoiser le brouillage culturel. Pour les migrants, hommes ou femmes, nés au Québec, il s'agit plutôt de concilier les divergences et les convergences entre leurs cultures: familiale, natale, locale, que chacune de celle-ci soit unique ou multiple.

Poser la question des paroles transgressives et du métissage culturel au féminin ne saurait donc se limiter à la seule parole des femmes migrantes. Il s'agit d'une problématique qui se développe de façon multidirectionnelle et que l'on doit explorer aussi dans un mouvement pluriel, en se gardant d'affirmer que telle ou telle œuvre représente la pensée des migrantes ou celle d'un groupe ethnique particulier, ou encore une certaine pensée postmoderne. Le va et vient d'un espace culturel à un autre, cette mouvance incontournable, et les paradoxes de déterritorialisation/reterritorialisation, déracinement/enracinement et appartenance/non appartenance, entre autres, constituent des composantes intrinsèques de ces œuvres métissées. Ainsi que le montrent Brydon et Tiffin au sujet de la littérature postcoloniale au Canada anglais, en Australie et dans les Antilles anglaises, la littérature métissée et *postnationale*, pourrait-on dire pour le contexte québécois,

> … takes us from the monocentric into the polyphonic, from the dominance of a single culture into convergent cultures, from pure ancestry into hybridisation, from the novel of persuasion to the novel of carnival. (33)

Cette écriture de la convergence se développe dans la perméabilité aux autres discours sociaux; elle les reprend, s'y oppose, les prolonge, en montre leur caractère labile et trace des pistes pour un avenir différent. Il convient de se demander, à l'instar de Marc Angenot, «qu'est-ce qui se dit *ici* [dans le cas de cet article, la littérature] qui ne saurait se dire là» (37), c'est-à-dire dans les autres pratiques cognitives du discours social.

Mon étude du métissage culturel dans les œuvres de femmes se situe dans un projet de recherche portant sur la production littéraire des femmes au Québec depuis le début des années 1980. C'est donc comme facteur dynamique de la littérature au féminin, ainsi que de la littérature québécoise en général, que l'écriture des femmes migrantes m'intéresse. De plus, comme femmes et comme migrantes, ces auteures subissent une double marginalisation. Enfin, des concepts tels que le pays, la patrie, la nation, l'appartenance au pays d'origine comme celle au pays d'accueil se présentent, me semble-t-il, de façon différente selon qu'il s'agit d'auteurs migrants masculins ou féminins. Je me limiterai ici à la représentation culturelle dans quelques œuvres d'auteures migrantes, auteures que je considère avant tout, ainsi que l'affirme Spivak (140), comme agentes de connaissances plutôt qu'objets d'étude. À l'écoute de leurs œuvres, je tenterai donc de comprendre ce qu'elles ont à m'apprendre, ce qu'elles disent dans l'*ici* de leurs œuvres. Par l'étude nécessairement limitée et partielle de la représentation du seul concept de la langue (paroles et/ou écriture) perçue comme stratégie de résistance et d'appropriation, il s'agira de voir comment l'identité culturelle y est pensée et représentée.

Le contact avec la langue – plus ou moins familier, plus ou moins difficile – s'établit dans la négociation entre les cultures et les langues en jeu, négociation parfois féconde, parfois impossible. Cette interpellation de la langue, des langues, mobilise les auteures selon leur propre spécificité; pour entrer dans cette zone d'échange, commençons par les rapports en apparence les moins problématiques, soit les rapports entre la langue et les «migrantes» nées au Québec. Pour elles, c'est surtout l'affirmation de leur singularité et de leur appartenance à une société moderne, en mouvement, qui compte; le métissage culturel, langagier parfois, qui sous-tend leur généalogie particulière n'apparaît pas nécessairement dans leur écriture. Elles ne se «sentent aucune mission par rapport au sort du langage.» (Bertrand 50) Elles ont séparé, dirait Danielle Zana, elle-même une migrante fortement métissée[5], le territoire idéologique du territoire imaginaire (Zana 37). C'est le cas de Marie-Françoise Taggart, de Désirée Szucsany, de Lisa Carducci. Ces migrantes non immigrées connaissent les codes langagiers et l'accent québécois et se représentent spontanément, à l'intérieur de la parole québécoise, leur langue natale – à tout le moins au niveau sonore dont elles sont imprégnées. Elles n'ont souvent plus conscience de l'accent. Ces écrivaines ont été élevées au Québec et ont, la plupart du temps, fréquenté les écoles francophones. Très tôt, elles ont été placées à un carrefour de bilinguisme puisque leur langue maternelle – l'anglais, l'arabe, le créole, le grec, l'italien, etc. – diffère de leur langue natale, la langue d'usage majoritaire du Québec, le français. Cette situation d'une double langue se complique parfois par l'apprentissage d'une troisième, même d'une quatrième langue, notamment lorsque l'environnement est anglophone ou les parents sont de langues différentes. De plus, l'apprentissage du français et de l'anglais se fait quelquefois de façon simultanée; il y a alors présence de deux langues natales.

L'union de la langue maternelle et de la langue natale, des langues natales parfois, ne va pas toujours sans aliénation. C'est alors la confusion et parfois l'incapacité d'accéder à une langue, qu'elle soit maternelle ou natale. Carole David, une jeune auteure québécoise née à Montréal dans une famille métissée – mère italophone, père francophone – représente cette quasi mutité dans l'une de ses nouvelles, intitulée «Le roman de Lina». Le mot «roman» ici laisse entendre un récit long à raconter, une fiction dont le personnage principal sera Lina. Il s'agit toutefois d'une brève nouvelle d'à peine deux pages, puisque Lina n'est que le double de Rosita, qui loin d'être un personnage central, incarne plutôt le décentrement. Rosita/Lina confond trois langues : le français, l'italien et l'anglais et «tout ce qu'[elle] écrit demeure incompréhensible» (David 60). Accusée de meurtre, elle veut s'expliquer, mais n'y arrive pas. Loin de la propulser hors de son mal de vivre, le meurtre, ce geste ultime d'aliénation, l'enfonce plus loin dans la schizophrénie et le dédoublement. À la fin de la nouvelle, Rosita annonce à la narratrice (féminin des deux premiers participes passés) que Lina sera internée.

C'est l'échec de l'unité intérieure; le roman de Lina ne sera pas écrit faute d'une langue appropriée, dans le double sens de langue adéquate et de possession d'une langue. Loin d'être une richesse, les trois langues de Rosita/Lina participent plutôt de la pauvreté; des bribes mal assimilées de trois langues ne peuvent remplacer une langue unique bien appropriée; ici, le bilinguisme réel n'a pas lieu. La narratrice anonyme de cette courte nouvelle veut pourtant que le roman de Lina s'écrive afin de dire l'aliénation et la difficulté, voire l'impossibilité d'une réconciliation entre la langue maternelle et les langues natales. Pour la narratrice, l'écriture se veut stratégie de réconciliation, d'affirmation et de quête du soi. L'écriture – ainsi que le rappelle le titre du recueil de David, *L'endroit où se trouve ton âme* – serait un lieu intime d'exploration et de mouvement vers l'autre, souligné par le possessif «ton». Rosita/Lina reste sans voix, mais la narratrice prend la relève et tente de dire le décentrement de la pauvre femme. Toutefois, en l'absence d'une langue appropriée de la part de Rosita/Lina, cette longue histoire d'aliénation est vouée à la brièveté; la narratrice affirme l'importance du roman, mais ne peut l'écrire à la place de Rosita. Elle ne peut non plus parler à sa place.

L'aliénation langagière n'occupe pas le centre de l'écriture de Carole David, mais, ici et là, elle sert d'indicateur d'un malaise, voire d'une attitude schizophrène devant le décentrement culturel non résolu, et aussi devant les autres formes de dérives. Le cas de Rosita/Lina ne permet pas de généraliser et d'affirmer qu'il y a nécessairement dérive et malaise au sein de l'écriture des femmes migrantes nées au Québec; il s'agit plutôt d'une représentation singulière de l'appropriation du soi et de la culture, ici confuse. À dire vrai, c'est l'impossibilité de cette appropriation.

Pour les écrivaines migrantes nées à l'étranger, le dépaysement, la nécessité d'une reterritorialisation, d'un repaysement, le métissage culturel, le sentiment d'exil et la méconnaissance des codes jouent souvent un rôle d'importance, qu'elles soient originaires des pays du Sud, des pays de l'Est ou des pays francophones européens; selon Zana, ces dernières sont volontiers vouées au silence:

> L'immigrant et surtout le Français, quelles que soient ses appartenances idéologiques, s'il reste fidèle à lui-même, continue d'être perçu en conquérant. (Zana 70)

Simultanément on lui rappelle constamment sa différence (Robin 139), son incapacité à comprendre la culture québécoise. De façon corollaire, les francophones venus d'ailleurs ne reconnaissent pas toujours l'accent québécois, notent souvent la différence de ce parler français dans une pensée américaine (Robin 83). Ainsi Soria, la narratrice française de *La convention* de Suzanne Lamy, se retrouve à Montréal «toujours un peu perdue. Ne serait-ce que par l'accent des Québécois» (Lamy 34). Comment dire cette «étrangeté» (Robin 51) qui traverse l'écriture de plusieurs femmes migrantes, même issues des pays francophones européens, cet «exil dans sa propre langue» (Robin 93) où l'on se comprend dans «le malentendu» (Robin 52)?

Maya, une jeune femme arabe immigrée, personnage principal du *Printemps peut attendre* d'Andrée Dahan (née en Égypte) est venue au Québec à cause de sa langue maternelle, le français, pour faire coïncider langue maternelle et vie quotidienne. Elle confronte plutôt le choc de deux cultures, de deux codes; l'impossibilité d'interpréter de petits gestes anodins, des mots inconnus; l'impossibilité de communiquer. L'écart entre les «savoir-dire, savoir-faire, savoir-vivre» (Médam 138) demeure, dans ce premier roman de Dahan, infranchissable. L'ethnicité, invisible dans le pays d'origine de Maya, devient manifeste et s'affiche (Médam 139) malgré elle. La jeune femme enseigne dans une école secondaire et les élèves refusent son accent et son enseignement. Elle se retrouve sans travail et meurt littéralement de peur. Tout à fait décentrée dans sa langue et dans son savoir, elle a de plus en plus peur, s'égare dans l'école, s'y retrouve seule, sans secours; lorsqu'elle trouve enfin une porte ouverte sur l'extérieur, une violente rafale de neige souffle et elle meurt sur un banc de neige, à deux pas d'un arrêt d'autobus qu'elle ne voit pas.

Le motif de la langue à la fois identique et différente provoque ici des prises de position figées chez Maya comme chez les élèves et l'administration scolaire, un rejet circulaire qui s'auto-nourrit et alimente les tensions. C'est l'échec de la parole; Maya ne peut ni se faire comprendre ni comprendre les autres. De part et d'autre, le métissage n'a pas lieu; au contraire, le refus des interférences culturelles domine. De plus, pour Maya, le pays qu'elle a quitté volontairement pour s'accomplir, au fond pour des raisons féministes, devient presque le paradis perdu, tant l'angoisse l'habite. La langue, celle de Maya comme celle des élèves, n'est ici qu'un outil d'aliénation quasi insurmontable. Pour tous la langue se fige dans la résistance et empêche l'avènement d'une complicité inédite.

L'incommunicabilité se présente autrement dans *Soigne ta chute* de Flora Balzano. À cause de son accent français au Québec et de son accent québécois en France, la narratrice constate qu'elle fait partie de la minorité audible (38), qu'elle n'a pour langue maternelle que le silence (60); sa généalogie culturelle brisée, croisée depuis des générations, la voue à l'éternelle errance.

La différence audible chez Balzano devient stratégie d'intégration par le refus de l'aliénation dans le silence:

> On va m'entendre, donc. Je tiens absolument à faire partie de quelque chose. Après tout, nous, les handicapés verbaux, ne sommes-nous pas des gens comme, n'avons-nous pas les mêmes besoins que, les autres? (38)

Par la parole transgressive, par la mise en son de sa différence et enfin par l'écriture, la narratrice tente de se resituer, de se repayser, d'appartenir au nouveau pays tout en conservant sa fierté d'être née, non pas de l'érable, mais du croisement d'un tremble et d'un saule pleureur (41) plantés dans des sables mouvants.

L'ironie traverse ce premier livre de Flora Balzano, un roman selon la précision générique de la page couverture. Du roman, il n'a que le nom; c'est un livre sans centre, qui bouge dans toutes les directions; ni le prologue ni l'épilogue, par exemple, ne jouent leur rôle habituel; chacune des parties se juxtapose plutôt que de s'enchaîner ou de s'expliquer; la structure est éclatée comme le sont les voix multiples de la narratrice. Tout le livre repose sur des sables mouvants. Comment pourrait-il en être autrement, puisqu'il n'y a pas d'unité identitaire et que la globalisation accompagne l'angoisse auto-ironique de la narratrice, ou devrais-je dire des narratrices? Néanmoins, par la parole et l'écriture, cette narratrice plurielle instaure sa propre réalité, dans un contexte territorial qui la nie en lui prêtant d'office une culture autre, et simultanément, l'autorise à s'avouer Québécoise. Pour Jacques Hassoun, l'intégration réelle serait «capable de déclarer que la culture de tel citoyen est celle qu'il avoue» (Hassoun 42) et non celle qu'on lui prête. *Soigne ta chute* ne réconcilie pas ces deux positions – culture choisie, culture prêtée – mais les problématise et montre, par l'ironie, certaines failles du discours d'autorité.

Marilú Mallet a aussi abordé cette notion de culture choisie, de façon plus métaphorique, dans une nouvelle intitulée «La mutation» (47-54), où Pépito, fils d'émigrés hispanophones, apprend le hongrois dans une garderie francophone pour communiquer avec son meilleur ami, mais n'apprend ni le français ni l'espagnol ou même l'anglais. Mallet démontre l'impossibilité pour les parents de transmettre à l'enfant leur langue maternelle, l'enfant marquant sa différence, dès sa naissance, par ses cheveux blonds. La mutation culturelle s'engage malgré les parents, malgré leur désir de lui donner une double culture, la leur et celle du pays d'accueil. Ici l'enfant choisit sa langue d'usage, sa voix, en dehors de celle des parents et de celle du pays. Toutefois, avant que le père ne découvre par hasard la langue de son fils, la façon de parler de ce dernier inquiète, est suspecte et échappe à tous les spécialistes, le dernier d'entre eux voulant envoyer Pépito chez les fous. Cette nouvelle place donc le rôle des parents, et celui des autres voix d'autorité, en périphérie devant le devenir culturel des enfants, les pairs ayant plus d'impact que le monde des adultes. C'est la reconnaissance implicite du caractère de plus en plus perméable, de plus en plus aléatoire, de l'identité culturelle.

Cette question de langue, parole, écriture ne saurait être expliquée ni par le décentrement schizophrène (David), ni par le décentrement meurtrier (Dahan), ni par l'appartenance conflictuelle, à la fois refusée et réclamée (Balzano), ni par la mutation culturelle spontanée (Mallet). Ces attitudes diverses indiquent plutôt un réaménagement culturel et langagier encore confus, une reconfiguration multidirectionnelle en cours et souvent conflictuelle[6]: la langue véhiculaire, ici le français, s'imprègne d'une pensée autre, de cultures autres, venant à la fois de pays européens et des pays du Sud et de l'Orient; elle se colore d'images d'ailleurs, emprunte des mots et se transforme lentement. Avec ce mouvement de mutation encore trop actuel pour pouvoir bien le cerner, la culture change également et les rapports entre les gens et les langues se modifient. Toute langue vivante a ainsi bougé et bouge encore, mais l'histoire des langues montre que toute transformation d'une langue, et conjointement d'une pensée, d'une culture, a lieu à la fois dans la résistance et dans la complicité. Force est d'admettre le pouvoir transgressif de la langue, car, outre son pouvoir déstabilisateur, elle est aussi initiation, univers à explorer, médiation, réconciliation des codes ou source d'inédit. Je pense ici à l'œuvre de Mona Latif-Ghattas ou à celle de Bianca Zagolin, œuvres qui explorent surtout le versant intégrateur de la langue au-delà de l'inquiétant décentrement qu'elles mettent simultanément en mots.[7]

La problématisation de la migrance culturelle ne saurait donc être comprise à partir d'une position unique, d'une époque, d'une catégorie, d'une loi. Ainsi, Monique Bosco, dans *Babel-opéra,* une œuvre récente, met à distance le discours du décentrement, l'éloigne d'elle, de son époque, même si parfois elle s'y insère de façon autobiographique et contemporaine; devant la longue histoire de l'hybridité des cultures, Monique Bosco situe les notions d'exode, de *Babel,* là où les scribes anciens les ont transcrites. Dans *Babel-opéra,* c'est à partir du «bagage de déportation» dont parle Ezéchiel dans la *Bible* que la narratrice explique son exil et son propre bagage si mince devant l'histoire longue de la migrance. Le titre d'ailleurs annonce ce lien ancien avec les langues de Babel et les exodes millénaires; par le mot «opéra», il inscrit aussi un mouvement de va et vient entre la voix solo et les voix des chœurs, entre la singularité et la collectivité. Ce titre chargé d'histoire et de voix plurielles résume l'œuvre. En effet, Monique Bosco, par l'accumulation de strates culturelles, anciennes et modernes, relativise le paradis perdu et la terre promise, et surtout refuse l'enfermement dans une chronologie, dans une géographie et dans une langue. Seule la parole compte, peu importe la langue, puisque pour elle, «il vaut mieux blasphémer que de se taire» (9). Certes, cette importance donnée à la parole ne saurait s'appliquer à toute l'œuvre de Bosco[8] qui, maintes fois, a représenté la femme soit muette soit se livrant sur le ton intime de la confidence. Ici, il importe surtout de montrer le rôle fondateur de la parole, puisque c'est dans et par l'exploration des voix de Babel que la quête de la narratrice se concrétise et que sa vision du monde prend forme. Indirectement, *Babel-opéra* célèbre sa prise de parole.

Plus l'auteure migrante se place au carrefour des cultures, plus le code langagier importe, plus il faut, à la fois, le décoder, le décanter, le transformer afin de venir à la parole, puis à l'écriture.

S'interroger sur le français constitue une tentative de subvertir le pouvoir marginalisant de cette langue dominante au Québec, cette langue du centre (même si elle est elle-même marginalisée au sein de la société nord-américaine). C'est aussi rappeler, par la présence de mots italiens, grecs, arabes, etc., que l'autre langue n'est pas nécessairement l'anglais. Pour l'écrivaine migrante, la langue d'usage, par son double pouvoir d'intégration et d'exclusion, doit avant tout permettre de rapprocher, de communiquer: écrire, dit Anne-Marie Alonzo, c'est «rejoindre l'autre dans les lignes» (109).

La langue n'est qu'un code permettant de recevoir et de transmettre; l'essentiel se situe au-delà de la langue nommée, au-delà des frontières géographiques et langagières. C'est en quelque sorte un français «polyglotte» que les auteures migrantes désirent afin de rapprocher du lectorat leur singularité de femme et de culture, et simultanément de permettre l'émergence de l'inédit culturel.

Mot par mot, l'écrivaine migrante s'enracine dans un territoire en transmutation et contribue à sa métamorphose. Il y a certes déracinement face à la culture d'origine ou déplacement entre les cultures en jeu, une quête avortée parfois, mais il y a aussi échange et accueil:

> Et je me dis que je te dois [à Montréal] les
> espaces infinis où se tracent mes poèmes
> D'exil ou de demeure
> D'entaille ou de convalescence
> D'hier ou d'à venir encore dans les saisons de tes promesses
> Où dorment des printemps
> En attente d'éclore.
> (Latif Ghattas, *La triste beauté du monde* 100).

NOTES
1. Cet article est une version remaniée d'une communication présentée au Congrès 1993 de l'ACSUS, à la Nouvelle-Orléans.
2. La notion d'identitaire élargit le concept d'identité, car elle met l'accent sur le mouvement, le processus évolutif, le dynamisme. C'est, selon le collectif de *Stratégies identitaires*, l'identité considérée du point de vue de «l'interaction sociale qui préside à la définition de soi, non pas seulement au niveau interindividuel mais au niveau structurel ou superstructurel (la culture, les institutions, l'histoire, l'idéologie...)» tel que cité par Jeanne-Marie Clerc dans *Le renouveau de la parole identitaire*, Mireille Calle-Gruber et Jeanne-Marie Clerc, (dir.), Montpellier et Kingston, Université Paul-Valérie et Université

Queen's, 1993, 7. Voir aussi Sherry Simon, Pierre L'Hérault, Robert Schwartzwald et Alexis Nouss, *Fictions de l'identitaire au Québec*, Montréal, XYZ, 1991.

3. Le père Joseph-Marie, un capucin, estime les gens non pas pour leur religion, mais pour leur valeur intrinsèque. Il rend service à sa voisine, Mrs. Macfarlane, une méthodiste qui, par la suite, lui donne son harmonium et en la personne de Kathy Macgregor, il trouve une organiste; celle-ci est presbytérienne. Enfin, c'est l'enseignante du village, une protestante, qui enseigne le catéchisme aux petits catholiques (187-196). Il n'y a pas pour ces gens de frontières étanches entre les religions, car, au-delà des différences ils partagent un même système de valeurs et vivent dans une même société.

4. Selon Janet Paterson, «on peut affirmer qu'une pratique littéraire est "postmoderne" lorsqu'elle remet en question aux niveaux de la forme et du contenu, les notions d'unité, d'homogénéité et d'harmonie. [...] le postmoderne est avant tout un savoir hétérogène qui n'est plus lié à une autorité antérieure mais à une nouvelle légitimation fondée sur la reconnaissance de l'hétérogénéité des jeux de langage» Voir *Moments postmodernes dans le roman québécois*, édition augmentée, Ottawa, Presses de l'Université d'Ottawa, 1993, 2.

5. Danielle Zana, née en France et immigrée au Québec, affirme dans son journal son métissage familial sans toutefois l'expliquer. À cause de sa généalogie familiale, le sentiment d'être étrangère l'habitait déjà en France même si, de par sa naissance, elle était française. Ce sentiment d'être étrangère dans leur pays natal se retrouve chez d'autres auteures migrantes, entre autres dans l'œuvre d'Anne-Marie Alonzo, Mona Latif Ghattas, Flora Balzano, Nadine Ltaif, car la famille de leur narratrice respective est déjà marquée avant même la naissance de celle-ci par des migrations antérieures, des mariages mixtes du point de vue culturel ou encore la présence quotidienne de plusieurs cultures ou plusieurs religions. L'appartenance au pays natal s'avère ainsi incertaine, surtout parce qu'elle est mise en doute par la voix de la majorité.

6. L'anglais parlé à Montréal serait aussi en voie de transformation influencé à la fois par le français et les autres langues qui y sont parlées abondamment. Il va de soi que les langues étrangères, l'italien, l'espagnol, l'arabe, par exemple, sont également perméables aux influences du français et de l'anglais.

7. Voir Lucie Lequin, «Elles disent leur dépaysement et bâtissent leur repaysement», *Les Bâtisseuses de la cité*, Évelyne Tardy et al. (dir.), ACFAS, Les cahiers scientifiques, no 29, 1993, 307-319.

8. Pour une étude récente de l'évolution de l'œuvre de Bosco, voir Pierre L'Hérault, «Les mythologies de Monique Bosco» dans *Multi-culture, multi-écriture. La voix migrante au féminin en France et au Canada*, Lucie Lequin et Maïr Verthuy, (dir.), Paris, L'Harmattan, 1996, 50-71.

TAMARA PALMER SEILER

Multi-Vocality and National Literature: Towards a Post-Colonial and Multicultural Aesthetic

Many would doubtless agree with historian Russell Jacoby's recent critique of post-colonial theory. Calling it "… the latest catchall term to dazzle the academic mind" (Jacoby 30), he finds it fuzzy and contradictory, a "bloated" theory that "breeds obscurity and solipsism" (37). Doubtless, one could find evidence to support this negative assessment; however, there seems to be considerable evidence of the theory's explanatory power and positive impact. In particular, it has led to a variety of important reassessments of various power structures and discourses, and of their interrelatedness. It has opened up new areas of literary study and suggested new approaches to that enterprise. Finally, the post-colonial perspective seems particularly useful for clarifying the various positions and interrelationships of minority literatures in Canada.

Post-colonial studies grew out of the work of Frantz Fanon, whose *Wretched of the Earth* (1961) described the lingering cultural effects of imperialism, suggested the significance of language in creating and sustaining those effects, and called passionately for a blend of national and cultural liberation. They also were influenced by the work of Michel Foucault, whose early books, such as *Madness and Civilization* (1965), attempted to uncover the codes that create the reality we perceive. Since then, a variety of analyses such as those of Edward Said in *Orientalism* (1978) and *Culture and Imperialism* (1993), Bill Ashcroft, Gareth Griffiths, and Helen Tiffin in *The Empire Writes Back: Theory and Practice in Post-Colonial Literatures* (1989), Homi K. Bhabha in *Nation and Narration* (1990), Gayatri Chakravorty Spivak in *The Post-Colonial Critic Interviews, Strategies, Dialogues* (1990), and Arnold Harrichand Itwaru and Natasha Ksonzek in *Closed Entrances, Canadian Culture and Imperialism* (1994) have explored the ways in which literature – defined as literary texts and the institutional infrastructures that publish, distribute, critique, and teach them – serves as an important site of struggle for self-determination, for political, social, and cultural power. Not surprisingly, Canadian writers and critics have contributed in no small way to the development of post-colonial theory over the past 30 years. For example, in their wide-ranging exploration of post-colonial literatures, Ashcroft, Griffiths, and Tiffin draw on the work of many Canadians and posit Canadian writing as a major example of a post-colonial literature.

In my view and for my purposes here, the usefulness of post-colonial theory stems in large part from its having emerged from post-colonial spaces and sensibilities and from its subsequent emphasis on local particulars. Post-colonial theory not only draws attention to a body of literatures that are linked by their having "emerged in their present form out of the experience of colonization and asserted themselves by foregrounding the tension with the imperial power, and by emphasizing their differences from the assumptions of the imperial centre" (Ashcroft et al. 2), but also suggests a reading strategy appropriate to our polyphonic postmodern era, in which the methodology historically linked with the study of English is dangerously outmoded.[1] That methodology involved "the fixing of texts in historical time and the perpetual search for the determinants of a single, unified and agreed meaning ... proceed[ing] from a single ideological climate ... and 'enthroned' [in] a 'privileging norm'" that *ipso facto* denied the value of anything from the margins (*Ibid.* 3).

In the following discussion, which is meant to be suggestive rather than exhaustive or definitive, I suggest the particular need for a new, post-colonial methodology or reading strategy within the current Canadian context. I do so by looking at two current issues from the perspectives offered by post-colonial theory: first, the long-standing concern over the need for and difficulty of nurturing a strong and "authentic" Canadian culture; and second, the currently high profile (but also long-standing) concern over the need for and difficulty of nourishing the cultural expressions of groups heretofore largely marginalized in Canada. This approach is useful, it seems to me, because it reveals some of the important ways these two concerns are interrelated, and because it directs teachers, writers, and critics from a variety of ethnocultural spaces towards a critical practice appropriate to hearing the diverse literary voices in contemporary Canada.

The first issue, that of developing a strong and authentic national culture, expressed in a variety of forms (including literature), has long been a part of a continuing discussion, primarily among Canadian intellectuals, about Canadian identity and nation. That literature might indeed express national culture was assumed fairly widely in English-speaking Canada from at least the time of Confederation to the 1970s. That the name "Confederation Group" was given to the late-nineteenth-century poets who expressly "sought plainer ways to record the beauty and reality of the Canadian landscape" is a graphic illustration of this assumption (New 1018). Indeed, the history of Canadian literature has often been constructed as the story of its evolving (in the eighteenth and nineteenth centuries) from a small collection of merely imitative colonial texts to (by the mid-twentieth century) an impressive collection of "indigenous" texts. The latter were seen as products of a confident nation that, with "Hugh MacLennan's 1941 novel *Barometer Rising*, experienced a period of liberal reassessment of Canadian culture, a period which declared Canada's freedom from external constraints, a Canadian role in world affairs, and the viability of Canadian subjects in literature" (New 1019).

Nourished by the Canada Council (established in 1957), Canadian literature continued to be seen by many during the 1960s as a reflection of national culture. During this period of assertive nationalism in English-speaking Canada, literature (including literary criticism) was widely regarded as a site where the remnants of the old colonial relationship with Britain and the new colonial relationship with the United States could be resisted, i.e., subverted. English Canadian writers and critics – Margaret Atwood, for example, in her novel *Surfacing* (1972) and more explicitly in her critical work *Survival* (1972) that attempted to illuminate the quintessential patterns of Canadian literature; Robert Kroetsch in a variety of works; and Dennis Lee, particularly in his article, "Cadence, Country, Silence: Writing in Colonial Space"(1974) – waged what we might now call a post-colonial struggle partly aimed at deconstructing "false" images but particularly aimed at asserting an authentically Canadian voice. Even as the Quiet Revolution was setting the stage in Quebec for the rise of separatism, some critics in English-speaking Canada saw a common literary tradition emerging from Canada's "two solitudes," based on a shared sensibility deriving in part from a perpetual awareness of the other "founding group" and of the complex inter-relationships between the two (Sutherland 1971, 1977).

Canadian culture continues to be seen as a site of struggle, particularly *vis-à-vis* the United States, and many Canadians are concerned about national unity in the wake of the Quebec referendum of 1995. They are also concerned about what they see as the fragmentation of Canadian society and culture perpetuated by official multiculturalism – an anxiety articulated, for example, by Neil Bissoondath in *Selling Illusions* (1994) and reflected in the appeal of the Reform Party of Canada. The idea is virtually dead, however, that either of Canada's two major literatures – that produced in English Canada and the literature of Quebec – might be regarded as constituting a single voice representative of nation. As W.H. New puts it,

> As far as the 1970s and 1980s are concerned, historians essentially gave up any fixed notion of the "whole" society; the whole was inapprehensible, in flux. Criticism, too, edged away from seeing literature as foremost an expression of a single national character. Recent research in psychology called into question a related notion about the wholeness of the self, an idea which bears upon some readings of interrupted literary sequences (whether in poetry or in short fiction).... Such attitudes ... call attention to the shifting limits of knowledge. (xxxii)

The idea that Canadian literature could express a single national character is no longer fashionable or even tenable in light of the insights offered by postmodernist and feminist criticism (Hutcheon 1988) and perhaps also in the context of increasing globalization. Yet interestingly and perhaps not surprisingly, it is clearly in important ways related to the idea of multiplicity that has replaced it. Stated simply, the concern with the problematics of discovering, creating, and championing an authentic national literature can be seen as a post-colonial attempt at decolonization. As Ashcroft, Griffiths, and Tiffin make clear,

> The development of national literatures and criticism is fundamental to the whole enterprise of post-colonial studies. Without such developments at the national level, and without the comparative studies between national traditions to which these lead, no discourse of the post-colonial could have emerged. The study of national traditions is the first and most vital stage of the process of rejecting the claims of the centre to exclusivity. (17)

This also applies, of course, to the concern with the problematics of minority literatures in Canada. Both "national" literatures and the literatures of various "minority" groups within Canada (for example, Aboriginal, South Asian, Ukrainian) emerged

> in their present form out of the experience of colonization and asserted themselves by foregrounding the tension with the imperial power, and by emphasizing their differences from the assumptions of the imperial centre. It is this which makes them distinctively post-colonial." (Ashcroft et al. 2)

Significantly, the post-colonial critics Ashcroft, Griffiths, and Tiffin quote both Kroetsch's "Unhiding the Hidden: Recent Canadian Fiction" (1974) and Lee's "Cadence, Country, Silence: Writing in Colonial Space," which delineate the barriers to authentic expression faced by Canadian writers and, in the latter case, at least, also offer a kind of cultural nationalist manifesto that captured the literary *zeitgeist* of the late 1960s and early 1970s. Kroetsch observes that while he had once thought the Canadian writer's task to be that of naming, he came to realize that it is, rather, "to unname." This seems remarkably congruent with concerns expressed recently by Aboriginal writers and critics:

> The Canadian writer's particular predicament is that he works with a language within a literature, that appears to be his own.... But ... there is in the Canadian word a concealed other experience, sometimes British, sometimes American. (quoted in Ashcroft et al. 141)

Compare, for example, Kimberly Blaeser (in an article on developing an appropriate critical response to American Indian literature) quoting Louis Owens's discussion of American Indian writer N. Scott Momaday as perceptively capturing the dilemma faced by the Native writer and critic: "The task before him was not simply to learn the lost language of his tribe but rather to appropriate, to tear free of its restricting authority, another language – English – and to make it accessible to an Indian discourse" (quoted in Blaeser 55). Similarly, Dennis Lee's comments seem to resonate with the contemporary concerns of Native writers and critics:

> The colonial writer does not have words of his own.... Try to speak the words of your home and you will discover – if you are a colonial – that you do not know them.... To speak unreflectingly in a colony then, is to use words that speak only alien space. To reflect is to fall silent, discovering that your authentic space does not have words. And to reflect further is to recognise that you and your people do not in fact have a privileged authentic space just waiting for words; you are, among other things, the people who have made an alien inauthenticity your own. You are left chafing at the inarticulacy of a native space which may not exist.... (163)

As the pioneering post-colonial theorist D.E.S. Maxwell points out, literatures produced on the margins of empire share a paradoxically crippling and enabling awareness of a gap between language and place that distinguishes them from the English literary tradition. In fact, the distinction he makes between settler colonies and invaded colonies provides a fruitful way of identifying the very real similarities and equally profound differences between the mindset that produced writers and critics concerned with fostering an authentically Canadian national literature and that which has produced many minority writers who resist just such a unitary vision. Maxwell distinguished two "broad categories" of post-colonial literatures:

> In the first, the writer brings his own language – English – to an alien environment and a fresh set of experiences: Australia, Canada, New Zealand. In the other, the writer brings an alien language – English – to his own social and cultural inheritance: India, West Africa. Yet the categories have a fundamental kinship.... [The] "intolerable wrestle with words and meanings" has as its aim to subdue the experience to the language, the exotic life to the imported tongue. (quoted in Ashcroft et al. 25)

It seems clear, then, that what fuels the desire to see literature as a site for asserting a distinctive and unified national voice is a desire to be out from under imperial domination: to decolonize one's political, social, and cultural space by bridging the gap between language and place, between representation and experience. And it seems equally clear that while "mainstream" Canadian writers such as Margaret Atwood have "written back to the empire" from the particular post-colonial space they occupy, the centre and the margin that define their project are different from those that define the project many contemporary Aboriginal writers see themselves engaged in, which is also one of decolonization.

Native writer and activist Jeannette Armstrong explains that "Indigenous peoples in North America were rendered powerless and subjugated to totalitarian domination by foreign peoples." And in her view, Native writers have a "tremendous" responsibility to redress this disempowerment by "The dispelling of lies and the telling of what really happened until *everyone*, including our own people understands that this condition (the disempowerment of Native peoples) did not happen through choice or some cultural defect on our part ..."(Armstrong, "Disempowerment" 209).

But while "national" writers such as MacLennan, Atwood, and many others might see or have seen themselves as the disempowered, writing to decolonize the marginal space they occupy as Canadian writers, Native writers such as Armstrong, Tomson Highway, Lenore Keeshig-Tobias, and others would see them as part of the oppressive structures of imperial domination. Their respective projects are, in fundamental ways, at odds. Post-colonial analysts are right when they tell us that an assertive national literature is an important site for the settler colony's efforts at decolonization, which are centred primarily in adapting the imported language to local experience. So too are they right when they highlight Native literature as an important site for the invaded Aboriginal culture to struggle against the settler colony.

That these two enterprises are clearly at odds is nowhere more evident than in the settler colony's efforts to seek connection with the "new world" it occupies through appropriating various elements of Aboriginal culture. "Appropriation" or "the process by which the language is taken and made to 'bear the burden' of one's own cultural experience" is vital to the decolonization process for "settler" colonies. It follows "abrogation," that is to say the "refusal of the categories of the imperial culture, its aesthetic, its illusory standard of normative or 'correct' usage, and its assumption of a traditional and fixed meaning 'inscribed' in words" (Ashcroft et al. 38). Appropriation is essential to carrying forward the momentum of abrogation, which otherwise "may not extend beyond a reversal of the assumptions of privilege, the 'normal'... all of which can be simply taken over and maintained by the new usage" (*Ibid.*).

Such is the process we see at work in Canada in the appropriation of words from Native languages for naming Canadian spaces; in the numerous depictions in Canadian literature in English of Native characters (Godard, "Politics of Representation"; Francis); in the use of Native symbols (often inaccurately rendered) and in the construction of region (as, for example, in the use of images of teepees and ceremonial headdress to symbolize the West).

Ironically, the settler culture's efforts to make the imported language "appropriate" to its "new world" experience (to decolonize the space it inhabits in the imperial structure by asserting its difference from the centre through language and story "authentic" to its emerging national space) construct further barriers to decolonization for the invaded Aboriginal peoples.

Clearly, then, the problems inherent in "writing back to the empire" are not quite the same for Native writers as for "settler" writers. The former, though "not forced to adapt to a different landscape and climate," nevertheless experience a more profound dislocation in having "their own ancient and sophisticated responses to them marginalized by the world-view which was implicated in the acquisition of English" (Ashcroft et al. 25). Tomson Highway captures this complexity in describing the process he sees himself engaged in as a Native writer:

> To make a long, complicated story short, it came to encapsulating that incredible collision of two cultures as symbolized by the meeting of the two mythologies, the two theologies. In this case, it's Christian mythology/theology that underlies all mainstream white society in this country. In my case, Cree mythology is the mythology/theology that I know best from what little I've been able to get back.... One mythology almost destroyed the other, took away the dignity of the other mythology. One god took away the dignity of another god. Now what has to happen is that the god who lost their dignity has to take it back. Just a simple act of taking it back.... (7)

As Highway clarifies, the project of decolonization is considerably more complex and many-layered from the invaded position than that from the settler position. For North America's Aboriginal peoples, European languages were not merely inadequate for expressing local experience, they also embodied a world view very different from, even hostile to, their own. As Highway sees it, the invading culture was male, the invaded female: "Along comes this incredibly patriarchal religion and God as a woman ran smack dab into God as a man and the male God raped the female God" (*Ibid.* 17).

Nor, in delineating the fundamental similarities and differences between the dynamics of "national" literatures in Canada on the one hand and those of Aboriginal literatures on the other, can one see the latter as representative of or synonymous with minority literatures in Canada. Like Native literature, the literature produced in Canada by immigrants and their children whose backgrounds were neither British nor French has until very recently been marginalized, that is, not viewed as being "Canadian" literature in the same sense as the work produced by Canada's "two founding nations." It too is, in a very real sense, post-colonial literature; however, the position from which it has been written is not only different from that of the "national" mainstream writers, but also from that of Aboriginal writers. One commentator who makes this difference particularly clear, though writing over 20 years ago and not writing about literature *per se*, is George Melnyk. In response to an Alberta Native leader's call for Native peoples to follow the paths of upward mobility well established by "ethnic" immigrants in Canada, Melnyk suggests why he sees this advice as misguided:

> Initially, the comparison between native and ethnic makes sense when one is aware of their historical affinity as outcast minorities. But why did their histories diverge?... The answer lies in the ethnic's immigrant status. The very thing that gave him some problems at first was what assured his mobility. The white conquest was an immigrant conquest and the ethnic was part of it, while the Indian was its victim.... He was the loser in the battle and he carried the scar. Not being white, he could not blend into the European mosaic. For the ethnic to identify with the victor is understandable; but for the native to do likewise is a travesty....
>
> The native peoples are the *other* half of Western history. They are not a numerical half, but a psychological and metaphysical one. Without their participation, the Western identity is incomplete. (52-58 *passim*)

The "ethnic" voice has been marginalized in Canadian society and in Canadian literature; however, while the latter have been "invaded" by the imperial centre, the former have been "dominated." This distinction, developed by Max Dorsinville in *Caliban Without Prospero* (1974), accounts for the complex hierarchies of social and cultural power that exist in heterogeneous societies by highlighting "linguistic and cultural imposition" and thereby enabling "an interpretation of (say) British literary history as a process of hierarchical interchange in internal and external group relationships" (Ashcroft et al. 33). Thus, while in Canada writers from backgrounds such as Ukrainian, Italian, South Asian, Japanese, or Caribbean cultures have been marginalized by "hierarchical exchange," in this case by the privileging of British and French ethnicity and often by an added level of linguistic displacement, these writers nevertheless share with the English/ French centre the position of interloper and sometimes invader *vis-à-vis* Aboriginal peoples.

The "two nations" ethnic hierarchy did, however, relegate to the margins of settler society the increasingly diverse immigrants and their descendants who migrated primarily to the western provinces and central Canada in several waves throughout the late-nineteenth and twentieth centuries. This increasingly polyglot immigration included such diverse groups as the Chinese who settled in British Columbia in the late 1850s; the Icelanders who settled in Manitoba in the 1870s; the Eastern-European Jews who began settling in Montreal, Toronto, and Winnipeg in the last decades of the nineteenth century; the Ukrainians who settled in northern Alberta and other parts of the prairie provinces between 1896 and 1930 and in the cities of Ontario after the Second World War; the Italians who came to Toronto, Montreal, and other urban centres in the 1950s; and the South Asians,

Southeast Asians, and Caribbeans who came to Canada in ever-greater numbers after the liberalization of immigration regulations in 1967.

This "third force," as they came to be called in the mid-1960s in the context of the Royal Commission on Bilingualism and Biculturalism, was composed of the "Canadianized" descendants of pioneer immigrants many of whom came from Eastern Europe in the early years of the century, and of first-generation immigrants, often highly skilled, educated, and articulate, who arrived from a variety of (primarily) European countries after the Second World War. Both cohorts demanded a legitimate space in Canada, one that would be defined by symbolic and cultural as well as legal equality. The political synthesis that emerged, in part as a result of "third force" activism, was official "multi-culturalism" (Burnet and Palmer 223-24).

With the potential to be a very radical, post-colonial vision of Canadian society, multiculturalism, both as ideology and public policy, had to be pragmatically adapted to the socio-political (bi-cultural) realities of Canada. Hence the official definition of Canadian culture that emerged in the policy announced by Pierre Trudeau in October of 1971 was "Multiculturalism within a bi-lingual framework," a phrase that arguably highlighted Canadian culture as the site of a complex process/struggle over the nature of Canadian identity and nationhood. The issue at the heart of these struggles, a remnant of Canada's colonial history, was (and is) the contradiction between not only ethnic hierarchy and an inclusive, horizontal vision of nationhood, also a unitary (or binary) vision of cultural expression and a multiplistic one (Seiler 1993).

This struggle has been evident not only in the political institutions and discourses related to immigration and diversity, but also in the institutions and discourses of "high" culture, including literature (Craig; Padolsky, "Canadian Ethnic"). An instructive example is the history of critical response in English-speaking Canada to the literary texts produced by those outside the privileged centre of the "two founding peoples." Most of this work was virtually absent from the literary canon of English-speaking Canada until the 1970s and has only been embraced by major cultural arbiters in the last decade or so. The work of Watson Kirkonnell, in particular *Canadian Overtones* (translations of poetry written by "new Canadians" in languages other than English and French) and his section on "New Canadian Letters" in the *University of Toronto Quarterly* (1937 to 1964), was the exception. Otherwise, until the 1980s, most English-speaking literary critics in Canada ignored the substantial body of *émigré* literature being produced in Ukrainian, Hungarian, Icelandic, Yiddish, Italian, and more recently in South-Asian languages such as Urdu. During the 1980s *Canadian Fiction Magazine,* under the editorship of Geoff Hancock, broke this silence and produced several "translation issues."[2]

Nor until recently did English Canada's critical establishment seem able or willing to respond to the works written in English, largely in the interwar years and post-Second World War era, by second- and third-generation writers such as Vera Lysenko, Laura Goodman Salverson, John Marlyn, Adele

Wiseman, and others. Again, it was not until the mid-1980s that *Canadian Literature* produced several issues devoted to Italian-Canadian, Caribbean-Canadian, and Slavic-Canadian literature. A typical example of this critical neglect is the response to *Yellow Boots* (1954), Vera Lysenko's important fictionalization of ethnic experience on the prairies, which languished largely unnoticed as an out-of-print hardcover on obscure library shelves until it was re-issued in 1992 by NeWest Press to at least some critical notice by mainstream cultural authorities.

An artful telling of the story of Lilli Landash, the daughter of Ukrainian immigrants who settled in Manitoba in the early years of the century, *Yellow Boots* challenged traditional notions of genre. At once folk tale, analysis of folklore, and female *bildungsroman*, Lysenko's narrative is also an early envisioning of a multicultural Canada and a hymn to nationhood (Rasporich 1991). Through her musical artistry Lilli, "a new world singer of old world songs" (Lysenko), not only asserts her legitimacy and claims her place as a Ukrainian and as a woman, but also bridges the differences among diverse groups – creating a new song, a new voice, and thereby an inclusive symbol of national identity.

An apostle of interculturalism in *Yellow Boots*, where she describes immigrants from "almost every European and Asiatic origin" (351) coming together in unity at a Lilli Landash concert at the end of the story, Lysenko creates in Lilli's personal odyssey an apt fictional symbol for both the personal and collective cultural experiences of immigrants from "other" cultural backgrounds.[3] For example, the literary history of virtually every "non-founding" immigrant group in Canada is a chronicle of struggle, first to find a voice and then to have that voice heard and appreciated (Padolsky, "Canadian Ethnic"; Seiler). Typically, the evolution in Canada of the literature of later ("non-founding") immigrants, like that of Aboriginal peoples, of various British groups, and of the French, has been based on the rich traditions of folk culture and oral tales that reside with early generations. Gradually incorporating Canadian subject matter, often related to the joys and sorrows of immigration, these forms, along with the writings of a few who constituted the intelligentsia of the group, were sometimes published in religious and/or ethnic periodicals, some with a local, others an international, distribution directed not only to the home country but to other immigrant communities in the United States and elsewhere.

During the earlier waves of immigration, the intelligentsia was most often the community's religious leaders; after the Second World War, they were more apt to be political dissidents, some of them displaced writers such as the Czech-Canadian Joseph Skvorecký, who came to Canada after the 1968 uprising in what was then Czechoslovakia. Extending the pioneering legacy of Lysenko, and in particular of immigrant writers such as Illia Kiriak, whose epic novel about Ukrainian pioneers was translated into English as *Sons of the Soil* in 1959, Skvorecký, along with other more recent *émigré* writers, expanded the boundaries of Canadian literature to include (in English translation) such works as his sophisticated, humanistic *The Engineer of Human Souls* (1984), which juxtaposes and blends the starkly contrasting landscapes and mindscapes of his communist-occupied homeland after the Second World War and 1980s Toronto. That it won the 1984 Governor General's Award for fiction in English suggests the degree to which Canadian literature in English has gradually been recognized as being polyvocal.

Typically, the next stage in this literary evolution has been the recognition of the work in English of second- or third-generation writers like Lysenko who (both willingly and unwillingly) have played the difficult role of mediator or apologist, interpreting their group's experiences to the larger community and, in so doing, often critiquing both. Such works constitute an extremely rich, significant, and rapidly growing feature of Canada's literature in English. Despite the uniqueness of each artist's vision, second-generation fictions often share certain post-colonial features. A recent anthology of Chinese-Canadian literature is representative: expressly entitled *Many Mouthed Birds* (1991) by editors Bennet Lee and Jim Wong Chu, it celebrates those who break certain cultural codes by talking too much (i.e., writers who are willing to tell a previously untold story). This and other "second-generation" literature is often framed as confessional, a somewhat risky act of "breaking the silence" (Pivato, *Contrasts*, "Italian-Canadian Women"; Padolsky "The Place of Italian-Canadian"). Such diverse works as Laura Goodman Salverson's *Confessions of an Immigrant's Daughter* (1937), Frank Paci's *Black Madonna* (1984), Rudy Wiebe's *Peace Shall Destroy Many* (1962), Joy Kogawa's *Obasan* (1981), more recently, Denise Chong's *The Concubine's Children* (1994), and interestingly, the work of many Aboriginal writers, such as Maria Campbell's *Halfbreed* (1973), use this narrative strategy that works to subvert distanced, "official" stories.

Like Lysenko's *Yellow Boots*, such fictions are often cast in the literary form of the *bildungsroman*, or coming-of-age story. John Marlyn's *Under the Ribs of Death* (1957), Mordecai Richler's *The Apprenticeship of Duddy Kravitz* (1959), and Adele Wiseman's *Crackpot* (1974), are all coming-of-age fictions that depict the perilous world in which the children of immigrants must serve their apprenticeships as North Americans. The spaces in which they negotiate their coming-of-age are marginal ones where they must master different, often contradictory, codes of behaviour. Another characteristic feature of this "other" voice in Canadian literature, both that of the first and of subsequent generations, is its focus on, indeed its near obsession with, duality. Story after story and novel after novel, as well as numerous poems and plays, articulate a profound sense of dislocation through a series of interlocking binary patterns – typically, the dichotomies of old world/new world, success/failure, remembering/forgetting, and revelation/concealment (Mandel; Kroetsch "Grammar of Silence"; Palmer "Fictionalization," "Mythologizing").

Not surprisingly a large part of the immigrant story in Canadian literature is the fictional exploration of journeying, of displacement, and of finding a place in Canadian society through comparing the new country with the old.

Such a comparison fuels much of the work of early first-generation immigrant writers such as Frederick Philip Grove, whose 1946 "autobiography" *In Search of Myself* was itself fictionalized in *In Search of America* (1927). Contrasts and connections between Europe and America are also central to the Jewish-Canadian writer Henry Kreisel's short stories and novel *The Rich Man* (1948). More recently, both first- and second-generation immigrants have also explored the comparisons of their own: Italian-Canadian Caterina Edwards in *The Lion's Mouth* (1982); Caribbean-born Austin Clarke in *Nine Men Who Laughed* (1986); and South Asian immigrant writers Rohinton Mistry in his *Tales from Firozsha Baag* (1987), Uma Parmeswaran in her poetry and in short stories, such as "How We Won the Olympic Gold" (1992), and M.G. Vassanji in *No New Land* (1991). In these and many other literary explorations of immigrant experience the old/new binary can be seen as a decolonizing strategy, since it enables the text to stand somewhat outside each cultural space and from this marginal position to critique both.

The fictional landscape that is portrayed by these writers often is the Canada that George Woodcock characterized as "a land of invisible ghettoes" (Mandel 59). The Jewish-Canadian writer Mordecai Richler is probably the most celebrated creator of such a fictional world, but there are many others. Guy Vanderhaeghe's "What I Learned from Caesar" (1987) reveals the price paid by a Dutch immigrant in his ultimately doomed attempt to prosper in Canada. Denise Chong in *The Concubine's Children* (1994), Sky Lee in *Disappearing Moon Cafe* (1990), and Paul Yee in "Prairie Night 1939" (1991) similarly reveal the confined spaces occupied by their Chinese-Canadian characters. Contemporary fictions such as these (and many earlier works) portray a profoundly stratified world and, in so doing, illuminate the barriers, illusions, and topsy-turvy values associated with the immigrant journey in Canada.

The increasing diversity of Canadian immigration throughout the twentieth century ultimately has transformed not only the country's demography, but also its culture. The evolution of literature in English-speaking Canada provides a telling example. Once limited to those works reflecting Anglo-Canadian sensibilities, Canadian literature in English is increasingly being recognized as pluralistic and polyphonic. The literature produced by "other" voices, from the 1920s to the present, has been central to effecting this re-visioning. Like Joy Kogawa's silence-breaking and award-winning novel, *Obasan* (1981), which portrays the experience of Japanese-Canadians interned during the Second World War, and its sequel *Itsuka* (1992), this literature has been both the source and the product of social and cultural transformation and change. As such, it coincides with an evolving post-colonial struggle against a constrictive, hierarchical construction of ethnicity, including the notion of a unitary Canadian literature.

The post-colonial struggle of minority ethnic writers in Canada throughout this century, a struggle that has helped to effect a variety of changes in Canadian social, political, and cultural institutions, is both similar to and different from that in which contemporary Aboriginal writers are engaged. The differences remind us of Melnyk's distinction between Native and ethnic positions in Canadian society and culture: the object of ethnic struggle has been inclusion; that of the Aboriginal struggle a much more radical re-thinking of North American history and its underlying values and assumptions. As Jeannette Armstrong makes clear, Native writers share with "ethnic" writers the goal of subverting the racist hierarchy that Canada's history as a European colony has bequeathed us:

> the dominating culture's reality is that it seeks to affirm itself continuously and must be taught that *numbers* are not the basis of democracy, *people* are, *each one* being important. It must be pushed, in Canada, to understand and accept that this country is multi-racial and multi-cultural now and the meaning of that. ("Disempowerment" 209-10)

But Armstrong also makes clear that the Native writer's project is larger, since it entails writing against centuries of ethnocentric constructions of Native peoples and against a world view that is virtually the opposite of that embedded in Native cultural practices. Thus, for her, the task is twofold: "To examine the past and culturally affirm a new vision for all our people in the future, arising out of the powerful and positive support structures that are inherent in the principles of cooperation" (*Ibid.* 210).

One could well argue, however, that a further important distinction should be made among "ethnic" writers in Canada, one that sees the position of writers of colour as being much more similar to that of Aboriginal writers than to ethnic writers of European descent. One might see, for example, South Asian writers – whether from India or the Indian diaspora that followed the map of empire – as writing from an invaded position as well as from a dominated one. Viewed this way, a text such as M.G. Vassanji's *No New Land*, which insightfully depicts the continuing displacement in Canada of East African immigrants of South Asian background – who are, of course, veterans of and refugees from life in various parts of the former British empire – might be seen to have as much in common with the work of Tomson Highway or Thomas King as with that of, say, John Marlyn or Mordecai Richler, with which it also has important affinities. Exploring such connections among the texts emerging from the various post-colonial spaces that Canada's particular evolution has created would seem an important part of a reading strategy appropriate for Canada's literatures, one that could enhance the dialogic power of these texts.

What kind of critical aesthetic might provide an appropriate strategy for reading the diverse texts currently being produced in Canada from the variety of post-colonial positions I have attempted to suggest above? Bringing together several key points made from diverse post-colonial spaces may suggest a clear direction, if not a fully elaborated strategy. One important guideline is suggested by a key point made by Robert Kroetsch and Dennis Lee over 20 years ago. Speaking as "national" writers, they apprehended and began to articulate a solution to the complex challenge of

appropriating the imperial language to give voice to Canadian experience. As
Lee put it in 1974,

> But perhaps – and here is the breakthrough – perhaps our job was not
> to fake a space of our own and write it up, but rather to find words for
> our space-lessness – instead of pushing against the grain of an external,
> uncharged language, perhaps we would finally come to writing with
> that grain. (163)

"Going *with* that grain," as Lee saw it, meant embracing silence. Not the
silence, I would argue, of a frustrated inability to speak, but the silence necessary
to really listen, to begin to hear the voices that emerge from one's "marginal
space." Kroetsch's (1974) notion of "unhiding the hidden," of "unnaming," is
closely related to Lee's in that such an endeavour demands silence as well as
voice. In comments made in 1991 by the Native poet and playwright Daniel
David Moses we can see the significance of that silence and appreciate the way
it might open up space for other voices:

> I think the concern with appropriation (of Native culture) has more to
> do with the fact that most people aren't sensitive listeners, so they are
> not sensitive transmitters of stories, partly because the cultures have
> different values. When someone from another culture hears a story I
> tell, they perceive only the things that relate to their values. If they try
> to retell my story they are going to emphasize those things that are
> important to them. That only makes sense. So all we're saying is don't
> retell our stories, change them, and pretend they are what we're about
> because they are not. (Moses and Goldie xx)

Thus some of the very real and formidable problems in contemporary
Canadian literary space as Moses sees it (I think rightly) emerge from an
inability to listen well to the stories of the "other," a lapse that is likely caused
by a kind of general laziness, but also more importantly by too much "noise"
in various forms: cultural constructions and biases that inevitably make
listening/reading a selective process that distorts what is perceived.

What might the silence Lee points to enable us to hear? What unnaming
might it facilitate? Productive silence has already enabled ethnic voices that
have, largely in the past 20 years, transformed what is now regarded as
Canadian literature in English from having one voice, largely genteel and
Anglo-Celtic, to having many. Aboriginal voices are just beginning to be part
of that multiplicity, including, very recently, the voices of Aboriginal critics.
Jeannette Armstrong rightly insists in her introduction to *Looking at the Words
of our People: First Nations Analysis of Literature* (1993) that the Native critical
voice is essential to "an acknowledgment and recognition that the voices are
culture-specific voices and that there are experts within those cultures who
are essential to be drawn from and drawn out in order to incorporate into the

reinterpretation through pedagogy the context of English Literature coming from Native Americans" (7).

In Armstrong's ground-breaking volume, the Native American critic Kim Blaeser makes several vitally important assertions that, in my view, point towards an appropriate multicultural aesthetic. The first concerns the limitations of imported literary theory for interpreting Native literature. She notes that like Native writers, Native critics must appropriate existing critical discourse in order to "make that language accessible to an Indian discourse." She also acknowledges the usefulness of some "universalizing theory" (for example Mikhail Bakhtin's distinction between monologue and dialogue and between linear and pictorial writing styles) and admits her "complicity" in using some "imported" theories such as postmodernism to analyze Native literature. Blaeser asserts strongly, however, that Native literature is distinctive and consequently insists that "reading Native literature by way of Western literary theory clearly violates its integrity and performs a new act of colonization and conquest" (55). Her point is that critics must begin "working from within Native literature or tradition to discover appropriate tools or to form an appropriate language of critical discourse...." (Blaeser 56)

Interestingly, and this constitutes the second point I find particularly important, Blaeser notes that this task is made even more difficult, more complicated, by the fact that

> the literary works themselves are always at least bi-cultural: Though they may come from an oral-based culture, they are written. Though their writer may speak a tribal language, they are usually almost wholly in the language of English. And though they proceed at least partly from an Indian culture, they are most often presented in the established literary and aesthetic forms of the dominant culture (or in those forms acceptable to the publishing industry). The writers themselves have generally experienced both tribal and mainstream American culture and many are in physical fact mixed-bloods. Beyond this, the works themselves generally proceed from an awareness of the "frontier" or border existence where cultures meet. The criticism, too, even if written by Native Americans, is also, (and for many of the same reasons) at least bi-cultural. Perhaps to adequately open up the multicultural texts of Native American literature, it must be.... [However] I still do not rescind my call for an "organic" native critical language. If we need a dual vision to adequately appreciate the richness of Indian literature, the native half to that vision has still been conspicuously absent. (56, 57)

Thus, Blaeser acknowledges that North American, post-colonial space is remarkably hybrid and fluid – that, as Edward Said asserts, "Partly because of empire, all cultures are involved in one another; none is single and pure, all are hybrid, heterogeneous, extraordinarily differentiated, and unmonolithic" (*Culture and Imperialism* xxvi). Said's observation is part of his admonition (particularly fundamental to developing a multicultural aesthetic) about the dangers of what he calls the "paranoid nationalism" so often part of the educational agenda whereby "children as well as older students are taught to venerate and celebrate the uniqueness of their tradition usually and invidiously at the expense of others" (*Ibid.*). The challenge, however, as Blaeser makes clear, is to appreciate and respond appropriately both to this syncretic innovation and to the traditions underlying it. And, as she insists, making space for and learning to listen to Native critical perspectives is vital to the multicultural aesthetic appropriate to appreciating literary texts produced in Canadian cultural space. This is particularly true for appreciating Native literary texts, but it applies to others as well – the perspectives of Native critics on a variety of non-Native texts should inform a multicultural aesthetic.

The third point that Blaeser makes that I find particularly relevant to developing an appropriate strategy for reading Canadian literary texts is the importance of proceeding inductively, that is, by beginning with the texts themselves. Such a method, itself a kind of decolonizing strategy since it insists on beginning from the post-colonial margins rather than from the imperial centre, enables the critic to appreciate a wide variety of texts – from the traditional and highly contextualized to the highly innovative and/or syncretic. Interestingly, several writers, perhaps most explicitly the writer and critic Kateri Damm, actually embody this hybridity in the person of the "mixed-blood" writer who explodes stereotypes and mediates across cultural spaces:

> Already the voices of mixed-bloods play an important role in the breaking of silences, the telling of Indigenous perspectives, the dispelling of lies and stereotypes, the creation of Indigenous literature.... The idea that mixed-bloods have a dual perspective and can bridge the gap between Indigenous and white societies through writing is one which recurs and echoes in the work of many Indigenous writers around the world. For example, one needs only to look at the work of Indigenous literature "pioneers" such as E. Pauline Johnson and Beatrice Culleton in Canada, Patricia Grace and Keri Hulme in New Zealand, Sally Morgan in Australia and Leslie Marmon Silko and N. Scott Momaday in the United States to see how prevalent these issues have been all along and how important the voices of mixed-bloods still are in the development of Indigenous literature. (Damm 7)

What I am suggesting, then, is that the two different ways of looking at Canada, embodied in the emphasis on a unified national culture versus the emphasis on multivocality, are not ultimately incompatible. A post-colonial, multicultural aesthetic can allow an appreciation of both as discourses that, in complex interaction, express Canadian experience on the margins of several empires – an experience that continues to be shaped not just by difference, but by various kinds of difference, as well as by complex hybridity that is never static.

In his *Reconciling the Solitudes: Essays on Canadian Federalism and National- ism*, political philosopher Charles Taylor asserts that the way out of the country's current political malaise is

> To build a country for everyone … to allow for a second-level or "deep" diversity, in which a plurality of ways of belonging would also be acknowledged and accepted. Someone of, say, Italian extraction in Toronto or Ukrainian extraction in Edmonton might indeed feel Canadian as a bearer of individual rights in a multicultural mosaic. His or her belonging would not "pass through" some other community, although the ethnic identity might be important to him or her in various ways. But this person might nevertheless accept that a Québécois or a Cree or a Dene might belong in a very different way, that these persons were Canadian through being members of their national communities. Reciprocally, the Québécois, Cree, or Dene would accept the perfect legitimacy of the "mosaic" identity. (183)

Furthermore, Taylor asserts, imported paradigms of citizenship that demand uniformity do not fit Canada's experience; they are "a straitjacket for many societies" and Canada and the world need "other models to be legitimated in order to allow for more humane and less constraining modes of political cohabitation," models that are "exploring the space of deep diversity" (*Ibid.*). A careful look at Canada's literary history and at its current multiplistic literary expression suggests that the critical aesthetic appropriate to – indeed that grows out of – Canada as a political, social, and cultural space, is one that is analogous to the strategy of federalism embodied in Taylor's phrase, "exploring deep diversity." While neither uniform nor tidy, such a strategy would likely enrich and enlarge our collective imaginings.

NOTES
1. Some critics, such as Stephen Slemon, "Monuments of empire: allegory/ counter-discourse/post-colonial writing," *Kunapipi* 9.3 (1987): 1-16, have sug- gested that post-colonialism is best thought of as a transformative reading practice rather than primarily a body of literatures.
2. Space does not permit a discussion here of the similar dynamic that has occured in Quebec. See Sherry Simon and David Leahy, "La recherche au Québec portant sur l'écriture ethnique," *Ethnicity and Culture in Canada, The Research Landscape*, eds. J.W. Berry and J.A. Laponce (Toronto: University of Toronto Press, 1994) 387-409 for a useful overview of the growing scholar- ship in this area.
3. The term "other" in this context derives from the discourse of the Royal Commission on Bilingualism and Biculturalism and in particular from Book IV of its Report, *The Cultural Contribution of the Other Ethnic Groups* (Ottawa: Queen's Printer, 1967). This book was written in response to protests from non-British and non-French ethnic groups, primarily from the West, whose efforts could be seen as those of decolonization; however, in the language of its title, it clearly reflects the very ethnic privilege it also worked to subvert.

JEAN JONASSAINT

Migration et études littéraires.
Essai de théorisation d'un problème ancien
aux contours nouveaux[1]

À CV qui m'offrit l'occasion de cette réflexion. Pour mes amours de Gaudreau qui ne cessent de soutenir ma démarche.

Au cours des dernières décennies, l'intensité et la diversité des flux migratoires du Sud ou de l'Est vers les pays du nord ou du centre[2] ont provoqué des changements démographiques perçus comme significatifs dans ces états, et la prolifération d'œuvres dites ethniques ou minoritaires en marge (ou au sein) de leurs productions littéraires dites nationales. Prenant acte de ces nouvelles données culturelles, certains chercheurs ont introduit dans le champ des études littéraires les notions de littérature ou d'écriture migrante, de littérature ou d'écriture ethnique ou raciale (*ethnic or racial literature/ethnic or racial writing*), de textes de minorités ethniques ou raciales (*ethnic or racial minority texts*), ou plus simplement ou globalement, d'études ethniques (*ethnic studies*).

Que couvrent ces termes? Permettent-ils de cerner objectivement le statut d'écrivains migrant d'une langue à l'autre, d'un espace politico-culturel à un autre? Quelle est leur opérationalité pour établir des corpus d'écrivains migrants ou transnationaux dans nos littératures actuelles de plus en plus post-nationales?

Voilà des questions qui seront abordées dans le cadre de cet article. Pour atteindre cet objectif, j'ai analysé les résumés soumis pour le colloque Windy Pine (24-27 août 1995) «Ethnic/Racial minority writing and Canadian/ Quebec literatures»[3]. Malgré l'ampleur du corpus d'études relié à ces termes, comme le prouvent les centaines de titres indexés sous ces termes tant au catalogue informatisé de Harvard University qu'à la bibliographie informatisée du MLA, cet échantillonnage de jugement, pour emprunter un concept de la «recherche marketing», devrait permettre d'arriver à des résultats assez fiables compte tenu du caractère exploratoire de cette réflexion. Car cet échantillon est constitué des travaux fort stimulants des plus réputés chercheurs canadiens du domaine tels Bannerji, Lequin, Mukherjee, Padolsky, Palmer Seiler, Pivato, Verduyn (voir bibliographie).

Puis dans un second temps, je tenterai de redéfinir quelques-uns de ces termes, et de soumettre pour des fins de discussion de nouveaux concepts pour circonscrire les divers objets ou faits littéraires qui sont généralement étudiés sous les rubriques telles: littérature ou écriture ethnique ou raciale, écritures migrantes.

D'un détour terminologique

Un rapide survol de la terminologie des uns et des autres montre bien qu'il n'y pas d'unanimité, pour ne pas dire qu'une certaine confusion règne dans ce nouveau champ des études littéraires.

Dans le texte d'invitation à ce colloque, qui devait s'intituler «Ethnic/ racial minority writing and Canadian/Quebec literatures»[4] Christl Verduyn a utilisé les termes *ethnic or racial minority writing,* qui sont des plus courants, des plus usités avec des variantes telles: «racial and ethnic minority writing»; «racial /ethnic minority texts»; «racial and ethnic minority literatures», ou simplement «ethnic literatures». Ces notions sont fort rapprochées sans être équivalentes, et d'une formulation à l'autre le focus est mis non sur des individus ou des sujets écrivants mais sur un certain mode d'écriture (ou un certain type de textes) qui serait fonction d'un certain statut socio-historique ou socio-politique: le minoritaire ethnique ou racial.

C'est un point de vue différent, il me semble, qu'adopte Himani Bannerji qui traite plutôt de literature *produced by writers from non-white communities –* «people of colour or non-white people», «others». Ici l'accent n'est plus porté sur l'écriture, mais plutôt sur le sujet écrivant: «writers from non-white communities». Implicitement cette désignation/délimitation de l'objet d'étude («littérature produite par des écrivains de communautés non-blanches») souligne un clivage historique, le conflit plus que séculaire entre «blancs» et «noirs», entre «white» et «non-white people», entre Européens et non-Européens, ou plus brutalement entre «colonisateur» et «colonisé». C'est une perspective nettement sociologique ou socio-historique qui s'inscrit dans une remise en question tant des normes littéraires («the canon») que des politiques éditoriales et académiques qui tendent à marginaliser, et même occulter les productions de ces sujets canadiens. Dans cette approche, la stratégie n'est pas d'étudier des textes, mais plutôt de se poser la question du statut d'un certain nombre d'écrivains, donc une question qui porte plus sur l'institution littéraire que sur la littérarité des textes.

Quant à Lucie Lequin, elle utilise une terminologie toute particulière: «écriture de la migrance et de l'altérité». Ici semble s'établir une équivalence, ou une complémentarité, entre migrance et altérité qui crée une certaine imprécision sur l'objet d'étude. Car écrire la migrance et écrire l'altérité ne sont pas du même ordre. De plus, ces termes ne renvoient pas nécessairement à des sujets écrivants de communautés spécifiques – tel que les écrivains non-blancs, les écrivains de couleur, ou même les écrivains immigrants – mais ils réfèrent d'une part à une situation individuelle ou collective, la migration; d'autre part à une situation toujours collective ou sociale, l'altérité. Nous ne pouvons être Autre qu'en rapport à d'autres. L'altérité est indissociable de la sociabilité. L'autre se définit toujours en relation avec une collectivité, un Nous qui se veut Un. Mais l'important reste encore l'écriture, le texte comme forme d'un contenu, un topos: migrance ou altérité.

Par ailleurs, il importe de souligner que Lequin introduit ici un nouveau paradigme dans un champ qui jusqu'à maintenant se définissait, dans le contexte québécois du moins, en fonction de la migration («écritures migrantes»), non de l'altérité qui est un facteur plus englobant et aucunement spécifique aux immigrants. Ce changement terminologique serait-il signe d'une critique d'une notion, «écritures migrantes», qui, il faut l'avouer – depuis sa première formulation publique au Québec dans mes entretiens avec Émile Ollivier dans *Le Pouvoir des mots, les maux du pouvoir* (1986), et surtout la lecture éclairante que Robert Berrouët-Oriol a fait de cet ouvrage dans «L'Effet d'exil»[5] – a connu une extension d'usage qui lui a fait perdre son sens premier (écritures de migrants, d'écrivants migrants) et peut-être même tout sens et opérationalité.

Enfin, dans le résumé d'Enoch Padolsky apparaît un concept très courant et plus englobant que ceux déjà analysés qui sont liés aux notions d'écriture ou de littérature: *ethnic studies*. Cette terminologie («les études ethniques»), largement utilisée dans la sphère politico-administrative canadienne, rendrait-elle compte de tous les phénomènes qui nous intéressent? Il me semble que non. À moins de faire de l'ethnique ou de l'ethnie une catégorie fourre-tout, un vague synomyme d'étranger et d'atypique, ou encore, dans le contexte canadien, tout sujet d'origine autre que française ou anglaise, il est difficile de classer sous cette appellation tous les sujets écrivants qui nous intéressent (ou pourraient nous intéresser.) D'autre part, les «études ethniques» étant généralement d'ordre sociologique ou historique, la littérature semble être le parent pauvre de ces études dites ethniques qui d'ailleurs sont souvent empreintes de misérabilisme.

Au passage, il est intéressant de noter que malgré les études statistiques ou autres qui tendent à prouver que les immigrants au Canada participent activement au développement culturel canadien[6], la tendance générale est de les percevoir comme un frein à l'élaboration d'une culture «canadienne» ou «québécoise». Certains, trop enfoncés dans leurs préjugés, vont même jusqu'à exclure du groupe dit ethnique tout artiste ou écrivain qui connaît un certain succès, qui bien sûr resombrera dans l'«ethnique» sitôt qu'il commet une erreur (ou perd sa réputation), comme nous le rappelle si bien le supposé déclin (l'instant d'un test «anti-doping») de Ben Johnson du statut de «champion canadien» à «athlète jamaïcain (ou d'origine jamaïcaine)». Ce préjugé me semble être sous-jacent à la thèse de Bissoondath notamment du «multiculturalisme» comme frein à l'intégration des immigrants, et la construction d'une «identité» canadienne[7], comme si la plurilinguicité (ou même pluriethnicité) suisse ou sénégalaise aurait été un frein à l'établissement d'une citoyenneté suisse ou sénégalaise. Au fond, s'il y a méprise, pour reprendre le sous-titre français de Bissoondath, elle n'est pas du côté du multiculturalisme qui (n'en déplaise à certains maîtres-penseurs qui lisent cette politique à la lumière de leur vision dixneuvièmiste de l'État-Nation: un peuple, une langue, une culture, une âme, un génie, et j'en passe[8]) est sans doute, malgré ses limites manifestes ou latentes, l'une des politiques les plus intelligentes de l'État canadien dont une preuve nous a été donnée récemment par les succès commerciaux canadiens en Asie. Mais mieux, la politique du multiculturalisme, dans le déni officiel qu'elle apporte à la thèse des deux peuples fondateurs ou son corollaire «the two solitudes» fonde ce qu'on pourrait appeler le caractère post-national (ou postmoderne si l'on veut, bien que les deux termes ne soient pas interchangeables) de l'État canadien.

En fait, ce discours anti-multiculturaliste n'est, sous son masque progressiste ou libéral, que l'ultime forme du conservatisme renaissant et triomphant. Et ce n'est pas par hasard qu'aux États-Unis l'anti-multi-culturalisme (avec sa variante obligée, la lutte contre le bilinguisme, notamment anglais/espagnol, et pour l'unilinguisme anglais et une langue officielle américaine, bien sûr anglo-saxonne) soit – avec l'anti-political correctness[9] – les principaux chevaux de bataille de la droite conservatrice, comprenant bien sûr la lutte contre l'immigration (aujourd'hui sous sa forme dite clandestine, demain sous toutes ses formes, sans doute). Voilà une donnée qui devrait faire réfléchir plus d'un qui persiste encore à se méprendre sur le sens réel de tout fantasme identitaire ou nationalitaire, comme s'il pouvait avoir un bon nationalisme (qui serait non ethnique).

Critique de la raison ethnico-racialo-minoritaire
Qu'importe la désignation retenue, à l'exception de la lecture ou du lecteur, l'accent est mis sur l'un ou l'autre des facteurs ou aspects du phénomène littéraire – l'écriture, le texte, les écrivains – toujours couplé à des concepts sociologiques ou ethnologiques comme ethnique, racial, migrant, non-blanc, gens de couleur. Globalement, il appert que le focus est parfois porté sur des critères textuels (formels ou thématiques), avec des expressions telles: *ethnic/ racial minority writing or text, écritures migrantes, écriture de la migrance*. D'autres fois, le focus est mis sur les sujets écrivants: *literature produced by writers from non-white communities* – people of colour. Enfin, l'accent peut être mis sur la production littéraire: ethnic literature (littérature ethnique).

Or, il existe des différences significatives entre race, non-blanc ou gens de couleur, ethnie, immigrant ou migrant, comme il existe, du moins en français, des différences notoires entre écriture, littérature, texte. Car en anglais «writing» traduit à la fois écrit (texte) et écriture[10], comme «literature» tend à se confondre parfois avec «écrit sur» dans des formulations comme *literature about a subject* ou *review of the literature*. Mais je ne débattrai pas de ces concepts littéraires pour centrer mon analyse sur les qualificatifs sociologiques et anthropologiques – «racial, non-white, ethnic, immigrant, migrant» – et tenter de démontrer l'inadéquation de ces formulations/ désignations pour cerner l'ensemble (ou même des aspects) des problèmes qui faisaient ou devaient faire l'objet du Windy Pine Colloquium.

Commençons par les maillons les plus faibles: *racial* et *non-white*, car ce ne sont là que des constructions idéologiques: nous n'avons qu'à penser aux Indiens (de l'Inde bien sûr) qui ne sont dans le spectre racial et raciste ni blanc ni noir, ou encore aux dits Latinos qui sont perçus comme non-blancs en Amérique du Nord, notamment aux États-Unis. Pour s'en convaincre, on n'a qu'à se reporter à n'importe quel formulaire d'un bureau d'action positive

(Affirmative Action Office) d'une grande entreprise américaine, ou encore aux définitions américaines des Ethnic/ Racial Identity où l'on retrouve des perles telles:

> WHITE (Not of Hispanic Origin): A person having origins in any of the original peoples of Europe, North Africa, or the Middle East[11].
> AFRICAN-AMERICAN (Black/ Not of Hispanic Origin): A person having origins in any of the Black racial groups of Africa.
> HISPANIC: A person of Mexican, Puerto Rican, Cuban, Central or South American [incluant bien sûr les Brésiliens de langue portugaise] or other Spanish culture or origin, regardless of race.
> AMERICAN INDIAN OR ALASKAN NATIVE: A person having origins in any of the original peoples of North America and who maintains cultural identification through tribal affiliation or community recognition.

Par ailleurs, au-delà de la non-scientificité de ces notions de race et de non-blanc, elles sont trop étroites pour rendre compte des productions des Hongrois-Canadiens ou des Allemands-Canadiens, par exemple, l'un et l'autre groupe étant dits de «race» blanche. Aussi les concepts de *racial minority text*, *racial minority writing* ou *racial minority literature* sont peu opératoires, même dans le contexte américain (états-unien) où l'on pourrait penser la littérature dite afro-américaine comme «racial literature». Mais il n'en est rien car la notion de littérature afro-américaine ne couvre pas l'ensemble de la production littéraire des «noirs» des États-Unis. Ainsi les productions des Haïtiens Américains, par exemple, y sont exclues. La même remarque s'applique à la notion de «Hispanic American Literature» qui exclut la production des Brésiliens Américains, bien que selon la nomenclature des statistiques de population du gouvernement américain les Brésiliens soient classés Hispanic ou Latinos[12]. Ces exemples nous montrent qu'une littérature ne se définit jamais selon un seul critère (qu'il soit fonction du sujet écrivant ou du texte), mais plutôt selon un faisceau de critères qui est fonction des sujets écrivants et des textes en tant que forme et contenu, donc signe. Mais ce signe n'est pas simple (ou simple signe), son signifiant étant déjà signe. Il s'agit bien là du mythe de Roland Barthes. Et ce n'est pas sans raison (ou passion) que les instances de consécration accordent tant d'importance à la langue d'écriture, et que les littératures (nationales ou régionales) se définissent d'abord en fonction de cette langue: celle du Père, de la Loi de l'État-Nation, Un et indivisible, qui impose grammaire et sens.

Quant au qualificatif «ethnique», si d'un point de vue théorique, ses fondements scientifiques semblent plus solides, il reste que la tendance généralisée à désigner comme ethnique tout individu ou sujet non-assimilable à l'image que la société se fait d'elle-même ou de ses sujets, ou tout groupe d'individus plus ou moins atypiques d'une société, est assez perverse et crée des aberrations que, déjà dans son résumé, Enoch Padolsky laisse entrevoir avec cette question fort judicieuse: «Are European "ethnic" minority groups becoming merely "white"?»

Cette tendance est d'autant plus perverse qu'au Québec et au Canada, par exemple, ne sont perçus comme ethniques ni les sujets britanniques ni les sujets français. Par contre les Belges, les Suisses (même francophones) sont considérés officiellement, du moins au Québec, comme minorités ethniques ou culturelles.[13] Une telle perception laisse à penser l'ethnie comme une nationalité ou une citoyenneté. Et qu'il y aurait une ethnie britannique et une ethnie française (une et indivisible) qui font corps aux ethnies canadiennes française et anglaise (également une et indivisible). Or, cette supposée homogénéité, des deux côtés de l'Atlantique, n'est que leurre, phantasme identitaire ou nationalitaire. Les conflits larvés ou ouverts entre Acadiens, Franco-Ontariens, Franco-Québécois et immigrants français (dont l'expression québécoise «maudits français» n'est qu'un signe parmi d'autres) sont là quotidiennement pour nous le rappeler. Et l'espace de l'État français, comme celui de l'État britannique, est peuplé d'ethnies assez différentes. Pensons, entre autres, aux Martiniquais, aux Bretons, aux Basques (en France), aux Gallois, aux Ecossais (en Grande-Bretagne).

De plus, l'ethnicité implique une certaine histoire, un certain ancrage historique, une certaine masse critique, un certain poids démographique et/ou politique, et bien sûr une certaine mythologie de l'occupation de l'espace de peuplement (le territoire)[14]. Autant de facteurs déterminants que ne possède certainement pas la communauté haïtienne du Québec, et, sans l'ombre d'un doute, la communauté irakienne du Québec qui, à ma connaissance, n'a donné qu'un seul écrivain de langue française au Québec, le Juif Naïm Kattan.

Aussi, il me semble que la notion de *ethnic minority writing*, sans même prendre en compte le débat sur ce concept d'écriture, reflète mal les enjeux liés aux productions littéraires en contexte migratoire. Car chaque immigrant ou groupe d'immigrants qui écrivent au Canada n'appartiennent pas *de facto* ni *de jure* à une ethnie (canadienne ou autre). Par ailleurs, il ne faudrait pas oublier qu'une ethnie s'identifie généralement à un espace régional, une région qui est aussi un espace géo-politique (mythique ou réel). Or, au Canada de telles conditions ne sont réunies que par très peu de groupes dont les principaux sont les Amérindiens, les Acadiens, les Franco-Québécois, les Anglo-Québécois, les Métis de l'Ouest, et possiblement les Noirs de la Nouvelle-Écosse.

Je ne dis pas qu'il n'existe pas un corpus qui serait de l'ordre de l'*ethnic minority writing*. Mais ce concept, compte tenu des définitions que l'on peut induire de son utilisation dans de nombreuses études, me paraît peu opératoire. En tout cas, il me semble inapproprié pour désigner les productions littéraires en contexte migratoire (émigration ou immigration). Bien sûr, un tel concept peut faire sens pour parler des littératures acadienne, franco-manitobaine ou amérindienne, mais je vois mal la production des Haïtiens ou des Italiens du Québec dans un tel paradigme, à moins d'un abus de langage du même ordre que le «vote ethnique» de l'ex-premier ministre québécois, Jacques Parizeau.

Quant à l'expression *écriture de la migrance et de l'altérité*, bien qu'il y ait ou puisse avoir effectivement une «écriture de la migrance et de l'altérité», il s'agit d'abord de topos et de posture, de forme, donc d'un certain type de texte lié à un certain type de sujet écrivant. Et ce concept ne nous permet pas de rendre compte des phénomènes migratoires dans les études littéraires, ni de l'apport migratoire dans les littératures nationales, celles des pays d'immigration comme celles des pays d'émigration. D'ailleurs, il est fort étonnant que Lequin abandonne les concepts d'«écritures migrantes ou métisses», plus productifs et généralement usités au Québec du moins, bien que problématiques dans sa généralisation outrancière.

Vers de nouveaux paradigmes
Les limites des différents paradigmes étudiés sont assez évidentes, malgré la richesse ou la justesse des diverses études qui les sous-tendent. D'une part, ils ne tiennent compte que d'aspects fort particuliers du phénomène littéraire en contexte migratoire ou de société multiethnique ou multinationale; d'autre part leurs objets d'étude sont plutôt mal définis. Je suis donc porté à recentrer le débat sur les productions littéraires en contexte migratoire[15], car c'est beaucoup plus la poussée migratoire que la pluriethnicité ou la multi-nationalité qui fait problème aujourd'hui. Aussi, prenant acte que ces nouvelles données littéraires et sociales affectent tant les pays d'immigration que les pays d'émigration, je propose de penser les littératures des États ou sociétés à grandes poussées migratoires non plus en terme de littératures nationales mais plutôt postnationales. C'est-à-dire des littératures qui se font de plus en plus par des écrivains qui participent à plus d'une tradition littéraire, à plus d'une littérature. En d'autres termes, des littératures qui intègrent des écrivains de citoyennetés, de langues ou d'espaces divers, mais aussi des écrivains transnationaux, qu'ils soient polyglottes ou non.

Car la réalité de ces états à forte migration (immigration et/ou émigration), c'est qu'ils ont (produit) des citoyens à double ou même à triple citoyenneté, ou à multiple appartenance (nationale, régionale ou linguistique), donc des citoyens tout à fait dans la transcitoyenneté (j'emprunte cette expression à Michel Laguerre), qui peuvent à la fois participer dans la culture ou les affaires (politiques ou autres) de leur pays de naissance et de leur pays de résidence ou d'adoption. Ainsi, Charles Aznavour, chanteur français par excellence, est aussi représentant à l'UNESCO de son pays d'origine, l'Arménie. Aussi est-il doublement ambassadeur: ambassadeur de la France sur le plan artistique, et ambassadeur de l'Arménie au niveau administratif et politique. De fait ou de droit, Aznavour transcende (culmule) et la nationalité (ou la citoyenneté) française et la nationalité (ou la citoyenneté) arménienne. Il est de ces citoyens typiquement transnationaux.

En littérature nous retraçons le même phénomène. Certains écrivains participent à plus d'une littérature soit parce qu'ils écrivent dans deux ou plusieurs langues comme l'Irlandais Samuel Beckett (français et anglais), l'Algérien Rachid Boudjedra (français et arabe), la Canadienne Nancy Huston (français et anglais), l'Haïtien Michel-Rolph Trouillot (français, haïtien et anglais) par exemple; soit par leur stature et leur statut, bien qu'écrivant dans une langue, parce qu'ils participent à deux ou plusieurs littératures – donc produits et reçus comme écrivains de plus d'une littérature. Un cas fort célèbre et intéressant: le poète T.S. Eliot à la fois écrivain anglais et américain. Ici le rapport avec la métropole, ou plutôt l'ex-métropole, est inversé: l'Américain T.S. Eliot naturalisé anglais est une figure fondatrice de la poésie contemporaine anglaise. Donc T.S. Eliot écrivain d'un état post-colonial, pour reprendre une expression à la mode, est aussi une figure de proue de l'espace national de l'ex-métropole, l'Angleterre[16]. Un autre exemple plus près de nous encore, et tout aussi intéressant: le poète, romancier, critique littéraire et éditorialiste Gérard Étienne qui participe à la fois aux littératures d'Haïti (où il est né), d'Acadie (où il vit) et du Québec (où il publie, et a vécu).

Et nous voyons se dessiner de plus en plus à l'horizon des littératures des grandes langues de communication (notamment l'anglais) ce genre d'écrivains. Je pense entre autres à un écrivain comme V.S. Naipaul qui participe à la fois aux littératures anglo-caraïbéenne et anglaise. Il y aurait aussi un Derek Walcott qui, de par son inscription (ou son statut) dans l'espace américain, est écrivain américain. Mais c'est aussi un écrivain saint-lucien (caraïbéen) qui par sa stature est une figure importante des littératures de langue anglaise[17].

Ces divers exemples nous montrent bien les problèmes inédits qui se posent massivement et structurellement à l'historien et au critique littéraire qui doivent sous pression de la production rompre avec les approches mono- ou unilinguistique et ethnorégionale de la littérature. En effet, un Beckett est à la fois écrivain irlandais et français, mais aussi écrivain de langue anglaise et française. Étudier son œuvre implique la maîtrise de deux langues, et sa possible inscription dans trois espaces littéraires différents (ceux de l'Irlande, de la France, et de la Grande Bretagne). Et cet écrivain immigrant – qu'il se nomme Samuel Beckett, Tahar Ben Jelloun ou Naïm Kattan – peut produire des textes dans l'une et/ou l'autre langue de son choix (celle de la naissance ou celle d'adoption) qui peuvent être récits de migration ou non, comme le montre entre autres l'œuvre d'une romancière immigrante tel qu'Elisabeth Vonarburg qui n'est centrée, du moins manifestement, ni sur l'espace du pays de départ ni sur celui du pays d'arrivée, mais sur un univers science-fictionnel, a-référentiel[18].

Aussi, l'écrivain immigrant, qu'il soit polygotte ou non (c'est-à-dire écrivant dans plus d'une langue ou non), ne se définit pas en fonction d'une ou certaines formes spécifiques – comme l'écriture de la migrance ou de l'altérité, le récit d'immigration – et son œuvre n'est pas à être jugée en fonction d'une certaine authenticité ou adéquation de l'expérience d'écriture avec l'expérience migratoire. Écrivain comme un autre, j'ai même tendance à dire plus qu'aucun autre car jouissant de plus de liberté, l'écrivain migrant (immigrant ou émigré) est souvent au centre de plusieurs mouvements d'avant-garde (formalistes ou non). Je pense entre autres, en France, aux Tzara (dadaïsme), Isou (lettrisme), Ionesco (le théâtre de l'absurde) et même Duras (le nouveau roman); au Québec, aux Alonzo (formalisme et féminisme) et Straram (contre-culture).

Pour conclure, je dirai qu'il n'y a pas de littérature migrante (immigrante ou émigrante) mais des productions (littéraires) migrantes: textes ou écrits de migrants – écrivains immigrants ou émigrants, c'est-à-dire de sujets qui ont laissé leur lieu (ou pays) de naissance (ou d'origine) pour un autre lieu, un autre pays. Par ailleurs, s'il y a une première, une deuxième ou une nième génération d'écrivains immigrants, il n'y a pas d'écrivains de première et de deuxième génération d'immigrants. On a migré ou on n'a pas migré. On naît dans un pays ou un autre. Il n'y a pas d'entre deux, de moyen terme. Cette expression fort courante, «deuxième génération d'immigrants», utilisée pour désigner les enfants d'immigrants nés ou non au pays d'immigration, est un abus de langage, ne fait aucunement sens surtout en Amérique du Nord où les législations tant américaines que canadiennes donnent le droit de cité à tout sujet né sur le territoire. Que les écrivains fils ou filles d'immigrants nés au pays d'arrivée ou d'accueil soient des transcitoyens, ou mieux comme le suggère Ismael Reed[19], des auteurs à multiple tradition culturelle («authors of a multicultural heritage») – oui, mais n'étant ni émigrants ni immigrants, ils ne sauraient être écrivains migrants. Certes, ils sont d'éventuels écrivains transnationaux (polyglottes ou non) de possibles littératures post-nationales (celles de leurs lieux de naissance ou de leurs parents), ou même de simples écrivains nationaux ou ethnorégionaux.

Le grand défi est d'articuler ces nouvelles données socio-historiques dans une nouvelle approche (ou théorie) de l'histoire et de la critique littéraires qui ne serait plus surdéterminée par des traits ni génériques (histoire ou critique de l'évolution des formes), ni linguistiques (littérature d'une langue X ou Y), ni ethno-régionaux (littérature d'un pays certain ou incertain, d'une race ou une ethnie négro-X ou judéo-Y), mais qui tiendraient compte de l'éclatement et de la multiplicité des situations d'écrivains (migrants ou transnationaux) de langue indigène ou allogène, unilingue ou plurilingue. Plus explicitement, c'est le défi d'une théorie de l'histoire et de la critique littéraires qui rendrait compte à la fois de la canadianité et de la francité d'une Nancy Huston (dans sa correspondance avec Leïla Sebbar), de sa double inscription dans les littératures anglo- et franco-canadiennes (avec un ouvrage comme *Cantique des plaines*), et de sa polygraphie (journaliste, essayiste, romancière).

Une telle théorie nous amenerait forcément à recentrer les études littéraires sur les sujets écrivants et sur leurs rapports à l'histoire de nos sociétés, et bien sûr à donner un souffle nouveau à l'histoire littéraire. D'autre part, elle placerait sans doute la linguistique comparée au centre des préoccupations littéraires, car la plurilingualité (individuelle) ou pluri-linguicité (sociale) aurait préséance sur l'intertextualité.

NOTES
1. Cet article s'inscrit dans le cadre d'une recherche sur l'apport migratoire dans la littérature québécoise subventionnée par le ministère du Patrimoine cana-dien que je remercie pour sa générosité.
2. À noter que ni cette densité ni cette diversité ne sont nouvelles. Le flux migra-toire du début du siècle était aussi important sinon plus, et assez diversifié

bien qu'essentiellement européen à cause des lois restrictives de l'immigration tant au Canada qu'aux États-Unis jusque dans les années 1960-1970. On n'a qu'à se rappeler l'héritage colonial (Amérindien, Canadien-français, Canadien-anglais, métis, africains); et l'héritage migratoire (Chinois, Japonais, Ukranien, etc.).

3. Selon les résumés de Bannerji, Lequin, Mukherjee, Padolsky, Palmer Seiler, Pivato, van Herk, et le «General topic» du texte d'invitation de Christl Verduyn.

4. Il importe de signaler que ce glissement dans la désignation de ces rencontres est fort significatif. En effet, le passage d'un colloque titré thématiquement («Ethnic/ racial minority writing and Canadian/Quebec literatures») à un colloque titré rhématiquement («Windy Pine Colloquium») est symptôme d'un malaise, du moins de la difficulté à nommer les phénomènes littéraires (et sociaux) qui devaient nous réunir à Windy Pine. À savoir: comment penser ou repenser les champs littéraires canadiens ou québécois pour tenir compte des nouvelles données sociologiques et politiques de notre fin de siècle, plus spécifiquement la diversité socio-culturelle ou socio-historique des sujets ou citoyens de l'État canadien actuel dont l'un des signes les plus évidents est l'émergence d'une population canadienne assez significative d'origines non-européennes.

Il est à noter également que le nouveau discours (néo-colonialiste) canadien (tant anglophone que francophone) est encore incapable de penser le fait amérindien, occultant systématiquement (avec naïveté ou cynisme) le fait colonial canadien (l'actuelle colonisation interne dont l'expression la plus manifeste est le concept des deux peuples fondateurs, et son corollaire «the two solitudes»). Le refus d'une bonne partie de l'élite canadienne (française ou anglaise) de penser la partition du Québec advenant l'accession de la belle Province à l'indépendance est une autre face visible de ce néo-colonialisme qui s'ignore ou fait semblant de s'ignorer. Néo-colonialisme dont la face cachée est bien sûr le racisme larvé que les notions de vote ethnique (de Parizeau), et de femmes blanches (de Bouchard) devront faire réfléchir ceux qui pensent encore de bonne foi qu'il pourrrait exister quelque part un possible nationalisme non-ethnique, non-chauvin, un éventuel nationalisme qui ne porterait pas en germe l'exclusion systématisée.

5. Voir: J. Jonassaint, *Le Pouvoir des mots, les maux du pouvoir. Des romanciers haïtiens de l'exil* (1986:93); R. Berrouët-Oriol, *L'Effet d'exil* (1987); Berrouët-Oriol et Fournier (1992), Domaradzki (1990); Lequin et Verthuy (1992 et 1993), et Nepveu (1988: 197-220).

6. Cf. entre autres les études du ministère de la Culture du Québec sur les habitudes de consommation culturelle des communautés culturelles au Québec cf. *Chiffres à l'appui*, vol VIII, no. 4, mars-avril, 1995 (Ministère de la Culture et des Communications du Québec).

7. Neil Bissoondath, *Le Marché aux illusions. La méprise du multiculturalisme* (1995).

8. Il importe de souligner que ces penseurs souvent pseudo- ou cripto-marxistes n'ont jamais pu comprendre que la notion de classe telle que formulée par Marx, et autres penseurs marxistes, est la négation même d'un possible État-nation, Un et indivisé. Mais, il ne faudrait pas leur tenir rigueur, car le Maître lui-même, et ses principaux disciples, se sont tous gourés dans le fantasme d'un nouveau «Un» prolétarien, source d'une nouvelle culture Une et indivisible, une nouvelle Loi d'un nouveau Génie, le Prolétariat, nouvelle appellation contrôlée du Peuple.

9. Loin de moi l'idée de cautionner globalement le «political correctness». Comme tout discours idéologique ou hégémonique, il a sa langue de bois,

mais il me semble moins dangereux que le «national correctness» qui voudrait le supplanter.

10. Cf. les titres des traductions de Alan Bass de *L'Écriture et la différence* de Derrida (*Writing and Difference*) ou de Barbara Johnson des *Écrits* de Lacan (*Writing*) dans son article "Writing" in *Critical Terms for Literary Study* (Chicago University Press, [1990] 1995, 39-49. Barbara Johnson dans son article «Writing» montre bien qu'il y a un glissement entre «writing» (écriture) et «writing» (écrit, équivalent de texte), terme utilisé en lieu et place de littérature (trop idéologiquement marqué) ou genre (terme trop flou ou mal défini). C'est sans doute la difficulté à trouver un équivalent anglais juste pour le terme français «écrit» qui porte un éditeur anglais des *Écrits* de Lacan à garder le mot français dans le titre, voir: *Écrits: A Selection* (London, 1977).

11. Il est intéressant de souligner que si aux États-Unis le Nord-Africain et le Moyen-Oriental sont considérés comme «White» (blancs), en France, ils sont, notamment les Maghrébins, d'abord Arabes, ni blancs ni noirs («bougnoules»).

12. Voir entre autres l'introduction de N. Kanellos à son ouvrage *Hispanic American Literature. A brief introduction and anthology* (1995), 1-8, et H. Augenbraum et I. Stavans, *Growing up Latino. Memoirs and Stories* (1993).

13. Voir entre autres: Miska (1990) et Sutherland (1986).

14. Cette relation obligée entre ethnicité, territorialité et poids démographique et/ou historique est surdéterminante. Quelques individus éparpillés un peu partout dans le monde ou sur un même territoire ne peuvent constituer une ethnie au sens ethnologique ou scientifique du terme. Par ailleurs, il ne faudrait jamais oublier que l'ethnie n'est toujours que construction, comme le soulignent fort justement Gérard Prunier et Jean-Pierre Chrétien dans leur ouvrage *Les Ethnies ont une histoire* (Paris, Karthala, 1989), et leur commentaire, «Ethnies, ethnicité, ethnicisme: un autre point de vue» (Afrique contemporaine, 155, 1990: 80-82) sur l'article de Dominique Darbon, «De *l'ethnie* à l'ethnicisme: réflexions sur quatre sociétés *multiraciales*: Burundi, Afrique du Sud, Zimbabwe et Nouvelle-Calédonie» (*Afrique contemporaine*, 154, 1990).

15. Ce recentrement sur la production des immigrants déjà en œuvre dans mon article sur les «Productions littéraires haïtiennes en Amérique du Nord» (1980), et le travail de Sutherland, *No Longer a Family Affair: The Foreign-born Writers in French Canada* (1986), que j'ai tenté de théoriser dans l'introduction du supplément de *Lettres québécoises*, De l'autre littérature québécoise, *Autoportraits* (1992), a trouvé un écho fructueux dans l'ouvrage de Helly et Vassal, *Romanciers immigrés: biographies et œuvres publiées au Québec entre 1970 et 1990* (1993).

16. Il est intéressant de noter que deux ouvrages de référence de Columbia University Press publiés à cinq ans d'intervalle, *Columbia Literary History of the United States* (1988) et *The Concise Columbia Encyclopedia* (1983), inscrivent T.S. Eliot, l'un dans la littérature américaine, l'autre dans la littérature anglaise.

17. Voir le discours de réception du Nobel de Walcott, *The Antilles. Fragments of Epic Memory* (1993), et sa place dans l'anthologie de HarperCollins, *The Literature of Contemporary America: Poetry* (1996).

18. Un autre exemple fort intéressant: la poète Anne-Marie Alonzo dont l'œuvre n'a pas été (et n'est pas encore) perçue au prime abord comme écriture de migrante. Voir sur ce point le stimulant article de Louise Dupré, «La Prose métisse du poème: sur Anne-Marie Alonzo» (1992/1993).

19. Voir son avant-propos au HarperCollins Literary Mosaic Series (cf. S. Wong, *Asian American Literature*, 1996, xi).

ARITHA VAN HERK

The Ethnic Gasp /
the Disenchanted Eye Unstoried

My concern as a writer preoccupied with contemporary fiction that might be designated as ethnic has led me to examine the in-sight, the epiphanic seeing that – like some version of thunderstorm – clarifies the troubled and often uneasy space that the ethnic subject occupies. I would like to believe that there is an epiphanic moment that enables the ethnic subject to begin the self-interrogation that must accompany the subject's recognition of him or herself as, if not other, other than.... But there are two trajectories to this possible, laden, implicated narrative, this moment of arrival at such an intensified space. This first is a narrative afterword, a readerly recognition – that of audience to ethnic, observers beyond claim yet claimants (those watching, defining, partial voyeurs, partial censors) to the act of the gaze.

In the summer of 1995, I attended a funeral. Not unusual, of course; funerals pace themselves through time, reminding us of the larger shared space of death. But as intensified space, combined with ritual (however sanitized or embalmed), the funeral has shuffled itself into a strange compliance with death – and yet, it is perhaps most obviously through funeral observances that a possible ethnic inscription can re-assert its presence in a more and more homogenized culture. And so this funeral, which took place in the tiny (yes, singularly tiny, some 150 people live there) village of Resolute Bay, in the Nunavut region of what southerners call the Northwest Territories. Resolute Bay is one of the Inuit settlements that the government artificially created, transporting a number of Inuit families there in order to consolidate its sovereignty over the North. The families who live there are marked by that transportation and its effects, and yet Resolute Bay is a cohesive and powerfully aware community contributing a great deal to the political voice and developing self-governance of the land of Nunavut. The settlement is not the most northerly of Canada's permanent communities (that honour goes to Grise Fjord), but it is close. At 75 degrees north, it crouches on the shoreline of Cornwallis Island, next to the only temporarily open ice of the Arctic Ocean, and relies on airplanes and a summer sealift to bring in supplies and to maintain its connection to the south – although that connection is a touristic one at best and an exploitative one at worst. Resolute lives as a village of komatiks and sled dogs, of stretched seal and caribou skins, and yet both the telephone and the television maintain their steady hum, as if to contradict the archaeological remains of the pre-Dorset village just a few miles out of town, visible and preserved by the dryness and cold of this winter desert.

North is not an ethnic designation in Canada; the notion of north is tossed about as casually as if it were nothing more than a direction, rather than a destination or even – quite possibly – an act of the imagination integral to Canada's collective ethnicity. In geographical space, Resolute Bay inhabits not the genteel and manageable muskeg and scrubby treed region of the near North (of Yellowknife and Whitehorse, for example) but the far North, that area of polar desert that reaches past the tree line to the permanent ice cap of the polar regions, which are dauntlessly and certainly nothing less than extreme North. Such designations are not ethnic, yet, in strange ways, they recite an ethnicity that might afford the unstoried eye an ethnic (although that term is fissured and fraught) narrative.

The funeral that I flew seven hours (from Calgary) to attend in Resolute Bay was that of a man named Bezal Jesudason. Bezal was as close as possible to being a true northerner; no tourist or temporary government official, he had lived and worked in the North for 20 years. But he was also Tamil, and born in Calcutta, a city he left when he went to Germany to study electrical engineering. He was fluent in German, Tamil, English, Japanese, Inuktituk, and, I believe, Spanish. From Germany he immigrated to Canada, where he worked for the Northwest Territories government. Fed up with its bureaucracy and in total disagreement with its treatment of the North and its peoples, he moved to Resolute Bay in the 1970s and set up a business as an expeditor and outfitter, combining his knowledge of the landscape and the climate with a community responsibility that was genuinely remarkable. He became, for all that he was an English-speaking Tamil with a German education, a Canadian Inuk, living and working in an Inuit world that enfolded him with gentle acceptance.

His funeral enacted exactly what I would describe as unblinded identi-fication, providing an epiphanic seeing of Bezal as ethnic subject, both central and other. He was certainly Indian, without a doubt his face and his skin and his history proclaimed that inheritance. But he was dressed for death in the ubiquitous clothing of northerners, a padded fleece vest, a knitted Inuit cap, the very clothes he wore throughout the winter and spring and fall – in effect for 11 months of the year, as summer only lasts one brief month in the extreme Arctic. That conjunction of Inuit and northerner focussed an intensified ethnic gaze, a connection between sight and recognition. His casket (plain wood) was open, and the entire community of Resolute Bay, from its youngest member, a week-old Inuit baby, to its oldest, 75-year-old Annie, one of the last Inuit women to practise the great gutterals of throat singing, attended the funeral in the community gymnasium. The funeral was noisy and alive, with children running underfoot and dogs howling outside. It was also absolutely confrontational: every member of the community, child and adult, walked up to the coffin and gazed directly into

Bezal's face. Every person in Resolute Bay, from the baby to Annie, touched the face of this Tamil man – so other, so alien, and yet so completely a part of their world – and then sat down to participate noisily and without hush or undue ceremony in the Anglican service for the dead, based on the *Book of Common Prayer*, but conducted in Inuktituk.

I admit that I was shocked, not by the apparent lack of ceremony, but by the unflinching directness with which Bezal was included in the collective gaze of this community, a gaze that seemed directed to an intensified space of experience. I faced wildly contradictory evidence that ethnicity as the pristine state of origin was a chimera that could be both embraced and ignored. It was a Christian service, but it reached beyond the apparatus of Christianity, made more specific by the children racing up and down the aisles, by the crooked hem of the priest's cassock, by the blue jeans and boots of the participating audience.

If there was self-interrogation at work, if it were possible to make a distinction between the origin and the adoption, that interstitial smuggle-ment was so complex and intricate that one could never unravel or identify it, except perhaps in the geographical location: this othered community inhabited the space of a hegemonic erasure that Canada insists on naming multicultural.

If it had been winter, the funeral procession would have included Ski-Doos as well as trucks. But it was summer, and in the shaley gravel of the permafrost, the grave yawned soft and muddy, and the sled dogs, tied down by the shore, howled to be fed. From the back of the van that served as hearse, the community lifted the coffin, carried it down into the earth, together, many hands lifting that body's weight. Their gaze did not falter or turn aside from the fact of burial, and after scattering sharp handfuls of flint and gravel, they began together to fill in the grave, under each other's eyes, everyone taking their turn at a shovel. That burial took a long hour while the wind blew off the ice-packed Arctic Ocean, and the children ran between the graves to warm themselves. The wooden marker that was put in place inscribed Bezal's name in both English and Inuktituk.

It is impossible to articulate the visible ethnic crisis depicted in this story. It is impossible for me to pretend to be anything but a stranger, a voyeur, a recorder, a friend, but distant, from another place, politely other. In this narrative, there is a mixture of ethnicities, a collision of ethnicities, a collusion of ethnicities that both refuses and embraces recognition, that acts out an ethnic epiphany without postulating ethnicity as such. Such a story and its living is both hybrid and particular, both authentic and contaminated.

But that suggests a second possible narrative, the more fraught narrative that is not afterword but foresight, again an enactment of a particular moment of a gaze, with all the difficulties that the gaze projects. I would like to call this dis-enchanted eye and its narrative moment of recognition *fluency*, a gesture towards articulation, of course, but also a fluency of sight that precedes the constructedness of articulation, the saying, speaking, and writing (which often works towards closure) of the purely ethnic identi-fication. This fluency is the glimpse that blinks past before the trained and analytical glance takes over, the fleeting cuff of recognition that waives expectation and inhabits a pivotal turning point, the moment when one endures the personal shock of knowing oneself "ethnic."

Many literary texts examine and make narrative climax a recognition of difference or otherness, the quixotic and often painful apocalypse that accompanies the intellectual placement of the self as "other" or "beside." But the peripheral glance that occurs before an adjustment to definition and subjugation, the eyeblink that sees the moment before the moment arrives, is often and carelessly laid aside. In the fluency of glance – and it is after all visual erasure that enables passing – there is an intensification that precedes the definitions and distortions of identification, a designation that now insists on accompanying every narrative, so that hyphen becomes a mode of reading: Ondaatje – Sri Lankan; Skvorecký – Czechoslovakian; Lee – Chinese; Kogawa – Japanese; Mistry – Indian, until the narrative of origin reinscribes the mime of geography, whether that geographic map is completely tangential or not. And if geography is too far-fetched, there is still the closure of blood, family, kin, as if inheritance were fluid enough to survive its own implosion.

Which returns and returns to that intensified space, the personal shock of knowing oneself "ethnic," of glimpsing oneself in an oddly angled ethnic mirror a moment before one is declared so "other," that moment I would call the fluency of the look, the gasp of the eye before the tongue finds its root. How to determine this glimpse, this quickening? It is easy to identify any gaze as racial or national, but is it merely so? Are other gestures implicated, so intricate that it is impossible to separate their intent from their cause? Class? Politics? Sexual orientation? All of them hesitate on the brink of the ethnic wedge and turn back, resist their own sightlines, as if to refuse the eye that would pull them into a vortex. Is there "a simple definition of self when one works from an ethnic posture" (Kroetsch, *Identifications* 75) – too tempting to be shunned? Is there a belabourment of nostalgia that slips past economic colonization (that the ginger candy I am so fond of is packaged in French, German, Dutch, and Korean because it comes from Indonesia)? Does realism become an obstacle? Does uninflected experience become a wall? Does linguistic vernacular become a terrain? And is creolization part of every ethnic narrative, to make audible a distinct voice within the cacophony of voices, to see the note of knowledge and pain before it articulates itself?

In the partisan, political, cultural, tonal, connotative, religious, psycho-logical acknowledgement of the crisis of ethnicity – I am that ethnic being talked about, that stupidly stubborn and Calvinistically motivated Dutch woman – someone cannot be somewhere else. I become, so othered, the mote in the homogeneous eye, the intake of breath before the subject asserts an ethnic identity (only too easy to disclaim multicultural platitudes, and to assent to the needfulness of diversity). Such resounding *clichés*, rotund with good intentions, like liberal multiculturalism with its nod to a national configuration of "good" Canadian, fail to narrate that sceptical glance, refuse the glimpse of denial and rage that precedes speaking.

Perhaps the ethnic narrative that we watch and read so subtly encodes and encloses this glimpse of recognition that it is subsumed by the larger trajectories of event and speaking, of rising action and dénouement. But like every intensified space, it creates its own energy, asserts a field that outlasts the thematic or the plot-driven mechanism of identity as a finding, a discovery, and an obligation. *Obbligato* duplicitous – a step past emigration or immigration or asylum or refugeehood towards a visual anatomy that sees and sees again, foreseeing the repeated shock of being "other."

When I began school in central Alberta – hardly a site of liberalism – I could already read, draw my alphabet and add. But I had a secret ear for that most indignant of languages – ugly, gutteral, spit-phlegm-sorted, but most of all, my mother tongue, for it was what I heard day in and out at home – Dutch. Smart as I was, they'd sent me to a school in a foreign language, English. But the language was nothing, the language was merely a collection of words and intonations, learnable, memorizable, manageable.

The worst shock of my ethnicity was a combination of religion, class, and economy. Oh, there was no doubt that I was white, northern European, capable of assimilating without a hitch and without a shudder, despite being female, near-sighted, and not particularly healthy, despite being prone to respiratory problems, someone whose TB test always came back positive, despite the fact that we used an outhouse, that my parents droned prayers in a strange resistance to Canada. I was what my now-colleagues disparagingly refer to as "poor white," well, not quite "trash," but certainly dirt-on-the-hands-working-class. And the glance that still skips past that instant of ethnic crisis has been burned into the back of my neck, spiralled into a repudiated narrative that cannot be told without my becoming ludicrously sodden with its poverty and clumsiness, its disdain and its dismissals.

This ethnic gasp of pain, I am repeatedly told, is nothing much, meaningless, without substance. But that erasure I repudiate, refusing to succumb to the powerlessness of invalidating my own invalidation. In my sub-cultural dialect of class, I de-territorialize my own abjection. No, poverty is not romantic, nor do I believe in authenticity, and as for aesthetics, they are a mixed bag, a nostalgic threat, all that depiction and delegation sitting in judgment over the alterity of power and its geography, the various gaps between theory and practice. No one needs to save me from oblivion, no one that is, but my own problematized and imprisoned ethnic, reconstructing her lost and imprisoned narrative. Traffic and glossary, discursive construction, what are they to someone with holes in their shoes, when merely to lick the palimpsest of language is audacious, impossible, a taxonomic sin. This melancholic space is always already an act of translation and its transgressions, always already a traffic of violent censorship, beyond arbitrative ideology and its good intentions. In any hybrid site, how easy is it to erase one's own balkanization?

Whose ethnic is where? What community can be imagined if the subject is divided, contesting herself and her own complicity in the disjunctive fractures and exfoliative gestures of economies and cultures? Some choices are limited indeed. Deportation or death? And no question is innocent, no exchange without coinage, no icon without worshippers, no language without silence. Camouflage saves no one from the fire, and the body betrays itself, has nothing to become but bone and ash.

NADINE LTAIF

Ecrire pour vivre l'échange entre les langues

Il faut transcender le concept d'appartenance culturelle pour vivre l'échange. Pour qu'il y ait véritablement échange, il faut que la diversité soit proclamée. Car la création littéraire se nourrit de l'échange et de la diversité. C'est en lisant d'autres cultures que les portes de l'imaginaire s'ouvrent. Et l'écriture ne survit pas dans la fermeture. Que soit reconnues les influences autochtones, francophones, anglophones, et autres, celles des immigrés qui vivent et écrivent soit en français, soit en anglais. J'en connais même qui, comme Hossein Sharang, écrivent en «farsi» (persan) et vivent à Montréal. Ces derniers arrivent avec leur mémoire, leur culture, leurs langues d'origine, souvent leur bilinguisme. Ils viennent partager l'expérience nord-américaine dans la langue de leur choix, soit en français ou en anglais. Il faut que les anglophones et les francophones se réconcilient au sujet de la question linguistique. Je suis une francophile. je n'aime pas la désignation de francophone, car l'interprétation politique du mot francophone me dérange. La question linguistique ne devrait plus être une barrière. L'important c'est d'écrire. Peu importe la langue choisie. Il ne faut plus qu'il y ait de barrières linguistiques pour les créateurs. Je cherche au contraire à établir des ponts, des dialogues entre les peuples et les cultures. Je suis pour l'échange, le partage, pour sortir de l'isolement des deux communautés. Les rares rencontres culturelles annuelles anglophones-francophones, symboliques et mythiques, ne sont pas suffisantes. Je ne supporte pas l'exclusion des anglophones de la vie culturelle montréalaise, mais je ne supporte pas non plus ni leur suprématie linguistique dans le milieu des affaires, ni le non-respect de l'identité québécoise. Je suis pour le partage : partager un territoire, recevoir un nombre illimité d'immigrants. Il y a toujours de la place pour le partage. Il faut que tout bouge et soit repensé : les valeurs et les lois. Entre deux êtres il faut la même dynamique; pour le social et pour l'individu, le même combat. Entre deux êtres de culture différente, le même échange se produit. Chez Lévinas, la pensée de l'autre c'est l'écoute de l'autre en tant qu'autre, non en tant que le même ou le semblable. C'est parce qu'il est irrémédiablement autre qu'il m'intéresse. Ce n'est pas son exotisme, ce n'est pas le fait qu'il vient de la même culture. Le respect de la différence fait naître l'amour: l'écoute attentive de l'inconnu. Respecter ce qui n'est pas moi.

Le thème de la migration des langues me touche dans la mesure où je transporte avec moi la langue arabe quand j'écris en français. Comme un grand nombre d'écrivains franco-arabes je continue à me traduire en français (instinctivement) quand j'écris. L'arabe reste l'inconscient de mon texte : le rythme qui scande la phrase, la composition musicale du poème. C'est comme chanter en français une langue arabe. Nancy Huston a vécu à sa manière le chant albertain : d'où l'originalité de son texte. L'inconscient de son français porte sa création en langue anglaise. Pour un québécois francophone l'inverse se produit. Chez lui il y a aussi migration linguistique. d'abord, il traduit la langue de l'enfance (comme tout créateur d'écriture); ensuite, il y a en lui l'autre langue, l'anglais, qu'il côtoit et avec lequel la communication ne se fait souvent pas, sauf dans sa création littéraire où il y a nécessairement levée du refoulement, rencontre avec l'autre. Il entend la langue anglaise depuis son enfance. Il entretient des rapports d'amour-haine avec cette langue. L'originalité de sa création littéraire québécoise résulte du métissage français-anglais. La création littéraire est au carrefour des langues, le point de rencontre des cultures.

J'ai écrit sans penser que le lieu d'origine allait être objet d'une classification des écrivains. Les classer devenait un geste politique regrettable, avec connotation discriminatoire, même si l'intention de départ des critiques était éxactement l'inverse. Il a été un temps où la désignation «écriture migrante» était nécessaire. Elle nous donnait une voix. Mais cette même désignation a fini par nous enfermer dans une boîte d'où nous trouvons difficile de sortir aujourd'hui. Je préfère qu'on soit considéré d'abord écrivains ensuite immigrés, et non l'inverse. J'espère qu'il n'existe pas de quota de sélection : un certain nombre d'immigrants, de femmes, de gens «de couleur», pour les postes, les bourses, les prix etc. Car le nom de l'écrivain ne doit pas précéder la qualité de son écriture.

J'ai vécu dans l'incompréhension du lieu d'acceuil pendant plus de cinq ans. J'ai tenté de faire le deuil par écrit sur une période de dix ou même quinze ans. Chacun son rythme et sa capacité de vivre les ruptures avec le passé. Aujourd'hui je reconnais que ce que je nommais froideur ou indifférence était le respect, la non-ingérence dans la vie quotidienne de l'autre. Je reconnais que c'était la liberté. Cette liberté coûte chère; elle est au-delà des compromis. Pour la préserver il fallait me méfier des engagements politiques qui tombaient dans le piège des partis-pris. La véritable dénonciation politique se faisait dans la marge. il fallait renoncer au pouvoir pour ne pas succomber à la tentation du pouvoir, pour être écrivain, ascète, «moine bouddhiste zen», pour préserver sa liberté et celle d'autrui. Car la vie existe au-delà du désir de pouvoir. Pourquoi nous oblige-t-on à nous prononcer sur notre appartenance politique? Ecrivons-nous pour le Québec ou pour le Canada? Nous écrivons pour des lecteurs pour qui la question nationale n'est pas le seul critère d'inspiration. Dans les discours politiques manquent les nuances. Il y a manipulation de notre propos. Rien de pire pour un écrivain que d'être mal interprété. Pour nous classer idéologiquement, certains n'hésitent pas à sauter aux conclusions. Je préfère donc rester dans le terrain neutre, celui qui ne fait partie d'aucun clan, pour mieux écouter les uns et les autres. Je me méfie des extrêmes comme des extrêmistes, ou des fanatico-intégristes. Je me méfie des discours qui déshumanisent.

Mon écriture est-elle désengagée politiquement? Je ne crois pas. Mon premier texte *les Métamorphoses d'Ishtar* dénonçait la guerre civile libanaise et la pauvreté au Caire, deux réalités que j'ai ressenties viscéralement dans mon enfance et mon adolescence. Aujourd'hui beaucoup de Libanais nient la désignation de «guerre civile». Par la suite écrire pour dénoncer m'a semblé un piège, celui de tomber dans le sujet à sensation. Quand je vois dans les médias des horreurs, les mots me manquent. Je ne me suis préoccupée que de l'amour et de l'amitié. La relation à l'autre occupait tout mon esprit. Mais l'amour aussi est politique, comme l'ont écrit Michèle Causse, Nicole Brossard, ou Lise Harou, quand l'amour remet en question des traditions bien ancrées. Un jour je dénoncerai encore une fois la condition de la femme dans les sociétés arabes pour aider à son émancipation. La liberté je l'ai aquise ici, cela je ne l'oublierai pas. Mais c'est vrai que je reste marginale dans les débats politiques. pourtant, quand j'écris j'assume mon identité d'arabe, de québécoise "francophone" et d'écrivaine. C'est-à-dire que je fais partie d'une petite société qui vit, je continue de l'espérer, une solidarité dans la marginalité, qu'elle s'impose comme règle pour sa survie, pour échapper à la récupération, et à la banalisation de notre discours. Cette société d'écrivains n'est pas seulement québécoise: elle est canadienne, trans-linguistique et internationale. L'écrivain, s'il ne transcende pas l'origine, le fanatisme, ne pourra pas vivre l'échange entre les langues, ni la traduction qui est l'écoute la plus respectueuse de l'autre, et qui est l'essence même de la création littéraire. En écrivant nous libérons notre imaginaire, notre mémoire, et nous établissons le pont : un dialogue sans fin. Ne sommes-nous pas traducteurs de nos sens, de nos images et de nos cultures? Qu'est-ce que le dessein d'un écrit s'il n'est lu? La lecture donne les sens du texte. Et la diversité du sens d'un poème se découvre au fil des ans, des lecteurs, des générations. Le sens d'un poème se renouvelle s'il parvient à transcender les décennies. Peut-être dans dix ans continuera-t-on à nous lire sous un autre angle que celui de l'écriture migrante?

KATERI AKIWENZIE-DAMM

We Belong To This Land:
A View of "Cultural Difference"

Boozhoo. My name is Kateri Akiwenzie-Damm. I am Anishnaabekwe from the Chippewas of Nawash First Nation, at Neyaashiinigmiing (the Cape Croker reserve). It's on the Saugeen Peninsula, on Georgian Bay.

The issue of cultural difference, which is at the core of my comments, is one that I believe demands that I speak as truthfully as possible from within my own cultural base. My oratory at Windy Pine and the essay which follows, are my attempt to do so within the limitations and utilizing the opportunities presented by each of these respective forms of communication.

* * *

we are the land.... More than remembered, the Earth is the mind of the people as we are the mind of the earth (Gunn Allen, "Iyani").

The Native peoples of this land *are fundamentally different from anyone else. We are fundamentally different from anyone else in this land, fundamentally different from Canadians. The basis of the difference is the land, our passion for it and our understanding of our relationship with it. We belong to this land. The land does not belong to us; we belong to this land. We believe that this land recognizes us and knows us.* In the broadest and most fundamental ways we are inextricably connected to this land. It holds the bones of our ancestors. This land provides for us and for our children. It is a birthright granted to us by the Creator. In return it is our responsibility to care for and protect the land. It is our connection to the land that makes us who we are, that shapes our thinking, our cultural practices, our spiritual, emotional, physical, and social lives. Our cultures and spirituality arise from our relationship with the land.

we are part of the land. it is in our songs and prayers. it is part of everyday life. giving and talking with the land. loving. rich dark forests. enjoying. (northSun)

It is the land that makes us who we are and that binds us. Land, community, culture, and spirituality are intricately woven together. This interconnectedness is expressed and reinforced through our arts, language, ceremonies, songs, prayers, dances, customs, values, and daily practices, all of which have been developed over generations, over thousands and

84

thousands of years of living on the land. The land, therefore, is central to this process. Who you are as an Indigenous person arises from your connection to the land and to all others who share it. Your community thus includes everything that is connected to the land: the human, the natural, and the supernatural. So your connection is complex because it is woven of strands of kinship and, for us, to be kin is about more than bloodlines. It is about love, and respect, honesty and truth. It is a weave that encompasses all that is around us.

As Anishnaabe we understand that we are an essential part of the weave. Each of us has a place within it; each of us is an integral part of it. Together, we help form the pattern and strengthen the weave. This is how we come to understand who we are: through the weaving that stretches out around us. Each of us stands at the centre of a web that reaches far beyond us, and yet each of us is at the centre: the place where we stand, where all elements in the circle of life intersect in each of us. Standing at this intersection we develop our sense of personal and social identity. We come to understand that behind us are our ancestors, in front of us our descendants. We come to understand our individual relationship to all others around us, to all aspects of creation. This is how we come to know who we are. Thus, we find meaning and purpose as human beings, as Anishnaabek, as people of good intentions, in connectedness, in community. We are supported and sustained within a web of relationships. And it begins with the land.

> So we say truly that the land is our mother, Mother Earth.
> People who come here from different immigrant backgrounds don't usually have that. It's possible to have the connectedness to the land, but it's not the land all your stories took place on, the land all the myths come from, your ancestors. (Hogan 128)

As Indigenous people of this land, our view of the world and our daily experience differs significantly from that of other people in Canada, of Canadians. Our daily experience differs because we are a part of the land. And the land, indeed all of Mother Earth, the entire planet, is under attack.

> The dominant culture – the colonized mind – is at war with nature, and so by definition is at war with all peoples of nature. The more natural the people, the greater the degree of hostility the dominant culture manifests toward them.
> This is an alienation from nature so profound and so virulent that no one in the dominant flow of things wants to acknowledge that it even exists. Theirs is the normal and correct ordering of consciousness to relate to the world, they say, they assert, they insist. (Churchill 163)

Our connection to the land, our role as protectors of the earth, and our willingness to stand our ground in protecting what is sacred to us all make us a threat to the colonizers, with their deeply inculcated ideas of their exclusive "dominion" over nature and all other beings. This, combined with consumerism, has created some new and deadly strains of colonization. In addition to everything else, Indigenous people now face corporate colonization, nuclear colonization, aesthetic colonization, and, most recently, genetic colonization. And in every case it is because of our connection to the natural world. The dominant culture, for all its "progress" in civilizing the world, wants most what it lacks – unfortunately the very things that Indigenous people have retained and protected. We have what they want. But no longer are colonizers simply after our land. That is just the beginning. They now want everything we have: land, spirituality, stories, even our genetic material.

Indians have been called "wild" and seem to represent an unfathomable mystery to Christians and to European colonists. This is because of the connection to land, the recognition that life itself resides in everything, the understanding indigenous people have of how the forces and cycles of nature work. The fear of wilderness, the fear of indigenous people, and the fear of not having control are all the same fear. (Hogan 123)

And what it comes down to is that politics is a part of our daily reality: the politics of colour, the politics of race, the politics of imperialism, the politics of poverty, the politics of language, the politics of identity, the politics of voice, the politics of culture. It informs everything that I do, it informs everything that people around me do.

As an Anishnaabe *my reason for being differs.* My purpose in life is geared to my community, to forming and strengthening connections, to preserving my bond to the earth, to maintaining my link to creation. I strengthen myself, I learn, I accumulate experience and knowledge, not for personal gain but because ultimately I know that personal development is a necessary tool for contributing to the community, to the earth, to life. All aspects of my life, my work, my learning, my spirituality, are geared to this, all are interconnected. They are not separate. They are bound by the need to give back which is an outcome of the one true motivating force – love.

At the same time, I am surrounded by certain political realities. Realities like racism, imperialism, colonization, genocide. These are part of the daily reality of being an Indigenous person in a society that has spent more than 500 years trying to kill you one way or another.

In truth, genocide has always been at the forefront of the colonial agenda. Unfortunately, it has been an extremely successful campaign, not only in Canada but around the globe. For those of us in the Americas it has been a 500-year-long nightmare. Regardless of the duration of contact, colonization has resulted in a global holocaust of staggering proportions – a holocaust which has seen some Indigenous populations reduced to five per cent or ten per cent of what they were prior to contact with the colonizers. Some, like the Beothuk, were completely annihilated. Yet the decimation of Indigenous peoples here on

Turtle Island and elsewhere around the world is a holocaust that remains completely unacknowledged. So far, no one other than Indigenous peoples will face it. Denial runs deep. This, of course, does not simply leave the holocaust unacknowledged, it allows it to continue. And it does. Today, Indigenous people are being murdered and destroyed all over the world. The dead fall like trees.

A quick look at the statistics for Indigenous communities easily reveals some of the real impacts of racism and genocide. Even in places where the violence may not seem overt, the impact is staggering. For example, in Canada our average life expectancy is well below that of the average Canadian. *Our infant mortality rate is three times the national average. Youth suicides in some communities are about eight times the national average. We are about three per cent of the Canadian population but we comprise the majority of people who are incarcerated in federal institutions. We are disproportionately represented in prisons and cemeteries.* Why? Certainly not because we are involved in organized crime nor because of any fault or defect of our own. We are there because this society fears and hates us. *That is the reality of life. That is the way we live and the way that our thinking evolves and the way that our activism evolves.*

The impact of colonization does not simply fall upon us and our communities. It affects all. It is an issue for everyone to consider. The destruction of the earth and the people will not remain within the man-made boundaries of "Indian reserves." It cannot. So as human beings we have to seriously look at what we want from life, what we want from government and other institutions, what we want for the earth and for our children. We have to look seriously and bravely at what is currently happening.

More than 500 years after Indigenous peoples discovered settlers, institutions of colonization and oppression continue to operate on this land. Notably, the education system continues to help the government colonize and oppress us by feeding children a constant diet of misinformation. Reactions to our recent struggles to protect our lands have shown how effective this is. Through the education system most Canadians are taught to remain ignorant about colonization, about treaties, about the Indian Act, about the taking of Indigenous land. In Canadian schools today, Canadians do not learn about the history of this land and its First peoples. As long as this continues, as long as Canadian children are ignorant about the devastation that has been taking place here, as long as the lies and silences continue, Canadians will continue to hurl stones, they will continue to accept the assertion that those of us who protect sacred sites are "militants" and "criminals," they will continue to support the use of armed force against us, they will continue to believe that living in poverty on a reserve is a privilege and that increasingly limited exemptions from certain taxes are exorbitant reimbursement for having your land, your language, your ceremonies, your sacred sites, and your children ripped away from you.

Another of the cultural differences that has arisen as a result of the education system is that our literature, our relationship to words, and our use of language (including English) continues to remain a mystery to the dominant culture.

Many of us have some degree of understanding of "mainstream" language and literature, of the tradition behind them, and of the symbols and meanings that enrich them. After all, we have been forced through an educational system that has ensured, at great cost to us, that we do. But the reverse is not true. Those immersed in white Euro-Canadian culture learn nothing about our literature, the tradition that is its foundation, the layers and layers and layers of meaning that have accumulated over generations since we were first placed on this land. Our languages, our symbols and imagery, our stories, are generally not known, and if they are, they are rarely understood.

> Intellectual apartheid of this nature helps create and maintain political apartheid; it tends to manifest itself in the practical affairs of all societies that subscribe to it. Contrary to popular and much of scholarly opinion in Western intellectual circles, aesthetics are not extraneous to politics. And because political conquest necessarily involves intellectual conquest, educational institutions in this country have prevented people from studying the great works of minority cultures in light of critical structures that could illuminate and clarify those materials in their own contexts. The literatures and arts of non-Western peoples have thus remained obscure to people educated in Western intellectual modes. Moreover, non-Western literature and art appear quaint, primitive, confused, and unworthy of serious critical attention largely because they are presented that way. (Gunn Allen, *Spider Woman's* 3-4)

Our stories are rarely understood and are routinely dismissed as simplistic. Often, our traditional stories and sacred stories are categorized as "children's literature." This kind of "aesthetic colonization," as Paula Gunn Allen calls it, is a reality for Indigenous writers, storytellers, and artists. At "Returning the Gift," a gathering of Native writers in Oklahoma in 1992, Greg Young-Ing, a poet and the managing editor of Theytus Books, spoke about the experience of being faced with this kind of ignorant appraisal of our stories. Greg had been at another conference where a university professor walked up to him and in the course of their discussion said that Native writing was "too simplistic." Greg said he thought to himself "that's because you just don't get it, man!" But he considered his response carefully and answered in a way that he thought would be correct – with a story. Not surprisingly, the professor still did not get it.

> Literature is a facet of a culture. Its significance can be best understood in terms of its culture, and its purpose is meaningful only when the assumptions it is based on are understood and accepted....
>
> American Indian literature is not similar to western literature because the basic assumptions about the universe and, therefore, the basic reality experienced by tribal peoples and westerners are not the same.... This difference has confused non-Indian students for centuries, because they

have been unable or unwilling to grant this difference and to proceed in terms of it.

For example, the two cultures differ greatly in terms of the assumed purpose for the existence of literature.... The tribes seek, through song, ceremony, legend, sacred stories (myths), and tales to embody, articulate, and share reality, to bring the isolated private self into harmony and balance with this reality, to verbalize the sense of the majesty and reverent mystery of all things, and to actualize, in language, those truths of being and experience that give to humanity its greatest significance and dignity. The artistry of the tribes is married to the essence of language itself, for in language we seek to share our being with that of the community, and thus to share in the communal awareness of the tribe. (Gunn Allen, *Sacred Hoop* 222-23)

For many of us, writing, storytelling, performance, and multi-media art are forms of activism, are creative (and therefore positive and giving) ways both to maintain who we are and to protest against colonization. In the simplest terms, we protest by dispelling lies and telling our own stories, our own histories, in our own ways, according to our own concepts of truth and beauty.

Tribal art of all kinds embodies the principle of kinship, rendering the beautiful in terms of connectedness of elements in harmonious, balanced, respectful proportion of each and to all-in-All.

What this signifies is a fundamental difference between the Western and the tribal sense of the beautiful.... Nor does the tribal community of relatives end with human kin: the supernaturals, spirit people, animal people of all varieties, the thunders, snows, rains, rivers, lakes, hills, mountains, fire, water, rock, and plants are perceived to be members of one's community. Ultimately, Indian aesthetics are spiritual at base; that is, harmony, relationship, balance, and dignity are its informing principles because they are principles that inform our spiritual lives. (Gunn Allen, *Spider Woman's* 10-11)

For us, writing and literature are important. In part, this is because we do not separate the intellectual debate from the reality of practical life, from what we need to do in order to work with our people, and to contribute back to our communities and to all of creation. Most of the people I know are able to do something, are not totally oppressed by the system to the point of inaction, but the ones who are able to do something, do it because of the idea of giving back. It is very fundamental to who we are as Anishnaabek, who we are as Indigenous people. As Linda Hogan says, "all the people I know who write, write because they feel it's important to do so, and that it contributes to some kind of change" (130). It is a way to share, to reaffirm kinship, to connect with the sacredness of creation.

When Indigenous people study and come to understand our own literatures, languages, cultures, and aesthetics, there comes the realization that everything is connected. There comes the realization that there are few simple answers except when there is no understanding, or when understanding is so profound that connections can be understood at a glance, with language and meaning carved into a simple design that reflects the larger pattern. There comes the realization that words are sacred.

> ... words are heavy with meaning
> they are the true survivors
> echoing into infinity
> when we have become bones cradled by ahki....

Words are heavy with meaning.

> ... Words have a great potential for healing, in all respects. And we have a need to learn them, to find a way to speak first the problem, the truth, against destruction, then to find a way to use language to put things back together, to live respectfully, to praise and celebrate earth, to love. (Hogan 120)

Love. Land. Words. Healing.

Love. Family. Community. Land. Each of us is born into a family, into a community in a specific place. Because of this, because we are born into a certain family and community and because the family and community and land know and welcome us, we are who we are as Indigenous people. Family and community give us a knowledge base, a way of being, a world view. This is provided to us through arts, language, ceremonies, songs, prayers, dances, customs, values, practices, all of which have been developed over generations, over thousands and thousands of years of living in kinship with the land.

The connections we have are reciprocal; each of us has a responsibility to them. To maintain our responsibility each of us must be a giver as well as a receiver. If we do not work to maintain the connection, if one of us rejects our responsibility by failing to contribute, to give back, that person will ultimately lose his or her sense of self. That person will become lost, drifting, disconnected. When that happens the person loses the spiritual base as well – a spiritual base which is founded on love and respect. This lost, disconnected person then becomes capable of all sorts of destructive behaviour – behaviour that can be internalized or that can be unleashed on the earth. This is why the connection to our homelands is so vital; without it we cease to exist as people.

> Land is people.... These are the kinds of relationships we must never forget. Our land is our strength, our people, the land, one and the same, as it always has been and always will be. Remembering is all. (Hobson 11)

For me as Anishnaabekwe, this is an issue of resistance, it's an issue of empowerment, it's an issue of survival.
Meegwetch.

MYRNA KOSTASH

Imagination, Representation, and Culture[1]

I come to these themes from two important experiences in my life as a Canadian writer. The first was the publication of my first book, *All of Baba's Children*, in 1978, with its account of the lives of the first generation of Ukrainian-Canadians (not the pioneers) in a small town in Alberta, and the publication of my fourth book, *Bloodlines: A Journey into Eastern Europe*, in 1993, which extended the first book's concerns with ethnicity into a meditation on the meaning of ancestral identity for a hyphenated Canadian.

The second informative experience was that of chairing The Writers' Union of Canada, from 1993 to 1994, during the planning of the "Writing Thru Race" conference and the uproar in the media about it. The conference continues to be a flashpoint in the arguments of critics of multiculturalism even though civilization as we know it was still intact the day after the conference ended. As one might have predicted, the media were generally uninterested in the proceedings of the conference itself and its outcomes.

In the 15 years between these two experiences, the discourses framing my concerns changed dramatically. As a third-generation Ukrainian-Canadian, I had begun with the idea of ethnicity as a generative identity – well past the immigrant experience – that forms part of a broad "culture of resistance" in Canada to coca-colonization. In those days, third-generation ethnicity felt like the leading edge of the cultural debate and I imagined broader and broader common fronts of cultural subversives (feminists, immigrants, eco-guerrillas, Métis, artists, gays, and lesbians) challenging the globalization of culture. By the 1990s, however, I was no longer speaking in those terms, although I wanted to. What had happened in the interval was the articulation of race and colour. It wasn't that we had never talked about them in the speech around multiculturalism; it's that we had subsumed them within the familiar categories of "otherness," "assimilation," "community," and of course "ethnicity." For example, in 1983, the year of the first "Women and Words" conference in Vancouver, Lillian Allen, Kristjana Gunnars, and I could still be on the same panel discussing the relationship between ethnicity, feminism, and our writing, as though the one thing we had in common – that none of us was "Anglo" – was the most meaningful.[2] In a word, I had discovered that, in the new terms of the discourse, I was white. I was a member of a privileged *majority*. I was part of the problem, not the solution.

This had immediate consequences for how one could think about political action to deal with the problem. Solidarity was no longer the point. Power and privilege, mine, were the point. As the language of difference seemed privileged over all other political speech, the interests of the majority and minority were seen as incompatible, a point made so effectively that it appeared no one spoke for anyone else, as in the troubling "voice appropriation" debates. No one had the right to extrapolate from another's experience. No shared territory could be assumed. In its place stood the acute self-consciousness of particularity. Identity, released from false universalisms, no longer had an investment in the whole human project either. As a result of these developments it has become problematic to argue for commonality of purpose among people who in many cases want the same thing.

There are very real differences among us, which is a large part of the burden of the new multiculturalist consciousness. The older liberal, humanistic ideals of "transcending" class and ethnic difference have manifestly not dissolved social and economic distinctions. As Judy Rebick has argued, in *Clash of Identities*, "Identifying with a group that faces discrimination is not identity politics, it is a reality of life" (31) because of the way in which their location in the group affects their lives, the *real* social divisiveness being racism and discrimination.

Taking another tack, postmodernists query the universalist assumptions of the so-called Enlightenment project (that there is a universal knowledge accessible to and true for all humanity), and argue that we must now deal with the world in terms of the tentative, indeterminate, contingent, and provisional. What, then, could compel us back to togetherness from our estranged positions when even *we* is a problematic pronoun?

Some Canadians have noisily raised the alarm about this development. They mistrust group identity as a coarsening of the speech of civil society and cultural diversity as a fragmentation of the social fabric. They – especially if they are on the Right – call on Canadians to practise their ethnicity within the privacy of their homes and to be "Canadians" outside, as though one's ethnic self were not part of a social identity; as though, to borrow an analogy used by philosopher Ian Angus, in his *A Border Within: National Identity, Cultural Plurality, and Wilderness*, the "deep diversity" of multicultural politics could threaten our national integrity any more than the bio-diversity of an ecosystem undermines the unity of that system. For one of the great achievements of official multiculturalism in the 1970s was the legitimization of cultural diversity as an "everyday part of public discourse and consideration" and the "crucible" in which we in fact all live, in the words of Dr Manoly Lupul, former director of The Canadian Institute of Ukrainian Studies at the University of Alberta. The socio-cultural achievements of our minorities belong to the whole community of Canadians, and multiculturalism encodes that fact as "public philosophy" – which is one of the things that enrages its critics. We should remind

Canadians that multiculturalism as a public policy has its roots in a protest against the idea of an "official culture," in a vision of socio-economic justice for minorities consistently un/under-represented in the governing elites and in the politics of what Stuart Hall calls "relations of representation" – which group gets maximum access to representation in public life.[3] To label and dismiss this policy commitment by the Canadian state as caving in to "special interests" is deeply offensive: what could be more representative of *communal* goals than the desire of minorities to be enabled and to be respected, to be accountable, to be visible? To *belong*, in a word. "Amid charges of essentialism or political correctness," writes Larissa Lai in *Bringing It Home*, "we forged strategies to insist on our presence" (202). In *Frontiers: Essays on Racism and Culture*, Nourbese Philip employs the moving image of "mothering" – of the need of the Africans in the New World so violently "othered" by slavery and racism to be finally "m/othered" by Canada.

This brings me to the crux of my current concern: how can I reconcile this one idea of multiculturalism – as a demand on and achievement of *public culture* – with the theory of identity as a "fractured and evanescent"[4] variable of *stand-point*? Since I believe that multiculturalism is perennially about social justice, what happens, from the perspective of identity politics, to those old political questions of "who gains, who loses, who bears what costs?"[5] Who, even, is this "who" that is being theorized into discontinuity and dissipated totality?

These are perilous times in the life of our Canadian "commons." Our national collectivity is threatened by a globalizing capitalism with its virtually unchallenged hegemonic corporate practices. Meanwhile, in a rapture of cultural theory about decentred, non-totalizing, and self-reflexive representation, we the people are said to live in habitats not countries, socialities not communities, and fluid pluralities not classes. So we (citizens, artists, immigrants) have to be diverse and decentred but *they* (bond traders, CEOs, Disneyland) get to be monopolistic and ubiquitous.[6] The new global capitalism, with its think tanks, trade agreements, and mega-mergers, goes from strength to strength as the one "meta-narrative" that has *not* been deconstructed.

It is with considerable urgency, then, that I want to make the case for solidarity among people and their communities. Or at least raise the possibility of practising what I like to call the "politics of resemblance." Even in our solitudes, our autonomous diversities, we have spoken of our attachment to the ideas of justice and peace and self-determination. We are involved with each other in a dialectic of community and society in which no single identity defines us. We are, at one and the same time, persons of a certain sex, profession, religion, birthplace, language, ethnicity. There is no single ghetto into which we can withdraw and still be whole.

In the turbulent wake of deconstructionist cultural criticism, is there perhaps enough social lumber left lying around with which to begin to speak of reconstruction? Are there traditions, however deeply flawed, in the so-

called Eurocentric Enlightenment dream of a universal knowledge, that can
be the foundation of a new cultural politics? Is there a common culture that
evokes this knowledge as one we still hold in common in the pursuit of
liberation and justice?

I have been fascinated to read writers who think so – Cornel West, for
instance, in *Out There: Marginalization and Contemporary Cultures*. West
believes there is a knowledge in the shared quest for the "precious ideals" of
individuality and democracy. Coalitions across "empire, nation, region, race,
gender, and sexual orientation" are admittedly fragile but their democratic
goals overlap and provide the skeletal structure of expanded latitudes of
freedom. James Littleton, editor of *Clash of Identities*, makes much the same
case for Enlightenment values as "consistent with" ideas of human equality
and human progress. The danger has lain in isolating identity politics from
the broad social agenda and the big ideas of the Left that have historically
contested the centres of power.

As Todd Gitlin argues in *The Twilight of Common Dreams*, what is required
is a "culture of commonality" – what he calls democracy – precisely within
which aggrieved minorities articulate the discourse of human and civil rights
and strategize their emancipation. As expansive capitalism marches on,
shattering the collectivities and common experience of citizens that
accumulated over generations, such a "culture of commonality" may,
ironically, be minorities' best guarantee of their own identities, a kind of self-
defence against arbitrary power of representation.

Finally, Ian Angus, surveying the devolution of nations and collectivities
to regional and local tendencies, worries, in *A Border Within: National Identity,
Cultural Plurality, and Wilderness*, that "we seem to be losing the key
mediation that linked local and regional concerns to universal ones." Do we
really have to choose between an interest in ourselves and human
universality? Angus thinks that the "politics of multiculturalism" holds the
key to the answer. That multiculturalism might be a search for both our
similarities and our differences. Interestingly, by employing the concept of
multiculturalism instead of *identity politics*, he is able to expose identity's *social*
process: it is not just an individual possession, it is formed collectively and so
multiculturalism becomes the means for minorities to demand of the state
that their ethnicity be developed within the matrix of civil society.

This is not just about "retention" of an identity but its development within
a larger social context. And so we can see that, at least as an ideal,
multiculturalism does not ask that we choose between our ethnicity and a
national identity but that the one is a "key content" of the other. In what I
think is a particularly felicitous formulation, Angus invites us to understand
the issue of multicultural understanding as an "us/we relation, not an
us/them" in which the "us" is our own ethno-cultural group and the "we" the
multicultural civic society of Canada. If a subculture is not taken up into the
larger identity, Angus warns, then the "passage" between the particular and
the universal is blocked for that subculture and those who live in it are

trapped in the us/them relation. But if their "otherness" is instead respected, then the particular is given access to the universal in the relation of us/we. "Particularity is not the opposite of universality but its condition...."

I find very hopeful these struggles for a rearticulated idea of the common cause that cannot fulfil itself without enabling subcultures to be fully present in public life and that go beyond the usual contradictions of majority and minority, centre and margin, self and other, ethnic and universal, whose resolutions usually involve the demonizing of the one in order to satisfy the demands of the other. Instead we have here an idea that forms an organic whole, if I can put it that way: my ethnic identity is not only continuous with the life of the "commons" but in fact guarantees it.

NOTES

1. A version of this essay was presented at the "Encounter Canada" conference, at York University, Toronto, Ontario, 6 March 1997.

2. Lillian Allen and Kristjana Gunnars are Canadian writers of Carribean and Icelandic background respectively.

3. Cited in Cornel West, "The New Cultural Politics of Difference," *Out There: Marginalization and Contemporary Cultures*, ed. Russell Ferguson (Cambridge Mass.: MIT Press, 1990).

4. See Frances Fox Piven, "Globalizing Capitalism and the Rise of Identity Politics," *Socialist Register* 1995.

5. Cornel West, contemplating deconstruction's ahistoricism, in "The New Cultural Politics of Difference," *Out There: Marginalization and Contemporary Cultures*.

6. Todd Gitlin, in *The Twilight of Common Dreams: Why America Is Wracked By Culture Wars* (New York: Metropolitan Books, 1995) wonders that certain intractable facts of American society – the "stupefying degree of inequality," the escalating student debt, the sustained attack on university budgets, the horrendous unemployment among young African Americans – were passed over in magisterial silence by both identity politicians and neo-conservatives, all of whom had points to make instead about reading lists.

JANICE KULYK KEEFER

"The Sacredness of Bridges":
Writing Immigrant Experience

The first part of this essay's title is taken from Michael Ondaatje's novel *The English Patient* (1992). His earlier work, *In the Skin of a Lion* (1987), made the act of bridge-building a key feature of that novel's plot and symbolic structure. Perhaps it's because bridge-blasting plays so significant a role in *The English Patient* that Ondaatje underlines the sacredness of bridges such as the one the novel constructs between the Canadian nurse Hana and the Sikh sapper, Kip, a bridge of eros that spans daunting gaps between cultures, races, and histories; a bridge shattered by the bombing of Hiroshima. If I emphasize the sacredness of bridges in this essay, it's not to call upon conventional pieties or duplicitous nostrums urging us all to just get along together – to "just do it" as the Nike ad urges. We live in a world where the bridges we desperately need to enable us to connect, in spite of profound differences, are under threat of demolition or else disintegration through neglect, deliberate or inadvertent.

I want in this essay to sketch out a possible trope or paradigm through which the writing and dissemination of immigrant experience can be effectively conceptualized, and also to unpack and rearrange some elements of that loaded term "immigrant." I'll go on to speak in a general way about that highly problematic "ism," multiculturalism, and some of the ways in which it has made it possible for the experiences of various immigrant communities to contribute in highly influential and significant ways to the making of contemporary Canadian culture. And I shall conclude by speaking of my own delayed exploration of immigrant experience in my most recent writing.

In referring to "immigrant experience" I deliberately refuse to preface this phrase by the definite article. I'm uncomfortable with the universalizing ring "the immigrant experience" conveys, as if there were only one kind of immigrant, one narrative of experience to be told. And yet I'm also aware that I'm speaking of these matters from a situation and point of view very different from, for example, those pertaining to a Nourbese Philip or Fred Wah. I also know that I can't claim to speak for European immigrants or even Eastern-European immigrants to Canada – nor can I attempt to present "the Ukrainian-Canadian" point of view, since I situate myself on the margins of my highly fractured ethno-social group, belonging not to those Ukrainian-

Canadians who are part of the prairie homesteading saga, nor to those descendants of prairie pioneers who become *emigrés* to Toronto, but to those Ukrainians who arrived in Toronto just before or after the Second World War. Thus, I speak for myself, hoping that what I have to say will resonate for others who share my particular ethnic background as well as for immigrants and children of immigrants from different ethnic communities. When I speak of immigrants in general it is with the consciousness that much of what I say might be found contentious or even alien.

With these provisos in mind, let me turn to Margaret Atwood's famous saying about Canadians: "We are all immigrants to this place, even if we were born here" (*Journals* 62). This remark becomes highly simplifying and occlusive when one imagines the "We" to be, for example, people of the First Nations. And are the experiences of Black or Asian immigrants to Canada not significantly different from those of members of the "Charter groups" – Anglo-Celtic Canadians or French Canadians? The experiences of a British family coming to Toronto in the early 1950s from Manchester or south London, and those of a Ukrainian family arriving at Union Station straight from a Displaced Persons (DP) camp in Bavaria would be so vastly different as to make the homogenizing "all" in Atwood's dictum immediately contentious. That said, let it be admitted that the experiences of that Ukrainian DP family and, say, a Chinese family who had already been in Canada for 30 years by the time the DPs arrived would be critically different. Despite the shared difficulty of learning an utterly strange new language and alphabet, the Ukrainians, given the sheer fact of the colour of their skin, would find that their children, or perhaps only their grandchildren, would be able to pass, should they so choose, for unhyphenated, "established" Canadians. They would never be asked that condescendingly racist question posed so often by "tolerant" WASPs – the kind of WASPs that Joy Kogawa skewers so neatly in *Obasan* – "and when did you come to this country?"

It's perhaps the inevitable lot of witty, important people who, like Atwood, have become cultural icons, to make flashpoint statements that then get torn to pieces when submitted to analysis. Yet while Atwood's definition of Canadians as perpetual or eternal immigrants is hugely reductive, it is also, in a strange way, dead-on, once all the hidden differences and specificities have been teased out and acknowledged. If by "immigrant" we mean the single generation that makes "the crossing" from one country and culture to another, often traumatically different, then no, Conrad Black is not an immigrant in Canada in the way that his wife Barbara Amiel has been – I believe we've made Britain the gift of her person, as well as her politics. But if the immigrant status Atwood confers on all Canadians has a metaphysical resonance – in the sense that, as the button says, we are all "just visiting this planet" and that, to use a line from poet bill bissett, "nobody owns the earth" – then one could only hope that Mr Black will become more aware of his recent and timebound, rather than olde-established, status than he currently is. As importantly, an awareness that we are all immigrants in Canada can help us undertake a crucial correction to the ideology of our national anthem – a correction that is frequently sported on T-shirts worn by the more politically aware of my students at the University of Guelph: Canada is *all* Native land. One could conceivably argue that Canada's Native peoples have been made *de facto* immigrants in the political construct, Canada, that was carved out of their ancestral lands.

What happens when the term "immigrant" is enlarged or loosened from the borders imposed on it by too strict, too literal an application of factors of time and space? Why should the word "immigrant" be applied to the experience of my mother, who left Poland for Canada in 1936, but not to myself, born 16 years later in suburban Toronto? To recognize that we are all immigrants, and that the term is a far more flexible, capacious, ramiferous one than we have allowed it to be in the past is to de-stigmatize the word "immigrant," to valorize those to whom the term most insistently applies, to make of that status not something to be got through and forgotten or hidden as quickly as possible, but rather something to be explored, its problematic features adumbrated. In the neo-liberal mood of a downsizing-doomed Canada, immigration policy has become a political hot potato. Despite all the reputable studies that show how positive a contribution immigrants make to the economic as well as cultural life of the country, the prevailing opinion – one whipped up and sustained by much of the media – is that an influx of immigrants, especially Blacks and Asians, is destroying the country. Wierdly enough, writers of colour like Neil Bissoondath have been found to articulate and in many ways embrace this opinion, as his recent *Selling Illusions, The Cult of Multiculturalism in Canada* so sadly shows.

I differ greatly from Neil Bissoondath in being a supporter of multi-culturalism – of what an authentic and progressive multiculturalism could be. Multiculturalism is a term that can so easily be manipulated to mean nothing more than state-defined and controlled ethnic chic/kitsch. I believe that a re-interpretation, an enlarging and unloosing of the term "immigrant experience" is crucial to the salvaging and reconfiguration of multiculturalism as a dynamic force in Canadian life, so that it can finally achieve its full potential as a social and political as well as cultural force. One of the salient features of multiculturalism has to do with what I would call the fraught continuum of immigrant experience. This continuum insists that while there cannot help but be a world of difference between the experiences of, say a Birmingham mechanic, a Trinidadian university student, a Bosnian refugee, all of whom immigrated to Canada at some point in the last 50 years, their common experience of displacement as opposed to specific instances of that experience – instances particularized by factors of race, class, gender, education – places them together on this continuum. The long, complex, and often scandalous history of Canada's reception of its immigrants also forms a part of that continuum, so that the experiences of those perceived by the dominant culture as "visible" – and therefore threatening minorities – the first Ukrainian settlers in the prairies, for example, with their sheepskin coats and incomprehensible speech, as well as Chinese labourers imported to work (or is slave the more appropriate verb?) on the railways, can be brought to speak to one another. Such speech is crucial, I would argue, in the struggle against forgetting, a struggle particularly important to non-Anglo-Celtic immigrants who, because of the ease with which their skin colour allows them to pass for "English," may just as easily become part of the anti-immigrant backlash currently extended to immigrants of colour.[1]

No two immigrants are alike, of course, and there's a crucial distinction to be made between those immigrants who, under duress, have come from one place that has always been home to a strangeness they must make familiar, and somehow their own, and immigrants whose condition would be better described by the term mobility than migrancy. By the latter group of immigrants, I mean those privileged enough, through education and often, though not always, through wealth to cushion their dislocation and preserve an air of the voluntary about their movements, past and future. Immigrants who've come to Canada to acquire a university education here, be they Michael Ondaatje, Austin Clarke, or Dionne Brand, are in "a different boat" from those who arrive as and remain labourers. It would seem to me that within any given ethno-cultural group, significant divisions will abound; that bridges are always being built whereby, for example, those immigrants privileged enough to attain a university education and a status or profession that allows them to interact with those in positions of power within the dominant culture can continue to communicate with and represent those in their communities who lack such privilege or status. The gap between the poor and disadvantaged of a given community and those who, however hard they fight to give a voice to the impoverished in their community, are or have become members of an elite, and whose children will benefit from the privileges they've accrued – this also has to be bridged.

There are endless differences to be acknowledged in the sketching-out of the continuum I've alluded to, and I only have space to gesture towards another difference that I find crucial to my own situation as the child and grandchild of immigrants. This is the distinction that needs to be drawn between those who are actual and those who are conceptual immigrants: those who can still feel the weight of their suitcases in their hands, and those who reflect on what that weight must have been like, or who hear, and perhaps write down the stories that describe that weight so that it becomes palpably real to others.

To undergo physical and cultural displacement and to image or conceptualize this displacement are both experiential activities, but there are important differences in the nature of the experience. It's not that the former is always more authentic, more real and significant than the latter, but that it cannot be articulated and communicated without the latter. This can be illustrated by the traditional situation of the immigrant family whose members actually made the crossing between "old" world and – to them – "new," yet who are incapable of articulating the experience except, perhaps, to family. It's often only the members of the second or third generation who are able to achieve a public form of this articulation, weaving together fragments of ancestral stories, memories of other people's memories, and their own awareness of their fractured, hyphenated, multiple selves into a text or painting or film – into art.[2] Yet even here, conditions have greatly changed, so that educated immigrants – Rohinton Mistry is a case in point – seem able to "bridge the gap" between the actual and the conceptual in their own person.

To speak of placing immigrants on a continuum, is to make or summon a metaphor, one that has to do with the bridging or joining of parallel experiences. So let me speak for a moment of the bridge I have in mind. It is not, I hasten to say, a coca-colonized Benetton-built bridge teaching the world to sing in Colourful and Happy Harmony. Nor is it modelled on those symphonies in stone that grace the capitals of western Europe – the Charles bridge in Prague, for example, or Paris's *Pont Neuf*. Rather it is like those swaying, alarmingly light suspension bridges you may have walked or staggered over when visiting Capilano Canyon near Vancouver. It's a bridge, in other words, in which mobility vies with stability, a bridge over which people are constantly passing, jostling one another and stopping to exchange opinions or interpretations of the view. This kind of bridge points as much to the intractable chasm it was built to span as to the fact that a means of crossing that chasm now exists; it also insists on its own constructedness, the immense labour it takes to build and maintain it. Anyone who talks about bridging the differences in immigrant experience must acknowledge at the outset that bridge and chasm are interdependent terms, and that their interrelation is one characterized by dramatic tensions.

Finally, this is a bridge that's continually changing and being changed by those who walk over it. If you can't step into the same river twice, neither can you walk over the same bridge more than once, or over the same chasm.[3] And it's constructed both out of material substances and that less substantial and reliable substance, memory, whether individual or collective, and the narratives memory impels. As for the material substance from which this swaying suspension bridge is constructed, it is an amalgam of paper and ink, canvas and pigments, celluloid, the wood and metal of sculpture and musical instruments, the boom and whisper of the human voice and body. For it's in the realm of cultural making that the private, tenuous memories of individual subjects – memories that often find expression in stories told within the family – become something larger and more durable, become part of the collective memory and thus consciousness of a whole country, by entering a public realm in which transmission and, most importantly, exchange is possible.

What this swaying bridge facilitates, of course, is movement. It is the product of the writer's ability to travel, through imagination and memory, across time and space, to represent or reinvent the experience of long-dead or long-silent family, as Nino Ricci does in *Lives of the Saints* (1990) or Wayson Choy in *The Jade Peony* (1995). If the writer's work is compelling enough, we become capable of the same kind of travel, both while we read the text and afterwards. The distance between ourselves and others becomes something we can traverse; it also becomes something no longer static, monumental, but dynamic, transformable. An Italian-Canadian who has read *The Jade Peony* will hopefully understand something of what it means to be Chinese-Canadian in a way that may have been totally inaccessible to her or him before. She or he will be able to cross back and forth between *Lives of the Saints* and *The Jade Peony* and in so doing achieve not that minimalist virtue, tolerance, but what Milan Kundera, in *The Unbearable Lightness of Being* (1984), discusses as *Mitleid*, something stronger than compassion – the ability to feel something happening *with* as well as *to* an Other.

But before I'm accused of going soppily Dickensian and celebrating art's ability to spur a vital change of heart, let me reiterate that intractable feature of bridges: that they acknowledge as well as overcome the fact of significant distance. Let me refer to something less grandiose than the narrow or swaying bridge of culture that I've just extolled. Let me speak of the far more makeshift and timebound affairs that individual immigrant families slap together to prevent themselves from being totally disabled by a form of experiential schizophrenia. This kind of bridge between old, lost, or abandoned world and new, *faute de mieux* world exists in time, through the continuum that memory constructs, and in space, through the trans-portability of objects, for example – the handwoven *kilims*, the goosefeather quilts my grandmother brought to Canada in 1936, not just to remind her of home but to recreate home in a foreign place, since these objects were to have formed essential parts of my young aunt's and mother's dowries. But such temporal and spatial bridges never stop signifying the immense, intractable nature of "distance from," once "distance to" has been forgotten.

The reality for the immigrant – and this is compounded for that special category of immigrant *in extremis*, the refugee – is that distance is always double, if not multiple. One's distance from the country and culture of origin is always measured in terms of losses as well as the gains one makes – that "better life" you promise your children, sacrificing your own happiness for theirs. And as a newcomer, a foreigner, you keep or are forced to keep your distance from the centre of things in the adopted country – "centre" being the place where those with power and agency, even just assurance, at-homeness, hold sway. Distance can also be measured in terms of actual deprivation and an acute anxiety that may persist long after material success has been achieved. My mother's family, arriving in Toronto in the thick of the Depression, was told by other immigrants never to apply for relief, no matter how hard things got. "They" – the ones at the centre – would ship you back home at once if you dared to signal your presence in the margins. My aunt, who has had a successful medical practice in Toronto for almost 50 years now, is still in many ways the 12-year-old child who was terrorized, on her arrival in Canada, to learn that her family's ability to get enough food to eat depended on their ability to earn pieces of green paper. Back in Poland, their few scattered fields, however narrow and difficult to maintain, had always kept the family from going hungry.

But it's not just this doubled sense of distance as loss and deprivation as well as new-found opportunity that inflects immigrant life; it's also the phenomenon of what I'd call middle distance. "You can never go home again," we've been told – or if you do go home, it will only be to find out that "home" has shifted ground, relocated itself neither there or here, in old or new country, but somewhere maddeningly in-between. This is the situation in which Danny Smiricky finds himself in Josef Skvorecky's novel *The Engineer of Human Souls* (1984). For Skvorecky's alter-ego Smiricky, home, the country of the heart, is ultimately neither the Nazi-occupied Czechoslovakia of his boyhood nor contemporary Toronto, but that quasi-mythical "Bohemia" that he's made into prime imaginative territory.

For my grandfather, who first came to Canada in 1927 not as an immigrant but as what would not until years later acquire that euphemistic title, *Gastarbeiter* (foreign guest worker) the situation was rather different. Being a reflective and deeply intelligent man, he found himself increasingly a "foreigner" on his return visits to Poland, disgusted with the oppressive policies a martial regime had enacted against ethnic minorities such as the Ukrainians. And yet when he returned to Toronto smack in the middle of the Dirty Thirties, he found himself taking up an increasingly oppositional stance to authority as well, becoming an active trade unionist when he finally found steady work during the war boom. Perhaps it was his political orientation that made him an occupier of the "middle distance," casting a critical eye on there and here, oriented always to that imagined country of possibility in which true justice and an order based on equality rather than privilege would prevail.

Middle distance – this is the site where the immigrant artist, or perhaps any artist positions herself, the fiction of "halfway" between those other fictive but necessary constructs: then and now, there and here, responsibility and desire, family and self, community and individuality. From my own experience, I would argue that artists who write of an ethno-cultural minority community in which they grew up, but from which they have removed or in crucial ways distanced themselves, are always performing balancing acts between their sense of loyalty to origins and solidarity with "their own" and their sense of critical curiosity, of imagining how things could be different, more equitable, more open in their home communities. This is particularly true for minorities within minorities – for instance, for the lesbian, Marxist writer in those Black communities that tend to privilege traditional forms of female sexuality or uphold traditional roles and aspirations within the family and economy in a given social formation.

But this "middle distance" occupied by the immigrant artist – a middle that suggests not compromise and bland restfulness, but continual struggle and alertness – is only half of the equation of possibility. For no immigrant artist writing of a non-Anglo-Celtic country of origin, writing of growing up in a minority community in Canada, could hope to publish her work and have it received in any significant way, in a socio-cultural context that utterly silenced or marginalized the "ex-centric," the pieces at the very corners or bottom of the notorious Canadian mosaic. In other words, for immigrant experience to have taken persuasive hold of a country's imagination, as it has done in Canada, shaping and restructuring its collective sense of self, something significant must have happened to create the agency presupposed by this "hold." This "significant something," I would argue, was the advent and development of that highly contentious phenomenon, multiculturalism.

Multiculturalism – a phenomenon found in many countries besides Canada – is the legally enshrined culture of this country. In its officially sanctioned form it is viewed with scepticism and even hostility not only by many First Nations peoples and Québécois, but also by writers from – as offensive official jargon has it – the "visible minorities" of the country, many of whom have found multiculturalist practice to be permeated with racist assumptions and perpetuative of inequalities. Defenders of multiculturalism have argued that at its inception, this "ism" was meant to be far more than a jazzy cultural icing on the stodgy Canadian cake. In insisting on the right to equal opportunity in all sectors of life – economic, educational, political, cultural – multiculturalism would create a truly democratic society in which the rich, ever-renewed, and ever-changing mix of cultures that make up Canada would not be showily celebrated and exploited, but would work to change fundamentally the status quo.[4]

It hasn't, alas, turned out the way those defenders envisaged it – but neither has it proved an abject failure in all respects. Small "m" multiculturalism – as practised in the artistic community and at the grass-roots levels in neighbourhoods and civic communities across the country – keeps struggling to open doors and borders, to create possibilities of change and exchange within and between ethno-cultural groups. It's this kind of substantive, progressive multiculturalism that has come under attack by conservative groups, among them Preston Manning's Reform Party and its sympathizers, and also, I would argue, successive federal governments that have devoted fewer and fewer resources to making multiculturalism a vital and constructive force for change.

Multiculturalism has had a profound impact on the arts. To confine the picture to the literary and publishing community, I would claim that the explosion of literary talent and the enthusiastic publication of new voices fostered by multiculturalism is the direct successor to that amazing cultural flowering of the 1960s, when Atwood and Ondaatje, Cohen and MacEwen changed the stuffy-demure demeanour of Canlit. Lee Maracle and Tomson Highway, Hiromi Goto and Sky Lee, Matt Cohen and Anne Michaels, Dany Laferrière and Claire Harris, Ven Begamudré and Shyam Selvadurai – these and others already named in the course of this essay are just a few of the "transcultural"[5] writers who have grown up in or entered into a multicultural Canada that had changed enough to encourage instead of silencing their talent, so that their work could be published not only here but often abroad as well and to great acclaim.

These writers either created or inherited the *donnée* that a poem or novel or short story could deal with Bombay, Sri Lanka, Trinidad and never once mention death-in-the-snow, wheatfields, or the autumnal tides of gold and crimson sweeping over the Laurentians – and still be intensely Canadian. They could also deal with a reserve or "rez" instead of Rosedale, Chinatown instead of Cabbagetown, with the internment camps set up for Canadians of Japanese birth or heritage during the Second World War, instead of the Halifax explosion of the First World War – and introduce their readers to an experience of Canadianness that was no less authentic than the "traditional" experiences recognized by the Charter Groups. What their work tells us is that it's as much in the subject position of the writer as in his or her geographical location or regional identity that "Canadianness" lies. It's the writer's being situated on the bridge between cultures, and thus free to turn her or his gaze in any direction, to critique, to defend, to redress wrongs – not just in the adopted but in the home culture as well – that makes him or her Canadian. And all Canadians, whatever their colour or ancestral culture, are the richer for it.

I want to end this discussion of writing the immigrant experience by giving some idea of my own trajectory as a writer who has spent a long while in a limbo of denial, contestation, and flight from the inherited facts of her conferred rather than self-constructed identity.

I was born in a pre-multicultural Toronto in 1952, when it was not "fun to be ethnic" as a host of T-shirts would later proclaim; and when the McCarthyite spirit flourished in the True North Strong and Free, though it may not have been as strongly and freely expressed *chez nous* as it was south of the border. When my parents were warned not to let my older sister speak "Russian" in the schoolyard, when my father was turned away from the American border when attempting to drive to Detroit to take part in that most subversive of all activities, a dental convention – on the grounds that as a child he'd played violin in the Ukrainian Labour Temple Orchestra – they responded by ceasing to speak Ukrainian in our home except as the language of secrets – things children weren't supposed to hear or know about.

Another member of my family had participated in similar musical crimes. At about the same time that my father was refused entry to the United States, my aunt, who'd learned to play the mandolin at the same Labour Temple, was being interviewed for her first job. She'd learned to speak fluent English in the first two years after her arrival in Canada; she'd fought to be admitted to Medical School at the University of Toronto, which had actively discouraged anyone with a name like "Solowska" from applying, and after completing the regular six-year course in five years, had graduated tenth in a class of 170, completing her internship with flying colours and distinguishing herself in a postgraduate programme in pathology at the Children's Hospital of Michigan. She seemed, in other words, fully qualified to work at any hospital in North America. But at the end of a job interview that she'd thought had gone very well, a certain Dr Feesbee had taken my aunt by the elbow and walked her over to the window of the hospital, which overlooks Bathurst Street. He directed her gaze towards number 300, the façade of the Labour Temple, and said: "That is where you grew up – that is where you belong." To her enormous credit my aunt, who is not given to acts of bravura or self-assertion, detached her elbow from Dr Feesbee's grasp, looked him straight in the eye and said, "I wouldn't work in your hospital even if you begged me," and walked out of the room. She subsequently refused to change her name to "Smith" in order to take up an invitation to join a prestigious paediatric practice at the Medical Arts Centre at St George and Bloor – she'd been told that people wouldn't want their children being touched by someone with an "immigrant" name like Solowska. Instead, she started her own, neighbourhood practice – one in which her patients were mainly new immigrants, Italian as well as Ukrainian and Polish – and became a respected consultant at Toronto's Hospital for Sick Children. But even after her marriage – to an Irish immigrant, as it turned out – she always practised medicine under her maiden, conspicuously ethnic name.

I relate these stories to demonstrate a little of that heavy baggage the immigrant or conspicuously "ethnic" citizen of a pre-multicultural Canada might have carried. I also want to suggest that for those born to immigrant parents and raised in two cultures and languages – for my parents did send me to Saturday morning Ukrainian school after the "red scare" had passed – a conflicted rather than mindlessly celebratory mode of existence and identity can become the norm. If I received signals from my parents and grandparents, my Ukrainian school teachers, the leaders of the Ukrainian youth organizations and summer camps that I attended, that having a Ukrainian background was something to be proud of, I received equally strong signals that it was also something to dissemble or disavow. The fear and instability my family had felt about being immigrants was always in the background during my childhood. The battles within Toronto's Ukrainian community, fiercely split as it was for complicated historical reasons, between Greek Catholic and Greek Orthodox religions, between Left- and Right-wing politics, were another unsettling feature of growing up *Ukrainski*, instead of fading into the WASP woodwork.

The prejudice that could still show itself – as when a WASP neighbour who lived on the suburban street where my parents moved in 1957, came up to introduce herself to my mother and said, on learning that our name was Kulyk, "I thought people with names like yours cleaned the houses of people with names like mine" – was a vivid influence on my upbringing, and while I can't emphasize enough how mild this prejudice was compared to what would have been served up to a Black or Asian family who'd been able to move into Toronto's west end, it was still there, and it still hurt.

Finally, as I grew into my teens and went on to university, where my reading of East-European history began to displace the sagas of Kievan 'Rus and myths of Cossack glory that had passed for history at Ukrainian school, I became aware of intensely problematic features of my Ukrainian, and indeed, Eastern-European, heritage: the ingrained misogyny of the culture and what seemed an endemic anti-Semitism. Both these features seemed to me inextricably woven up with the claustrophobic spirit of ethnicity as it was then constructed – a spirit I associated with the Ukrainian word *nashi*, meaning "our own." *Nashi* was, of course, a means of surviving as a community in a dominant, Anglo-Celtic culture bent on homogenizing and subordinating all differences into its own mould. But it was also a way of keeping out the Other, whether the familiar Others of the Old Place or the just-discovered Others of the "New." At that time in my life, the only response I could make to claustrophobia was flight. I got as far away from my ethnicity as I could, through marriage to what my community called an *Anglik* or Englishman, though his family had come to Canada as United Empire Loyalists, and through moving for a period of six years to England.

It was only when my husband and I moved back to Canada in 1980 that I started in any serious way to try to publish anything I'd written while doing postgraduate study on the work of two paradigmatically displaced writers, Henry James and Joseph Conrad. My first poems and stories appeared under my married name, Keefer, which gave no hint of my hyphenated identity, and for the most part I kept resolutely away from anything that smacked of the "ethnic," having decided that it would be the kiss of death to become known as a writer whose imaginative world could be of interest only to other Ukrainian-Canadians. I published a collection of poems, two books of short stories, and two novels, none of which made any reference, except in minor or peripheral ways to the fact that I'd grown up as the child of immigrants. It's only been in the last seven years that I've been able to write actively of and through my ethnicity, and this has been due to three main factors: my reading in the area of contemporary Canadian fiction in the transcultural mode; the emergence of Ukraine as an independent country in 1991; and my discovery, at about this time, of a number of Ukrainian-Canadian artists working in Toronto in different fields, among them the painter Natalka Husar, with her risky, iconoclastic explorations of ethnicity and gender.

By 1996, when *The Green Library* was published, I had realized that the past I'd worked so hard to hide had a large hand in the making of the present and its possibilities. It's significant, however, that I chose to make the protagonist of my novel a woman who discovers, by accident, and when she is into her 40s, that she is half Ukrainian, her biological father a DP, her mother an *haute* WASP. What she discovers in pursuing the tangled lines of her past, both in Canada and Ukraine, is that public history – an exceedingly troubled history – is the prime constituent of ethnicity.

In my new book, *Honey and Ashes*, I am confronting my ethnicity and formation as the child of immigrants in a much more direct and head-on way, by attempting a work of creative non-fiction in the combined genres of family memoir and travel narrative. Out of a mass of bits and pieces – various passports, photographs, immigration cards, steamer tickets that have somehow managed to survive a transatlantic voyage and 60 years in the dark of various desk drawers – I am attempting to weave a story made up of the many stories I heard while growing up in two countries, two houses, two landscapes at once – suburban 1950s and 1960s Toronto and a rural, almost feudal Poland without telephones or automobiles, hospitals or running water, but filled with wars, curfews, and border guards who shot to kill. I am also trying to tell the story of my own belated journey "back" to a place I've never been except through familial narrative – a story of the collision between imagined and actual worlds.

For me, *Honey and Ashes* is a bridge between past and present, private and public history, sanctioned and secret stories, and the fraught, often tragic narratives of Poles, Jews, Ukrainians, all of them sharing the charged ground of "the Old Place" – a literal translation of the name of my mother's village, Staromiszczyna. It will be a controversial text, and its eventual reception by my family, as well as the Ukrainian, Polish, and Jewish communities in Canada will, I'm sure, be problematic. But I've come to think of it as the most important work I've ever attempted, in terms of what drove me to write this particular book, and where it's taking me.

For I wrote *Honey and Ashes* in order to rescue, from an ocean of silence and forgetting, the remarkable story of my grandparents and their children, a story of radical and often traumatic displacement, and of the kind of struggle – social, economic, political – through which they made themselves at home in Canada, as much as human beings can ever be at home on this earth. And through this act of writing I am also performing my own act of homecoming, in the sense of crossing into an awareness of the need to talk not only to the dead, but to the living, to begin a dialogue with those "Others" whom my family's stories exclude or only barely mention, who shared with them the crowded living space of the "Old Place" and who share with me the relatively open space of the country where I was born. This dialogue is with Jewish-Canadians and, by extension, all the other "Others" that the term *nashi* or "our own" would exclude – everyone else on that swaying, ever-changing bridge that is, perhaps, the only home we have here, an enactment of commonality over the differences between us.

The possible commonality – not universality – of experience: whatever it is that says, I am interested in, may even have undergone something similar to what is happening in your community; that *our* communities, whether Hungarian or Haitian, are, inescapably, part of one another[6] – this is what can prevent what Charles Taylor refers to as "the politics of difference" from splintering and disempowering its adherents. I am thinking in this context of the ugly *contretemps* between Blacks and Jews in Toronto's "Showboat" controversy of a few years ago. I am also thinking of the fact that all artists/cultural producers in this country, regardless of race, gender, class and ethnicity, are equally threatened by such phenomena as the MAI negotiations, which would "allow any country to import its commodities and services [to Canada] with no conditions attached ... [so that] [a]ny foreign company could have access to any domestic grant, loan, tax incentive or subsidy, with no local requirement or public-interest distinction allowed."[7]

On the eve of the millennium, to draw upon that much-hyped phrase, we find ourselves at a juncture when a common purpose, deriving from our sense of sharing an experiential and historical continuum – a bridge between our differences – is crucial. We cannot effectively oppose neo-conservative ideologies or the corporatist agenda of which John Ralston Saul warns us so convincingly in *The Unconscious Civilization* (1995) without that common purpose. In this context, the phrase "the sacredness of bridges" resonates with the sense not of conventional piety but of a trust that is the opposite of what may prove to be our own version of *la trahison des clercs* – not a sell-out to the state, but an inability to join forces to oppose those powers that seem to be so busily selling us down the global-capitalist-corporate river.

NOTES

1. While there certainly are Eastern-European immigrants, among others, who distance themselves from the plight of immigrants such as Sikhs or Somalis so that they end up parroting the kind of racist, anti-immigrant-speak in which the *Toronto Sun* excels, I do not believe that such behaviour is an indelible and intrinsic marker of East Europeans, making them, as Himani Bannerji asserts, vigorous participants in white supremacist politics. The political formation and outlook of certain generations of Eastern-Europeans have to be understood – not condoned – in the light of complex socio-economic and -cultural factors: class, linguistic disempowerment, and the legacy of an oppressive colonialism imposed by that other great imperial power, Tsarist or Soviet Russia are all part of the story. See Bannerji's article in this volume.

2. I am using the term artist in the sense of someone who makes something qualititatively different from shoes or software. That the process of making is inevitably influenced by the conditions of cultural production is indisputable; so, to me, is the fact that artists are persons possessing and practising a vocation which obliges them to acquire skills and disciplines to work in ways that both privilege and very often impoverish them, given negligible funding for the arts and the non-commodifiable nature of such arts as poetry, for example.

3. I am grateful to Michael Keefer for pointing out to me that Heraclitus further observes that it's not the same you who steps twice into the river – or by extension, crosses the endlessly changing bridge.

4. See Kas Mazurek's essay "Defusing a Radical Social Policy: The Undermining of Multiculturalism," *20 Years of Multiculturalism, Successes and Failures,* ed. Stella Hryniuk (Winnipeg: St John's College Press, 1992).

5. Transcultural art insists on exchange, on the permeability of borders between formerly ghettoized groups, on the kind of working hybridity that occurs when we read or listen to or watch the Other not as a representation of something safely exotic, but as an obliquely-angled version of ourselves.

6. It's regrettable that some writers and theoists of race/ethnicity take up ideological positions that prevent them from acquainting themselves with the history of other immigrant groups in Canada. Misrepresentation is often the result, as when Himani Bannerji, for example, accuses "the Ukrainians" of only now seeking to construct and represent themselves as ethnics in Canada

"because the price to be paid is no longer there." The history of Ukrainians in Canada, their struggle to preserve and validate their ethnicity, not just as a museum-case display, but as an evolving historical process impacted by events in their oppressed originary homeland as well as within Canada itself has been amply and accessibly documented in such works as Myrna Kostash's *All of Baba's Children* (Edmonton: NeWest Publishers, 1987), Jaroslav Petryshyn's *Peasants in the Promised Land: Canada and the Ukrainians, 1891-1914* (Toronto: Lorimer, 1985), and Orest Subtelny's *Ukranians in North America: An Illustrated History* (Toronto: University of Toronto Press, 1994). See Bannerji's article in this volume.

7. See Merilyn Simonds's "Cultural Agenda Lobby Committee Report," The Writers' Union of Canada Newsletter 25.4 (September 1997): 8. In the opinion of informed followers of this controversy, the MAI, though temporarily derailed, will be back "in business" under another name all too soon.

EVA C. KARPINSKI

Multicultural "Gift(s)": Immigrant Women's Life Writing and the Politics of Anthologizing Difference

Multiculturalism has been part of Canadian public discourse for more than 20 years, at least since Pierre Trudeau's 1971 pronouncement of a "Policy of Multiculturalism within a Bilingual Framework," later enshrined in the 1988 *Canadian Multiculturalism Act.* The anxieties that have grown around multiculturalism during these years seem to be partly related to the multiple coding of the term. Multiculturalism has been constructed as a demographic fact, institutionalized as policy, and variously deployed as rhetoric in such fields as politics, pedagogy, Canadian studies, social studies, or literature. Significantly, a greater openness to "multicultural climate" coincides with the turn towards postmodernism and post-colonialism, traditionally seen as marked by the demise of unifying narratives of history; the aesthetics of multiplicity, heterogeneity, and fragmentation; as well as the increased political mobilization of the oppressed peoples. As a discursive construct parallel to postmodernism, multiculturalism, too, is caught up in many contradictions and competing claims that have been played out in the shifting dialectic of resistance and celebration.

In this essay, I read multiculturalism from the marginal space of immigrant women's life writing.[1] The latter represents an aspect of Canadian cultural production that has been largely neglected by mainstream critics, even those who write about ethnic minority authors. Given Canada's reputation as a nation of immigrants, it is a surprising gap, especially if one looks across the border at the United States where in the last 20 years the study of immigrant life writing has blossomed into an industry. Immigration and ethnic historians, literary and cultural critics, and feminist scholars have turned to first-person narratives such as autobiographies, memoirs, diaries, journals, oral histories, and reminiscences in order to locate sources documenting experiences of silenced or marginalized groups (Bergland 103). In Canada, immigrant women's life writing is no less diverse, ranging from oral histories, "as tolds," and short autobiographical essays, to "ethnographic self-portraits" (Kadar 121), fictionalized memoirs, spiritual autobiographies, and extremely sophisticated, highly self-conscious autobiographical metafiction. For my purpose, I want to limit myself to one particular form of publication where such narratives can appear, namely to edited anthologies of immigrant life writing.[2] I look at two types of such collections that have been published between 1977 and 1997: those that profile women of a single ethnic group and those that provide a multi-ethnic mix. They are both involved differently in the metonymic relation to the "real" world out there, since the former, through the part/whole play of repetition with a difference, can be seen as offering fragments of diversity, while the latter, by virtue of their mosaic-like arrangement, can function as suitable "icons" of multiculturalism. Among the texts examined here are anthologies edited by Gloria Montero, Milly Charon, Catherine Warren, Sheelagh Conway, Makeda Silvera, Tomoko Makabe, and Arun Mukherjee, as well as the *Jin Guo* project. Spanning some 20 years of Canadian history, they collectively gauge changing experiences, attitudes, and accompanying discursive constructions of multiculturalism.

My exclusive focus on how women's experiences are used in the construction of the larger narrative of multicultural plurality explains why, rather than attending to subjectivity and textual strategies employed by different writing subjects, I pay attention to the way these subjects are discursively framed as "multicultural."[3] The reason why I have selected immigrant women's voices is that the intersection of ethnicity, race, gender, and class – often ignored in public discourse of multiculturalism – is precisely where the mosaic cracks. It is a good place to conduct a critique of strategies of containment and diffusion of potentially divisive issues within the multicultural framework.

If my decision to tackle the question of multiculturalism by reviewing how anthologies are made seems a bit idiosyncratic, I would like to draw readers' attention to the fact that it is not such an unusual idea. In *Around 1981* (1992), Jane Gallop creates a precedent when she reads feminist anthologies, approaching them allegorically as a collectively authored "text" that might yield insights into individual editorial and institutional politics involved in the production of the academic field of feminist literary theory. Closer to home, Evelyn Hinz's special issue of *Mosaic*, "Idols of Otherness" (September 1996), similarly challenges the boundary between the genre of the review essay and critical essay; the most interesting theorizing happens in the review section that features several multicultural anthologies.

The published texts that are the basis of my discussion here have a role in shaping the Canadian multicultural imaginary. Each of them captures a particular moment in history, supposedly "reflecting" Canadian multicultural reality. Yet, a closer look at their apparently innocent mimetic façade reveals a hidden paradox of representation: to a large extent, these collections construct and enact models of what they purport to "represent." As such, they disclose much about changing attitudes to otherness and different uses of multicultural rhetoric. The questions we can ask of the editors who assemble these anthologies are the same ones that might be asked of "editors" of multiculturalism at large. What position do they occupy in relation to the anthologized voices? How do they justify their mediating role between different groups? How do they use their power to include/exclude? Whom do they address through their texts – the powerless groups or the dominant culture for whose consumption the anthology has been prepared? The principles of selection and compilation of "representative" voices parallel the politics of multiculturalism as a site of power struggle over the definition of what constitutes Canada's commonality as a nation, a struggle often fuelled by assimilationist, benign pluralist, or racist tendencies.

Even a cursory glance at some earlier multi-ethnic collections such as Gloria Montero's *The Immigrants* (1977), Milly Charon's *Between Two Worlds: The Canadian Immigrant Experience* (1982), or Catherine Warren's *Vignettes of Life: Experiences and Self-Perceptions of New Canadian Women* (1986), reveals that the editors privilege the immigration pattern associated with assimilative narratives and ethnographic attitudes to difference over exilic or diasporic paradigms, which in their own ways refuse integration into the affiliative order.[4] A pioneer trying to create a multi-ethnic mosaic of immigrant voices, Gloria Montero uses the word "immigrant" without any historical specificity – as a collectively "heroic" category of people, both men and women, engaged in individual pursuit of happiness. The overall "narrative of immigration" constructed by her stories corresponds to a mythical rite of passage: from rejection, through struggle, to "acceptance as a Canadian." Foregrounding similarity rather than difference, Montero's collection represents an "optimistic" variant of multiculturalism, where a Canadian is defined as someone who "wears a wide array of skin colours, speaks in a fascinating range of accents, has a collective life experience that spans all cultures, all continents" (12).

Similarly, Milly Charon's two volumes of oral history, *Between Two Worlds* (1982; rev. ed. 1988) and *Worlds Apart: New Immigrant Voices* (1989), are inspired by an optimistic belief in the benefits of pluralism, although in the second volume she demonstrates greater sensitivity to difference. The first book is hopelessly Eurocentric: only a fraction of her 26 chapters introduce people of other races, and only five of these chapters feature women. Charon presents her project as a collection of "articles, essays, short stories, interviews, and personal testimonials in celebration of our diversity. Each piece is a unique thread in the national fabric" (*Between Two Worlds* 14). Her purpose is twofold: to exemplify "the values of our immigrant parents and grandparents" and to show "how much Canada means to the immigrant" (*Ibid.*). In the 1982 book Canada is unproblematically constructed an "an ideal place" for immigrants. Charon's consciousness of racial conflicts was evidently raised, however, between the publication of the first and second volume. This is symptomatic of a generally growing awareness of the issue of racism in the context of Canadian multicultural rhetoric. This is suggested by the title – *Worlds Apart* – and the book's dedication to "the visible minorities whose resettlement and integration have been slower, more difficult, and which require more understanding, patience, and assistance." Charon's wording, however, not only constructs being a "visible minority" as a problem, but it also renders "the visible minorities" as helpless and passive recipients of "our" (white) benevolence. The volume comprises 24 texts, of which five (!) qualify as "visible minorities." Given the book's epigraph, this seems a token gesture. The gender breakdown, though, has been much improved, and there are more stories by women. As editor, Charon works from the liberal-pluralist assumptions that "one day we may all benefit from the many cultures in Canada and, in the process, discover that racism has finally disappeared from our pluralistic society" (*Worlds Apart* 12).

A similar liberal pluralist perspective is shared by Catherine Warren, although she elaborates a more gender-conscious awareness. Warren collected 24 interviews with women associated with the Calgary Immigrant Women's Centre in the early 1980s. In a lengthy "scientific" framing of her data, she constructs her subjects as "typical." Their life stories are not only theorized so as to illuminate the issue of "the attitudinal bridging processes," but at the same time they are aestheticized so they can be read "like creative works of art" (Warren 7). Immigrant women's experience is thus presented by Warren as material for academic research as well as material to be consumed for pleasure. One can detect a pedagogical subtext in her use of her immigrant subjects whose life writing "may be read for the inspiration and interest which autobiographical writing affords by allowing the strands of the lives of others to intersect with our own" (Warren 5). Significantly, speaking on behalf of immigrant women, she fails to stress racism and sexism in immigration policies that offer subsidized English language programmes for "head of the household" only. Consequently, her multicultural "pedagogy" is geared to her own functionalist view of "newcomers" as potential contributors of "real talents" and "fresh perspective."

The views described above hint at potential tensions present among different – often contradictory – foundational philosophies of Canadian society, including capitalism, liberal democracy, and multiculturalism. As Lisa Jakubowski's analysis of the duality of law in capitalist democracy demonstrates, various forms of anti-discriminatory legislation, including Canada's *Immigration Act* and the *Multiculturalism Act*, on the level of human rights "may be defined as gains for the less advantaged populations. These gains, however, can simultaneously benefit those in positions of power by subtly reinforcing already-existing structural or systemic forms of inequality" (Jakubowski 46). In fact, the *Multiculturalism Act* seems to echo directly the sentiments expressed by mosaic-makers like Montero, Charon, or Warren. Scott McFarlane shows that the language of the *Act* is steeped in liberal-democratic rhetoric, contextualized as it is in relation to rights legislation and constitutional law – both of which are Eurocentric, Enlightenment-derived concepts (22). Like these anthologies, the *Act* exhibits its parasitical concern with "cultural contribution [to an ideal Canada] as opposed to the cultural relations that produce race discourse" (*Ibid.*). McFarlane also signals the presence of a nationalist agenda underlying the anthropological violence of the *Act*, which resembles the agenda of the above-mentioned multicultural collections:

> "Canada" functions as the transcendental signified, because all the exterior signs of cultural difference always already refer back to a homogenizing Canadian interiority and spirit. That is to say, within the multicultural paradigm, the "living principles" of Black culture or Asian culture and their intersections are understood primarily in relation to the ideal: Canadian "multi-culture." (*Ibid.*)

The pseudo-universalism of the liberal-pluralist attitude of "We are all immigrants or hyphenated Canadians" is not only oblivious to history, but from the point of view of minority cultures, it makes multiculturalism look like a variant of cultural neo-colonialism. What these anthologies illustrate is that very often calls for multicultural content turn into different forms of containment. This became apparent recently when the issue of voice appropriation, of who speaks for others, as opposed to speaking with them, galvanized Canadian writing communities. The women whose voices are framed by multicultural practices, however, employ their own strategies to resist containment. There are moments in Charon, Montero, and Warren, when the official discursive frame adopted by the editor is at odds with the actual experiences it frames. For example, although Catherine Warren hides behind polite silences when confronted with "controversial" issues, carefully avoiding any politically radical statements even in the face of her respondents' desperation, sometimes what a woman is not saying is more striking than what she does say in her interview. As Mary from Yugoslavia, who feels "less important here," puts it in response to Warren:

> I find your interview is okay. I mean, you are at least trying to give an opportunity to us immigrants to talk to you freely. But I still don't think this will solve all our problems…. I still think that even if I learned good accents it might not still be enough for Canadians to accept me. (39)

The two-facedness of multicultural society[5] is further exacerbated in the experience of racial minority women whose stories clearly show that assimilation is not a choice for everyone. They persistently challenge the benign image of Canada as a pluralistic paradise and are also more sceptical about the endless opportunities supposedly offered by the capitalist free market economy.

Writing in the American context, E. San Juan Jr. warns that it is a serious error to apply "the paradigm of the white immigrant experience as the controlling model for understanding the plight of all [racial] groups" (216). They have been differently affected by the differential positioning of groups in relation to power. Even when the paradigm employed by the editor is "progressive" with respect to one aspect of immigrant struggle, for example class, it is not sufficient if it remains blind to other forms of oppression based on race, gender, or sexuality. Gloria Montero's approach illustrates the dangers of selective recognition of factors of inequality. Herself an immigrant of Spanish-Australian background, she seems to be influenced by reductive economic determinism that underplays other forms of oppression except class:

> No one [in this collection] is identified by ethnic background.... I found that ethnicity is not what determines how well an immigrant lands on his or her feet in Canada. A ruthless economic system dispenses quickly with such differences. What's more, many of the difficulties encountered by immigrants are identical to the serious problems lived each day by Canada's Indian and Inuit people, by Canadian migrant workers and mothers on welfare. (Montero 11)

Ironically, against this clearly pronounced downplay of racism and sexism, the material collected in Montero's book often recounts incidents of racial discrimination, and thus undermines her agenda and refuses to corroborate her claims.

Much more "subversive" in relation to traditional discourses of gender and assimilation are those collections whose editors foreground their subjects' fight against multiple forms of oppression. Sheelagh Conway's *The Faraway Hills Are Green: Voices of Irish Women in Canada* (1992) is a rare example of editorial work informed by the awareness of "whiteness" as a privilege. What distinguishes Conway's project from the ones published in the previous decades is her staunch commitment to feminist standpoint, class analysis, anti-racism, and self-reflexivity. She views her work as that of "recovery" of the Irish heritage, insisting that the story of Irish women in Canada be seen as part of Canadian history. She alerts the reader to "class distinctions" within different communities and cutting across ethnic differences. Similarly, she insists on making a distinction between the situations of different kinds of immigrants, based on the privilege of race. According to Conway, Canadian immigration patterns "reflect both racism and sexism rooted in a history of colonialism and imperialism. In this context, while Irish women today encounter sexism they do not meet with the pervasive discrimination embedded in racist ideologies and practices that women of colour experience" (25-6). She also considers the tensions between the editor's agenda and the women's voices in a collection like hers. Aware of her "intervention in transcribing and editing these stories," she admits that some women may be at odds with her multiple locations as a feminist, a nationalist, or an activist, which all inform the way she has constructed the histories (Conway 28).

Women of Afro-Canadian, Asian, and other racial minority backgrounds have been the most vocal in addressing the question of systemic inequalities and racism in the context of multiculturalism. Makeda Silvera's work of oral history, *Silenced* (1983), sets a standard for life writing that is openly political and interventionist. Silvera's presentation of the voices of 10 West Indian women, who are economic migrants employed as domestic workers in Canada, exposes "the labour of women of colour from Third World countries" (11) as legalized slavery. Low pay, long hours, sexual harassment are all sanctioned by the Canadian government implicated in "supplying substantial amounts of cheap imported labour to fill the domestic needs of upper and middle class Canadian families" (Silvera 16). Silvera's collection provides space for the most marginalized women whose "silence is the result of a society which uses power and powerlessness as weapons to exclude non-white and poor people from any real decision-making and participation" (19). Documenting the multiple oppressions of race, gender, and class in the lives of domestic workers, Silvera shows how race and class differences problematize identity based on gender, for example, in the image of "the feminist woman-as-mistress" for whom legal exploitation of another woman is a way to solve "the housework question" (123). On the other hand, cross-racial and cross-ethnic solidarity around class issues is also possible, as evidenced by coalitionist politics of women of colour, organizing to change discriminatory immigration laws. What is important is that Silvera's book, by capturing the precise moment when the immigrant dream of the land of opportunity is shattered in confrontation with racism, manages to debunk the Canadian myth of benevolent multicultural society. One is reminded here of Dionne Brand's statement that for her, too, racism rather than immigrancy was the focus of her encounter with Canada (Hutcheon and Richmond 272).[6]

Other collections edited by racial minority women, sharing Silvera's goal of retrieving forgotten or neglected women's histories, are *Jin Guo: Voices of Chinese Canadian Women* (1992), Arun Mukherjee's *Sharing Our Experience* (1993), and Tomoko Makabe's *Picture Brides: Japanese Women in Canada* (1995). Makabe's oral history attempts to correct the male bias in immigration history, especially of Japanese-Canadians. It is a translation of the book first published in Japanese in 1984. The author, herself an immigrant from Japan, came to Canada to study sociology and "made a firm resolve to live in a foreign society as a woman alone" (1). Her book reveals fascination with the stories told to her by the Issei (first-generation). The five women featured in Makabe's book all grew up in Japan in the Meiji period (1868-1911), a period associated with male privilege. Makabe deals with the issues of the "ordinariness" of their experience, their poverty and suffering, and the problem of exclusion and discrimination. She emphasizes the fact often overlooked by immigration historians that, in addition to their domestic duties, women worked equally with their husbands in the production process, including farming and the fishing industry. Part of her analysis concerns the differences between women's and men's approaches to such topics as anti-Asian racism, and her perception that Japanese women generally tend to downplay discrimination.

Makabe's approach contrasts sharply with that of Arun Mukherjee, whose collection is much wider in scope as it focusses on "the diverse experience of racial minority and Aboriginal women" (*Sharing Our Experience* i), viewed through these women's own subjectivities. Mukherjee argues eloquently that oral history projects like this one, which she helped to prepare for the Canadian Advisory Council on the Status of Women, are inescapably political:

> [History] should also be about the political reality that keeps so many women disenfrenchised in this society. History should highlight the roots of inequality and oppression. It should illustrate that these roots are very different for women belonging to different groups. Life histories shed light on the multiple ways in which women are oppressed. They can play a significant role in the decolonization of our minds and institutions. (*Sharing Our Experience* ii)

Combining Mukherjee's awareness of the political role women's life writing can have in our understanding of immigrant history and Makabe's goal of filling in some of the gaps in male-oriented histories of diverse ethnic groups, the *Jin Guo* project is truly groundbreaking, although its editors modestly refuse to see their book as "the definitive history of Chinese Canadian women" (22).[7] First of all, the editors, who identify themselves as The Women's Book Committee of the Chinese Canadian National Council, subvert the traditional concept of authorship by presenting their book as a collective work of oral history, without putting their names on the cover. By this they symbolically assert that their contribution is of no greater importance than those of the women included in the volume. Pointing out common themes and threads running through the book, the editors carefully avoid any essentializing gestures and facile generalizations which tend to oversimplify history, reminding the reader of "an endless number of interwoven factors [that] have come into play in our lives. We are neither passive victims of uncontrollable social forces - nor are we superhuman heroines" (Women's Book Committee 23). A truly outstanding element of *Jin Guo*, however, is a coda called "Keep Listening," which reproduces fragments from "an informal, round-table, wrap-up session," where the editorial committee discusses the project after its completion. They bring together their research and activism, viewing the book in conjunction with other actions that "need to be taking place – to make real changes in people's lives" (227). In other words, they see the book "as more of a means, rather than an end" (228). The desired fallout of the project was the establishment of a Chinese Canadian women's network to counter sexism in the community, improve visibility of Chinese Canadian women, and work out strategies for survival in the recession. The editors also register concern about whom the volume will reach, discussing the problem of language and economic barriers. They point out omissions, especially the limited presence of working-class and lesbian women. They express their hope that this project will put to rest "the old stereotype of Chinese women being submissive and passive" (229). The last word is on racism, which "lumps together" different peoples and must be resisted through coalitions with other communities. Julia Tao, one of the participants, makes an important point, challenging narrow notions of identity politics that compartmentalize anti-racist and anti-sexist struggle and absolve groups such as white Canadians or men from taking any responsibility for change in both these areas: "It seems that fighting racism and sexism is seen as the responsibility of the visible minorities or women. I think that these should be issues for all Canadians to address – not just issues of Chinese-Canadians or Canadian women" (233).

As Sneja Gunew observes, the reality of racism is indisputable, unlike that of "race," which has been hijacked from racist discourse to become "an unstable and decentred complex of social meanings constantly being transformed by political struggle" ("Feminism and the Politics" 9). Indeed, the anthologies of multicultural life writing I am discussing, by enacting a contest over categories of naming clustered around the axis of race/ethnicity and ethnicity/immigrancy, might be viewed as discursive interventions trying to fix the terms in the ongoing debate on multiculturalism. As different critics have pointed out, emphasis on "ethnicity" has often been used to diffuse issues of racial discrimination and inequality. For the historian Robert F. Harney, who subsumes race under ethnicity in his juxtaposition of "immigrant" and "ethnic," "immigrant conjures up the thresholds of acculturation while ethnic implies a permanent quality of otherness" (68). Or as Smaro Kamboureli puts it, "an immigrant is an outsider whose difference is defined by her or his origins, whereas the ethnic subject's difference (however visible or pronounced its traces of difference might be) is defined by the surrounding culture" ("Technology of Ethnicity" 208). Used as an all-embracing concept characterizing Canada, ethnicity in the context of the *Multiculturalism Act* "loses its differential marker, and becomes instead a condition of commonality: what all Canadians have in common is ethnic difference" (*Ibid.* 209).[8] Arun Mukherjee counters this tendency, proposing a useful distinction between such categories as "ethnic minority women" and "racial minority and Aboriginal women," even as she rejects the concept of "visible minority" as having negative undertones. She criticizes the dangers of using the terms "ethnic," "racial minority," and "immigrant" interchangeably – a common government practice – which leads to denying "the specific oppression that racial minority women experience in Canadian society" (*Sharing Our Experience* 6). In other words, she suggests that it is necessary to distinguish between oppression caused by institutionalized racism and by immigration. Mukherjee's views on this point concur with Sneja Gunew's reading of race as a category imposed from without, in contrast to ethnicity, which has "the quality of the self-chosen appellation" ("Feminism and the Politics" 9).[9] This explains why race is used as group identity while ethnicity is seen as part of individual identity (*Ibid.*).

"Race" in anthologies such as the one edited by Arun Mukherjee, however, is raised to the status of "self-identified" category and embraced strategically "as a way of signalling ... determination to resist assimilation and to pursue cultural difference and autonomy" (*Sharing Our Experience* 10). Mukherjee's Introduction records these changes as she recounts the process of the volume's inception and production, in the course of which the originally used category "immigrant women" was abandoned for the expression "racial or ethnic minority women." When too many self-identified "(white) ethnic minority women" responded to the call for papers, the editors decided to include only the voices of racial minority and Aboriginal women in a conscious effort to avoid their further marginalization. The category "immigrant experience" has left its trace only in the thematic index. Strategic exclusions like these coincide with what different writers recognize as the increasing "racialization" of multicultural discourse.[10] Interestingly, several "white" critics warn against the possibility that such deployment of race may homogenize whiteness (Loriggio, *Social Pluralism* 12), or may succumb to "the temptation of Othering the dominant power group" (Goddard, *Intersexions* 27) and reinstate traditional essentialist constructions of race (Gunew, "Feminism and the Politics" 10). In the context of the history of immigration, Francesco Loriggio identifies the costs of racializing history through "the 'Europeanization' of the white ethnics" as a total amnesia with regard to the specificity of their migration histories; to racialize multicultural history is "to take away the shadows, to de-culturalize history ... to substitute another symmetry to the sometimes too linear neatness of the immigrant narrative [espoused by assimilationists]" (*Social Pluralism* 13).

If the collective strength of the anthologies discussed here lies partly in their ability to infuse multicultural history with specificity, they are even more important insofar as they help to historicize the terms that are so hotly contested in multicultural debates. It is a sobering experience to see how "race," "racism," "immigrant," "Canadian," or "multiculturalism" circulate in different historical contexts. For example, in recent years, the content of the word "multiculturalism," no doubt under the influence of racialized discourse, has begun to comprise Native peoples as well, as in Arun Mukherjee's anthology, although initially they were excluded from the *Multiculturalism Act*. Similarly, one might be surprised to learn that not so long ago, Italians, Ukrainians, Jews, and the Irish were regarded in terms of "race" rather than "ethnicity." In one of the earlier oral history projects, *No Streets of Gold: A Social History of Ukrainians in Alberta* (1977), Helen Potrebenko problematizes both the concepts of "Canadianness" and "multiculturalism" by raising accusations against the capitalist and racist culture of Canada. According to her, "racism" manifests itself in the enforced isolation of immigrants from both the old and new cultures (299). "Multiculturalism" is a word that masks real pressure towards "instant assimilation" that is demanded of new immigrants. Although she speaks from an identifiably white position, as a representative of a minority culture struggling to preserve its ethnic difference against the forces of assimilation, Potrebenko bitterly denies that Canada is a cultural mosaic. Catherine Warren rejects the word "immigrant" because of its negative connotations of discrimination. She remembers "an ongoing discussion" among the women at the Immigrant Women's Centre in Calgary, concerning the Centre's name:

> Some of the women feel that the word "immigrant" is pejorative and that "new Canadian" or "women from around the world" should be used; others think "immigrant" is the most accurate description. Regardless of how the issue is resolved, the women at the Centre are reacting to discriminatory attitudes toward immigrants. (Warren 15)

Ironically, Warren herself opts for "New Canadian Women" as a key descriptor in the title of her collection. She also inadvertently problematizes the concept of unitary Canadian identity by profiling a woman born in Canada who has had difficulty achieving a sense of Canadian identity due to abuse, isolation, and lowered self-esteem, and by including such comments as this one by a Finnish woman: "Sometimes I feel I am not Canadian, and I am not Finnish" (Warren 71). Given the frequent semantic shifts undergone by the key terms in multiculturalist discourse, it seems wise to heed Barbara Godard's call for "an ethics of responsibility to the historical particularities of usage" (*Intersexions* 12).

It is through the problem of absent language, towards which these anthologies repeatedly gesture, that we can identify another hidden paradox of multiculturalism. Whenever we hear that editors (or sometimes translators) of immigrant women's life writing feel "compelled to revise the vocabulary and syntax" (Charon 12) or admit that "grammar was corrected" (Warren 4) and "the peculiar language and expressions used by the women" were smoothed out (Makabe vii), we are reminded of the erasure of other languages performed by translation and editorial practices. A related "sanitizing" procedure, transcription from tapes, effectively removes from recorded voices traces of orality such as accent, dialect, or non-auditory cues. These various forms of forcing "others" into the regime of "standard English" disguise the greatest logistic impossibility of multiculturalism, that is, the absurdity of multiculturalism without multilingualism. As Barbara Godard comments on the sacrifice of other languages to bilingualism: "Multiculturalism, as culture without language(s) and authority, or voices reconcilable in one voice (English speaking), figures an end of dislocation (transposition or translation) as figuration of alterity in a fiction of unanimity" (*Intersexions* 15). In a sense, the grounds for this linguistic hypocrisy are laid in the *Multiculturalism Act*, which enlists the users of languages other than English and French in the cause of "strengthening the status and use of the official languages of Canada" (*Canadian Multiculturalism Act* 3(1)(i)). Premised on the idea of translatability of cultures, multiculturalism – through its contextualization within the framework of official bilingualism – in fact forecloses the possibility of intercultural translation and reveals the haunting of colonialism in Canada's present. Perhaps one can detect here a residue of the fear of "foreign languages" seen as threatening, fear which Sneja Gunew associates with Julia Kristeva's notion of the abject: "Words are feared because unlike food they cannot be assimilated, and words in another language emphasize the split within subjectivity. Words are able, like the non-introjected mother, to devour from within" ("Feminism and the Politics" 17).

Read collectively, the anthologies of immigrant women's life writing which I have used as my "multicultural text" visualize clearly what "doesn't work" in the model of multiculturalism endorsed by the Act. Throughout, multiculturalism emerges as a site of ideological power struggle and contestation of meanings, often polarized between traditional assimilationist, liberal-pluralist, or anti-racist rhetoric. The anthologies signal that multi-culturalism is a failure because it does not recognize the need to attend to the realities of gender, race, and class. It must align itself with anti-racism and anti-sexism struggle. From the feminist perspective, the question as to whether multiculturalism is a utopian ideal or a livable reality is a moot point if we consider that our societies, on the level of sexual difference, still exemplify the male-dominated mono-culture. The texts examined here also point to the danger of containment present in multiculturalist discourse, while at the same time revealing different counter-hegemonic strategies employed by the subjects "disciplined" by its rhetoric. No less important is the fact that the anthologies put the usage of highly contested terms (including names such as "immigrant," "ethnic," or "racial minority") in the historical perspective. Finally, the collections disclose the inescapable contradiction of a declared commitment to plural cultures within the framework of official bilingualism.

So what are we to do with the "gift" of multiculturalism? And who is a recipient of this gift? What kind of debt is incurred in the giving? Giving a slightly unexpected twist to Derrida's reading of the problematics of the gift, the vocabulary of the gift, applied to multiculturalism via the reading of immigrant women's life writing, opens up the possibility of rethinking the economy of cross-cultural exchange. Life writing as a gift of life from the "other" speaks to the need of reconfiguring the relations between subjectivity and alterity. The gift refers to mutuality, reciprocity, to the establishment of community and communication. Yet the unacknowledged debt in this exchange is that of the dominant culture to those whose labour was needed to build Canada. Moreover, the gift of multiculturalism comes as a poisoned gift, hiding the ugly secret of racism. In the giving, two kinds of economy meet: the spendthrift economy of the *Multiculturalism Act* and the potlatch (one is almost tempted to say "potluck") economy of multicultural contributions, offerings, and samplings. But despite a rather limited vision of Canada offered by the *Act*, it is precisely this perpetual crisis that calls for radical interventions to be made. Paradoxically, it is multiculturalism's problematic character as discourse and policy that mobilizes resistance and production of counter-discourses, which have the potential to lead to transformations of social perception and to institutional empowerment for oppressed or marginalized groups. If there is any movement towards "justice and equality" invoked by the *Act*, it occurs not as a consequence of its implementation, but rather as a result of dialogical challenge and opposition to it mounted as part of anti-discrimination struggle.

NOTES

1. For a variety of life writing genres, see Marlene Kadar's typology developed in her introduction to *Reading Life Writing* (ix-iv). Some examples of oral histories and "as tolds" include Makeda Silvera's *Silenced* (1983), Trudy Mitic's *Canadian by Choice* (1988), the *Jin Guo* project (1992), Tomoko Makabe's *Picture Brides* (1995), Apolonia Kojder's *Marynia Don't Cry* (1995), and Giovanna Del Negro's *Looking Through My Mother's Eyes* (1997). Ibolya Grossman's *An Ordinary Woman in Extraordinary Times* (1990) and Nelma Sillanpaa's *Under the Northern Lights* (1994) are ethnographic self-portraits. Leah Rosenberg's *The Errand Runner* (1981) and Aili G. Scheider's *The Finnish Baker's Daughter* (1986) are good examples of fictionalized memoir, while formally experimental autobiographies by immigrant women include Maria Jacobs's *Precautions Against Death* (1983), Smaro Kamboureli's *in the second person* (1985), or Eva Hoffman's *Lost in Translation* (1989). Jacobs's text, along with post-Holocaust accounts by Mina Deutsch or Elizabeth Raab belong to a separate subgenre which Kadar calls "survivor narratives" (121). Dorothee V. Kleist's *Love's Loss, Love's Gain* (n.a.) is a spiritual autobiography.

2. Consequently, I have to ignore such potential sources of first-person immigrant narratives as periodicals (there are special issues of *Polyphony*, *Tiger Lily*, and *Canadian Woman Studies* devoted to immigrant women), and multicultural college readers and anthologies. Furthermore, since my focus is on first-generation accounts, I have to exclude fascinating examples of life writing produced by second-generation immigrants such as Myrna Kostash's *All of Baba's Children* (1977), Adele Wiseman's *Old Woman at Play* (1978), Fredelle Bruser Maynard's *Raisins and Almonds* (1972; 1985), or Denise Chong's *The Concubine's Children* (1994), as well as Laura Goodman Salverson's *Confessions of an Immigrant's Daughter* (1939) written much earlier.

3. Although some multi-ethnic collections, such as the ones edited by Gloria Montero, Milly Charon, or Evelyn Huang, include both male and female accounts of immigration, I selectively use women's narratives only. Generally speaking, there is an interesting correlation in the texts that insist on "gender balance" between accepting liberal-pluralist ideology of multiculturalism and embracing more conventional gender concepts.

4. I use these terms following Shirley Geok-Lin Lim's distinction between immigration, exile, and diaspora. In contradistinction to immigration and exile, which are both conditions of voluntary or involuntary separation from the natal order, she defines diaspora as "a condition of being deprived of the affiliation of nation, not temporally situated on its way toward another totality, but fragmented, demonstrating provisionality and exigency as immediate, unmediated presences. The discourse of diaspora is that of disarticulation of identity from natal and national resources, and includes the exilic imagination but is not restricted to it." (297)

5. Norman Ravvin recognizes this two-facedness as "characteristically Canadian: public acknowledgement of the multicultural ethos alongside a privately nurtured nausea upon encountering actual cultural cross-fertilization" (122).

6. It seems that the experience of racism is precisely what aligns Silvera's book, as well as such narratives as Joyce Fraser's *Cry of the Illegal Immigrant* (1984) or Rosemary Brown's *Being Brown* (1989), with life writing by non-immigrant Afro-Canadian women, such as Carrie Best's *That Lonesome Road* (1977),

Carol Talbot's *Growing Up Black in Canada* (1984), or Karen Shadd-Evelyn's *I'd Rather Live in Buxton* (1993).

7. The unique value of *Jin Guo* is particularly striking when confronted with Evelyn Huang's glossy showcasing of the voices of Chinese-Canadian business community and cultural establishment, in a collection that came out in the same year.

8. Note a different use of the term "ethnic" in the American context, where in common practice "ethnic" refers to European nationalities while "racial minority" refers to Blacks, Asians, etc. In the United States, as in Canada, in current discourses of ethnicity, ethnicity is used to replace race. San Juan Jr. argues that we should "avoid confusing racial and ethnic differences; blurring them entails blindness to white racism as a causal/historical force in the shaping of US society and a justification of economic and political inequalities sanctioned by 'colour-blind' state policies" (218).

9. Similarly, Antonio D'Alfonso, who in his "defence of ethnicity" insists that identity can only be ethnic,writes that deterritorialized ethnicity "offers a vast array of identities from which to choose today. Instead of reverting to the loaded ideas of territory, nation, or blood relationship, I welcome identity that is entrenched in free choice" (125).

10. One more example of a shift from "immigrancy" to "race" as an organizing paradigm of multicultural history is Dionne Brand's *No Burden to Carry*, the oral history project sponsored by the Immigrant Women's Job Placement Centre, which includes only one woman born outside of Canada: "Most of the women ... turned out to be Canadian-born, their people having come to Canada in the 1830s-1960s" (31).

HIMANI BANNERJI

On the Dark Side of the Nation: Politics of Multiculturalism and the State of "Canada"

I am from the country
Columbus dreamt of.
You, the country
Columbus conquered.
Now in your land
My words are circling
blue Oka sky
they come back to us
alight on tongue.

Protect me with your brazen passion
for history is my truth,
Earth, my witness
my home,
this native land.

"OKA NADA" (K. Bannerji 20)

The Personal and the Political: A Chorus and a Problematic

When the women's movement came along and we were coming to our political consciousness, one of its slogans took us by surprise and thrilled and activated us: "the personal is political!" Since then years have gone by, and in the meanwhile I have found myself in Canada, swearing an oath of allegiance to the Queen of England, giving up the passport of a long-fought-for independence and being assigned into the category of "visible minority." These years have produced their own consciousness in me, and I have learnt that also the reverse is true: the political is personal.

The way this consciousness was engendered was not ideological, but daily, practical, and personal. It came from having to live within an all-pervasive presence of the state in our everyday life. It began with the Canadian High Commission's rejection of my two-year-old daughter's visa and continued with my airport appearance in Montreal when I was interrogated at length.

125

What shook me was not the fact that they interviewed me, but rather their tone of suspicion about my somehow having stolen my way "in."

As the years progressed, I realized that in my life, and in the lives of other non-white people around me, this pervasive presence of the state meant everything – allowing my daughter and husband to come into the country; permitting me to continue my studies or to work, to cross the border into the United States and back; allowing me the custody of my daughter, although I had a low income; "landing" me so I could put some sort of life together with some predictability. Fear, anxiety, humiliation, anger, and frustration became the wire-mesh that knit bits of my life into a pattern. The quality of this life may be symbolized by an incident with which my final immigration interview culminated after many queries about a missing "wife" and the "head of the family." I was facing an elderly, bald, white man, moustached and blue-eyed – who said he had been to India. I made some polite rejoinder and he asked me – "Do you speak Hindi?" I replied that I understood it very well and spoke it with mistakes. "Can you translate this sentence for me?" he asked, and proceeded to say in Hindi what in English amounts to "Do you want to fuck with me?" A wave of heat rose from my toes to my hair roots. I gripped the edge of my chair and stared at him – silently. His hand was on my passport, the pink slip of my "landing" document lay next to it. Steadying my voice I said, "I don't know Hindi that well." "So you're a PhD student?" My interview continued. I sat rigid and concluded it with a schizophrenic intensity. On Bloor Street in Toronto, sitting on the steps of a church – I vomited. I was a landed immigrant.

Throughout these 25 years I have met many non-white and Third World legal and illegal "immigrants" and "new Canadians" who feel that the machinery of the state has us impaled against its spikes. In beds, in workplaces, in suicides committed over deportations, the state silently, steadily rules our lives with "regulations." How much more intimate could we be – this state and we? It has almost become a person – this machinery – growing with and into our lives, fattened with our miseries and needs, and the curbing of our resistance and anger.

But simultaneously with the growth of the state we grew too, both in numbers and protest, and became a substantial voting population in Canada. We demanded some genuine reforms, some changes – some among us even demanded the end of racist capitalism – and instead we got "multi-culturalism." "Communities" and their leaders or representatives were created by and through the state, and they called for funding and promised "essential services" for their "communities," such as the preservation of their identities. There were advisory bodies, positions, and even arts funding created on the basis of ethnicity and community. A problem of naming arose, and hyphenated cultural and political identities proliferated. Officially constructed identities came into being, and we had new names – immigrant, visible minority, new Canadian, and ethnic. In the mansion of the state small back rooms were accorded to these new political players on the scene.

Manoeuvring for more began. As the state came deeper into our lives – extending its political, economic, and moral regulation, its police violence and surveillance – we simultaneously officialized ourselves. It is as though we asked for bread and were given stones and could not tell the difference between the two.

Part I
In or Of the Nation? The Problem of Belonging

> Face it there's an illegal
> Immigrant
> Hiding in your house
> Hiding in you
> Trying to get out!
> * * *
> Businessmen Customs officials
> Dark Glasses Industrial Aviation
> Policemen Illegal Bachelorettes
> Sweatshop-Keepers Information Canada
> Says
> "You can't get their smell off
> the walls."

(Bhaggiyadatta 23)

The state and the "visible minorities," (the non-white people living in Canada) have a complex relationship with each other. There is a fundamental unease with how our difference is construed and constructed by the state, how our otherness in relation to Canada is projected and objectified. We cannot be successfully ingested or assimilated or made to vanish from where we are not wanted. We remain an ambiguous presence, our existence a question mark in the side of the nation, with the potential to disclose much about the political unconscious and consciousness of Canada as an "imagined community" (B. Anderson). Disclosures accumulate slowly, while we continue to live here as outsider-insiders of the nation that offers a proudly multicultural profile to the international community. We have the awareness that we have arrived into somebody's state, but what kind of state; whose imagined community or community of imagination does it embody? And what are the terms and conditions of our "belonging" to this state of a nation? Answers to these questions are often indirect and not found in the news highway of Canadian media. But travelling through the side roads of political discursivities and practices we come across markers for social terrains and political establishments that allow us to map the political geography of this nation-land where we have "landed."

We locate our explorations of Canada mainly in that part where compulsorily English-speaking visible minorities reside, a part renamed by

Charles Taylor and others as "Canada outside of Quebec" (COQ).[1] But we will call it "English Canada" as in common parlance. This reflects the binary cultural identity of the country to whose discourse, through the notions of the two solitudes, survival and bilingualism, "new comers" are subjected.[2] Conceptualizing Canada within this discourse is a bleak and grim task since "solitude" and "survival" (with their Hobbesian and Darwinist aura) are hardly the language of communitarian joy in nation making.

What, I asked when I first heard of these solitudes, are they? And why survival, when Canada's self-advertisement is one of a wealthy industrial nation? Upon my immigrant inquiries these two solitudes turned out to be two invading European nations – the French and the English – which might have produced two colonial-nation states in this part of North America. But history did not quite work out that way. Instead of producing two settler colonial countries like Zimbabwe (Rhodesia) and South Africa, they held a relationship of conquest and domination with each other. After the battle at the Plains of Abraham one conquered nation/nationality, the French, continued in an uneasy and subjected relation to a state of "Canada," which they saw as "English," a perception ratified by this state's rootedness in the English Crown. The colonial French then came to a hyphenated identity of "franco-something," or declared themselves (at least within one province) as plain "Québécois." They have been existing ever since in an unhappy state, their promised status as a "distinct society" notwithstanding. Periodically, and at times critically, Quebec challenges "Canadian" politics of "unity" and give this politics its own "distinct" character. These then are the two solitudes, the protagonists who, to a great extent, shape the ideological parameters of Canadian constitutional debates, and whose "survival" and relations are continually deliberated. And this preoccupation is such a "natural" of Canadian politics that all other inhabitants are only a minor part of the problematic of "national" identity. This is particularly evident in the role, or lack thereof, accorded to the First Nations of Canada in the nation-forming project. Even after Elijah Harper's intervention in the Meech Lake Accord, the deployment of the Canadian Army against the Mohawk peoples and the long stand-off that followed, constant land claims, and demands for self-government/self-determination, there is a remarkable and a determined political marginalization of the First Nations. And yet their presence as the absent signifiers within Canadian national politics works at all times as a bedrock of its national definitional project, giving it a very particular contour through the same absences, silences, exclusions, and marginalizations. In this there is no distinction between "COQ" or English Canada and Quebec. One needs only to look at the siege at Oka to realize that as far as these "others" are concerned, Europeans continue the same solidarity of ruling and repression, blended with competitive manipulations, that they practised from the dawn of their conquests and state formations.

The Anglo-French rivalry therefore needs to be read through the lens of colonialism. If we want to understand the relationship between visible minorities and the state of Canada/English Canada/COQ, colonialism is the context or entry point that allows us to begin exploring the social relations and cultural forms that characterize these relations. The construction of visible minorities as a social imaginary and the architecture of the "nation" built with a "multicultural mosaic" can only be read together with the engravings of conquests, wars, and exclusions. It is the nationhood of this Canada, with its two solitudes and their survival anxieties and aggressions against "native others," that provides the epic painting in whose dark corners we must look for the later "others." We have to get past and through these dual monoculturalist assumptions or paradigms in order to speak about "visible minorities," a category produced by the multiculturalist policy of the state. This essay repeats, in its conceptual and deconstructive movements, the motions of the people themselves who, "appellated" as refugees, immigrants, or visible minorities, have to file past immigration officers, refugee boards, sundry ministries, and posters of multi-featured/coloured faces that blandly proclaim "Together we are Ontario" – lest we or they forget!

We will examine the assumptions of "Canada" from the conventional problematic and thematic of Canadian nationhood, that of "'Fragmentation or Integration?" currently resounding in post-referendum times. I look for my place within this conceptual topography and find myself in a designated space for "visible minorities in the multicultural society and state of Canada." This is existence in a zone somewhere between economy and culture. It strikes me then that this discursive mode in which Canada is topicalized does not anywhere feature the concept of class. Class does not function as a potential source for the theorization of Canada, any more than does race as an expression for basic social relations of contradiction. Instead the discursivities rely on hegemonic cultural categories such as English or French Canada, or on notions such as national institutions, and conceive of differences and transcendences, fragmentation and integration, with regard to an ideological notion of unity that is perpetually in crisis. This influential problematic is displayed in a *Globe and Mail* editorial of 29 March 1994. It is typically pre-occupied with themes of unity and integration or fragmentation, and delivers a lecture on these to Lucien Bouchard of the Bloc Québécois.

> It has been an educational field trip for Lucien Bouchard. On his first venture into "English Canada" (as he insists on calling it) since becoming leader of Her Majesty's Loyal Opposition, Mr. Bouchard learned, among other things, there is such a thing as Canadian Nationalism: not just patriotism, nor yet that self-serving little prejudice that parades around as Canadian Nationalism – mix equal parts elitism, statism, and Anti-Americanism – but a genuine fellow-feeling that binds Canadians to one another across this country – and includes Quebec.
> (*Globe and Mail*)

Lest this statement appear to the people of Quebec as passing off "English Canada" disguised as "the nation" and locking Quebec in a vice grip of "unity" without consent or consultation, the editor repeats multiculturalist platitudes meant to mitigate the old antagonisms leading to "separatism." The demand for a French Canada is equated with "self-serving little prejudice" and "patriotism" and promptly absorbed into the notion of a culturally and socially transcendent Canada, which is supposedly not only non-French, but non-English as well. How can this non-partisan, transcendent Canada be articulated except in the discourse of multiculturalism? Multiculturalism, then, can save the day for English Canada, conferring upon it a transcendence, even though the same transcendent state is signalled through the figure of Her Majesty the Queen of England and the English language. The unassimilable "others" who, in their distance from English Canada, need to be boxed into this catch-all phrase now become the moral cudgel with which to beat Quebec's separatist aspirations. The same editorial continues:

> Canada is dedicated to the ideal that people of different languages and cultures may, without surrendering their identity, yet embrace the human values they have in common: the "two solitudes" of which the poet wrote, that "protect and touch and greet each other," were a definition of love, not division.

But this poetic interpretation of solitudes, like the moral carrot of multicultural love is quickly followed by a stick. Should Quebec not recognize this obligation to love, but rather see it as a barrier to self-determination, Canada will not tolerate this. We are then confronted with other competing self-determinations in one breath, some of which ordinarily would not find their advocate in *Globe and Mail* editorials. What of the self-determination of the Cree, of the anglophones, of federalists of every stripe? What of the self-determination of the Canadian nation? Should Mr Bouchard and his kind not recognize this national interest, it is argued, then the province's uncertainties are only beginning. In the context of the editorial's discourse, these uncertainties amount to the threat of a federalist anglophone war. The "self-determination of the Cree" is no more than an opportunistic legitimation of Canada in the name of all others who are routinely left out of its construction and governance. These "different (from the French) others," through the device of a state-sponsored multiculturalism, create the basis for transcendence necessary for the creation of a universalist liberal democratic statehood. They are interpellated or bound into the ideological state apparatus through their employment of tongues which must be compulsorily, officially unilingual – namely, under the sign of English.[3]

"Canada," with its primary inscriptions of "French" or "English," its colonialist and essentialist identity markers, cannot escape a fragmentary framework. Its imagined political geography simplifies into two primary and confrontational possessions, cultural typologies, and dominant ideologies. Under the circumstances, all appeal to multiculturalism on the part of "Canada Outside Quebec" becomes no more than an extra weight on the "English" side. Its "difference-studded unity," its "multicultural mosaic," becomes an ideological sleight of hand pitted against Quebec's presumably greater cultural homogeneity. The two solitudes glare at each other from the barricades in an ongoing colonial war. But what do either of these solitudes and their reigning essences have to do with those whom the state has named "visible minorities" and who are meant to provide the ideological basis for the Canadian state's liberal/universal status? How does their very "difference," inscribed with inferiority and negativity – their otherwise troublesome particularity – offer the very particularist state of "English Canada" the legitimating device of transcendence through multiculturalism? Are we not still being used in the war between the English and the French?

It may seem strange to "Canadians" that the presence of the First Nations, the "visible minorities" and the ideology of multiculturalism are being suggested as the core of the state's claim to universality or transcendence. Not only in multiplying pawns in the old Anglo-French rivalry but in other ways as well, multiculturalism may be seen less as a gift of the state of "Canada" to the "others" of this society, than as a central pillar in its own ideological state apparatus.[4] This is because the very discourse of nationhood in the context of "Canada," given its evolution as a capitalist state derived from a white settler colony with aspirations to liberal democracy,[5] needs an ideology that can mediate fissures and ruptures more deep and profound than those of the usual capitalist nation state.[6] That is why usually undesirable others, consisting of non-white peoples with their ethnic or traditional or underdeveloped cultures, are discursively inserted in the middle of a dialogue on hegemonic rivalry. The discourse of multi-culturalism, as distinct from its administrative, practical relations, and forms of ruling, serves as a culmination for the ideological construction of "Canada." This places us, on whose actual lives the ideology is evoked, in a peculiar situation. On the one hand, by our sheer presence we provide a central part of the distinct pluralist unity of Canadian nationhood; on the other hand, this centrality is dependent on our "difference," which denotes the power of definition that "Canadians" have over "others." In the ideology of multicultural nationhood, however, this difference is read in a power-neutral manner rather than as organized through class, gender, and race. Thus at the same moment that difference is ideologically evoked it is also neutralized, as though the issue of difference were the same as that of diversity of cultures and identities, rather than those of racism and colonial ethnocentrism – as though our different cultures were on a par or could negotiate with the two dominant ones! The hollowness of such a pluralist stance is exposed in the shrill indignation of anglophones when rendered a "minority" in Quebec, or the angry desperation of francophones in Ontario. The issue of the First Nations – their land claims, languages, and cultures –

provides another dimension entirely, so violent and deep that the state of Canada dare not even name it in the placid language of multiculturalism.

The importance of the discourse of multiculturalism to that of nation-making becomes clearer if we remember that "nation" needs an ideology of unification and legitimation.[7] As Benedict Anderson points out, nations need to imagine a principle of "com-unity" or community even where there is little there to postulate any.[8] A nation, ideologically, can not posit itself on the principle of hate, according to Anderson, and must therefore speak to the sacrificing of individual, particularist interests for the sake of "the common good" (chapter two). This task of "imagining community" becomes especially difficult in Canada – not only because of class, gender, and capital, which ubiquitously provide contentious grounds in the most culturally homogeneous of societies – but because its socio-political space is saturated by elements of surplus domination due to its Eurocentric/racist/colonial context. Ours is not a situation of co-existence of cultural nationalities or tribes within a given geographical space. Speaking here of culture without addressing power relations displaces and trivializes deep contradictions. It is a reductionism that hides the social relations of domination that continually create "difference" as inferior and thus signifies continuing relations of antagonism. The legacy of a white settler colonial economy and state and the current aspirations to imperialist capitalism mark Canada's struggle to become a liberal democratic state. Here a cultural pluralist interpretive discourse hides more than it reveals. It serves as a fantastic evocation of "unity," which in any case becomes a reminder of the divisions. Thus to imagine "com-unity" means to imagine a common-project of valuing difference that would hold good for both Canadians and others, while also claiming that the sources of these otherizing differences are merely cultural. As that is impossible, we consequently have a situation where no escape is possible from divisive social relations. The nation state's need for an ideology that can avert a complete rupture becomes desperate and gives rise to a multicultural ideology which both needs and creates "others" while subverting demands for anti-racism and political equality.

Let me illustrate my argument by means of Charles Taylor's thoughts on the Canadian project of nation making. Taylor is comparable to Benedict Anderson insofar as he sees "nation" primarily as an expression of civil society, as a collective form of self-determination and definition. He therefore sees that culture, community, tradition, and imagination are crucial for this process. His somewhat romantic organicist approach is pitted against neo-liberal projects of market ideologies misnamed as "reform."[9] Taylor draws his inspiration, among many sources, from an earlier European romantic tradition that cherishes cultural specificities, local traditions, and imaginations.[10] This presents Taylor with the difficult task of "reconciling solitudes" with some form of a state while retaining traditional cultural identities in an overall ideological circle of "Canadian" nationhood. This is a difficult task at all times, but especially in the Canadian context of Anglo-French rivalry and the threat of separatism. Thus

Taylor, in spite of his philosophical refinement, is like others also forced into the recourse of "multiculturalism as a discourse," characterized by its reliance on diversity. The constitution then becomes a federal mosaic tablet for encoding and enshrining this very moral/political mandate. But Taylor is caught in a further bind, because Canada is more than a dual monocultural entity. Underneath the "two solitudes," as he knows well, Canada has "different differences," a whole range of cultural identities which cannot (and he feels should not) be given equal status with the "constituent elements" of "the nation," namely, the English and the French. At this point Taylor has to juggle with the contending claims of these dominant or "constituent" communities and their traditions, with the formal equality of citizenship in liberal democracy, and with other "others" with their contentious political claims and "different cultures." This juggling, of course, happens best in a multicultural language, qualifying the claim of the socio-economic equality of "others" with the language of culture and tolerance, converting difference into diversity in order to mitigate the power relations underlying it. Thus Taylor, in spite of his organicist, communitarian-moral view of the nation and the state, depends on a modified liberal pluralist discourse which he otherwise finds "American," abstract, empty, and unpalatable.[11]

Reconciling the Solitudes and *Multiculturalism and the Politics of Recognition* are important texts for understanding the need for the construction of the category of visible minorities to manage contentions in the nationhood of Canada. Even though Taylor spends little time actually discussing either the visible minorities or the First Nations, their importance for the creation of a national ideology is brought out by his discussion of Anglo-French contestation. Their visceral anxieties about loss of culture are offset by "other" cultural presences that are minoritized with respect to both, while the commonality of Anglo-French culture emerges in contrast. Taylor discovers that the cultural essences of COQ have something in common with Quebec – their Europeanness – in spite of the surface of diversity. This surface diversity, he feels, is not insurmountable within the European-Anglo framework, whose members' political imagination holds enough ground for some sort of commonality.

> What is enshrined here is what one might call *first level diversity*. There are great differences in culture and outlook and background in a population that nevertheless shares the same idea of what it is to belong to Canada. Their patriotism and manner of belonging is uniform, whatever their differences, and this is felt to be necessary if the country is to hold together. (C. Taylor 182)

Taylor must be speaking of those who are "Canadians" and not "others": the difference of visible minorities and First Nations peoples is obviously not containable in this "first level diversity" category. As far as these "others" are concerned the Anglo-European (COQ) and French elements have much in common in both "othering" and partially "tolerating" them. Time and time again, especially around the so-called Oka crisis, it became clear that liberal pluralism rapidly yields to a fascist "sons of the soil" approach as expressed by both the Quebec state and its populace, oblivious to the irony of such a claim. It is inconsistent of Taylor to use this notion of "first level diversity" while also emphasizing the irreducible cultural ontology of Quebec as signalled by the concept of a "deep diversity" (183). But more importantly, this inconsistency accords an ownership of nationhood to the Anglo-French elements. He wrestles, therefore, to accommodate an Anglo-French nationality, while the "deep diversities" of "others," though nominally cited, are erased from the political map just as easily as the similarity of the "two nations" *vis-à-vis* those "others." Of course, these manipulations are essential for Taylor and others if the European (colonial) character of "Canada" is to be held *status quo*. This is a Trudeau-like stance of dual unification in which non-European "others" are made to lend support to the enterprise by their existence as a tolerated, managed difference.

This multicultural take on liberal democracy, called the "politics of recognition" by Taylor, is informed by his awareness that an across-the-board use of the notion of equality would reduce the French element from the status of "nation" to that of just another minority. This of course must not be allowed to happen, since the French are, by virtue of being European co-conquerors, one of the "founding nations." At this point Taylor adopts the further qualified notion of visible minorities as integral to his two-in-one nation-state schema. For him as for other majority ideologues they constitute a minority of minorities. They are, in the scheme of things, peripheral to the essence of Canada, which is captured by "Trudeau's remarkable achievement in extending bilingualism" to reflect the "Canadian" character of "duality" (C. Taylor 164). This duality Taylor considers as currently under a threat of irrelevancy, not from anglo monoculturism, but from the ever-growing presence of "other" cultures. "Already one hears Westerners saying ... that their experience of Canada is of a multicultural mosaic" (C. Taylor 182). This challenge of the presence of "others" is, for Taylor, the main problem for French Canadians in retaining their equality with English Canadians. But it is also a problem for Taylor himself, who sees in this an unsettling possibility for the paradigm of "two solitudes" or "two nations" to which he ultimately concedes. In order to project and protect the irreducible claims of the two dominant and similar cultures, he refers fleetingly and analogically, though frequently, to aboriginal communities. "Visible minorities" also enter his discourse, but both are terms serving to install a "national" conversation between French and English, embroidering the dialogue of the main speakers. His placement of these "other" social groups is evident when he says: "Something analogous [to the French situation] holds for aboriginal communities in this country; their way of being Canadian is not accommodated by first level diversity" (*Ibid.*). Anyone outside of the national framework adopted by Taylor would feel puzzled by the analogical status of the First Nations brought in to negotiate power sharing between the two European nations. Taylor's approach is in keeping with texts on nationalism, culture, and identity that relegate the issues of colonialism, racism and continued oppression of the Aboriginal peoples and the oppression visited upon "visible minorities" to the status of footnotes in Canadian politics.

Yet multiculturalism as an ideological device both enhances and erodes Taylor's project. Multiculturalism, he recognizes at one level, is plain realism – an effect of the realization that many (perhaps too many) "others" have been allowed in, stretching the skin of tolerance and "first level diversity" tightly across the body of the nation. Their "deep diversity" cannot be accommodated simply within the Anglo-French duality. The situation is so murky that, "more fundamentally, we face a challenge to our very conception of diversity" (*Ibid.*). "Difference," he feels, has to be more "fundamentally" read into the "nation":

> In a way, accommodating difference is what Canada is all about. Many Canadians would concur in this.
>
> Many of the people who rallied around the Charter and multiculturalism to reject the distinct society are proud of their acceptance of diversity – and in some respects rightly so. (C. Taylor 181, 182)

But this necessary situational multiculturalism acknowledged by Taylor not only creates the transcendence of a nation built on difference, it also introduces the claims of "deep diversities" on all sides. Unable to formulate a way out of this impasse Taylor proposes an ideological utopia of "difference" (devoid of the issue of power) embodied in a constitutional state, a kind of cultural federalism:

> To build a country for everyone, Canada would have to allow for second-level or "deep" diversity in which a plurality of ways of belonging would also be acknowledged and accepted. Someone of, say, Italian extraction in Toronto or Ukrainian extraction in Edmonton might indeed feel Canadian as a bearer of individual rights in a multicultural mosaic. His or her belonging would not "pass through" some other community, although the ethnic identity might be important to him or her in various ways. But this person might nevertheless accept that a Québécois or a Cree or a Dene might belong in a very different way, that these persons were Canadian through being members of their national communities. Reciprocally, the Québécois, Cree, or Dene would accept the perfect legitimacy of the "mosaic" identity. (C. Taylor 183)

This utopian state formation of Taylor founders, as do those of others, on the rocky shores of the reality of how different "differences" are produced, or are not just forms of diversity. For all of Taylor's pleas for recognizing two kinds of diversity, he does not ever probe into the social relations of power that create the different differences. It is perhaps significant from this point of view that he speaks of the "deep diversities" of Italians or Ukrainians but does not mention those of the Blacks, South Asians, or the Chinese. In other words, he cannot raise the spectre of real politics, of real social, cultural, and economic relations of white supremacy and racism. Thus he leaves out of sight the relations and ideologies of ruling that are intrinsic to the creation of a racist civil society and a racializing colonial-liberal state. It is this foundational evasion that makes Taylor's proposal so problematic for those whose "differences" in the Canadian context are not culturally intrinsic but constructed through "race," class, gender, and other relations of power. This is what makes us sceptical about Taylor's retooling of multicultural liberal democracy by introducing the concept of "deep diversity" as a differentiated citizenship into the bone marrow of the polity, while leaving the Anglo-French European "national" (colonial and racist) core intact. He disagrees with those for whom

> ... [the] model of citizenship has to be uniform, or [they think] people would have no sense of belonging to the same polity. Those who say so tend to take the United States as their paradigm, which has indeed been hostile to deep diversity and has sometimes tried to stamp it out as "un-American." (C. Taylor 183)

This, for Taylor, amounts to the creation of a truly Canadian polity that needs a "united federal Canada" and is able to deliver "law and order, collective provision, regional equality and mutual self-help...." (*Ibid.*) None of these categories – for example, that of "law and order" – is characteristically problematized by Taylor. His model "Canada" is not to be built on the idea of a melting pot or of a uniform citizenship based on a rationalist and functional view of polity. That would, according to him, "straight-jacket" deep diversity. Instead,

> The world needs other models to be legitimated in order to allow for more humane and less constraining modes of political cohabitation. Instead of pushing ourselves to the point of break up in the name of a uniform model, we would do our own and some other peoples a favour by exploring the space of deep diversity. (C. Taylor 184)

What would this differentiated citizenship look like in concrete example, we ask? Taylor throws in a few lines about Basques, Catalans, and Bretons. But those few lines are not answer enough for us. Though this seems to be an open invitation to join the project of state and nation making, the realities of a colonial capitalist history – indentures, reserves, First Nations without a state, immigrants and citizens, illegals, refugees, and "Canadians" – make it impossible. They throw us against the inscription of power-based "differences" that construct the self-definition of the Canadian state and its citizenship. We realize that class, "race," gender, sexual orientation, colonialism, and capital cannot be made to vanish by the magic of Taylor's multiculturalism, managed and graduated around a core of dualism. His inability to address current and historical organizations of power, his inability to see that this sort of abstract and empty invitation to "difference" has always enhanced the existing "difference" unless real social equality and historical redress can be possible – these erasures make his proposal a touch frightening for us. This is why I shudder to "take the deep road of diversity together" with Charles Taylor (*Ibid.* 184). Concentration and labour camps, Japanese internment, the Indian Act and reserves, apartheid, and ethnic "homelands" extend their long shadows over the project of my triumphal march into the federal utopia of a multiculturally differentiated citizenship. But what becomes clear from Taylor's writings is the importance of a discourse of difference and multiculturalism for the creation of a legitimate nation space for Canada. Multiculturalism becomes a mandate of moral regulation as an antidote to any, and especially Quebec's, separatism.

Part II
On the Dark Side of the Nation: Considering "English Canada"

If one stands on the dark side of the nation in Canada everything looks different. The transcendent, universal, and unifying claims of its multi-culturally legitimated ideological state apparatus becomes susceptible to questions. The particularized and partisan nature of this nation-state becomes visible through the same ideological and working apparatus that simultaneously produces its national "Canadian" essence and the "other" – its non-white population (minus the First Nations) as "visible minorities." It is obvious that both Canada and its adjectivized correlates English or French Canada are themselves certain forms of constructions. What do these constructions represent or encode? With regard to whom or what are we otherized and categorized as visible minorities? What lies on the dark side of this state project, its national ethos?

Official multiculturalism, mainstream political thought, and the news media in Canada all rely comfortably on the notion of a nation and its state both called Canada, with legitimate subjects called Canadians, in order to construct us as categorical forms of difference. There is an assumption that this Canada is a singular entity, a moral, cultural, and political essence, neutral of power, both in terms of antecedents and consequences. The assumption is that we can recognize this beast, if and when we see it. So we can then speak of a "Pan-Canadian nationalism," of a Canada which will not tolerate more Third World immigrants or separatism, or of what Canada needs or allows us to do. And yet, when we scrutinize this Canada, what is it that we see? The answer to this question depends on which side of the nation we inhabit. For those who see it as a homogeneous cultural/political entity, resting on a legitimately possessed territory, with an exclusive right to legislation over diverse groups of peoples, Canada is unproblematic. For others, who are on the receiving end of the power of Canada and its multiculturalism, who have been dispossessed in one sense or another, the answer is quite different. For them the issues of legitimacy of territorial possession, or the right to create regulations and the very axis of domination on which its status as a nation-state rests, are all too central to be pushed aside. To them the same Canada appears as a post-conquest capitalist state, economically dependent on an imperialist United States and politically implicated in English and American imperialist enterprises, with some designs of its own. From this perspective "Pan-Canadianism" loses its transcendent inclusivity and emerges instead as a device and a legitimation for a highly particularized ideological form of domination. Canada then becomes mainly an English Canada, historicized into particularities of its actual conquerors and their social and state formations. Colonialism remains as a vital formational and definitional issue. Canada, after all, could not be English or French in the same sense in which England and France are English and French.

Seen thus, the essence of Canada is destabilized. It becomes a politico-military ideological construction and constitution, elevating aggressive acts of acquisition and instituting them into a formal stabilization. But this stability is tenuous, always threatening to fall apart. The adjective "English" stamped into "Canada" bares this reality, both past and present. It shows us who stands on the other side of the "Pan-Canadian" project. Quebeckers know it well, and so their colonial rivalry continues. And we, the "visible minorities" – multiculturalism notwithstanding – know our equidistance from both of these conquering essences. The issue at stake, in the end, is felt by all sides to be much more than cultural. It is felt to be about the power to define what is Canada or Canadian culture. This power can only come through the actual possession of a geographical territory and the economy of a nation-state. It is this which confers the legal imprimatur to define what is Canadian or French Canadian, or what are sub- or multi-cultures. Bilingual-ism, multiculturalism, tolerance of diversity and difference, and slogans of unity cannot solve this problem of unequal power and exchange – except to entrench even further the social relations of power and their ideological and legal forms, which emanate from an unproblematized Canadian state and essence. What discursive magic can vanish a continuously proliferating process of domination and thus of marginalization and oppression? What can make it a truly multicultural state when all the power relations and the signifiers of Anglo-French white supremacy are barely concealed behind a straining liberal democratic façade?[12]

The expression "white supremacist," harsh and shocking as it may sound to many, encodes the painful underpinnings of the category visible minorities. The ideological imperatives of other categories – such as immigrants, aliens, foreigners, ethnic communities, or New Canadians –

constellate around the same binary code. There is a direct connection between this and the ideological spin-off of Englishness or Frenchness. After all, if nations are "imagined communities," can the content of this national imagination called Canada be free of its history and current social relations of power? Does not the context inflect the content here and now?

At this point we need to remind ourselves that there are different kinds of nationalisms – some aggressive and others assertive. Benedict Anderson makes a useful distinction between an "official nationalism" of imperialism, and the "popular nationalism" of lived relations of a settled society and its shared historical/cultural relations (86).[13] The former, Anderson claims, is about hate and aggression; the latter, about love and sacrifice of a people for a shared culture, ancestral history, and a shared physical space. This "popular nationalism" in my view is clearly not possible for Canada whose context is the colonization and continued marginalization of the First Nations while seeking to build a liberal democratic state. In Canada, such "popular nationalism" contains legal/coercive strategies and the means of containment and suppression of all "others." The kinship or blood-ties of which Anderson speaks as elements of a nation are ranged along two contending sides (B. Anderson 19). On the side of Canada there is a history and kinship of European/English colonial and subsequently American complicity in domination, of bad faith and broken promises, and, at best, of guilt. On the other side is the labour-migration kinship of all who stand in the underside of this Canada, roped in by relations of colonialism and imperialism with their "race"-gender and cultural discrimination. This European domination is coded as "civilized" and "modernizing" and signified through "white,"[14] while global resistance or acquiescence to them are carried on by "others" who are colour coded as "visible," meaning non-white, black, or dark.

The case of Canada and its nationalism, when considered in this light, is not very different from the "official nationalism" of South Africa, erstwhile Rhodesia, or of Australia. These are cases of colonial "community" in which nation and state formations were created through the conquering imagination of white supremacy.[15] An anxiety about "them" – the aboriginals, pre-existing peoples – provides the core of a fantasy which inverts the colonized into aggressors, resolving the problem through extermination, suppression, and containment.[16] Dominant cultural language in every one of these countries resounds with an "us" and "them" as expressed through discursivities of "minority/sub/multi-culture." A thinly veiled, older colonial discourse of civilization and savagery peeps out from the modern versions. Here difference is not a simple marker of cultural diversity, but rather, measured or constructed in terms of distance from civilizing European cultures. Difference here is branded always with inferiority or negativity. This is displayed most interestingly in the reading of the non-white or dark body that is labelled as a visible and minority body.[17] The colour of the skin, facial and bodily features – all become signifiers of inferiority, composed of an inversion and a projection of what is considered evil by the colonizing society. Implied in these cultural constructions is a literal denigration, extending into a valorized expression of European racist-patriarchy coded as white.

This inscription of whiteness underwrites whatever may be called Englishness, Frenchness, and finally Europeanness. These national characteristics become moral ones and they spin off or spill over into each other. Thus whiteness extends into moral qualities of masculinity, possessive individualism, and an ideology of capital and market.[18] They are treated as indicators of civilization, freedom, and modernity. The inherent aggressiveness and asociality of this moral category "whiteness" derives its main communitarian aspect from an animosity towards "others," signalling the militaristic, elite, and otherizing bond shared by conquerors. The notion of Englishness serves as a metaphor for whiteness, as do all other European national essences. Whiteness, as many have noted, thus works as an ideology of a nation-state. It can work most efficiently with an other/enemy in its midst, constantly inventing new signifiers of "us" and "them." In the case of Canada, the others, the First Nations, have been there from the very inception, modulating the very formation of its state and official culture, constantly presenting them with doubts about their legitimacy. Subsequently, indentured workers, immigrants, refugees and other "others" have only deepened this legitimation crisis, though they also helped to forge the course of the state and the "nation."[19] "English," as an official language, has served to create a hegemonic front, but it is not a powerful enough antidote as an ideological device to undermine antagonisms that are continually created through processes of ruling; it is the ideology of "whiteness/Europeanness" that serves as the key bonding element. Even though the shame of being an Italian, that is, non-English, in Canada outweighs the glory of the Italian renaissance, "Italian" can still form a part of the community of "whiteness" as distinct from non-white "others." It is not surprising, therefore, to see that one key element of white supremacy in Canada was an "Orange" mentality connecting Englishness with whiteness and both with racial purity. Books such as *Shades of Right*, for example, speak precisely to this, as does the present day right-wing nationalism of "English"-based groups. Quebec's "French" nationalism has precisely the same agenda, with a smaller territorial outreach. In fact, racialization and ethnicization are the commonest forms of cultural or identity parlance in Canada. This is not only the case with "whites" or "the English" but also with "others" after they spend some time in the country. A language of colour, even self-appellations such as "women of colour" (remember "coloured women?"), echo right through the cultural/political world. An unofficial apartheid, of culture and identity, organizes the social space of "Canada," first between whites and non-whites, and then within the non-whites themselves.

Part III
A Rose by Any Other Name: Naming the "Others"

The transcendence or legitimation value of the official/state discourse of multiculturalism – which cherishes difference while erasing real antagonisms – breaks down, therefore, at different levels of competing ideologies and ruling practices. A threat of rupture or crisis is felt to be always already there, a fact expressed by the ubiquity of the integration-fragmentation paradigm in texts on Canada. Instead of a discourse of homogeneity or universality, the paradigm of multiculturalism stands more for the pressure of conflict of interests and dynamics of power relations at work. This language is useful for Canada since imagining a nation is a difficult task even when the society is more homogeneously based on historic and cultural sharing or hegemony. Issues of class, industry, and capital constantly destabilize the national project even in its non-colonial context. Gramsci for example, in "Notes on Italian History," discusses the problem of unification inherent in the formation of a nation-state in the European bourgeois context.[20] Unificatory ideologies and institutions, emanating from the elite, posturing as a class-transcendent polity and implanted on top of a class society, reveal as much as they hide. These attempts at unification forge an identifiable ideological core, a national identity, around which other cultural elements may be arranged hierarchically. It transpires that the ability and the right to interpret and name the nation's others forms a major task of national intellectuals, who are organic to the nation-state project.[21]

If this difficulty dogs European bourgeois nationalism, then it is a much more complicated task for Canada to imagine a *unificatory* national ideology, as recognized by members of the "white" ideological bloc espousing non-liberal perspectives. Ultra-conservatives in general have foresworn any pretence to the use of "multi-cultural" ideology. They view multiculturalism as an added burden to a society already divided, and accord no political or cultural importance to groups other than the French. The political grammar of "national" life and culture, as far as the near and far right are concerned, is common-sensically acknowledged as "English." According importance to multiculturalism has the possibility of calling into question the "English" presence in this space, by creating an atmosphere of cultural relativism signalling some sort of usurpation. This signal, it is felt, is altogether best removed. English/Europeanness, that is, whiteness, emerges as the hegemonic Canadian identity. This white, Canadian, and English equation becomes hegemonic enough to be shared even by progressive Canadians or the Left.[22] This ideological Englishness/whiteness is central to the programme of multiculturalism. It provides the content of Canadian culture, the point of departure for "multiculture." This same gesture creates "others" with power-organized "differences," and the material basis of this power lies both below and along the linguistic-semiotic level. Multiculturalism as the "other" of assimilation brings out the irreducible core of what is called the real Canadian culture.

So the meaning of Canada really depends on who is doing the imagining – whether it is Margaret Atwood or Charles Taylor or Northrop Frye or the "visible minorities" who organize conferences such as "Writing Thru Race." Depending on one's social location, the same snow and Canadian landscape, like Nellie McClung and other foremothers of Canadian feminism, can seem near or far, disturbing, threatening, or benign. A search through the literature of the "visible minorities" reveals a terror of incarceration in the Canadian landscape.[23] In their Canada there is always winter and an equally cold and deathly cultural topography, filled with the RCMP, the Western Guard, the Heritage Front and the Toronto Sun, slain Native peoples and Sitting Bull in a circus tent, white-faced church fathers, trigger-happy impassive police, the flight and plight of illegals, and many other images of fear and active oppression. To integrate with this Canada would mean a futile attempt at integrating with a humiliation and an impossibility. Names of our otherness proliferate endlessly, weaving margins around "Canada/English/ French Canada." To speak of pan-Canadian nationalism and show a faith in "our" national institutions is only possible for those who can imagine it and already are "Canada." For "others," Canada can mean the actuality of skinhead attacks, the mediated fascism of the Reform Party, and the hard-fist of Rahowa.[24]

It is time to reflect on the nomenclature extended by multiculturalism to the "others" of "Canada." Its discourse is concocted through ruling relations and the practical administration of a supposed reconciliation of "difference." The term visible minorities is a great example: one is instantly struck by its reductive character, in which peoples from many histories, languages, cultures, and politics are reduced to a distilled abstraction. Other appellations follow suit – immigrants, ethnics, new Canadians, and so on. Functional, invested with a legal social status, these terms capture the "difference" from "Canada/English/French Canada" and often signify a newness of arrival into "Canada." Unlike a rose, which by any other name would smell as sweet, these names are not names in the sense of classification. They are in their inception and coding official categories. They are identifying devices, like a badge, and they identify those who hold no legitimate or possessive relationship to "Canada." Though these are often identity categories produced by the state, the role played by the state in identity politics remains unnoticed, just as the whiteness in the "self" of "Canada's" state and nationhood remains unnamed. This transparency or invisibility can only be achieved through a constellation of power relations that advances a particular group's identity as universal, as a measuring rod for others, making them "visible" and "minorities."

An expression such as visible minorities strikes the uninitiated as both absurd and abstract. "Minority," we know from J.S. Mill onwards, is a symptom of liberal democracy, but "visible?" We realize upon reflection that the adjective visible attached to minority makes the scope of identity and power even more restricted. We also know that it is mainly the Canadian state and politics which are instrumental in this categorizing process and confers this "visibility" upon us. I have remarked on its meaning and use elsewhere:

> Some people, it implies, are more visible than others; if this were not the case, then its triviality would make it useless as a descriptive category. There must be something "peculiar" about some people which draws attention to them. This something is the point to which the Canadian state wishes to draw our attention. Such a project of the state needed a point of departure which has to function as a norm, as the social average of appearance. The well-blended, "average," "normal" way of looking becomes the base line, or "us" (which is the vantage point of the state), to which those others marked as "different" must be referred ... and in relation to which "peculiarity" [and, thus, visibility] is constructed. The "invisibility" ... depends on the state's view of [some] as normal, and therefore, their institution as dominant types. They are true Canadians, and others, no matter what citizenship they hold [and how many generations have they lived here?] are to be considered as deviations.... (H. Bannerji, *Returning the Gaze* 148)[25]

Such "visibility" indicates not only "difference" and inferiority, but is also a preamble to "special treatment." The yellow Star of David, the red star, the pink triangle, have all done their fair share in creating visibility along the same lines – if we care to remember. Everything that can be used is used as fodder for visibility, pinning cultural and political symbols to bodies and reading them in particular ways. Thus for non-whites in Canada,

> their own bodies are used to construct for them some sort of social zone or prison, since they can not crawl out of their skins, and this signals what life has to offer them in Canada. This special type of visibility is a social construction as well as a political statement. (*Ibid.* 149)

Expressions such as "ethnics" and "immigrants" and "new Canadians" are no less problematic. They also encode the "us" and "them" with regard to political and social claims, signifying uprootedness and the pressure of assimilation or core cultural-apprenticeship. The irony compounds when one discovers that all white people, no matter when they immigrate to Canada or as carriers of which European ethnicity, become invisible and hold a dual membership in Canada, while others remain immigrants generations later.

The issue of ethnicity, again, poses a further complexity. It becomes apparent that currently it is mainly applied to the non-white population living in Canada. Once, however, it stringently marked out white "others" to the Anglo-French language and ethos, while today the great "white" construction has assimilated them. In the presence of contrasting "others," whiteness as an ideological-political category has superseded and subsumed different cultural ethos among Europeans. If the Ukrainians now seek to be ethnics it is because the price to be paid is no longer there. Now, in general, they are white *vis-à-vis* "others," as is denoted by the vigorous participation of Eastern-Europeans in white supremacist politics. They have been ingested by a "white-Anglo" ethos, which has left behind only the debris of self-consciously resurrected folklores as special effects in "ethnic" shows. The ethnicities of the English, the Scottish, the Irish, etc. are not visible or highlighted, but rather displaced by a general Englishness, which means less a particular culture than an official ideology and a standardized official language signifying the right to rule. "Ethnicity" is, therefore, what is classifiable as a non-dominant, sub- or marginal culture. English language and Canadian culture then cannot fall within the ministry of multi-culturalism's purview, but rather within that of the ministry of education, while racism makes sure that the possession of this language as a mother tongue does not make a non-white person non-ethnic. Marginalizing the ethnicity of black people from the Caribbean or Britain is evident not only in the Caribana Festival but in their being forced to take English as a second language. They speak dialects, it is said – but it might be pointed out that the white Irish, the white Scots, the white people from Yorkshire, or white Cockney speakers are not classified as ESL/ESD clients. The lack of fuss with which "Canadians" live with the current influx of Eastern-European immigrants strikes a profound note of contrast to their approach to the Somalis, for example, and other "others."

The intimate relation between the Canadian state and racism also becomes apparent if one complements a discussion on multiculturalism with one on political economy. One could perhaps give a finer name than racism to the way the state organizes labour importation and segmentation of the labour market in Canada, but the basic point would remain the same. Capitalist development in Canada, its class formation and its struggles, predominantly have been organized by the Canadian state. From the days of indenture to the present, when the Ministry of "Manpower" has been transformed into that of "Human Resources," decisions about who should come into Canada to do what work, definitions of skill and accreditation, licensing and certification, have been influenced by "race" and ethnicity.[26] This type of racism cannot be grasped in its real character solely as a cultural/attitudinal problem or an issue of prejudice. It needs to be understood in systemic terms of political economy and the Gramscian concepts of hegemony and common sense that encompass all aspects of life – from the everyday and cultural ones to those of national institutions. This is apparent if one studies the state's role in the importation of domestic workers into Canada from the Philippines or the Caribbean. Makeda Silvera, in *Silenced*, her oral history of Caribbean domestic workers, shows the bonds of servitude imposed on these women by the state through the inherently racist laws pertaining to hiring of domestic workers.[27] The middleman/procurer role played by the state on behalf of the "Canadian" bourgeoisie is glaringly evident. Joyce Fraser's *Cry of the Illegal Immigrant* is another testimonial to this. The issue of refugees is another in which we can see the colonial/racist as well as anti-communist nature of the Canadian state. Refugees fleeing ex-Soviet bloc countries, for example, received a no-questions acceptance, while the Vietnamese boat people, though fleeing communism, spent many years proving their claim of persecution. The racism of the state was so profound that even cold-war politics or general anti-communism did not make Vietnamese refugees into a "favoured" community. The story of racism is further exposed by the onerous and lengthy torture-proving rituals imposed on Latin Americans and others fleeing fascist dictatorships in the Third World. In spite of Canada's self-proclaimed commitment to human rights, numerous NGOs, both local and international, for years have needed to persuade the Canadian state and intervene as advocates of Third World refugees. Thus the state of "Canada," when viewed through the lens of racism/difference, presents us with a hegemony compounded of a racialized common sense and institutional structures. The situation is one in which racism in all its cultural and institutional variants has become so naturalized, so pervasive that it has become invisible or transparent to those who are not adversely impacted by them. This is why terms such as visible minority can generate so spontaneously within the bureaucracy and are not considered disturbing by most people acculturated to "Canada."

Erol Lawrence in his Gramscian critique "Plain Common Sense: The 'Roots' of Racism," uses the notion of common-sense racism to explain the relationship between the British Blacks and the state. He displays how common sense of "race" marks every move of the state, including official nomenclatures and their implementation in social and political culture. Lawrence remarks on how hegemony works through common sense or expresses itself as such:

> The term common sense is generally used to denote a down-to-earth "good sense." It is thought to represent the distilled truths of centuries of practical experience; so much so that to say of an idea or practice that it is only common sense, is to appeal over the logic and argumentation of intellectuals to what all reasonable people know in their "heart of hearts" to be right and proper. Such an appeal can all at once and at the same time (serve) to foreclose any discussion about certain ideas and practices and to legitimate them.[28]

The point of this statement becomes clearer when we see how the Canadian state, the media and political parties are using "visible minorities," "immigrants," "refugees," and "illegals" as scapegoats for various economic and political problems entirely unrelated to them. For this they rely on common sense racism: they offer pseudo-explanations to justify crises of capitalism and erosion of public spending and social welfare in terms of the presence of "others." Unemployment, endemic to capital's "structural adjustment," is squarely blamed on "these people." This explanation/ legitimation easily sticks because it replicates cultural-political values and practices that pre-exist on the ground. These labelling categories with racialized underpinnings spin-off into notions such as unskilled, illiterate, and traditional, thus making the presence of Third World peoples undesirable and unworthy of real citizenship. Englishness and whiteness are the hidden positive poles of these degrading categories. They contain the imperative of exclusion and restriction that neatly fits the white supremacist demand to "keep Canada white." The multiculturalist stance may support a degree of tolerance, but beyond a certain point, on the far edge of equality, it asserts "Canadianness" and warns off "others" from making claims on "Canada." Through the same scale of values East European immigrants are seen as desirable because they can be included in the ideology of whiteness.

"Difference" read through "race," then, produces a threat of racist violence. The creation of a "minority" rather than of full-fledged adult citizens – the existence of levels of citizenship – adds a structural/legal dimension to this violence. Inequality within the social fabric of Canada historically has been strengthened by the creation of reserves, the Department of Indian Affairs, the exclusion of Jews, and the ongoing political inequalities meted out to the Chinese, the Japanese, and South Asians. These and more add up to the tenuousness of the right and means to existence, jobs, and politics of the "visible minorities." Being designated a minority signals tutelage. It creates at best a patron-client relationship between the state and "others" who are to be rewarded as children on the basis of "good conduct." Social behaviour historically created through class, "race," and gender oppression is blamed on the very people who have been the victims. Their problems are seen as self-constructed. The problem of crime in Toronto, for example, is mainly blamed on the Black communities. Black young males are automatically labelled as criminals and frequently shot by the police. It is also characteristic that an individual act of violence performed by any Black person is seen as a representative act for the whole Black community, thus labelling them as criminal, while crime statistics among the white population remain non-representative of whiteness.

Visible minorities, because they are lesser or inauthentic political subjects, can enter politics mainly on the ground of multiculturalism. They can redress any social injustice only limitedly, if at all. No significant political effectiveness on a national scale is expected from them. This is why Elijah Harper's astute use of the tools of liberal democracy during the Meech Lake Accord was both unexpected and shocking for "Canadians." Other than administering "difference" differentially, among the "minority communities" multiculturalism bares the political processes of cooptation or interpellation. The "naming" of a political subject in an ideological context amounts to the creation of a political agent, interpellating or extending an ideological net around her/him, which confers agency only within a certain discursive-political framework. At once minimizing the importance and administering the problem of racism at a symptomatic level, the notion of visible minority does not allow room for political manoeuvre among those for whose supposed benefit it is instituted. This is unavoidably accompanied by the ethnicization and communalization of politics, shifting the focus from unemployment due to high profit margins, or flight of capital, to "problems " presented by the immigrant's own culture and tradition. Violence against women among the "ethnics" is thought to be the result of their indigenous "traditions" rather than of patriarchy and its exacerbation, caused by the absolute power entrusted by the Canadian state into the hands of the male "head of the family." The sponsorship system through which women and children enter into the country seems calculated to create violence. Food, clothes, and so-called family values are continually centre-staged, while the fundamental political and economic demands and aspirations of the communities are erased through multicultural gestures of reconciling "difference." The agent of multiculturalism must learn to disarticulate from his or her real-life needs and struggles, and thus from creating or joining organizations for anti-racism, feminism, and class struggle. The agencies (wo)manned by the "ethnic" elements – within terms and conditions of the state – become managers on behalf of the state. In fact, organizing multi-culturalism among and by the non-white communities amounts to extending the state into their everyday life and making basic social contradictions disappear or be deflected. Considering the state's multicultural move therefore allows a look into the state's interpellative functions and how it works as an ideological apparatus. These administrative and ideological categories create *objects* out of the people they impact upon and produce mainstream agencies in their name. In this way a little niche is created within the state for those who are otherwise undesirable, unassimilable, and deeply different. Whole communities have begun to be re-named on the basis of these conferred cultural-administrative identities that objectify and divide them. Unrelated to each other, they become clients and creatures of the multicultural state. Entire areas of problems connected to "race," class, gender, and sexual orientation are brought under the state's management, definition, and control, and possibilities for the construction of political struggles are displaced and erased in the name of "ethnic culture." The politics of identity among "ethnic communities," that so distresses the "whites" and is seen as an excessive permissiveness on the part of the state, is in no small measure the creation of this very culturalist managerial/legitimation drive of the state.

What, then, is to be done? Are we to join forces with the Reform Party or the small "c" conservative "Canadians" and advocate that the agenda of multiculturalism be dropped summarily? Should we be hoping for a deeper legitimation crisis through unemployment and rampant cultural racism, which may bring down the state? In theory that is an option, except that in the current political situation it also would strengthen the ultra-Right. But strategically speaking, at this stage of Canadian politics, with the withdrawal and disarray of the Left and an extremely vulnerable labour force, the answer can not be so categorical. The political potential of the civil society even when (mis)named as ethnic communities and reshaped by multiculturalism is not a negligible force. This view is validated by the fact that all shades of the right are uneasy with multiculturalism even though it is a co-opted form of popular, non-white political and cultural participation. The official, limited, and co-optive nature of this discourse could be re-interpreted in more materialist, historical, and political terms. It could then be re-articulated to the social relations of power governing our lives, thus minimizing, or even ending, our derivative, peripheral object-agent status. The basic nature of our "difference," as constructed in the Canadian context, must be rethought and the notion of culture once more embedded into society, into everyday life. Nor need it be forgotten that what multiculturalism (as with social welfare) gives us was not "given" voluntarily but "taken" by our continual demands and struggles. We must remember that it is our own socio-cultural and economic resources which are thus minimally publicly redistributed, creating in the process a major legitimation gesture for the state. Multiculturalism as a form of bounty or state patronage is a managed version of our antiracist politics.

We must then bite the hand that feeds us, because what it feeds us is neither enough nor for our good. But we must wage a contestation on this terrain with the state and the needs of a racist/imperialist capital. At this point of the new world order, short of risking an out-and-out fascism, the twisted ideological evolution of multiculturalism has to be forced into a minimum scope of social politics. Until we have developed a wider political space, and perhaps with it keeping a balance of "difference," using the avenues of liberal democracy may be necessary. Informed with a critique, multiculturalism is a small opening for making the state minimally accountable to those on whose lives and labour it erects itself. We must also remember that liberalism, no matter who practises it, does not answer our real needs. Real social relations of power – of "race," class, gender, and sexuality – provide the content for our "difference" and oppression. Our problem is not the value or the validity of the cultures in which we or our parents originated – these "home" cultures will, as living cultures do in history, undergo a sea-change when subjected to migration. Our problem is class oppression and objectifying sexist-racism. Thinking in terms of culture alone, in terms of a single community, a single issue or a single oppression will not do. If we do so our ideological servitude to the state and its patronage and funding traps will never end. Instead we need to put together a strategy of articulation that reverses the direction of our political understanding and affiliation – against the interpellating strategies of the ideological state apparatus. We need not forget that the very same social relations that disempower or minoritize us are present not only for us but in the very bones of class formation and oppression in Canada. They are not only devices for cultural discrimination and attitudinal distortion of the white population, but also a mode of co-optation for "visible minorities." They show themselves inscribed into the very formation of the nation and the state of "Canada." Thus the politics of class struggle, of struggle against poverty or heterosexism or violence against women, are politically more relevant for us than being elected into the labyrinth of the state. The "visible minorities" of Canada cannot attain political adulthood and full stature of citizenship without struggling, both conceptually and organizationally, against the icons and regulations of an overall subordination and exploitation.

In conclusion, then, to answer the questions "How are we to relate to multiculturalism?" and "Are we for it or against it?" we have to come to an Aesopian response of "yea, yea" and "nay, nay." After all, multiculturalism, as Marx said of capital, is not a "thing." It is not a cultural object, all inert, waiting on the shelf to be bought or not. It is a mode of the workings of the state, an expression of an interaction of social relations in dynamic tension with each other, losing and gaining its political form with fluidity. It is thus a site for struggle, as is "Canada" for contestation, for a kind of tug-of-war of social forces. The problem is that no matter who we are – Black or white – our liberal acculturation and single-issue oriented politics, our hegemonic "subsumption" into a racist common sense, combined with capital's crisis, continually draw us into the belly of the beast. This can only be prevented by creating counter-hegemonic interpretive and organizational frameworks that reach down into the real histories and relations of our social life, rather than extending tendrils of upward mobility on the concrete walls of the state. Our politics must sidestep the paradigm of "unity" based on "fragmentation or integration" and instead engage in struggles based on the genuine contradictions of our society.

NOTES

1. This division of Canada into Quebec and Canada outside of Quebec (COQ) is used as more than a territorial expression by Charles Taylor in *Reconciling the Solitudes*.

2. For an exposition of the notions of "solitude" and "survival" see Margaret Atwood, *Survival: A Thematic Guide to Canadian Literature*.

3. For an elaboration of these concepts see Louis Althusser, "Ideology and Ideological State Apparatuses (Notes towards an Investigation)," *Lenin and Philosophy and Other Essays* (London: New Left Books, 1977).

4. On multiculturalism, its definition and history, see Augie Fleras and Jean Leonard Elliot eds., *Multiculturalism in Canada: The Challenge of Diversity* (Scarborough: Nelson, 1992).

5. On the emergence of a liberal state from the bases of a white settler colony see B. Singh Bolaria and Peter Li eds., *Racial Oppression in Canada* (Toronto: Garamond Press, 1988); also see Peter Kulchyski ed., *Unjust Relations: Aboriginal Rights in Canadian Courts* (Toronto: Oxford University Press, 1994) and Frank Tester and Peter Kulchyski, *Tammarniit (Mistakes): Relocation in the Eastern Arctic* (Vancouver: University of British Columbia Press, 1994). For a

"race"/gender inscription into a semi-colonial Canadian state see Patricia Monture-Angus, *Thunder in My Soul: A Mohawk Woman Speaks* (Halifax: Fernwood, 1995).

6. For an in-depth discussion of mediatory and unificatory ideologies needed by a liberal democratic, i.e., capitalist state, see Ralph Miliband, *The State in Capitalist Society* (London: Quartet Books, 1984) chapters 7 and 8.

7. For a clarification of my use of this concept see Jürgen Habermas, *Legitimation Crisis* (Boston: Beacon Press, 1975). This use of "legitimacy" is different from Charles Taylor's Weberian use of it in *Reconciling the Solitudes*.

8. See B. Anderson, *Imagined Communities*, Introduction and chapter 2. Anderson says, "I ... propose the following definition of the nation: it is an imagined political community – and imagined as both inherently limited and sovereign. It is *imagined* because the members of even the smallest nation will never know most of their fellow members, meet them, or even hear of them, yet in the minds of each lives the image of their communion" (6).

9. In *Reconciling the Solitudes*, chapter 4, on "Alternative Futures" for Canada, Taylor fleshes out his desirable and undesirable options for Canada. This is also found in his *Multiculturalism and "The Politics of Recognition"* (Princeton: Princeton University Press, 1992).

10. Taylor is quite direct about his German romantic intellectual heritage. In *Reconciling*, in an essay entitled "Institutions in National Life," he states, "In Herder I found inspiration, ideas that were very fruitful for me, precisely because I was from here, I was able to understand him from the situation I had experienced outside school, outside university, and I was able to engage with his thought, internalize it, and (I hope) make something interesting out of it" (136).

11. For an exposition of this idea, and Taylor's rejection of an "American" solution for "Canadian" identity, see "Shared and Divergent" in *Reconciling*.

12. On the development of active white supremacist groups in Canada, and their "Englishness," see Martin Robb, *Shades of Right: Nativist and Fascist Politics in Canada, 1920-1940* (Toronto: University of Toronto Press, 1992); also William Peter Ward, *White Canada Forever* (Montreal: McGill-Queen's University Press, 1978).

13. See also B. Anderson's chapter on "Official Nationalism and Imperialism."

14. On the construction of "whiteness" as an ideological, political, and socio-historical category see Theodor Allen, *The Invention of the White Race: Racial Oppression and Social Control* (London: Verso, 1994); David Roediger, *The Wages of Whiteness: Race and the Making of the American Working Class* (London: Verso, 1993); also Ruth Frankenberg, *White Women, Race Matters: The Social Construction of Whiteness* (Minneapolis: University of Minnesota Press, 1993).

15. On the use of "whiteness"/Europeanness as an ideology for ruling, including its formative impact on sexuality of the ruling, colonial nations, see Ann Laura Stoller, *Race and the Education of Desire: Foucault's History of Sexuality and the Colonial Order of Things* (Durham: Duke University Press, 1995).

16. On this theme see Joseph Conrad's *The Heart of Darkness*, E.M. Forster's *A Passage to India* and Edward Said, *Culture and Imperialism*.

17. On the reading of the black, dark or "visible minority" body see the collection of essays in Henry Louis Gates Jr. ed., "Race," *Writing and Difference* (Chicago: The University of Chicago Press, 1985), especially Sander Gillman, "Black Bodies, White Bodies."

18. See Stoller, *Race and the Education of Desire*, but also Mrinalini Sinha, *Colonial Masculinity* (Manchester: Manchester University Press, 1995).

19. The history of immigration and refugee laws in Canada and of the immigrants, indentured workers, and refugees themselves must be read to comprehend fully what I am attempting to say. See The Law Union of Ontario, *The Immigrant's Handbook* (Montreal: Black Rose Books, 1981); also *A Report of the Canadian Immigration and Population Study: Immigration Policy Perspective* (Ottawa: Department of Manpower and Immigration and Information Canada, 1974); and *Equality Now: Report of the Special Committee on Visible Minorities* (Ottawa: House of Commons, 1986).

20. Antonio Gramsci, "Notes of Italian History" in Gramsci, *Selections from the Prison Notebooks*, edited and translated by Quentin Hoare and Geoffrey Smith (New York: International Publishers, 1971).

21. On organic intellectuals as intellectuals who are integral to any ideological and class project, see Gramsci, "The Intellectuals" in *Ibid.*

22. This becomes evident when we follow the controversies which are generated by writers' conferences, such as "Writing Thru Race," or the Black communities' response and resistance to Royal Ontario Museum's exhibition on African art and culture – "Out of the Heart of Africa."

23. See, for example, Dionne Brand, *Winter Epigrams* (Toronto: Williams-Wallace, 1983); Krisantha Sri Bhaggiyadatta, *The 52nd State of Amnesia* (Toronto: TSAR, 1993); Himani Bannerji, *Doing Time* (Toronto: Sister Vision Press, 1986); and collections such as Diane McGifford and Judith Kearns eds., *Shakti's Words* (Toronto: TSAR, 1990).

24. The acronym for Racial Holy War, a neo-Nazi rock band.

25. On this theme of social construction of a racialized "minority" subject and its inherent patriarchy, see Linda Carty and Dionne Brand, "Visible Minority Women: A Creation of the Colonial State," and Roxana Ng, "Sexism, Racism, Canadian Nationalism," in H. Bannerji ed., *Returning the Gaze.*

26. See Donald Avery, *Reluctant Host: Canada's Response to Immigrant Workers, 1896-1994* (Toronto: McClelland & Stewart, 1995). Much work still needs to be done in this area in which class formation is considered in terms of both "race" and gender. But a beginning is made in Dionne Brand's *No Burden to Carry: Narratives of Black Working Women in Ontario, 1920s to 1950s*; and Dionne Brand and Krisantha Sri Bhaggiyadatta eds., *Rivers Have Sources, Trees Have Roots: Speaking of Racism* (Toronto: Cross Cultural Communications Centre, 1985).

27. This is powerfully brought forth through the issue of importation of domestic workers in Toronto from the Caribbean by Makeda Silvera, *Silenced: Talks with working class Caribbean women about Their Lives and Struggles as Domestic Workers in Canada*, 2nd edition (Toronto: Sister Vision Press, 1989).

28. Erol Lawrence, "Just Plain Common Sense: the 'roots' of racism," in *The Empire Strikes Back: Race and Racism in 70s Britain* (London: Centre for Contemporary Cultural Studies, Hutchinson, in association with the Centre for Cultural Studies, University of Birmingham, 1986).

JOSEPH PIVATO

Representation of Ethnicity as Problem: Essence or Construction

> My Italian identity started to come out more and more.
> By the end of the summer I started to dream in Italian.
>
> Mary di Michele

Let me begin with a scene from the Italian film, *Padre Padrone*, a scene that helps bring into focus some of the issues surrounding the question of representation. In *Padre Padrone* we see an Italy of the Third World – Sardinia, an island of shepherds, olive pickers, and poverty. The final scene in the film has Gavino Ledda, the author of the story on which it is based, explain to the audience why after finishing his graduate degree in linguisitics he did not take up a university position in Rome, but returned to the poverty of his small town to teach the peasant children. He explains that the university position gave him power over others, and implies that this power would have made him like his father – a padrone.

I was moved by this film because it recalled for me the poverty of the post-war Italy which I left behind in 1952. The film is set in the late 1960s when the poverty of Sardinia is in sharp contrast to the economic miracle taking place in most of Western Europe. I was shocked by its final scene: why, after trying to escape this poverty and an oppressive family throughout the narrative, should Gavino decide to return to his town?

The narrative of Gavino's brutal early life and his final political choice lends credibility to the representation of this story. The author speaks with the poor in his story and not just about them from a distance. Gavino, though a university graduate, wants to identify with the powerless children of his village. This final scene highlights that the important relationships in the narrative are those of power and property. We have witnessed the brutal murder of Gavino's cousin, and have seen Gavino's father eagerly inherit his olive grove. Gavino chooses to try to change these power relations by returning and teaching the children to read. He gives them the education that he was denied by his own father. The film opens with the father pulling the young Gavino out of grade school in order to send him into the wasteland to mind the sheep. Escaping to Rome and taking up a position of power would indicate that Gavino has allowed his brutal father, and those like him, to win.

He would have become like them. The brief final words by the adult Gavino Ledda tell us about the relationships of power and the representation of the subject. Gavino, the author, clearly states his position. He is an example of what Gramsci called an organic intellectual, one who emerges from and continues to identify with an oppressed class.

Authority and Authentic Voice
My starting point for a discussion of the representation of ethnicity is a political position. Who is speaking and from what place? In all my criticism of Italian-Canadian writing and other ethnic minority literature I have tried to be conscious of the position of the speaker. I have often focussed on the voice of the writer and his/her authority to speak about the minority experience. Nevertheless, I often get the impression that this idea of the authentic voice is dismissed by some of my colleagues as naïve. It is naïve from the poststructuralist point of view that sees all differences as socially and historically constructed and not based on any fixed properties of nature. Any discussion of the authentic voice and the appropriation of voice becomes involved in the larger debate between essentialism and social constructionism that has animated feminist writers for over three decades (Fuss). This debate between essentialism and constructionism is also influencing the discourse on ethnic minority writing in Canada. We cannot avoid the question of biology, if only because blood relations are so important within many ethnic communities (Kostash, *Bloodlines*).

The research and study of ethnic minority writing is such a new area that it is necessary to use the author's signature as a marker of minority status. Names like Pier Giorgio Di Cicco, Antonino Mazza, Mary di Michele, Marco Micone, Antonio D'Alfonso, and Mary Melfi, all with those final Mediterranean vowels, were not the kinds of names normally found on Canadian literature courses and so they stood out immediately. Linda Hutcheon has pointed out that women with Italian family names who married non-Italians lost these name markers and the "advantages" that went with them (Hutcheon, "Crypto-Ethnicity").

As immigrants and the children of immigrants these authors were speaking for the first time about their communities; in many cases they were the only speakers from these groups and so, willing or not, they have become the authority voices for these immigrant communities. Who decides that someone speaks for a particular group? We must assume that the groups consent to these writers speaking for them. Much like Gavino in the Sardinian film, the writers can speak with their community and can do so in their own authentic dialects. They have not left their communities to speak about them from a distance and in a foreign language. When these writers use English or French to speak about their communities these languages come from the immediate experience of these people. At one point in the Canadian documentary film *Enigmatico*, Antonio D'Alfonso complains that he is not happy with the quality of his writing. Though he can use English, French, and

Italian, he says he cannot master them as well as the native speakers of these standard tongues. This is exactly the point of authenticity – in his own body D'Alfonso reflects his community and its language problems. The people depicted in the writing of Frank Paci, Dino Minni, Mary di Michele, Caterina Edwards, and others demonstrate that no matter how many university degrees these characters earn they do not escape the language or identity problems of their families. Post-colonial theory and criticism have linked language and representation. In order to articulate, to represent the cultural difference of one's own group, one must speak their language. Using English or another colonial language often involves translation, a problem we can only discuss briefly here (Pivato, "Constantly Translating").

In her study of marginality Sneja Gunew cites Lacan's dictum that the unconscious is structured like a language, and she asks if that unconscious may be formed in relation to a particular language, rather than language in general (*Framing Marginality* 13). The quotation from Mary di Michele at the beginning of this essay is an example of the inscription of the original language in the body. During her first return trip to Italy and to the town of her birth, Mary di Michele began to dream in Italian once more as she must have done as a little girl.

Whether the immigrant writer uses the language of the old country or that of the new he/she is involved in translation. The representation of cultural difference through the old language in the new country may produce the deterritorialization of the dominant language (Deleuze and Guattari), but it also changes the minority language in terms of context, meaning, and even sound. How can it authentically represent the minority experience if it is itself changing in the new territory? The Italian of Maria Ardizzi's four Canadian novels is not the same language as that of Italy, because it is influenced by this process of deterritorialization. Ardizzi is translating while writing in standard Italian. Her heroine, Nora Moratti, is a Canadian character who speaks Italian.

The use of a new language such as English or French in the new country by the immigrant writer or his/her children presents other problems of translation. Representing the immigrant experience (originally lived in Italian or in Japanese or in Bengali) in English changes the experience. The ethnic minority writer is involved in the process of translation, in the search for the authentic presentation of the experience. With Joy Kogawa, the use of the Japanese culture also involves the use of silence, an element which is difficult to translate into another language, especially a dominant language such as English. On the other hand, Hiromi Goto uses whole Japanese sentences to capture the untranslatable in *Chorus of Mushrooms*:

What do you mean? *Eigo hitotsu mo hanashitenal to omou kedo.* Haven't we been talking Japanese all along? (197)

In Goto's narrative there are some Japanese characters and many Japanese terms which are written phonetically in the Roman alphabet and so have already undergone one transformation.

Appropriation of Voice

Translation and the appropriation of voice are linked activities. All forms of translation have been practised for centuries out of a variety of needs. Translation assumes that a given author or text cannot speak for itself and needs someone to interpret into another language. Appropriation of voice, on the other hand, appears to be a recent development with all kinds of undesirable political dimensions. Given the many problems involved in both translation and the search for the appropriate expression of the minority experience we can understand the gravity of the problem of appropriation of voice. It is an activity that seems to assume that the minority person cannot speak for himself/herself, when in fact they can and should be given every opportunity to do so. For a person from outside the minority group to presume to speak about the experience of (and for) persons from the marginalized group is not just a political problem but an aesthetic one as well. It cannot be explained away by appealing to the freedom of the imagination of the artist. When power is involved there is no real freedom of the imagination for the artist. Appropriation of voice, by definition, is not a dialogue among equals but an exercise of power by the appropriator over the minority person, who is thus made an object and not a subject.

While I am well aware of the dangers of biological essentialism, I am equally sensitive to the power relations in the major languages and literatures that also belong to and were used as instruments by colonial powers. It would be absurd to maintain absolutely that only people of Italian blood could write about Italians. This would eliminate half the plays in Shakespeare's canon, and when we look closely at the example of Shakespeare, we see that the power relations do not put Italy at a disadvantage. The powerful city-states of Italy were leaders of the Renaissance, and the English playwright was simply imitating what was considered the most fashionable and popular culture of his time. Shakespeare was not appropriating the voices of Italians, since their artists, writers, and musicians were speaking for themselves very loudly all over Europe. There was no unequal power relationship between the languages and cultures of England and Italy at the time.

If we look at a more recent example of borrowing from another culture, though, we may find that the power relations are very unequal. Take the case of W.P. Kinsella and his short stories about a Native community in Alberta, in which the stories are fiction and the characters all imaginary, but the location of the reserve is similar to that of a real reserve near Hobbema, Alberta. The fact that the stories are humorous and depict Native peoples in comical situations can be seen as degrading, maintaining the negative stereotypes of Native peoples as not very intelligent. As an Italian I can appreciate the situation of seeing your own people depicted as either foolish clowns or as evil. But the problem of appropriation here depends on the disparity in the power relations of the two. Kinsella is a successful, published writer with a

North American audience, whose books have been made into popular movies and who has access to all the media and the most powerful publishers. And he has taken advantage of all these forms of communication to denounce his critics and accusers as "the thought police." The Native peoples of Hobbema have few avenues of self-expression about this issue or any other. Their weak economic position gives them little ability to exercise agency and to contest the representation of negative stereotypes. The very fact that the case against appropriation in this case was taken up by other white writers and academics in Canada rather than by the Native peoples of the community supports this view of their position of powerlessness. Sadly, it also reveals the paternalistic position in which this particular group of Native peoples still finds itself. Even their white advocates are guilty of speaking for them. Many Native writers happily speak for and to their own communities. Tomson Highway and Drew Hayden Taylor address their own communities.

In Rudy Wiebe's books depicting Native peoples, we see an historical encounter between the dominant white world and that of the Native peoples. In *Discovery of Strangers* Wiebe tries to place the two cultures on more or less equal ground. Can he too be accused of appropriation of voice when he puts English words into the mouths of these long dead Native figures? For African-Canadian writer Nourbese Philip the answer to this question is yes:

> For the white artist/writer/painter/musician – particularly the male of the species – the world is his oyster, and if he wishes to use Asian, African or Native culture in his work, then why the hell not? What does white mean, if it does not mean being able to lay waste and lay claim to anything you may happen to set your mind to? That is the moral turpitude at the heart of white "civilization." (219)

In his important book, *Orientalism*, Edward Said makes some cogent observations about the problems of representation which can be applied to the European depiction of Native peoples and visible minorities. For Said, the West's construction of the Orient was mediated by a whole set of ethnocentric forces – political, ideological, religious, and cultural (*Orientalism* 203). In addition to the violence of Western imperialism in the Orient, there was the violence of the representation itself, of the power to select and exclude material, to translate and to interpret in terms of modern Europe, and all from positions and perspectives that were not visible to readers (121, 207-9). Elsewhere Said has observed that this violence is also due to the contrast between the act of representation and the calm exterior of the image, the text ("In the Shadow" 95).

The writer who studies other cultures must avoid trying to "master" them through the power of expertise. Does this acquired knowledge also give the writer the ability to speak for the marginal group, and thus appropriate its voice? Or is the writer an interpreter, a translator of the words for the minority people who may have another language? Does this privilege of speaking with them also require the writer to live with them, in the same location? Only from this position might the writer understand the differences between the Western tradition and the local culture. The writer who speaks with the minority group, whether his/her own or one from another culture, recognizes power relations and the agency of the other (see Fine 1994).

Contemporary theories have made us aware that even narratives of minority experience are susceptible to all the contradictions inherent in texuality. Even innocent biographical narratives come to us textualized as representations that may have done violence to the original events (Buss). No language is neutral. What is important is the position and power of those being depicted in the literary work. As Said observes, "What we must eliminate are systems of representation that carry with them the kind of authority which ... has been repressive because it doesn't permit or make room for interventions on the part of those being represented" ("In the Shadow" 95). Many ethnic minority writers themselves articulate their own difficulty with the power relations in representation. Frank Paci acknowledged the literacy problems among his own immigrant family members, their lack of access to his English language works, and wondered if film might give them the opportunity to participate in the discourse (unpublished correspondence, 3 March 1981).

Representation and appropriation of voice is a difficulty for all writers. Sneja Gunew points out that we use the term representation in at least two senses: as the depiction of a subject and as delegation (when someone speaks for a group or individual) (*Framing Marginality* 31). Writers and critics who are delegates for marginal or minority groups may find themselves in the situation of Gavino Ledda – from their position of power in the hegemony of Western civilization, how can they really speak for a powerless group? In using the language of the dominant culture and the discourse of sophisticated theory, can they still address the concerns of the marginal community? With every university degree there comes a level of separation between the writer and his/her community. And so we can see that the only concrete links this person may have with these original roots is to try to speak with and for these people. The task is not unproblematic (Paci, "Tasks of the Canadian" 47).

The case of the Italian-American writer and critic Frank Lentricchia illustrates the ambivalent feelings produced by academic training on the one hand and ethnicity on the other. In his two books on novelist Don DeLillo, Lentricchia praises him for his ability to escape Italian ethnicity (*Introducing Don DeLillo* 2). But in two other publications, especially his autobiographical *The Edge of Night*, Lentricchia obsessively reviews the meaning of his Italian background. In an interview he confesses,

But when I write, I'm aware, at some level – not always but intermittently – that I'm writing from a position as a critic who is not in a typical position in the American academy. That fact sometimes weighs heavily upon me. I can't say that it's shaped all of my work: if you read some of my early stuff, you'll see no relationship with my Italian-American working-class background. But, these days, I have to say that one of the things I'm aware of is that I'm not a gentleman scholar. And, especially in my last two books, this has made me wary of theories of literature that avoid the kinds of differences you can't avoid. ("Interview" 182)

The delegated critic who tries to speak about and for minority groups often finds that he/she must point to the norms of universality assumed by white western societies. These norms are so taken for granted as to be invisible to us. How can we understand the difference between the dominant cultures and the subordinate ones? Will the theories of European deconstruction help us here? In his work Said is critical of the separation between literary culture and social problems: "This has given rise to a cult of professional expertise whose effect in general is pernicious. For the intellectual class, expertise has usually been a service rendered, and sold, to the central authority of society. This is the *trahison des clercs* of which Julien Benda spoke in the 1920s" (Said, *The World, the Text and the Critic* 2). The problem of representing alterity is bound up with the questions of position and of power. Psychologist Michelle Fine advises researchers to "work the hyphen" in order to probe these power relations.

Representation and the Conventions of Realism
In the not-too-distant past ethnic minority writing was dismissed as work of low literary value because it was perceived as too sociological. The novels of Italian-American writers such as Pietro di Donato and John Fante were criticized as poor realism or naturalism. In general, ethnic minority writing was reduced to the oral history of immigrants or to the sociology of new settlement in ethnic neighbourhoods. I have always taken this dismissive criticism and turned it around. It is precisely because of this attention to the realistic representation of the immigrant story that the works of a Frank Paci or a M.G. Vassanji are valuable both as literature and as story. As I have argued elsewhere, writers such as Maria Ardizzi and Joy Kogawa strike a responsive chord in readers because they are reconstructing a history of immigrant women which has been lost and neglected. To me this biographical dimension increases rather than diminishes the literary value of their work.

In recent years the works of ethnic minority writers have been criticized in the context of contemporary theory. These works are often seen as stuck in the conventions of literary realism and not as experimental in their exploration of new forms of representing the subject. Some critics have tried to read these works as postmodern. And we can see how it is appealing to read many ethnic minority novels as open to postmodern theories that promote the "decentred subject," support the fragmentation of linear narratives, and show scepticism about master narratives. I have argued that many ethnic minority writers do not want to decentre the subject but simply to find or construct the minority subject for the first time. They do not use anti-narrative fragmentation because they are often trying to reconstruct a lost narrative for the first time from the chaos of fragmented oral histories (Pivato, "Shirt of the Happy Man").

Critical theory not only questions the intentions of the minority writer, but also the need to recognize the very existence of the author. Much contemporary criticism tries to avoid the role of the author by preferring the term "text" rather than "work" that implies the creation of an author. For Foucault and his followers the author is merely an "author function" in the discursive analysis of art. It has become a troubling issue that just at the point when minority writers find individual voices and assert their existence, postmodern theory seems to deny the need for this existence. In response to this obliteration of identity Francesco Loriggio has pointed out that the signature of the marginalized writer is an important marker: "The most idiosyncratic and most conspicuous feature of ethnic texts is also their most controversial one. It has to do with the function of the author" ("Question of the Corpus" 55). The recognition of the individual author is linked to the identity of the minority group and to their history. It is a history consisting not of momentous world events from history books, but of little stories, family chronicles, tales of displaced people, autobiographies of women and men. The discourse of feminist writers on the issues of essentialism and the body, and especially of those studying life writing, has helped us to re-evaluate the work of ethnic minority writers as literary works, as texts which reward reading, study, and research (Neuman, *ReImagining Women*, *Autobiography*; Kadar; Verduyn, *Lifelines*).

The conventions of literary realism are the ones that lend themselves most easily to the storytelling of ethnic minority groups. Conventional narrative permits the minority writer to tell the story in the most direct manner and to develop characters who exercise some form of agency. It is this agency that allows writers to critique the social values of both the old and the new country. Agency allows people the freedom to act in conformance with, in opposition to, or without regard for biological or social determinants (Rychlak 50).

Agency

Along with the preference for the conventions of literary realism often found in ethnic minority writing is the common use of the first person narrative. Examples are numerous: Frank Paci's *Black Blood*, Hiromi Goto's *Chorus of Mushrooms*, Gérard Etienne's *Le nègre crucifié*, and in Australia Rosa Cappiello's *Paese fortunato*. One of the attractive aspects of speaking in the first person, in one's own voice, is that it gives the illusion of power and control over one's life, a sense of self-determination that never existed in the real experience of dislocation. In a sense the agency of the main character in the narrative parallels that of the author with the freedom to tell his own or her own story.

In the past, critical theory was able to accommodate the intention and authority of the writer, but this has changed. Recent literary theories proclaimed the death of the author (Barthes). Reader-response theory privileged the interaction of the reader with the text. Umberto Eco claimed that the author is only a strategy of the text and that the real text is a product of the reader's consciousness. Wolfgang Iser agreed and maintained that the text only exists through the activity of the reader. We can see the gap here between the urban culture of Europe, with its self-reflexive theories that are meant honestly to do away with the cult of personality, and the basic activities of the minority writer who is trying to articulate an experience, develop an identity, and find a space in society.

In ethnic minority writing we have not only the recuperation of the author, but also the exercise of his or her authority as a voice in and for the community. This recognition of the authority of the author is one response to the appropriation of voice from outside the community. When we write about ethnic minority authors we are implicitly recognizing their vital role as voices in their communities. In her study of Dionne Brand's poetry, Himani Bannerji focusses on this important dimension in her writing:

> Dionne Brand, born in Trinidad, in Guaguyare (1953), immigrant to Canada, woman and black is another such poet. To read her poetry is to read not only about her but also about her people. Her identification with their struggles both in the metropole of Canada and in the hinterland of the Caribbean. (*The Writing on the Wall* 24)

In her study of Marco Micone's plays set in Quebec and written in French, Sherry Simon directly articulates his role in her choice of title, "The Voice of Authority." The plays not only provide Micone entry into the political discourse of Quebec, they also give him a voice for the Italo-Québécois community, a voice it did not previously have. These *Gens du silence* are never going to be silent again.

For Dionne Brand, Marco Micone, and Hiromi Goto putting words from the ethnic community into print is an exercise in agency, allowing them to question freely both the biological and the social determinants they confront everyday. Linda Hutcheon, despite her attachments to postmodernism, recognizes the value of intentionality when it comes to literatures of resistance. In her reinterpretation of the theory of irony she writes, "After all, the touchy political issues that arise around irony's usage and interpretation invariably focus on the issue of intention (of either ironist or interpreter). And it is because of its very foregrounding of the politics of human agency in this way that irony has become an important strategy of oppositional rhetoric"(Hutcheon, *Irony's Edge* 11-12). The representation of ethnic difference in literature takes many forms, combining the realities of blood relations and social construction. Implicit in the idea of difference is the freedom to resist these factors. Helped by the example of half-forgotten immigrants, we as writers and critics should constantly be engaged in questioning the categories of ethnicity, race, and gender.

I will end with an image from another film. This one is from the historical Italo-Québécois film, *La Sarrasine*, by Paul Tana and Bruno Ramirez. An Italian immigrant, Giuseppe Moschella, is arrested and imprisoned for an accidental death. He orders his wife Ninetta to return to Italy, but she refuses and instead stays in Canada to plead his case. She resists the bullying of Giuseppe's older brother and remains in Canada even after Giuseppe takes his own life in despair. In contrast to her husband, who gave up, Ninetta is a paradigm of agency inhabiting a marginalized figure. As a powerless immigrant woman in turn-of-the-century Quebec Ninetta's resistance is of three kinds: first, she wants to fight the legal system in order to get justice for her husband; second, she wants to decide for herself where she is going to live; and third, she wants to tell her own story in her own words, which in this case are Sicilian. The film ends with an image blending Canadian and Italian elements: the black-clad Ninetta standing in a field of snow gazing out at the horizon. It is by representing herself as visible that Ninetta can become a part of the new landscape.

ARUN P. MUKHERJEE

Teaching Ethnic Minority Writing: A Report from the Classroom

Anecdote One

This week, we are reading Claire Harris's *The Conception of Winter* (1989). The challenges a racial/ethnic minority text throws up for cultural outsiders are encapsulated in the following poem from "A Grammar of the Heart," a cycle of poetic laments about the death of Harris's mother.

> She was a spell
> a plot
> i could not be like her
> it was something
> i could not learn   the way
> i learnt
> to make buljol
> stuff cucumbers
> match patterns
> the way i learnt
> a woman must have a profession
> that way you aren't dependent on any man
> and yet
>
> now sometimes
> i come upon her suddenly
> and in shadow
> now perhaps my grave's clarity
> resolving itself
> i understand
> what passion forged the cool smile. (59)

The word that I did not know in the poem and had not worried about over the last three years that I had taught this text is "buljol." I could guess that it was some kind of dish that the poet learnt to make from her mother. But, somehow, this time we started talking about unfamiliar words in ethnic minority writing. When I told the students that I did not know what "buljol" was, and asked whether anyone in the class knew, four hands went up. I learnt that it is a favourite Caribbean dish made with salt cod, onions, and tomatoes.

You may wonder how this information adds to our interpretation of the poem. We all have our cuisines, and the world is full of cookbooks; how does it matter that what Harris learnt from her mother was "buljol" and not apple pie? It mattered to us in that classroom because we had been coming across references to salt cod in the work of other Caribbean Canadian poets. Cyril Dabydeen's poem "Letter" is one such example:

> You have not written
> these past weeks:
> a mail strike perhaps.
>
> I do not give up
> easily: remembering
> old words
>
> like salted cod
> in the penury of taste
> and the dim slaves
>
> with their leather
> tongues; the indentured
> also grew accustomed
>
> to neglect
> in the humid heat. (5)

Now that we realised that "buljol" was made with salt cod, the poem became linked up for us with Dabydeen's and Arnold Itwaru's work. The intertextuality between the works of Caribbean-Canadian writers was concretised once more for the class by just that one word. Salt cod, we had discovered, is a signifier loaded with cultural and historic memory for Caribbean-Canadians. It was the food given to slaves and, later, to indentured workers. Salt cod, sugar, molasses, and rum were signifiers we kept encountering in the writing of Dionne Brand, Cyril Dabydeen, Claire Harris, and Arnold Itwaru. And associated with them were other signifiers – so that sugar evoked references to the Middle Passage and chain and coffle.

All those memories were brought into action through the literature's reference to food. Food, we discovered, is a powerful carrier of group memory. Its procurement, its preparation, its smells, and responses to it from the dominant group trigger kinaesthetic responses in the reader. For example, when I asked the students who had explained how "buljol" is prepared, what effect the word had on them in the Harris poem, one said it made her hungry. I took that to mean that the word in the poem evoked memories of childhood for the student: home, kitchen, mother, native land, flora and fauna, and who knows what else. The poem, then, had for her, and for others who know the word and have eaten the dish, a very intimate meaning. It marks them as members of a cultural group at the same time as it adds to that belonging.

I realized that for me, and for others who did not "know" the word and the food that it signified in the same way, the poem could not have that kind of meaning. It could not be a self-recognition for us, as it was for those who knew. What it could be for us, though, was an example of how poems – and literature in general – work. We could go on to think about our own cultural heritages and their signifiers. And, as one Caribbean Canadian student said, we could appreciate Harris's contribution to the composite Canadian culture by introducing other Canadians to her Caribbean roots.

While we may not salivate at the uttering of "buljol," we may benefit by learning about Caribbean-Canadian connections that go back several centuries. "Buljol" could not have been prepared except for the trade between Canada and the Caribbean. Yet Kenneth McNaught's *The Penguin History of Canada* has just one sentence about salt cod: "The West Indian trade which exchanged codfish for rum, sugar, and molasses was substantial" (63). It is this "substantial" relationship, built on the bitter economy of sugar plantations, that Caribbean Canadian writers uncover for us. In doing that, they are writing a chapter of Canadian history that has been neglected for too long.

The one unfamiliar word in Harris's otherwise seemingly transparent poem, then, led me and my class into an elaborate excursion into history and culture and the power of words. As well, it taught me how important food is to one's identity. Its smells and tastes, imprinted through our neurons, lead us into a thicket of associations. While all texts may encode references to food, a minority writer's text makes its importance obvious to readers from other cultural backgrounds because of our unfamiliarity with its signifiers. One of my essay topics asked students to comment on the importance of food and clothes as signifiers in minority Canadian writers' texts. I have tremendously enjoyed the papers they have written on the works of Native, Caribbean Canadian, Chinese Canadian, and South Asian Canadian writers' works.

Anecdote Two

I have been teaching Sky Lee's *Disappearing Moon Cafe* for three years. The cover page displays three "Chinese" (Mandarin? Cantonese? – since I do not really know, I will call them Chinese) characters that I began to wonder about. What does it mean to have a Canadian novel in English utilizing another language and another script on its cover page? What does it mean to the reader who will not know what they mean? What, on the other hand, might it mean to the reader who does know what they mean?

I sent an e-mail inquiry to Lien Chao who has just completed her PhD dissertation on Chinese-Canadian literature. Here is her answer:

The three characters on Lee's novel mean the following:
First character: waning
Second character: moon
Third character: building, chamber, traditional Chinese architecture
style building
Together they sound quite poetic in Chinese (gee, that's a surprise!)

Lien's explanation makes me see how inadequate a substitution the expression "Disappearing Moon Cafe" is for the sentiments expressed in "Chinese." The closest approximation to the English title in my experience is the imagery of gothic fiction: moonlight making leafless trees and ruined buildings appear unfamiliar, almost otherworldly. The meaning of "Chinese" characters allowed me to visualize a Chinese landscape painting – elegant, "mysterious," and beautiful. This landscape, I presume, would have arisen in the imagination of patrons of Disappearing Moon Cafe or other similar restaurants.

The three "Chinese" characters on the cover are performing some very important functions. The gap between their expressivity and that of the English language title points to two very different sensibilities. The "Chinese" characters, it seems to me, want to capture an entire scene in what, for the lack of a better term, I would call a phrase: a scene with the moon and clouds and the movement of the clouds playing hide and seek with the moon. In languages relying on a phonetic script, one may describe such scenes in several poetic lines, but definitely not in three words. Hence, the English translation, "Disappearing Moon," is necessarily un-idiomatic, altogether un-English. And yet it does give a sense of what the original language was trying to portray. It also forces us to rethink how we organize the world through language. I presume that that is what the writer intended: to make the non-Asian or unilingual reader aware of other worlds and other sensibilities existing outside her immediate cultural currency.

Disappearing Moon Cafe is full of such un-idiomatic translations from the "Chinese": "There is so much to tell You," writes Fong Mei to her sister, "but as they say, 'When there are too many bright flowers, the eye knows not where to look'"(42). Mui Lan boasts that "no one can accuse the Wong family of having 'a wolf's heart and a dog's lung'" (S. Lee 61). Wong Gwei Chang, remembering Kelora, thinks of a poem that, again, can be translated only inadequately into English:

Pushed by his need to be outside of this, he stepped right up to the window's edge. There, as if searching, he stared up at the cloudless, brilliant sky, feeling an old tug on his heavy spirit. Away in the distance, he followed the movements of what might have been a pair of hawks or eagles circling in the sky. Maybe they were just crows, but suddenly he remembered a love poem:
  When a pair of magpies fly together
  They do not envy the pair of phoenixes. (78)

It is Sky Lee's prefatory words introducing the poem that help the reader grasp the inadequacy of the English translation. Her refusal to translate Wong Gwei Chang's and his contemporary Chinese Canadians' lives into English only is the author's way of alerting us to the mysteries and depths of cultures and human beings, an artistic decision and a triumph that literary criticism, developed on monolingual and monocultural principles, has yet to recognize. By making English carry the weight of Chinese *Weltanschauung* Lee concretizes for us the pluricultural nature of humanity on the one hand and the loss and deprivation felt by those transplanted to an alien cultural universe on the other hand.

For instance, the following passage acquired added poignancy for me when I reread the text in the light of my new knowledge:

> Disappearing Moon was divided into two front sections, with the kitchen and the storeroom at the back. The dining room was the largest in Chinatown, perhaps the most beautiful in all of Vancouver, with its teak carvings on the pillars and gateways.... Cultivated jade trees, with leaves like precious stones, overflowed the dragon pots. On the walls, long silk scrolls of calligraphy sang out to those patrons who could read them. It was a nostalgic replica of an old-fashioned chinese teahouse, which accounted for its popularity not only amongst its homesick chinese clientele but also outsiders who came looking for oriental exotica. (S. Lee 32)

Disappearing Moon's ambience, it seems, utilizes a whole semiotics, what Raymond Williams calls "a structure of feeling." It immerses us into a sea of culture, divides us into those in the know and those who can only respond to it as "exotica." I would suggest that Disappearing Moon as an iconic representation of this semiotics adds to the text's emphasis on rendering the autonomy and uniqueness of a culture.

Lee's experimentation with English idiom and syntax, however, was not looked upon kindly by many of her reviewers. The reviewer for *Canadian Literature* suggested that "the use of these registers of speech ... may trouble the reader. For instance, Sky Lee has opted for a kind of literal translation when her characters speak Cantonese, so that, although she is able to convey the character of colloquial Cantonese and its expressions, her characters' speech verges on pidgin" (Mostow 175). *Books in Canada*'s reviewer was similarly disapproving: "The prose is too frequently un-idiomatic and it is modified into the ground.... I think Lee's editors must take responsibility for what's gone wrong here. Lee has an important, interesting story to tell, and the writing faults erect a substantial barrier between the reader and the tale" (Draper 49). Such criticisms have also been made of other minority Canadian writers who include non-English words in their text. Here is *Fiddlehead*'s reviewer on Rohinton Mistry's *Swimming Lessons and Other Stories from Firozsha Baag*:

The attractive new design, however, cannot mask the fact that the book
... is flawed. Michael Darling, writing in *The Macmillan Anthology*, has
correctly noted that Mistry has, at times, a poor sense of diction, with
numerous non-English words used in an effort to create local colour....
The overuse, in Mistry's case, of unfamiliar Indian words slows down
the speed of the prose, giving sentences and whole paragraphs a
clumsy, jerky flow: the diction suffocates the Western reader. (Holmes
111)

Canadian critics are not alone, however, in responding in this negative way
to bilingual texts. Many "postcolonial" writers have been criticized for mixing
English and their native tongue, the implication being that the untranslated
words create a barrier between the reader and the text.

I am suggesting here that bilingual and bicultural texts demand a different
kind of response from their readers. They demand that we recognize the reality
of a multilingual, multicultural earth as well as the coming together of people
from different linguistic and cultural backgrounds. (AT&T has obviously
recognized this and is making money by providing the services of translators in
"just about every language from Arabic to Yoruba"). While many of us have
gained competence in English, for a variety of reasons often linked to
colonialism and migration due to economic and political imperatives, we have
also persisted in retaining our heritage cultures despite the tremendous
pressures to assimilate. Sky Lee's text, for instance, asserts the vitality of ongoing
connections with one's ancestral links. The narrator of *Disappearing Moon Cafe*,
writing in 1986, knows the language, spends time studying in China and
believes in the efficacy of Chinese dietary and herbal traditions. The text in some
sense becomes a metonymic representation of Chinese-Canadian culture.

What, then, can readers not familiar with the cultural universe of the text
do? I suggest that they ask. Information is all around us. For instance, a
student of mine gave a seminar on Rohinton Mistry's *Such a Long Journey* by
distributing a glossary of all the non-English words used in the text. She had
asked the assistance of her South Asian neighbour to translate them. In my
seeking out Lien on e-mail and Isla's seeking out her neighbour in person, the
text leaves the printed page to join our day-to-day oral culture and to
become embellished with further narrations. Such a hermeneutic, I believe, is
far more democratic than the expert-dominated literary criticism of the past,
where the trained critic spoke as authority. This hermeneutic is built on the
premise that knowledge needed to decode the text is dispersed in the social
environment the reader lives in and can be had through communicating with
friends, colleagues and neighbours.

Sometimes some aspects of the text are decoded later rather than sooner.
For instance, one might not find out that 1414 Osler Street, the address where
Janet Smith was killed and where Morgan Wong lives in the narrative present,
has a negative meaning for the Chinese – unless one were aware of an

interview Lee gave the *Vancouver Sun*: "The number 1414 in Lee's ancestral village means *yit-say yit-say*, roughly translated as 'death at once, death at once.'" Therefore, "no Chinese in their right mind would buy a house with that address."

I am familiar with the kind of games South Asian writers like Salman Rushdie or Rohinton Mistry or M.G. Vassanji play by utilizing linguistic code-switching. I "get" their jokes because I am fortunate enough to know the languages they are drawing on. I need help, however, when I read texts like *Disappearing Moon Cafe* or Farida Karodia's *Daughters of Twilight* that insert lexical units from languages I am not familiar with. And I have found that one can often get help when one seeks it.

In the classroom, I begin by saying that the minority Canadian texts we study situate us either as "cultural insiders" or "cultural outsiders." I insist that both positions have their advantages and disadvantages on the one hand, and on the other hand that they are fluid. If I am a "cultural insider" reading a South Asian-Canadian text, I lose that position when I read a Native Canadian or a Chinese-Canadian, or, for that matter, an Anglo Canadian text. I insist that one can ask interesting questions from both reading positions. And when several readers, both outsiders and insiders, come together in the classroom as a reading community, some of the most rewarding interchanges happen, as outlined in my first anecdote.

Anecdote Three

Basil Johnston's *Indian School Days* inscribes huge chunks of Ojibway (I presume) in its usage of English. His liberal use of Ojibway to report the speech of Native children at the residential school materializes for us the trauma these children underwent when, wrenched from the love and security of their homes, they were thrown suddenly into a sea of English-speaking strangers. Johnston's decision to transcribe whole sentences in incomprehensible (to us) Ojibway puts the shoe, figuratively speaking, on the other foot. It is also a declaration of cultural survival against insurmountable odds.

This time I had no one in my immediate community I could draw on to explain to me the intricacies of Ojibway. I must for the present stay satisfied with the gaps in my knowledge of the text. Those gaps themselves, however, are instructive. The interruption of English by Ojibway forces us to take cognizance of the colonial nature of the Canadian state, in that no Native language (except in the Northwest Territories) enjoys the status of "official" language in Canada. We are also forced to ponder the fact that Johnston's fluency in English was forced on him, while we did not have to undergo a forced immersion in Ojibway.

Besides discussing the political and textual significance of language itself, we wrestle with names and concepts such as "Manitoulin." I refer to Johnston's other writings to point out to the class that "Manitoulin" is not to be translated as equivalent to the Christian God. Having myself learned English the hard way, and as someone who is still not sure about some of her pronunciations, I am particularly fond of the following passage, one that wonderfully captures the oddities of English sounds and grammar:

> The tribal language operated quite well without the letters "r," "l," "f," "v," "x" and "th." Thus when the boys attempted these strange sounds they stuttered and muttered and made substitutions. "Xavier" became "Zubyeah"; "never" became "neber"; "Virginia" became "Bayzhinee"; "father" became "fauder"; "Cameron" became "camel"; "three" and "through" were pronounced "tree" and "true." In addition we all had some trouble with the English practice of separating the pronouns "he" and "she" in speech. It was hard to get away from tribal syntax in which "he" or "she" was embodied in the word and structure. (Johnston 9-10)

It is salutary for me and the class to think about the arbitrariness of gender construction and how cultures may construct gender differently. This point has provoked some very productive discussion when those of us with "ethnic" names discuss how our names often confuse "Canadians" who cannot tell our gender when they see our name on paper.

Indian School Days also makes visible for us the perils of translation. The following exchange between the two languages and their speakers, mediated by Johnston as a cultural go-between, is a good example of the encounters portrayed in the text. Clarence has run away from the residential school and Father Hawkins goes to the reserve with other schoolboys who can serve as translators:

> From Massey, Father Hawkins drove downstream along the Spanish River road some four miles or so before he stopped.
>
> "That's the Abitung house," he said, pointing to a log house on the opposite shore. Smoke was wafting from the chimney. "I want you to call Mr. Abitung or whoever's home. Tell them that they must hand over Clarence. Call them first, and I'll tell you what to say."
>
> We all got out of the car and stood on the bank of the river facing the Abitung residence, which apart from the wisp of smoke curling from the chimney, appeared uninhabited.
>
> "You can call now."
>
> "Heeey! Heeey! Heeey!" we all called.
>
> A man came out of the house.
>
> "Waeginaen baebau-nindoyaek?"
>
> "He says, 'What do you want?'" I told Father Hawkins, not telling him that from the tone of the man's voice he meant, "What the hell do you want?"
>
> "Ask him if he's Clarence's father."
>
> "Keen nah Clarence ossun?"
>
> "Ahneen gayae igoh nauh, ahneen dush?"
>
> "Yes. He wants to know why."

"Tell him I'm Father Hawkins and that I'm here to fetch Clarence."

I relayed the message to Mr. Abitung, who replied that he didn't give a damn who the priest was and that he wasn't about to surrender his son to Spanish again. (Johnston 105-6)

This exchange across the river wonderfully encapsulates the distrust and unequal power relations between the colonizer and the colonized, with the river as a perfect metaphor for the barrier between the two people. As readers we enjoy the trick played on Father Hawkins by the translator. And yet, it also reminds us of the daily reality of non-native speakers of English who must have esoteric legal and medical texts translated for them by translators who are not always very good or reliable.

Conclusion

Ethnic minority texts inform their readers, through the presence of other languages as well as through a whole repertoire of cultural signs, about the multicultural and multilingual nature of Canadian society. The texts affirm and celebrate the cultures they represent. It is unfortunate not only that the stylistic and structural aspects of these texts have not been noticed or understood, but also that they have been negatively received.

I believe that by foregrounding the heritage language for the purpose of code-switching, that is, for signifying heightened emotions, for expressing familial relationships for which English has no words, and for conveying culturally shared memories and meanings that once again have no English equivalents – these texts help us see how ethnicity, language, and culture are intertwined. By encountering what is unfamiliar to us, we may become aware that what we assume as normal within our cultural boundaries may appear unfamiliar to someone from another cultural group. Reading and teaching these texts may, in that case, lead to empathy and tolerance.

We live in a sea of Anglo conformity while paying lip service to the ideal of multiculturalism. Immigrants are constantly exhorted to become "Canadian." Such monoculturalism can lead to attitudes like the one described in the following anecdote by John Edwards in his book *Multilingualism*: "Recently, a school superintendent in Arkansas refused a request to have foreign languages taught at the secondary level. He said, 'If English was good enough for Jesus, it's good enough for you'" (204). Although Edwards thinks that the story may be apocryphal, the fact is that such arrogance and smugness about one's own culture are not hard to find. The belief in the universality of the English-language literary canon is only another manifestation of the same arrogance.

Certainly, bilingual and bicultural texts are not "universal" insofar as they seem to refuse transparent access. Unlike texts written strictly in English, they tease us with gaps in our comprehension. I have proposed that these gaps demand a different kind of hermeneutic effort from the reader than the one accorded to the canonical texts. Second, the linguistic texture of such works is closer to our lived experience of a multicultural and multilingual world where the sounds and rhythms of other languages routinely reach us without our fully decoding them.

I would like to close with the words of the Sri Lankan-Australian novelist Yasmine Gooneratne:

> It is difficult to write "between cultures," yet whether I like it or not, my experience of life seems to have given me that occupation. Luckily, knowledge of more than one language adds an edge to the pleasure of writing, since one can use linguistic puns purely for one's own pleasure. Some people may grasp them, some surely won't, but maybe there is a blessed reader somewhere who grasps both meanings. I imagine this is a modern equivalent for the eighteenth-century poetic pun....

It is no secret that a very large number of books in English today are being written by writers with backgrounds similar to Gooneratne. And they enjoy hopping and skipping between languages. I believe that reading these books can be a very stimulating and enjoyable experience for all readers, provided we are willing to go hunting for the meaning.

NOTES
I would like to thank my students Elaine Asare, Dania Gopaulsingh, and Jennel Mohamed for the discussion on "buljol." Isla Macpherson, by preparing a glossary of the Indian words in Rohinton Mistry's Such a Long Journey, opened up a whole new dimension of the text for me and the class. My heartfelt thanks to Lien Chao and Yasmine Gooneratne for their instructive correspondence on e-mail.

MAÏR VERTHUY

Pan Bouyoucas: le principe des vases communicants ou de la nécessité de «sortir de l'ethnicité[1]»

En 1994, dans le cadre d'un colloque[2] sur l'écriture des femmes migrantes en français en France et au Canada, une Québécoise «pure laine», Claudine Potvin, a proposé sa lecture de *La Québécoite* de Régine Robin[3]. Le roman de Robin fait peser sur Montréal, ses différents quartiers, ses différentes sociétés, un regard d'immigrante, d'immigrée française. À l'époque de sa publication, les très rares comptes rendus du livre avaient surtout été l'œuvre d'autres immigrants qui partageaient pour l'essentiel son point de vue. Tout à coup, plusieurs années plus tard, grâce à une «souche[4]», à la première image se superpose celle de la personne regardée, en train d'observer à la fois l'observatrice et ses observations. La Québécoise de souche ne reconnaît nullement son Montréal dans les descriptions de Robin; celle-ci se trouve abasourdie par la lecture que fait Potvin de son œuvre.

Il est tentant de voir dans cette rencontre entre les deux perspectives qui ne se reconnaissent pas une réminiscence aujourd'hui actualisée des *Deux Solitudes*[5] de Hugh MacLennan. L'on se souviendra que, dans ce roman-phare, écrit à l'issue de la Deuxième guerre mondiale, l'incompréhension ou l'incommunication (pour employer un néologisme) entre divers francophones et anglophones québécois aboutissent à la tragédie. Il nous semble nécessaire aujourd'hui de redéfinir, de raffiner ce concept. Les deux solitudes du Québec seraient ainsi, à l'heure qu'il est, composées moins des anglophones et francophones traditionnels que, d'un côté, des «souches» et, de l'autre, des «branches», et cela souvent mais pas toujours à l'intérieur de la même langue. En témoigne[6] le débat qui entoure la plaquette *L'arpenteur et le navigateur* de Monique La Rue et qui se trouve résumé dans une note de renvoi.

Cet échange ou l'absence d'échange réel que nous constatons au sein de ce débat semblent constituer une mise en abyme de la situation littéraire au Québec, bien que celle-ci évolue aujourd'hui. Malgré leur présence ancienne, les immigrants sont souvent remarquablement absents du roman des «souches[7].» Le roman des «branches», de son côté, évite non moins souvent toute vraie mise en scène de la population francophone majoritaire, se concentrant plutôt sur le milieu «culturel» dont était ou est issu l'auteur. Le

Québec n'aurait-il évité le rouleau compresseur de l'assimilation à la française que pour mieux s'installer dans ce que Robin appelle «le repli ethnique» propre à l'Amérique du Nord?

Il existe cependant quelques auteurs immigrants qui traduisent dans leurs écrits une version plus positive de la réalité surtout montréalaise, version dans laquelle, si les problèmes de communication et d'intégration ne connaissent pas tous et nécessairement une fin heureuse, la problématique existe et la possibilité d'une entente future se fait jour. La plupart de ces auteurs sont encore fort jeunes; l'on pense, par exemple, à la génération de Stanley Péan ou encore de Nadine Ltaif. mais la voie a été ouverte par une autre génération, dont un auteur qui publie au Québec depuis un peu plus de vingt ans déjà. C'est sur sa vision, son écriture, que je voudrais revenir ici.

Pan Bouyoucas, né au Liban de parents grecs, à la fin de la Deuxième Guerre mondiale, est arrivé au Québec vers l'âge de quatorze ans. Refoulé, à cause de sa religion, par l'école francophone et catholique romaine malgré ses études antérieures en français au Liban, il s'initie à son pays d'accueil par le biais du milieu anglophone. Il reste cependant fort attaché au français; presque tous ses écrits (romans, nouvelles, scénarii de film, pièces de théâtre[8]) sont rédigés dans cette langue. Tout en demeurant fidèle à une certaine culture grecque et à son milieu d'origine, il choisira néanmoins, après un certain nombre de péripéties, de ne pas s'y enfermer, d'aller vers le milieu des francophones de souche. Citons à titre d'exemple sa participation avec d'autres écrivains à la mise sur pied des Éditions Quinze.

Ces détails ont pour but de mieux situer l'engagement de cet auteur. Qu'en est-il de la vision qui se dégage de ses romans[9], dont deux, *Le dernier souffle* et *Une bataille d'Amérique*, remontent aux années 70 et dont les deux autres, *L'humoriste et l'assassin* et *La vengeance d'un père*, sont de facture très récente? Quelles conclusions peut-on tirer des textes de cet écrivain qui se veut Québécois à part entière[10], mais avec sa différence? Peut-on dans son cas parler de deux solitudes?

Devant l'interruption d'une vingtaine d'années à l'intérieur de sa production romanesque, il convient sans doute de commencer par étudier les deux périodes séparément. Cette approche permettrait dans un premier temps de relever les caractéristiques communes à chaque période, s'il y en a, et dans un deuxième temps de constater l'absence ou la présence relatives d'un changement d'optique chez l'auteur, toujours dans la perspective des deux solitudes éventuelles.

Alors qu'une première lecture encourage à conclure que l'action de ses quatre romans se passe à Montréal, cette affirmation demande à être nuancée dans le cas du premier. Celui-ci, entièrement onirique, narré à la troisième personne, met en scène les derniers instants d'un suicidé. Il s'agit d'un Canadien d'origine grecque, un marchand de poissons, qui, malgré sa réussite pécuniaire à Montréal, ne supporte pas l'isolement affectif qui est le sien et qui décide de mettre fin à ses jours. Ce mourant se trouve donc à Montréal mais le roman est entièrement consacré à la vision onirique de la Grèce fictive, atemporelle, qui occupe les ultimes secondes de la pensée de Lucas[11].

Dans sa société d'adoption où évoluent des personnages d'origine diverse
(japonais, italiens, j'en passe...), le paraître semble primer, particulièrement
chez les femmes immigrantes, qui souhaitent, peut-être pour se consoler de
leur exil, démontrer qu'il leur a réussi:

> Son associé, Stavro S., qui ne répondait plus qu'au nom de Steve, se
> moquait surtout de ses chemises blanches au col étroit et serré comme
> les hommes avaient l'habitude de les porter l'année où il les avait
> achetées. [...] mais à regarder Stavro, c'était Lucas qui avait envie de rire
> car il ressemblait à un perroquet tropical empaillé et oublié dans un
> marché de poissons parmi les pieuvres congelées et les huîtres crottées.
> Lucas soupçonnait madame S. d'être l'instigatrice de cet accoutrement
> théâtral de chemises, de cravates et d'habits truculents. (p. 10)

Surtout, la nouvelle société serait axée sur des valeurs purement
matérielles, situation qui aboutit au désespoir de Lucas qui, ayant tout sacrifié
à la poursuite de cette forme de réussite, constate en fin de compte que sa
victoire est creuse: «et ce magasin qui lui avait rongé tous les rêves et tous les
espoirs, pour ne le laisser que propriétaire d'une maison dont il ne voulait
pas, munie d'un garage large où, la veille au soir, il avait invité la mort...» (p.
187).

Le deuxième roman, *Une bataille d'Amérique*, est plus ambigu. Cette fois,
malgré quelques retours en arrière, l'action réelle se passe pour l'essentiel à
Montréal. Au commencement, la réussite financière semble loin; le livre met
en scène un jeune couple désœuvré: Nicolas, le narrateur, apprenti-écrivain
réduit à s'inscrire au Bien-être social; Camille, elle, graphiste sans emploi. Ils
ont un enfant.

Nicolas, d'origine grecque, bien qu'il se présente comme ayant vécu enfant
en Égypte, connaît plusieurs déchirements. Le premier oppose les valeurs et
l'ethnocentrisme de ses parents à son désir de s'ouvrir au monde, ce dont
témoigne son attachement à Camille. Le deuxième déchirement oppose son
désir et son besoin d'écrire à la nécessité de faire vivre sa petite famille et
donc à Camille. Le roman sera consacré à la résolution éventuelle de ces deux
problèmes.

Encore une fois, Bouyoucas nous propose le portrait d'une population aux
origines très diverses, qui ne se caractérise pas nécessairement par son
ouverture aux autres. Les enfants anglophones ne souhaitent pas apprendre
le français; leurs mères veulent qu'ils l'apprennent mais avec un accent
français de France. Par ailleurs, la population francophone majoritaire fait
souvent preuve dans le roman de xénophobie («Si vous n'aimez pas ça,
retournez chez vous, m'a-t-on déjà dit» p. 128), mais les immigrés ne sont pas
exempts de toute responsabilité car ils se replient souvent sur eux-mêmes.
Ainsi à Camille, Québécoise de souche, la belle-mère aurait préféré une bru
grecque. Les préjugés, nous indique Bouyoucas, ne sont pas à sens unique
même si, comme dans le débat dont il a été question au début de ce texte, le
pouvoir est inégalement partagé.

Aux autres malheurs de Nicolas viennent s'ajouter l'hiver (toujours la neige et le froid[12]) et la difficulté que connaissent les immigrés, grecs en l'occurrence, à trouver du travail. Nicolas attire peu d'élèves à qui donner des leçons de français. Malgré sa formation artistique, son meilleur ami, Théo, accepte d'être veilleur de nuit dans un hôtel: «Je veux me ramasser assez d'argent pour aller chercher fortune ailleurs. Ça fait presque quatre ans que je suis ici et j'arrive pas à trouver d'emploi ni comme acteur, ni comme metteur en scène. Ah! si seulement je parlais l'anglais !» (p. 55). Théo finit par se suicider.

Le sort de Nicolas ne sera pas nécessairement plus heureux même si ses deux problèmes trouvent leur résolution en même temps. Après une dispute, lui et Camille, de nouveau enceinte, se réconcilient; il accepte d'aller travailler pour son beau-père québécois qui a donc fini par ouvrir son cœur et sa porte à cet immigré. Les parents de Nicolas, heureux de constater que l'avenir de leur fils est assuré, ouvrent également leur cœur et leur porte à leur belle-fille. Tout est bien qui finit bien.

Nicolas cependant, pris enfin au piège de la réussite pécuniaire, privé de l'appui de sa famille qui épouse soudainement les valeurs matérielles, voit s'éloigner de lui toute possibilité d'une vie consacrée à l'écriture. Dans la dernière scène, quelque peu surréelle, il fait état de la perte d'une couille:

J'ai défait ma braguette [...] J'ai pris mes couilles dans une main pour mieux les replacer [...] Mais comme je les massais, celle de gauche s'est détachée et est tombée à mes pieds, pour rouler ensuite sur le plancher immaculé (...) Là [...] elle s'est ouverte en deux, comme si un couteau bien effilé l'avait tranchée, d'un coup. J'ai regardé ma couille droite. Elle semblait bien attachée [...] je suis reparti [...] laissant mon testicule par terre, même s'il n'est pas très poli de laisser traîner une couille sur le plancher des toilettes publiques. (p. 213)

Cette image constitue un *leitmotiv* à l'intérieur de ce roman. Nicolas affirme son droit de demander l'aide du Bien-être social afin de pouvoir encore travailler chez lui, de se consacrer à la littérature: «Est-on en quelque sorte *émasculé* si on reste chez soi, moins digne de sa raison d'être? Que nous restera-t-il alors si ce n'est qu'un misérable souffle de vie?» (C'est nous qui soulignons.) Quelques pages plus loin, dans une scène irréelle et onirique, il se fait dire par le préposé au bureau du Bien-être, avant que celui-ci ne fasse clouer les couilles de Nicolas à une chaise et coupe son pénis en deux: «C'est le règlement. Si vous voulez l'argent, il faut sacrifier quelque chose» (p. 60).

Toute l'opposition entre Nicolas et son entourage se trouve concentrée dans ce thème. Pour la société dans laquelle il se trouve, se consacrer à l'écriture, à la culture, c'est être moins qu'un homme; elle ne lui doit donc rien, le punit même de vouloir vivre ainsi. Pour Nicolas en revanche, être moins qu'un homme, c'est céder à la pression sociale, renoncer à l'écriture pour travailler à l'extérieur. Le voilà donc à la fin du livre émasculé, châtré, incapable dorénavant de re/produire.

Dans ces deux premiers romans, un gouffre sépare les «souches» des «branches.» Le matérialisme qui caractériserait la société d'accueil vient heurter les sensibilités culturelles des nouveaux venus, la réussite pécuniaire qui accompagne parfois l'exil se payant très cher, trop cher, nous disent les personnages.

Si le Québec, à l'intérieur de l'Amérique du Nord, présente dans ces livres un visage inculte, il faut s'interroger sur les valeurs que véhiculent les immigrés qui y évoluent – avant évidemment d'être «corrompus», comme les parents de Nicolas, par exemple, par le milieu ambiant.

Ces personnages sont pour l'essentiel porteurs d'un passé culturel ancien, celui qui se place à l'origine de la majeure partie de la civilisation occidentale, l'histoire et la mythologie gréco-méditerranéennes, avec quelques avatars plus récents. Devant ce qui paraît être l'omniprésence de valeurs monétaires, matérielles, Bouyoucas fait valoir ce monde antique dont il ne trouve pas toujours l'écho au Québec mais dont la pensée imprègne même les Grecs et d'autres Méditerranéens de condition modeste.

Lucas, le marchand de poisson suicidaire, par exemple, avait toujours caressé le rêve d'imiter un jour Schliemann[13], ce héros de son enfance. Persuadé que les colonnes d'Hercule avait jadis été érigées sur le rocher de Gibraltar, il espérait accumuler assez d'argent pour un jour pratiquer des fouilles et les ressortir au soleil (p. 9.) Alors qu'il dialogue avec un simple pêcheur arabe, celui-ci lui dit en riant: «Sacré Lucas [...] Ma fille avait bien raison quand elle m'a dit que tu ne vis que de rêve et que ton imagination ferait pâlir *Homère* lui-même» et il continue: «Tiens, moi aussi, quand j'étais jeune, j'ambitionnais. Je rêvais; je bâtissais et démolissais à ma guise, comme cela me prenait. Je m'étais juré de vivre ma vie amplement, d'user mon corps jusqu'à l'os et de ne rien laisser à *Charon*» (p. 63). (C'est nous qui soulignons.)

Le roman suivant, *Une bataille d'Amérique*, se présente sous le signe de Constantin Cavafy (Cavafis dans son orthographe française), célèbre poète néo-grec originaire d'Alexandrie, né en 1863, mort en 1933. Après une allusion homérique, aux Sirènes cette fois, Nicolas cite des vers de Cavafy qui traduisent bien l'angoisse qu'il ressent devant la page qui reste désespérément blanche, devant la léthargie qui le consume, le sentiment de perdre son temps:

Tu as dit: J'irai vers une autre terre, vers une autre mer.
Je trouverai bien une autre ville préférable à celle-ci où chacun de mes efforts est condamné d'avance, et où mon cœur est enseveli comme un mort.
Jusqu'à quand mon esprit restera-t-il dans le marasme?
Où que je tourne les yeux, où que je regarde, je n'aperçois ici que les ruines calcinées de ma vie, que durant tant d'années j'ai gâchée et gaspillée. (p. 23)

Incapable de poursuivre la citation, il évoque d'autres événements marquants – et tragiques – de l'histoire égyptienne ou plutôt de celle d'Alexandrie, ville fondée au 3ᵉ siècle avant Jésus-Christ et très longtemps le plus brillant centre de l'hellénisme et de la tradition intellectuelle, possédant une bibliothèque contenant 700 000 manuscrits dont la disparition dans un incendie priva le monde d'innombrables textes anciens: «J'essaie de me rappeler la suite du poème de Cavafy mais en vain. Est-il allé, lui aussi, rejoindre le Phare et le Musée, la Bibliothèque et la tombe de Cléopâtre?» (p. 23).

Ces quelques citations suffisent pour indiquer combien les personnages immigrés sont conscients d'être issus d'un espace historico-culturel ou vertical qui ne trouve pas son pendant dans le Nouveau Monde, davantage caractérisé par un espace géographique ou horizontal.

Mais la culture qui ne se conjugue pas à ses seules composantes intellectuelles est à prendre dans toutes les acceptions du mot. L'opposition en question se voit confirmer par divers autres éléments de l'univers de Bouyoucas, ne serait-ce qu'au niveau culinaire[13]!

Dans ces livres, l'on met l'accent sur l'absence de chaleur, de couleurs et de parfums au Québec où il semble constamment neiger («banlieue du Labrador» dit Nicolas, *Une bataille d'Amérique*, p. 11): «Demain les journaux raconteront avec saveur les faits et méfaits de l'hiver canadien, assaisonnant leurs pages de quelques photos bien à propos : embouteillages monstres, voitures ensevelies, personnes suffocant dans leurs limousines aux vitres et aux portières coincées, vieillards enterrés, gelés ou morts d'apoplexie à quelques pas de leur demeure» (p. 10).

Le pays délaissé, en revanche, même frappé par la misère («J'en ai assez de la misère et du soleil, de la pauvreté et du beau temps», *Le dernier souffle*, p. 111), se caractérise par des couleurs vives, un soleil éclatant: «Il but encore et son regard s'arrêta pour un bref instant au soleil, ce grand œil magnanime et plein d'amour qui avait régné sur son enfance, tout comme la mer» (p. 18), des odeurs de rose acacia, de jasmin aigre, de brise saline.

Similairement, à la solitude nord-américaine s'oppose la vie en plein air, les rencontres au café et ainsi de suite:

... toutefois j'ai passé la soirée à savourer de vieux souvenirs [...] surtout des scènes d'Alexandrie [...] Je me suis retrouvé devant la fenêtre de ma chambre, regardant le *cafénion* d'en face où Abu-Fouad se balançait [...] Des amis grecs lui payaient un verre d'*ouzo* que le cafetier lui apportait sur un plateau suspendu par trois chaînes dont le ballottement ne renversait pas une seule goutte [...] Le *cafénion* retentissait d'éclats de voix et de rires, du bruit sec des jetons contre les tables de trictrac et du glouglou onctueux de l'eau encore claire dans les narguilés. La clientèle était la même depuis dix, vingt, trente ans. Des Arabes et des Grecs, des Italiens et des Juifs, dans cette ville aux cinq races et aux cinq religions, certains portant leurs canotiers blancs avec élégance, d'autres leurs fez rouges avec nonchalance. (*Une bataille d'Amérique*, pp. 10 et 13)

Faute d'accueil, faute de compréhension, il en résulte que les personnages, comme l'indique cet extrait, sont largement tournés vers le passé, réel ou fictif. Nous avons vu que le premier roman se compose essentiellement d'une séquence onirique où Lucas revisite sur le mode surréel une Grèce au moins partiellement imaginaire. Mais la pensée de Nicolas se nourrit aussi d'un passé à la fois personnel (le *cafénion*, par exemple) et collectif (les allusions mythologiques.) Le recours au retour en arrière, assez fréquent dans ce deuxième roman, se justifie essentiellement dans ce contexte: «J'avais douze ans...» (p. 97); «Je faisais semblant de ne pas écouter, de ne rien comprendre. J'avais onze ans, peut-être dix, et ça passait bien...» (p. 107). Il s'agit moins de comprendre l'action au présent que de saisir toute la détresse de Nicolas pour qui vivre au passé constitue une consolation dans le désert qu'il croit vivre dans son quotidien montréalais.

Le portrait que nous brosse Bouyoucas de la vie immigrante à Montréal, pour ne pas être entièrement catastrophique, n'est pas particulièrement positif. Les deux solitudes paraissent insurmontables; séparées par une espèce de *no man's land*, branches et souches se regardent comme autant de chiens de faïence. Qu'en est-il alors des deux autres romans? La vision du monde qui s'en dégage est-elle plus optimiste? Le gouffre se comble-t-il?

Vingt ans se sont écoulés entre les deuxième et troisième romans. Il importe de signaler que dans celui-ci, *L'humoriste et l'assassin*, Bouyoucas franchit le pas, si l'on peut dire. Son personnage central est un Québécois de souche qui évolue tout à fait naturellement dans un Montréal de plus en plus multiculturel. Philippe Blais, humoriste québécois, reçoit une menace de mort; il dispose de soixante-douze heures pour la déjouer. Lecteurs et lectrices assisteront à toutes les démarches qu'il entreprendra durant cette période, tant en ville qu'à la campagne, tant dans les milieux intellectuels que dans celui des motards. La population diverse inclut cette fois-ci, en plus des Grecs (dont sa maîtresse, Despina, et le mari de celle-ci, Kosta, le propriétaire de l'immeuble qu'habite Blais) et Italiens traditionnels, des Juifs hassidim, des Latino-américains, des Sri-Lankais, des Arméniens et un Noir dont nous ne savons jamais s'il est de vieille souche québécoise ou d'arrivée récente.

Il n'existe cependant aucun lien organique entre la tension qui règne dans le roman, qui connaît une fin relativement heureuse, entre la problématique donc de celui-ci et une quelconque origine autre de l'un ou de plusieurs des personnages. Il s'agit tout simplement d'un roman, dont l'action se déroule dans une ville moderne, en l'occurrence Montréal, avec une population mixte. L'auteur se sent suffisamment intégré à la population majoritaire pour entreprendre de mettre en scène des personnages divers dont certains sont immigrés, d'autres pas. Dans la perspective que l'on cherche à développer ici, ce roman constitue un grand pas en avant, ouvre de nouvelles perspectives pour la littérature – et la société – francophone du Québec.

Le dernier roman à l'étude, *La vengeance d'un père*, publié au printemps 1997, prolonge, au moins partiellement, cette même veine. Il met en scène, de façon égale, deux pères de famille, l'un immigré grec, l'autre Québécois de souche. Bouyoucas continue, c'est évident, de se sentir libre de présenter indifféremment les pensées les plus intimes, les joies et les souffrances de ces deux personnages qui représentent deux mondes souvent opposés. Sa réussite, cependant, semble rester individuelle car l'univers de son roman présente une certaine contradiction avec celui de l'auteur.

Du côté «grec», nous sommes confrontés à une famille composée de la grand-mère, du père et de la mère, de trois enfants qui sont de jeunes adultes. Les trois jeunes fréquentent aussi bien des Québécois de souche que d'autres enfants d'immigrants. À la fin du roman, cependant, la fille aînée s'est suicidée; le fils qu'insupportent tous les jours davantage les débats autour du séparatisme, part pour les États-Unis; la troisième abandonne ses études. Le père sombre dans la démence.

Du côté «québécois», nous trouvons une famille plus dysfonctionnelle déjà au départ. Les parents sont divorcés, la mère étant alcoolique. Ils ont une seule fille dont il faut relever qu'elle fréquente le même milieu que les jeunes Grecs. À la fin du roman, elle est quadriplégique. Le malheur est sinon partagé au moins égal. De part et d'autre, l'avenir est gravement compromis.

La plupart de ces drames résultent de l'incompréhension entre les deux milieux. Au commencement du roman, la fille aînée de l'immigrant grec est agressée par un inconnu. L'on confie l'enquête au Québécois de souche. Interviennent ensuite tous les préjugés de part et d'autre, toutes les manipulations journalistiques et politiques de part et d'autre, qui ont pour résultat la destruction des deux familles et surtout de la génération à venir, l'avenir du Québec. C'est une belle mise en garde.

En 1997 comme en 1975, force nous est alors de conclure qu'il ne fait pas toujours bon être immigrant au Québec. La réussite matérielle accompagnerait certes ce déplacement mais le prix à payer peut demeurer lourd: le suicide, la perte au moins partielle de la virilité, la démence. La famille est fragilisée dans ce monde où les nouveaux venus sont frappés d'exclusion, en partie à cause de la méfiance exprimée à leur égard par la société dite d'accueil, en partie à cause de leur propre ignorance qui les rend sujets à manipulation. Tous, de part et d'autre, portent une lourde responsabilité.

Cela étant, comme il a été constaté plus haut, dans l'univers romanesque de Bouyoucas cette situation n'est pas non plus sans conséquences pour la société de souche. Là réside peut-être l'une des grandes différences entre les deux périodes de son écriture. Au départ, dans son univers, les différentes communautés, qui pourtant se côtoient, peuvent agir isolément l'une de l'autre, comme dans autant de bulles renfermées sur elles-mêmes; dans la société actuelle, la multiplicité de bulles cède la place à une seule bulle, ou au moins à des vases communicants, où se joue le sort de tous. Ainsi dans *L'humoriste et l'assassin*, l'on nous brosse le portrait indifférencié des diverses communautés culturelles, et, dans *La vengeance d'un père*, nous constatons combien le destin des uns se répercute chez les autres. L'on peut déjà conclure alors à la présence d'un changement profond dans la perspective de l'auteur.

Il faut aussi constater, même si les images hivernales demeurent omniprésentes – l'action de *La vengeance d'un père* se déroulant, par exemple, à partir de la Saint-Sylvestre – que certaines facettes de l'opposition entre les deux mondes s'amenuisent, sans doute parce que les Québécois de souche auront largement adopté ou assimilé plusieurs caractéristiques des nouveaux citoyens.

Il est vrai que pour le Nouvel An, la famille grecque de *La vengeance d'un père*, mange selon la tradition: *mélomakaroua, kourabiédès, vassilopitta*... Mais Despina, la femme grecque de *L'humoriste et l'assassin*, ne prépare-t-elle pas régulièrement pour son amant québécois des assiettées de *spanokopitta* (des feuilletés aux épinards) qu'il mange avec gourmandise? Celui-ci se fait d'ailleurs inviter dans un restaurant grec par une amie québécoise, Renée, avec qui il consomme une bouteille de *retsina* (p. 193).

Nous pouvons également faire remarquer que, dans ces deux romans, les allusions à la culture classique, devenues rares, sont le fait des Québécois de souche. Le voisin de Yannis Fokas lui parle du complexe d'Œdipe; Philippe Blais se remémore son voyage en Grèce où il a visité les théâtres antiques, et s'interroge sur la permanence des situations mythico-historiques: «Ou ils vous enchaîneront à un rocher[15], ou ils vous feront boire de la ciguë»[16] (p. 66).

Mais plus importante encore est la remise en question du bien fondé de ces bagages. Dans une scène fantasmée, Despina, en qui il voit la fille de la déesse de la mémoire, Mnémosyne, lui annonce:

> Je ne suis pas comme les autres muses. C'est pour ça que Zeus m'a engendrée. Quand il s'est rendu compte de ce que mes sœurs inspiraient... Rien que Clio, la muse des historiens, à elle seule ... Ça coûte cher l'histoire. Il suffit de regarder le Liban, la Yougoslavie ... Et Melpo[17], qui perpétuait sur scène toutes ces horribles tragédies ! Alors mon père a dit :«Il nous faut une muse pour inspirer l'oubli. Nous l'appellerons Despo» (p. 117).

Et là l'on peut remarquer que c'est au Québécois de souche que l'on reproche son obsession du passé. Cette même remise en question s'accompagne aussi pour la première fois d'un refus de la culture méditerranéenne, du moins dans certains de ses aspects:

> Il revoit le Maghrébin et se rappelle un incident survenu récemment en Algérie où des hommes bien fiers d'avoir un pénis ont fait irruption dans une classe, ont saisi une fillette de dix ans et l'ont traînée dans la cour pour l'égorger devant tous les enfants, afin de leur signifier que les filles ne doivent pas aller à l'école. Il repense à Lambron, qui n'est pas moins que le candidat à la mairie d'une métropole de deux millions, qui traverse un parc sans garde du corps. Et pour la première fois depuis longtemps, il se sent bien de vivre au Québec. (p. 87)

Pour comble de l'ironie, nous apprenons que le père de Yannis, ce «héros» de la résistance grecque, n'avait été pour sa famille qu'une brute (p. 299). Tous les mythes s'écroulent.

Tout se passe comme si l'auteur reniait ou faisait renier à ses personnages les valeurs que véhiculent ceux des deux premiers romans. D'une part, certaines différences entre «souches» et «branches» commencent à s'estomper, d'autre part, la culture non seulement n'est plus l'apanage des seuls immigrés mais encore elle peut constituer un frein à la compréhension entre les peuples.

Ce reniement apparent peut évidemment se lire aussi de façon à prolonger la vision qu'offrent les premiers romans selon laquelle le Québec se distinguerait surtout par son absence de culture *historique*. Nous avons vu que l'auteur se «québécise» davantage dans sa deuxième période, qu'il met aujourd'hui en scène en grand nombre des personnages «pure laine.» Il n'est pas exclu de penser que pour Bouyoucas, consciemment ou inconsciemment, cette évolution entraîne un abandon progressif des thèmes antérieurs. Ainsi, en épousant plus étroitement la société dans laquelle il se trouve et qui se caractérise essentiellement par sa (post)modernité, il s'insère de plain-pied dans celle-ci. L'ex-femme de Philippe Blais chante dans des concerts rock, son fils encore à l'école rédige des articles sur la drogue; la fille de Yannis Fokas joue dans une troupe de théâtre québécoise; son fils compose de la musique pour la guitare. La Culture cède peut-être le pas à la culture. Sans jugement de valeur.

Pour résumer, il paraît évident que pour l'auteur, l'insertion des immigrés demeure difficile. L'opposition se joue peut-être à d'autres niveaux mais, en fin de compte, le prix à payer demeure élevé. Il nous rappelle néanmoins non seulement que les immigrés portent une part de responsabilité dans cette situation mais aussi que la société d'accueil souffre également de son incapacité de se renouveler en acceptant l'apport des nouveaux venus. Les deux solitudes se prolongent dans l'univers qu'il décrit, provoquant cette fois des effets néfastes de part et d'autre.

En revanche, en 1996 et 1997, contrairement à ce qui se passe en 1975, l'auteur assume pleinement son rôle, créant, comme nous l'avons déjà signalé, un univers où il peut se couler dans la peau tant des «pures laines» que des «impures»! Plus objectif au sujet du bagage culturel des immigrants, Bouyoucas se montre également plus ouvert à la modernité qui l'entoure et aux changements qui ont eu lieu.

Voilà aussi le Montréal multiculturel familier aux immigrants, apprécié d'eux, un Montréal qui figure peu ou pas du tout dans les écrits de la majorité des Québécois de souche. Si le but à atteindre est l'univers de Robin tel qu'il est décrit entre autres dans «Sortir de l'ethnicité», où l'on s'intègre en gardant sa spécificité, où, avec ceux qui sont déjà sur place, l'on contribue à la création d'un nouveau monde toujours en mouvance, Bouyoucas avance à grands pas et annonce ainsi une société et une littérature à venir où toutes et tous ont leur place.

Bouyoucas a fait la moitié du chemin, fait ce qu'il a pu, comme certains auteurs immigrants plus jeunes, pour combler sa part du fossé qui sépare les Québécois de souche des néo-Québécois. Il faut espérer maintenant qu'en face, des écrivains «pure laine» se montreront capables de se couler dans la tête et le cœur d'un père grec, pour mettre fin à la dichotomie qui continue de caractériser actuellement la majeure partie de la production littéraire du Québec.

NOTES

1. Cette expression est empruntée à l' article éponyme de Régine Robin.

2. Organisé par Lucie Lequin et moi-même, Université Concordia, mai 1994.

3. Lucie Lequin, Maïr Verthuy dir., *Multi-Culture, Multi-Écriture : la voix migrante au féminin en France et au Canada*, Paris, L'Harmattan, 1996.

4. L'expression «Québécois de souche» est communément employée; pour y répondre, l'écrivaine immigrée d'origine algérienne, Nadia Ghalem, pour caractériser les néo-Québécois, a eu recours à l'expression «les branches,» expression que j'ai adoptée.

5. Hugh MacLennan, *Two Solitudes* (*Deux Solitudes*), 1945. Une tentative sympathique et sensible de dépeindre les tensions et les différences à l'intérieur du Québec bien avant la Révolution tranquille à laquelle elles devaient aboutir.

6. Dans cette plaquette, version écrite d'une conférence prononcée au Centre d'études québécoises (CETUQ) de l'Université de Montréal, Monique La Rue fait parler un «ami» écrivain tout fictif à qui elle prête des propos xénophobes au sujet des écrivains immigrés, qui «remporteraient des prix littéraires», qui «représenteraient le Québec à l'étranger», qui «imposeraient à la littérature québécoise un visage nouveau et inacceptable». Elle aligne, bien sûr, ces arguments, qui correspondent, il faut le préciser, à une certaine réalité, pour mieux les réfuter ensuite, dans une très belle réflexion sur la nature même de la littérature. Nul doute que La Rue n'endossait aucunement les remarques désobligeantes de son «ami.» L'on peut évidemment s'étonner qu'un tel débat puisse encore avoir lieu en 1997 mais, le débat existant, La Rue est du côté des anges.

Cette plaquette a fait l'objet d'un compte rendu négatif par la directrice de la revue *La tribune juive*, Madame Ghila Sroka, immigrée d'origine marocaine, qui en a peut-être fait une lecture un peu hâtive. On peut le regretter; on peut aussi le comprendre. Mais le plus curieux dans cet incident, c'est ce qui en a résulté. Le brouhaha qui s'est ensuivi aurait pu émaner du fameux «ami.» Les uns après les autres, les gros canons de la littérature québécoise ont tiré à boulets rouges, l'expression n'est pas trop forte, sur Sroka: des personnalités tels que Réginald Martel, Pierre Nepveu, Jeanne Demers, Lise Bissonette et d'autres encore. Sans doute fallait-il rendre justice à l'auteure de la plaquette et rétablir la vérité du texte d'origine. Mais l'on s'étonne que l'on ait cru qu'il fallait à La Rue toute une armée pour la défendre alors que son texte parle pour elle. Le compte rendu en question, même virulent, même erroné, justifie difficilement que, dans ce qui pourrait ressembler à une curée, l'on remette tant de fois et avec tant de force les pendules à l'heure. Une fois, voire une fois par journal, voilà ce qui paraît plus que suffisant pour rétablir les faits.

Les collègues et, il faut le dire, les compatriotes de La Rue ont probablement été peinés, indignés même, par l'article de Sroka. Il est néanmoins surprenant que, dans ce milieu intellectuel, l'on n'ait pas voulu établir une certaine distance, chercher davantage à comprendre la raison d'être de ce qui paraissait être une si mauvaise lecture. Demers elle-même signale que les propos attribués par La Rue à son «ami» correspondent à une certaine réalité québécoise. Sroka a sans doute fait fausse route, mais il se présentait là une occasion à saisir: non pas comme Nepveu, pour expliquer que son Centre d'études québécoises a effectivement reçu quelques immigrants par ci par là; non pas comme Martel pour tout simplement dénoncer Sroka dans les pages de *La Presse*; non pas comme Demers pour lui imputer une éventuelle (vicieuse) tentative de désinformation; mais pour tendre la main vers une personne manifestement écorchée, pour jeter un pont entre les deux communautés, celle des personnes de souche, celle des immigrés. L'occasion fut manquée. Deux solitudes, en effet.

7. Dans sa thèse de doctorat, Lucie Lequin a montré que, dans la période qui a suivi la Deuxième Guerre mondiale, seules certaines auteures semblaient sensibles à la présence d'immigrants au Québec.

8. Dans un article publié dans *Le Devoir* le 30 janvier 1993, intitulé «Différemment "pure laine"», et dans lequel Gilbert David fait le compte rendu d'une pièce de Bouyoucas, *Le cerf-volant*, le critique fait allusion à «l'ignorance quasi totale [des publics francophones] de ce que vivaient parallèlement les autres communautés culturelles» et dit de la production en cours: «Une distribution prometteuse qui prend le risque d'une parole "métèque" et qui invite à visiter l'âme d'une communauté montréalaise que l'on côtoie sans pour autant la connaître vraiment.»

9. Nous avons choisi de parler des seuls romans, ses textes dramatiques et ses scénarii n'étant pas disponibles au grand public.

10. Poser cette question, c'est évidemment reprendre à l'envers le questionnement de La Rue.

11. Rappelons que l'auteur est né au Liban et non en Grèce. Le pays, tel que représenté ici, est donc doublement mythique ou fantasmé.

12. Lucie Lequin et Maïr Verthuy ont signalé ailleurs et à plusieurs reprises la persistance de cette image de froideur, au sens propre et au sens figuré, dans les écrits migrants; cf. en particulier: «L'écriture des femmes migrantes au Québec: l'hétérogénéité et la culture au féminin,» *La recherche littéraire au Québec: objets et méthodes*, Paris-Montréal, Presses universitaires de Vincennes, XYZ.

13. Heinrich Schliemann, 1822-1890, archéologue allemand, ayant entrepris, contre tout avis professionnel, des fouilles à Hissariik près de l'Hellespont dans le but de découvrir l'emplacement de Troie. Là, il mit à jour plusieurs niveaux d'occupation de cette ville, dont le septième (Troie VII) semble correspondre à la Troie des récits homériques.

14. Si les Québécois mangent, par exemple, des omelettes, du homard et de la tarte aux pommes, boivent même du vin, les immigrés, eux, gardent le souvenir autrement plus parfumé de leur cuisine propre, celle qu'ils ont dû abandonner ou celle qu'ils continuent de pratiquer en famille: agneau rôti, huile d'olive, feuilles de câpre, bouteilles de retsina et d'ouzo, etc. dans *Le dernier souffle*; menthe, oignons, moussaka, yogourt, fromage de chèvre, fèves foules inondées d'huile et de citron, langoustes d'Alexandrie, j'en passe, dans *Une bataille d'Amérique*.

15. Allusion à Prométhée, fils de Titan, responsable d'avoir dérobé le feu au Ciel pour l'apporter sur Terre et l'offrir aux hommes. Il fut attaché par Héphaïstos sur la plus haute cime du Caucase, où un vautour lui dévorait le foie qui ne cessait de repousser.

16. Allusion à Socrate, philosophe grec, à qui il fut reproché d'avoir corrompu la jeunesse par ses idées; condamné à mort, il but dignement sa coupe de ciguë.

17. Melpomené, muse de la tragédie.

CHRISTL VERDUYN

Perspectives critiques dans des productions littéraires migrantes au féminin, au Québec et au Canada

This essay emerges from my ongoing study of writing by women in Quebec and English Canada. For the past several years, my focus has been on work by writers of racial or ethnic minority group identification. The terminology is problematic, as noted in essays throughout this volume, but broadly speaking I am referring to writing by women whose identification – imposed or chosen – is with groups having minority status on the basis of race or ethnicity. The matter of choice and the categories "race," "ethnicity," minority status, gender, and class, all raise questions about the locations from which they are perceived. In this essay, I write as a reader of Quebec literature living outside the province, whose (North European) immigrant family experience did not include many of the realities recounted in the literature under study here, though it helped sensitize me to their significance. Writers of "minority" identification have been producing work that poses many challenges and questions. The issue that interests me here is an apparent difference in what I shall term "political edge" in two bodies of work, one written in French, the other in English.

From its headwaters in the politically inspired writing of Quebec's *Révolution tranquille* in the 1960s, through its interaction with French feminist writing of the 1970s, the work of Quebec women writers has manifested a political edge which has not always been as striking in the work of colleagues in English Canada. This is not to suggest English-Canadian women's writing is devoid of social critique and political protest! But texts such as Michèle Lalonde's *Speak White* (1974), Louky Bersianik's *The Euguélionne* (1976), Nicole Brossard's *L'Amer, ou le chapitre effrité* (1977), and France Théoret's *Bloody Mary* (1977) – to name but these – enjoined readers towards social engagement and political commentary. This project had impact for English-Canadian writers such as Daphne Marlatt and Gail Scott, who engaged in dialogue with Quebec women writers. In the late 1980s and early 1990s in English Canada, authors such as Nourbese Philip, Dionne Brand, Himani Bannerji, and Lee Maracle – again, to name only a few – drew readers' attention with sharp-edged, politically provocative works. Not only did they deal with issues of gender within Canadian experience, they articulated the need for attention to considerations of race or ethnicity as well as class and gender.

The first part of this essay offers sample works as a foundation for the question that I wish to probe further: is there an equivalent body of work amongst women writers of racial or ethnic minority identification in Quebec? And if so, what is its political character? This is the focus of the second part of my essay. A third and final section considers very briefly some sociopolitical factors which may underlie these literary observations.

I

That language and representation are not neutral, but rather the site where social and political meanings are produced, as well as vehicles for the ideologies behind these meanings, has been the insight of contemporary linguistics and cultural movements such as feminism, postmodernism, and post-colonialism. Writers like Brand, Bannerji, Philip, and Maracle consciously locate their work at the intersection of language and society. They take up the struggle over meaning and representation, and their work has the potential to disrupt the ideologies that dominate contemporary society in Canada as elsewhere. In *Bread out of Stone* (1994) Dionne Brand writes that "the English Canada that I live in is always surprised by and resistant to cultural intervention from people it does not recognise as fitting into its imposed forms" (179). English Canadian culture, Brand elaborates,

> is not an oppressed culture and can impose this stasis on all discussion also, so we have the situation where in 1994 its artists and social commentators refuse to admit the existence of an ideology some five hundred or more years old through which their ancestors arrived and prospered ... we are unwilling and unable to be filled by this, just as we are unable inevitably to qualify for the grant of "whiteness." (*Bread out of Stone* 180)

In questioning societal assumptions, revealing injustices, and imagining new possibilities, works like those by Brand, Bannerji, Philip, and Maracle reveal that their language is not only literary but also political in inspiration. This writing often foregrounds political events or concerns – as in Afua Cooper's poem "The Power of Racism"[1] in which the poet asks how "the ROM could mount an African exhibition/without consulting Black people." Cooper is referring to the 1990 Royal Ontario Museum exhibit, "Into the Heart of Africa," which met protest from many members of Toronto's (and Canada's) Black communities, among them poet and novelist Nourbese Philip. Philip's fiction and essays articulate facts of racial prejudice within Canadian experience. "I wish them to know the contempt which the literary establishment of this country has for Black writers like myself," Philip writes in her collection of essays *Frontiers: Essays and Writings on Racism and Culture* (1992), citing by way of example

George Bowering, one of the preeminent members of this establishment, writing and publishing in the *Globe and Mail* that he had read my poetry and was very surprised to see that I was a good poet! I want them to know that racism is alive and kicking shit all across this country; that in Toronto, for instance, four Black people have been shot by the police in the last two years, in situations that didn't warrant those shootings; that similar shootings take place in Montreal; not to mention the long history of racism in Nova Scotia against the oldest Black population in this country. (264)

The conjunction of political and theoretical concerns relates to the authors' very position and identities as writing subjects. Writing as a Black or an Aboriginal Canadian woman becomes a political act in and of itself. Writing as process and practice is seen to be inherently and necessarily political, part of a larger struggle which often involves political action – frequently around women's issues or race relations. A well-known example of this is Philip's involvement with Vision 21[2] and the latter's intervention at the PEN international meeting in Toronto in 1989. In such instances, writing frequently bursts beyond the "limits of literature." To cite Dionne Brand again:

I've had moments when the life of my people has been so overwhelming to bear that poetry seemed useless.... At times it has been more crucial to wield a scythe over high grass in a field in Marigot; at times it has been more important to figure out how a woman without papers in Toronto can have a baby and not be caught and deported; at times it has been more helpful to organise a demonstration in front of the police station at Bay and College Streets. Often there's been no reason whatsoever to write poetry. There are days when I cannot think of a single reason to write this life down. (*Bread out of Stone* 182)

Another notable example is the work of dub poet Lillian Allen. In "I Fight Back," Allen gives voice to the familiar/unfamiliar "foreign domestic":

Here I am in Canada
bringing up someone else's child
while someone else and me in absentee
bring up my own

AND I FIGHT BACK
[...]
They label me
Immigrant, law-breaker, illegal, minimum wager
refugee
Ah no, not mother, not worker, not fighter

> I FIGHT BACK
> I FIGHT BACK
> I FIGHT BACK
> (*Women Do This Every Day* 139-40)

Numerous other examples might be cited, along with entire collections which have appeared in the 1990s, such as Makeda Silvera's *The Other Woman: Women of Colour in Contemporary Canadian Literature* (1995), Arun Mukherjee's *Sharing Our Experience* (1993), Carol Morrell's *Grammar of Dissent* (1994), and Carol Camper's *Miscegenation Blues: Voices of Mixed Race Women* (1994), among others.

Compelling, controversial, instructive, and sobering, these are writings whose equivalents seem less readily identifiable in Quebec. The sounding board provided by *La Parole métèque*, a review featuring immigrant women writers established in 1987, no longer exists. Work by Régine Robin (notably *La Québecoite* 1983) stands out, but appears to be relatively isolated, as is that of a writer such as Ying Chen, despite recent media attention.[3] A sense of collective critique seems harder to locate in Quebec than in English Canada at present. It is, however, possible to find.

Groups of South Asian, Black, or Native women writers are not as visible in Quebec as in English Canada. But there does appear to be an emerging group of Quebec writers of Arabic background – and a concomitant "racialization" of this group of writers.[4] In the second part of this essay, I will focus on works by a few writers of Arabic background, notably Andrée Dahan, Mona Latif Ghattas, and Nadine Ltaif.[5]

II

A travers une étude méticuleuse des expériences de la protagoniste Maya, *Le Printemps peut attendre* (1985) d'Andrée Dahan présente une critique déterminée du traitement des nouveaux arrivants au Québec. Sélectionnée par le département d'immigration du Canada, Maya, trente ans, dispose d'une carrière réussie dans l'enseignement de la biologie et d'une vie heureuse – jusqu'au moment des événements racontés dans le roman de Dahan. Alors qu'elle s'attendait à obtenir un poste d'enseignante une fois immigrée au Québec, Maya ne réussit à décrocher qu'une position de suppléante à temps partiel dans une polytechnique. L'école elle-même s'affirme être un microcosme de la société en général, de ses valeurs et de ses membres. Plutôt que des cours en biologie – sa spécialisation – Maya est contrainte d'enseigner un cours de transactions commerciales (la symbolique ne nous échappant pas) et ce, aux élèves difficiles et laissé/es-pour-compte de l'école. Elle a peu de chance de réussir. Mais c'est à partir de son rapport au langage et de ses usages particuliers que s'exprime l'échec d'insertion de Maya. De cette manière, le roman de Dahan illustre clairement l'affirmation selon laquelle le langage n'est pas neutre. Maya se rend compte que «les jeux de mots … l'excluent et l'isolent de plus en plus dans sa singularité» (25-26). «Ils ne parlaient pas la même langue. Ni celle des mots, ni celle du corps» (78). Bien qu'elle se démène contre le «décodage des signes de communication qui ne sont pas vraiment identiques aux siens,» Maya tombe dans «le piège de sa propre culture, seule référence possible» (26). Sous le tracé habile de Dahan s'exprime une projection interne d'une expérience minoritaire consciente des images et des stéréotypes qui lui sont associés. Ainsi Maya «voit clairement l'abîme infranchissable qui se creuse et il y a quelque chose de tragique dans l'idée que l'image qu'elle se fait d'elle-même ne se superpose plus du tout à l'image d'elle que la classe lui renvoie» (27): «... elle était passante transfuge dans une cité codée, frappée d'interdiction, où la seule promenade côtoyait l'insolite et éveillait la suspicion» (56).

Le roman dévoile les défauts de l'école qui mènent à des injustices, et par-delà le cadre éducatif, le texte expose l'inéquité de la société, de ses dirigeants et de leurs procédés: «Il y eut bien une contestation, mais, les élèves ne sachant pas pourquoi ils contestaient, la direction eut recours au procédé à la mode, remède à tous les maux, celui de la dynamique de groupe, à laquelle n'assistait aucun spécialiste» (75). L'adjointe au directeur, Mme Roy (le nom en dit long), «depuis les hauts lieux de l'autorité» (32) et par «une forme d'impérialisme du pouvoir» (32) annonce à Maya le diagnostic: «sa *surdité* [est] une des raisons de ses difficultés. Sous le choc, [Maya] était restée sans voix» (5). Maya n'a aucun problème auditif, mais elle est réduite au silence par l'injustice de son traitement. Au plus profond de son angoisse, Maya s'interroge, «Pourquoi attendre le printemps?» Sa mort dans une tempête de neige (*lietmotif* québécois/canadien par excellence) fait-elle suite à un des hasards de la vie ou répond-elle plutôt à un acte lucide mais tragique d'immigrante?

Dahan vient rejoindre d'autres auteures d'origine arabe qui portent un regard critique sur la société québécoise. Ainsi par exemple, Mona Latif Ghattas dans *Le Double conte de l'exil* (1990) offre une narration poétique axée sur des récits d'une expérience autre de la ville de Montréal. Madeleine est «une Ancienne du 'Kébec'» (127), c'est-à-dire qu'elle est d'origine amérindienne. Elle n'a pas eu la vie facile. Enfant, Madeleine travaillait déjà dans une taverne. A douze ans, elle est victime d'un viol. Adulte, elle doit toujours accepter un travail dur, cette fois dans une buanderie de l'est de Montréal. Un jour, Madeleine vient en aide à un homme connu seulement comme Fêve, réfugié d'un désert d'Anatolie balafré par la guerre. La buanderie s'avère le cadre de nombreuses observations critiques sur la société québécoise par l'intermédiaire des «Trois Clara.»[6] Ces trois travailleuses «implantée[s] dans la buanderie depuis quelques décennies ... fortes de leurs similitudes et de leur ancienneté ... s'octroyaient le droit de dévisager tout nouveau venu, de le scruter, de commenter ses comportements, de pointer du doigt sa différence, d'épier ses misères, de salir sa beauté si elle les poussait dans l'ombre, d'amoindrir ses qualités quand elles menaçaient de mettre à jour leurs lacunes, enfin, de bâtir sa réputation» (54). L'objet de leur critique actuelle est un jeune Asiatique qui travaille beaucoup et parle peu. De lui, «Clairette Légaré avait déjà affirmé qu'il sentait l''egg roll,' Clarence Lindsay avait décrété qu'elle n'aimait pas les Asiatiques et Clara Leibovitch, après qu'elle eut un peu hésité comme d'habitude, avait fini par renchérir en déclarant qu'il parlait mal et qu'elle ne comprenait rien de ce qu'il disait» (54). A travers ces personnages, l'auteure tire l'attention sur la réalité de la méfiance, voire de la haine,[7] qui existent vis-à-vis «l'autre,» ainsi que sur des réalités telles l'embauche des travailleurs au noir et le besoin de ceux-ci de travailler et de vivre en cachette. Si Fêve est heureux de travailler «sous la terre» (dans les égoûts d'une banlieue prospère à l'ouest de la ville, un trajet de deux heures en autobus), c'est «qu'[il] y risquait moins de se faire dénoncer» (90) que dans la rue. Ainsi que l'exprime Maya dans *Le Printemps peut attendre*, «être immigrant[e], c'est vivre entre parenthèses» (79).

Avec *Le Double Conte de l'Exil,* Mona Latif Ghattas dévoile la discrimination et l'expression de certains préjugés dans la société québécoise. Dans une section du livre tout particulièrement frappante,[8] l'auteure énumère les multiples groupes qui font face aux stéréotypes attachés à la race: Marocains, Sikhs, Haïtiens, Égyptiens, Chiliens, Salvadoriens, Colombiens, Iraniens, Juifs, Turcs, «et quoi encore, quoi encore, les urgences des hôpitaux engorgées, le métro où l'on se croit dans la tour de Babel, mon Dieu, mon Dieu» (103). La protagoniste Madeleine pense que son ami Fêve va pouvoir obtenir le statut d'immigré. Mais, conte d'exil, le livre de Ghattas trace en fait la déportation de Fêve et le désarroi de Madeleine, qui doit dorénavant reconnaître l'expérience d'exil de ses propres ancêtres autochtones.

Le regard critique posé sur la société québécoise par des auteures telles que Latif Ghattas and Dahan ne nie pas le fait que des conditions semblables se retrouvent ailleurs au monde. C'est ce que souligne Nadine Ltaif sans son recueil *Les Métamorphoses d'Ishtar* (1987) où l'horreur de guerre en Liban ressurgit dans la mémoire du «je» poète vivant maintenant à Montréal – «île du Naufragé,» (8) «île Magique» (26) «entre les fleuves,» selon le titre du deuxième recueil de l'auteure:[9]

> Voilà que je reviens sur la place
> de la douleur,
> et me regarde face à moi-même.
> Et regarde Montréal.
> Et je vois double: l'Est et l'Ouest.
> Je prends ma tête entre mes mains
> Je crois voir Beyrouth.
> Des lambeaux entre les deux.
> Et l'horreur et l'exil,
> une guerre entre mes deux coeurs
> (*Les Métamorphoses d'Ishtar* 40).

Ce regard par dessus les frontières nationales fait comprendre que le Québec (le Canada) n'est pas unique, mais pas exempté non plus lorsqu'il s'agit de conflits et de violence provenant de différences de race et/ou d'éthnicité. Dans *Les Métamorphoses d'Ishtar*, Ltaif finit par trouver une façon d'envisager le conflit basé sur des différences de race ou de culture. «Je suis Arabe. Tiens, et vous êtes Juive,» constate le «je» à la dernière page du texte: «Que c'est lourd, et le cœur, le cœur pèse, lorsque je chante, c'est le cœur de l'amour, c'est la terre antique qui aime, et la haine entre Agar et Sarah c'est de l'amour» (62).

On pourrait donc parler d'une conscience politisée ainsi que d'une critique sociale chez plusieurs auteures québécoises «migrantes» – notamment celles d'origine arabe dont nous venons de voir quelques extraits de livres. Ce sont des voix puissantes, et si elles s'élèvent de manière isolée plutôt qu'à travers un chœur communautaire, c'est peut-être que d'autres facteurs entravent l'expression d'une forte identité collective. Ces facteurs seraient à approfondir à l'aide d'analyses sociologique et politique. Dans la dernière partie de cette étude, j'aimerais seulement soulever quelques hypothèses de recherche.

III

Dans l'essai qu'ils ont contribué à l'imposant volume *Ethnicity and Culture in Canada: The Research Landscape* (1994), intitulé «La recherche au Québec portant sur l'écriture ethnique,» David Leahy et Sherry Simon affirment qu' «il n'existe évidemment aucun rapport de cause à effet entre l'origine socio-culturelle de l'auteur et la portée de son écriture. A cela il faut ajouter que le contexte intellectuel des années 80 est largement méfiant des certitudes identitaires» (393). Leahy et Simon écrivent avec raison que «la critique est soucieuse dans l'ensemble de souligner les *convergences* entre les écritures issues des communautés culturelles et les autres, de manière à reconnaître et à mettre en question la pertinence de la question de l'origine» (393). Mais est-ce ce dont témoignent les textes eux-mêmes, notamment ceux écrits par des femmes «migrantes» au Québec? [10]

Comment reconcilier l'affirmation de Leahy et de Simon, à savoir que «la spécificité culturelle de l'origine devient une matière privilégiée à exploiter, oui, mais elle ne détermine en rien le caractère de l'écriture» (394) avec ces vers de Nadine Ltaif qui, elle, en affirmant que «les Arabes ont le rythme avant d'avoir les mots"» (*Métamorphoses* 58), écrit:

> Mais comment vous avouer que mon inspiration vient d'ailleurs, que je ne suis pas d'ici, même si j'aime un loup à Montréal, que ma langue vient d'ailleurs, que l'écriture est d'ailleurs, que mon rythme à moi n'est pas celui de l'hiver, mais que ma passion pour vous me fait changer de langue, et je parle et je raconte, comme une femme arabe à une autre femme arabe (*Les Metamorphoses d'Ishtar* 26).

Le survol qu'offrent Leahy and Simon des études portant sur l'écriture ethnique au Québec confirme la très forte tendance de ces recherches vers une «réappropriation d'une québécité elle-même transculturelle» (401), ce qui a pour effet de réduire la problématique de l'écriture ethnique à celle de la littérature québécoise dans son ensemble (401): «Ainsi, c'est moins 'la littérature ethnique' comme telle qui doit être un champ privilégié de recherche,» concluent Leahy et Simon, «que les conceptions d'identité culturelle que véhicule le texte littéraire» (400). C'est là une trajectoire littéraire que ne respectent pas nécessairement les textes d'auteures migrantes au Québec, s'il faut croire les exemples cités ci-dessus. De par leur regard critique sur le milieu, ces textes se rapprochent davantage des écrits d'auteures comme Brand, Philip, Bannerji et d'autres au Canada anglais. Mais au Canada anglais, de telles auteures s'expriment non seulement en tant qu'écrivaines mais aussi en tant que critiques, que ce soit dans le domaine littéraire ou social. En contrepartie, mis à part les écrits issus de *Vice Versa* – et ce surtout à travers les écrits d'hommes – les critiques québécois dans l'ensemble sont issus de l'identité majoritaire. Ils portent un regard critique sur les textes littéraires à partir d'une expérience ancrée dans la culture dominante, ne vivant pas au quotidien les conséquences d'une appartenance à un groupe minoritaire. Cette différence fondamentale se doit d'être soulignée. Elle semble s'être confirmée dans le débat récent autour de la plaquette *L'arpenteur et le navigateur* de Monique LaRue, dont Maïr Verthuy offre le résumé dans son essai.[11] Les textes d'auteures comme Dahan, Ghattas et Ltaif visent à formuler une critique de l'idéologie que véhiculent la langue et le discours majoritaires au Québec. «Vous me faites changer de langue, et ce que je disais en arabe je le dis maintenant en français,» écrit Nadine Ltaif dans *Les Métamorphoses d'Ishtar.* «Qu'avez-vous fait de ma langue? Comment ai-je pu conserver ma voix? Au-delà de la mort, au-delà de la souffrance, vous avez une force!» (61). La protagoniste du roman d'Andrée Dahan pose une question semblable: «Qu'avait-on fait de son authenticité? Être ou paraître? Sa vie? Elle n'était qu'un amas d'apparence [...] Paraître ou disparaître» (77). L'écriture d'auteures comme Dahan, Ltaif et Ghattas semble communiquer, entre autre, une volonté de ne pas disparaître. C'est une écriture par laquelle commencer à paraître, à affirmer la différence. En cela, elle se rapproche peut-être plus qu'elle ne s'éloigne de l'écriture de femmes s'identifiant à des groupes minoritaires au Canada anglais. L'étude comparative plus approfondie de ces deux corpus littéraires suggère qu'une dimension «politique» se retrouve dans l'un et dans l'autre – mais différemment.

NOTES

This essay was first presented as a paper to the Association for Canadian Studies (June 1995), and revised for delivery at The Windy Pine Colloquium (August 1995). A modified version, written in English, has appeared in *Cultural Identities in Canadian Literature,* ed. Bénédicte Mauguière (New York: Peter Lang, 1998) 211-25. The research which underlies this essay has been assisted by support from SSHRCC.

1. In *Memories Have Tongue* 73. The full text of the poem is "The power of racism/the power of racism/the power of racism/is such that Neville who is six foot two and weights [sic] 210/could be threatened with assault by three

white children//The power of racism/the power of racism/the power of racism/is such that a Yusef Hawkins was killed in Brooklyn/due to the colour of his skin//the power of racism/the power of racism/the power of racism is such/that the ROM could mount an African exhibition/without consulting Black people."

2. Described by Philip, in an interview with Janice Williamson, as a multi-disciplinary, multi-racial group "committed to making sure that the practice of art in Ontario is free of racism, sexism, and economic disparity" (*Sounding Differences: Conversations with Seventeen Canadian Women Writers* 242). See Introduction footnote 2.

3. Chen is featured in the Québec literary magazine *Lettres québécoises* 98 (Printemps 1998) in two articles, Francine Bordeleau, "La dame de Shanghai," 9-10 and Robert Chartrand "Variations de thèmes d'exile," 11-13. She is also profiled in "Retour en Chine," *Châtelaine* (avril 1998): 26-28 and is the subject of a newly released film by Georges Dufaux, "Voyage illusaire" (ONF, 1998).

4. Perhaps witnessed by the recent rash of debates and publications around the question of wearing the hijab/tchador.

5. In a forthcoming essay, I look at the first novel (*Le Bonheur à la queue glissante*, 1998) by Quebec playwright Abla Faroud, also of Arabic background.

6. Les "Trois Clara" ne sont pas sans différences l'une de l'autre, ainsi que le communiquent leurs noms: Clairette Légaré, Clarence Lindsay, et Clara Leibovitch.

7. "Les Trois Claras ne voient pas cela du même œil que Madeleine, c'est évident. De leur angle de vision elles perçoivent des choses qui les déboussolent et aiguisent en elles une sorte de haine indéfinie, une haine, comme on dirait, épidermique, épidémique, qui peut même devenir contagieuse. Au fait, elles ne savent pas exactement ce qui, en lui [le jeune Asiatique] les rend furieuses. Et pourtant, ce genre de furie est toujours justifié par des images enfouies sourdement dans nos tiroirs à préjugés et dans le sac d'intolérance que nous avons hérité de l'Histoire" (100).

8. Voir pages 102-103.

9. *Entre les fleuves* (1991), d'où sont tirées les deux citations précédentes (8, 26).

10. Leahy et Simon citant Pierre Nepveu, 1989.

11. Verthuy's account appears in the notes to her essay. See also Patricia Smart, "The 'Pure Laine' Debate," *The Canadian Forum* LXXVI.864 (November 1997): 15-19.

GEORGE ELLIOTT CLARKE

Liberalism and Its Discontents: Reading Black and White in Contemporary Québécois Texts

The question of race is increasingly a concern of literature (Craig 21).

In their wry, picaresque travelogue, *Two Innocents in Red China* (1968), co-authors Jacques Hébert and Pierre Elliott Trudeau record the latter's quip that "Chinese Marxists are like Quebec collegians. On questions of religion and sex, they lose their sang-froid" (141). This incisive jest may also be applied to the Québécois intelligentsia, particularly if one adds *race* to M. Trudeau's taxonomy of disconcerting discourses.[1] Indubitably, since 1945, Québécois intellectuals have frequently deployed white/Black racial metaphors to dramatize the conflict between liberalism and nationalism, one that annexes all serious political discourse in *le bel état putatif.*[2] I am interested in the ways in which these metaphors both clarify and contradict the liberal *cum* nationalist ideologies of certain Québécois writers – principally, Suzanne Lantagne, Dany Laferrière, Eugène Seers, and Michel Garneau. Importantly, their depictions of blackness and whiteness, I will argue, call into question the triumph of liberalism as the incipient terminus of the chronology of philosophical evolution outlined in Francis Fukuyama's celebrated 1989 essay, "The End of History?"

To elucidate the nature of the challenge that these writers pose, perhaps unwittingly, to partisans of liberalism, it is necessary to revisit the clash between the two surviving, post-Cold War ideologies (a contest with obvious consequences for Quebec). According to Fukuyama, inchoately victorious liberalism entails "the universalization of Western liberal democracy as the final form of human government" (4). He summarizes the content of this "universal homogenous state" as "liberal democracy in the political sphere combined with easy access to VCRs and stereos in the economic" (8). In this "post-historical period there will be neither art nor philosophy, just the perpetual caretaking of the museum of human history" and "the endless solving of technical problems, environmental concerns, and the satisfaction of consumer demands" (18). Fukuyama's sense of a powerful utopian and millenarian liberalism is complemented in Canada by the stern, aggressive thought of Trudeau. In *Federalism and the French Canadians* (1968), his central text, Trudeau judges nationalism a *gauche* irrationality, parading in the guises of "chauvinism, racism, jingoism, and all manner of crusades, where right reasoning and thought are reduced to rudimentary proportions" (175). This delegitimation of nationalism and *de facto* liberation of capitalist individualism – the *Zeitgeist* blessed by Fukuyama and Trudeau – is opposed by the conservative vision of George Grant. In *Lament for a Nation* (1965), his incendiary defence of nationalism, Grant agrees that the erasure of national differences is the aim of classic liberalism, which he dubs "the perfect ideology for capitalism" in that it "demolishes those taboos that restrain expansion" (47). Vitally, he advises that "The classical philosophers asserted that a universal and homogeneous state would be a tyranny" (96), that is, "a society destructive of human excellence" (86). Grant insists, then, that only those who dread this threat "can assert consistently that parochial nationalisms are to be fought for" (85-86). Writing in 1994, Quebec nationalist Pierre Vallières follows Grant in repudiating liberal triumphalism:

> La réconciliation du peuple et du capital est impossible lorsque celui-ci multiplie les inégalités, augmente le chômage, désindustrialise des pans entiers de l'économie, provoque le démantèlement des services publics, détruit l'environnement, etc. Tous ces problèmes ne peuvent être résolus par le libre-échange et la "globalisation de l'économie." (99)

Announcements of the demise of nationalism seem egregiously premature.

The repeated appearance of racialized metaphors in Québécois literature illumines the oscillation between nationalist (collectivist-conservative) and liberal (individualist-universalist) ideologies, to utilize Grantian grammar, that is the contrapuntal tension inherent in all post-colonial literatures.[3] Seers, Garneau, Laferrière, and Lantagne all engage race in ways that re-inscribe romanticized or xenophobic constructions of the racial Other, even as they interrogate such reductive visions. In other words, the Black/white trope functions in their texts to delineate notions of both unfettered liberality and deep anxieties *vis-à-vis* potential assimilation. In this sense Toni Morrison's insight into the use of Black characters by American writers is applicable here:

> Through the simple expedient of demonizing and reifying the range of color on a palette, [blackness] makes it possible [for writers] to say and not say, to inscribe and erase, to escape and engage, to act out and act on, to historicize and render timeless. It provides a way of contemplating chaos and civilization, desire and fear, and a mechanism for testing the problems and blessings of freedom. (7)

My selected Québécois writers work with notions of blackness to achieve similar ends, even deploying, at times, deplorable racial imaginings.

In making this statement, however, I do not mean to tarnish Quebec; English-Canadian writers also have produced a bracing canon of sanguinely racist texts. Thomas Chandler Haliburton (of *Sam Slick* fame), for instance, in his day mongered derogatory caricatures of Africadians (Black Nova Scotians).[4] Terrence Craig reveals that John Murray Gibbon, the first president of the Canadian Authors' Association, "consistently displayed" in his writings "a vehemently anti-Semitic attitude as well as ... sympathy for eugenics..." (46). Pervasive anti-Orientalisms in Hilda G. Howard's novel *The Writing on the Wall* (1921) provoke Craig to label it "the most racist book in Canadian fiction" (51), while as recently as 1994 Laura Fairburn's novel *Endless Bay* produces a Mi'Kmaq character who seems a psychotic Heathcliff.[5] Craig stresses that racism has always shaded Canadian fiction, "whether as a mild form of xenophobia, or in one of the more fanatical forms of group-hatred such as anti-Semitism" (139).[6] In short, English Canadians cannot feel morally superior to francophones when it comes to their treatment of minority groups.[7]

Nevertheless, I have chosen to survey Quebec in this paper for two reasons: first, the nationalist *versus* liberal debate is sumptuously acute in that locale; second, Québécois writers have made steady, political use of racialized metaphor – festively so during *la révolution tranquille*. In his splenetic *cri-du-coeur*, *White Niggers of America* (1971), Vallières parallels the mutual marginality of blackness and proletarianized *francité* in North America: "The liberation struggle launched by the American blacks ... arouses growing interest among the French Canadian population, for the workers of Quebec are aware of their condition as niggers, exploited men, second-class citizens" (21). Vallières asks rhetorically, "Were [Québécois] not *imported*, like the American Blacks to serve as cheap labour in the New World?" (*Ibid.*). Sébastien Joachim reports that the Québécois narrator of the 1965 novel *Journal d'un Hobo* likens his compatriots to Jews and Blacks: "[Vancouver] manque de *Juifs* et de *Nègres*. C'est peut-être aussi bien, ces deux races ont des complexes et présentent des problèmes *comme nous*" (Joachim 238). Around 1968, Michèle Lalonde composed "Speak White," a conjoining of the felt experiences of Québécois and Black oppressions that critic Jean Royer terms "le poème-étendard de la poésie du pays": "speak white / tell us again about Freedom and Democracy / nous savons que liberté est un mot noir" (Royer 85). In Hubert Aquin's anti-colonial allegory *Trou de mémoire* (1968), "un Noir est au centre de l'intrigue" (Joachim 238). This long-standing linking of Black and Québécois subjectivities, I think, calls for a reading of white/Black metaphors as accounts of the ongoing liberalist-nationalist rivalry, both within Quebec and within the wider world.

II

In Eugène Seers's *Les Enfances de Fanny* (1951) (*Fanny* is the title of Raymond Y. Chamberlain's 1974 English translation) and in Dany Laferrière's *Comment faire l'amour avec un nègre sans se fatiguer* (1985) (*How to Make Love to a Negro* in David Homel's 1987 English version), the male protagonist in both cases is an immigrant-exile of racial minority status. Seers (who wrote under the pseudonym of Louis Dantin) introduces us to the pseudo-autobiographical Donat Sylvain, a white Québécois artist who has settled in Boston and taken

Fanny Lewis, an African-American woman, as his lover. In contrast, Laferrière sketches the yearnings and acts of Vieux, an equally pseudo-autobiographical Haitian refugee in Montréal (a demi-America), who covets the capitalist salvations of white women, lucre, and fame.[8] Suzanne Lantagne's short story "Histoire noire" (1995) narrates the bleak encounter between a white woman and an African immigrant. *Héliotropes* (1993), a drama by Michel Garneau, depicts a multi-racial group of prostitutes and a Black male pianist. These texts declare, as I will show, both a liberal openness to others – the alien, the exotic – *and* a nationalist or ethnocentric resistance to the same.

Of this quartet, only Laferrière's work is situated in Quebec; Seers's novel and Garneau's play are both located in the United States, Lantagne's in a generic, Canadian city. Still, the salient commonality of these texts is their engagement with the tradition of racialized metaphor adumbrated above. Nevertheless, to dislodge Max Dorsinville's curious submission in *Caliban Without Prospero: Essay on Black and Quebec Fiction* (1974) that "it is in the early sixties ... that the figure of the Black man, as symbol, image and myth, emerges in the French-Canadian consciousness" (10), a few earlier examples of metaphoricized blackness are in order.

Québec's *fin-de-siècle* poet Émile Nelligan manipulates blackness-as-metaphor in his poem, "Le Perroquet" (circa 1899). Nelligan portrays a "pauvre négresse," resident of a "coin hideux," who fancies that her parrot embodies "l'âme de son amant," a presumably white sailor who had told her that his being would inhabit the bird (111). This "crédule enfant d'Afrique" thus countenances the parrot's mocking utterance, "Ha! Ha! Ha! Gula, mes amours!" and perishes, eventually, of "la rancoeur" (111-12). Blackness signifies, in this late Symbolist poem, indigence, gullibility, and pathos. Whiteness, however, is construed, by its exact invisibility, as a positive opposite manifesting the kinds of virtues that Frantz Fanon catalogues in *Peau noire, masques blancs* (1952): "On est blanc comme on est riche, comme on est beau, comme on est intelligent" (43).

Nelligan's friend and editor Seers, in "Chanson javanaise," a poem of contemporaneous provenance with *Les Enfances de Fanny*, hallows blackness as the sign of impassioned being. In this poem, which recalls both Nelligan and Charles Baudelaire, a white sailor is granted succour and love by "c'te grande fill' d'Afrique," a Gauguin-like woman with "les bras ballants / N'ayant sur les seins et les hanches / Que sa court' chemise des dimanches" (Dantin, pseud. Seers 140). She is a *National Geographic* earth goddess, a "chaude fleur d'Afrique" (144), and her history admits the usual, fevered atavism:

> "Quand j'pens', dit-ell', que pour ma fête,
> Chaque année, on coupait vingt têtes,
> Et qu'tout l'mond' battait du tom-tom:
> Et m'v'là plus coulée qu'l'oncle Tom!" (142)

Seers's verse supports the finding of Joachim that "La foule africaine, c'est toujours la horde primitive à l'état pur" (Joachim 95). Seers concocts a Manichean polarity in which blackness marks, to cite Fanon again, "une fusion totale avec le monde, une compréhension sympathique de la terre, une perte de mon moi au coeur du cosmos..." (38). It implies the exotic, the sexual, and the savage, a series of associations that Herbert Marcuse also accepts, linking "black, violent, orgiastic" (42). Similarly essentialist fantasies mar Seers's novel.

Even in contemporary Québécois literature, however, blackness evokes license, force, and transgressive sexuality. Suzanne Pellerin promulgates these forbidding representations in her unhesitantly nationalist poem "La Cité des interdits" (1994).[9] Privileging a nurturing darkness over daylight, this lyric depicts a white female speaker, "fille de Piaf et [Juliette] Grèco," who attacks "La nouvelle race aryenne" (Pellerin 44) and "la cité aux phallus de béton" (46) represented by "deux Anglos blancs" (44). Their city is a sexless, commercial desert of "pâles mutants / Le corps désinfecté, le coeur déshydraté / Steak frites, verre de lait et condom" and "La passion plasmifiée... / Le sexe muselé par mille interdits" (*Ibid.*). The speaker spurns this whiteness *plat*, stating "Je me réfugie dans le noir / À la recherche des sources de la vie" (*Ibid.*). Not only is blackness superior to the white Anglos: the latter merit destruction, the speaker dreams of shattering their porcelain hearts (46). Pellerin perpetuates the cliché, *à la* Marcuse, that blackness signals "a desublimated, sensuous form of frightening immediacy, moving, electrifying the body, and the soul materialized in the body" (52). This superficially liberating, opulent blackness is an unabashed repetition of the civilized white's "nostalgie irrationnelle d'époques extraordinaires de licence sexuelle, de scènes orgiaques, de viols non sanctionnés, d'incestes non réprimés" (Fanon 135), a longing projected onto Blacks. In Nelligan, Seers, and Pellerin (in spite of her progressive politics), blackness is affianced to the sexual, "comme si," as Gérard Étienne alleges, "la sexualité était le seul critère existentiel de l'homme ou de la femme noirs, comme si nous ne vivions et ne respirions que par la sexualité, que le nègre et la négresse sont des bêtes toujours en rut" (Étienne 148).

As this overview attests, Québécois writers have often made a metaphor of race, even using it, as in the work of Vallières and Pellerin, to allegorize French-English relations. Québécois politicians lend further credence to the appropriation and territorializing of this trope. Queried about his reticence in defending bilingualism and national unity policies during the 1972 federal election campaign, for instance, Trudeau reportedly delivered the following analogy:

> He would in effect have been telling people they had to vote for him to prove they weren't bigots ... and he likened that to a black man asking a white woman to go out with him and insisting that a refusal could only be due to his colour. The woman might have 101 reasons for refusing, just as people might have 101 reasons for voting against him ... and he hadn't wanted to distort the issue. (Radwanski 261)

Quebec's *premier ministre* René Lévesque also delighted in politicizing blackness. He characterized the first francophone prime minister, Sir Wilfrid Laurier, as "a black king" (quoted in Grant 77) and the third, Trudeau, as "our

Negro King in a sports jacket" (quoted in Sullivan 302).[10] Lévesque viewed
these liberals as Québécois marionettes within the federal system. Yet
Trudeau also utilized this spectacular metaphor, condemning Quebec
independence as a "form of African tribalism that even the Negro kings don't
want for themselves" (quoted in Vastel 134). He denounced the idea of a
Quebec leader or lieutenant within the federal Liberal party caucus in equally
clear terms: "The concept of a Quebec lieutenant is really the black Negro
king theory translated into the federal field" (quoted in Sullivan 122).
Trudeau parades an extended analysis of this concept in *Federalism and the
French Canadians*:

> In politics, Anglo-Canadian nationalism took on the form of what
> André Laurendeau has so admirably named the "cannibal-king" theory
> [*théorie du roi-nègre*]. Economically, this nationalism has been expressed
> essentially in treating the French Canadian as *un cochon de payant*.
> Sometimes, magnanimously, they would go as far as putting a few straw
> men on boards of directors. These men invariably had two things in
> common: first, they were never bright enough or strong enough to rise
> to the top, and second, they were always sufficiently "representative" to
> grovel for the cannibal-king's favours and flatter the vanity of their
> fellow-tribesmen. (163)

No doubt should exist as to the potency of blackness as racialized metaphor
for both liberals and nationalists in Québécois political and literary
discourse.[11]

Assuredly, Lantagne's saturnine *conte*, "Histoire noire," sketches an actual
"Negro" King, that is to say, "un noir" named "King," who is just as abject a
figure as the mythological rulers conjured by Laurendeau, Lévesque, and
Trudeau. This Negro "King" lives up to Lantagne's single-white-female
narrator's expectations – or, more accurately, her prejudices. King is farcical
– a fantastic puppet – as weak and pitiable as those in Québécois political
lore. Lantagne's narrative welcomes the unwelcome, value-laden, binary
opposition that Fanon excoriates, the supposition that "Le péché est nègre
comme la vertu est blanche" (Fanon 114). To the anonymous protagonist,
then, King embodies soul, the earth, the flesh – in other words, to turn again
to Fanon, "l'instinct sexuel (non éduqué)" (145). The narrator confesses such
beliefs when, after having arrived "saoule dans [un] bar, avec une copine, pour
danser avec n'importe quel Noir chaud et sexy" (Lantagne 19), she revels, while
dancing with King, in an Anaïs Nin-like sensuality:

> Mon esprit divaguait, je lassais mon corps danser tout seul, je
> fermais les yeux et King me faisait bouger. La musique résonnait
> contre ma poitrine, les autres danseurs se perdaient dans une
> espèce de chaud brouillard; j'avais de l'écho dans la tête, des
> bourdonnements dans les oreilles, un voile épais devant les yeux,
> les jambes souples et le ventre comme un volcan. (19-20)

This lush evocation is chased by a chain of verbs supported by the eroticized repetition of the first-person direct and indirect object: "Mon partenaire noir me suivait ... me tenait, me provoquait, me manipulait, me consolait, me regardait, m'embrassait, me serrait, me faisait rire et fondre, me prenait" (20). Decadent, the speaker perceives King only as a bestower of pleasure. She disregards, cavalierly, his cultural identity, presuming that he is "probablement zoulou, ou quelque chose comme ça" (19). She rejects "un Blanc" as a potential partner, for "il regarderait autour, serait légèrement mal à l'aise et surtout ne saurait pas quoi faire de ses deux mains" (20). She prefers "ces hommes-là [qui] me parlent avec leur chair" (*Ibid.*). Like Pellerin, she espouses blackness as the source of life, of enjoyment.

Yet, if the first half of this two-paragraph-long story locates the narrator in a primeval paradise of the senses, a site of "chaleur" and bliss, the remainder portrays her fall into the cold, sordid, capitalistic world that she had sought, through mere *jouissance*, to obliterate. This *dégringolade* commences as soon as the music stops and serves to reduce King to a man whose name seems, in the end, "Une vraie farce" (Lantange 19). The narrator accompanies King home for "une chic aventure bien perverse" (20), an expectation which Fanon would attribute to the myth that black men keep "la porte impalpable qui donne sur le royaume des Sabbats, des Bacchanales, des sensations sexuelles hallucinantes..." (Fanon 145). But the affair decays into a debacle. King declines to purchase condoms, while the narrator prevails. He requests money; she feels insulted. At King's "correct mais laid" apartment block, his "triste réalité," the narrator fears, while showering, that he will filch cash from her purse (Lantange 21). Epiphanically the narrator discovers at this moment that "la vie avait ... un visage sans masque" (*Ibid.*). Hence, the once-charming King, "Maintenant qu'il savait qu'il pourrait enfoncer sa queue quelque part, il ne faisait plus le beau...." Now "lui, le roi," is "conscient d'être pitoyable au milieu de ses guenilles..." (*Ibid.*). The speaker's disillusionment assumes the form of spiritual panic: "La crudité de cette rencontre m'est apparue dans toute sa plénitude. Je n'étais pas devant un vide spirituel qui conduit à l'illumination, mais devant un effroyable trou sans fond et infiniment glacial" (22). Completing the picture of King's corrupted state, the narrator notes, after they have made love, that King possesses "un sexe décevant pour un Noir" (*Ibid.*), thus reinforcing a stereotype – "Le nègre est appréhendé avec un membre effarant" (Fanon 145) – even as it is eviscerated. Once King falls asleep, the narrator steals away, after checking her billfold, "dans l'hiver noir" – the polar negation of the bar's "chaud brouillard" (Lantange 20).

"Histoire noire" is a black comedy, one replete with images of black holes, a black winter, a negatively comic Black, and even an atmospere of black shirts, that is to say, of a faint fascism. I raise this possibility because of the narrator's fascination with the body, her mania for cleanliness, and her resolute adherence to regressively narrow racial beliefs. King is the reborn "négresse" of Nelligan, a slave to indigence and failure. Worse, he is a potential thief, almost impotent, a *faux* man. The narrator sleeps with him and experiences a glacial dark night of the soul.[12] Her encounter with the Other leaves her trapped more agonizingly in the prison of the self – and in the mercenary dystopia of late capitalism. Lantagne's story enacts a collision between whiteness and blackness, one which sullies both. *Histoire noire* bodes ill for the promulgation of multiculturalism in Quebec.[13]

I suspect, though, that Lantagne immerses her readers in the *merde* of ethnocentrism as a riposte to the misogynist and anti-white positions taken, even if only satirically, in Laferrière's consideration of the cruising bar milieu in *How to Make Love to a Negro*. There is a leaven of humour in Laferrière that Lantagne lacks, but his work anticipates her spendthrift way with racial stereotypes. If Lantagne's King administers squalor, Laferrière's hero, Vieux, with his Islamic friend Bouba, rules a run-down Montreal apartment. If Lantagne's narrator *drague les hommes noirs*, Laferrière's narrator dragoons white women. If Lantagne's barfly heroine denigrates white men as sexually maladroit, Laferrière's hero concurs:

> Streaming bodies. Eighteen-carat ebony. Ivory teeth. Reggae music. Combustion. Black fusion. A white/black couple practically copulating on the dance floor. Atomic shockwaves.... "Sexually, the white man is dead. Completely demoralized. Look at them [the Black/white couple] dancing. Do you know any white man who could keep up with that madness?" (*How to Make Love* 93)

If Lantagne envisions such dance-floor unions as a pseudo-tropical event, Laferrière agrees: "It's like moving into Amazon humidity. Bodies running with sweat. You need a machete to cut through this jungle of arms, legs, sexes and mingling smells. Spicy sensuality" (94). Like Lantagne, Laferrière grounds his narrative in the notion that, to sound Fanon, "c'est ... qu'avec le nègre commence le cycle du *biologique*" (133). For both writers, the African denotes the physical, the earthy, the sexual.[14]

Neither adheres to this construction entirely. Lantagne's heroine casts King as the key to orgasm, then recants from this construction, refusing the very narrative that Vieux validates, ironically, in a mock interview with Miz Bombardier: "She was beside herself. She had found her African. Her primitive" (112). Laferrière's hero seems hedonistic, but his sexual relationships engender finely honed dissertations. Laferrière produces a laid-back, bohemian atmosphere in which titillating, liberal coitus occurs between the *déclassé* Black narrator and his (largely English-speaking) bourgeois white partners, but, as in Sade, it is the commentary – a continuous, Black nationalist riff on North America society – that is paramount. Vieux and Bouba are, as Vieux admits, "Two Blacks in a filthy apartment ..., philosophizing their heads off about Beauty in the wee hours" (Laferrière, *How to Make Love* 30), but the emphasis is on the act of cogitation. The text details the tantalizing indulgences of reading, eating, drinking, lovemaking, sleeping, and barhopping, but it is more than an "erotico-satiric" novel (Homel 8). Rather, Laferrière showcases a potent Negro King, a Haitian-Canadian *roi soleil*, one whose ideology is written out in sperm.

Significantly, Vieux's subjugation of white women is putative reprisal for the sins of their imperialist ancestors:

> This Judeo-Christian girl is my Africa. A girl born for power. So what is she doing at the end of my black rod? ... I want to fuck her subconscious.... I catch a glimpse of my oiled thighs (coconut oil) against this white body. I take her white breasts firmly in my hands. The light down on her white marble body. I want to fuck her identity. Pursue the racial question to the heart of her being. (Laferrière, *How to Make Love* 60-61)

When Vieux enters Miz Literature's posh home for a tryst, he experiences an agreeable sensation of racial and class transgression: "This house breathes calm, tranquillity, order. The order of the pillagers of Africa" (76). In this *haute-bourgeois* oasis, he will "fuck the daughter of these haughty diplomats who once whacked us with their sticks" (*Ibid.*). An unarticulated revenge fantasy also spans the abrupt transition between Vieux's musings on American slavery – "Black bodies shining sensual, beaten by the cruel wind of the Deep South" – and his presumption of "Black desire obsessed with pubescent white flesh" (78).

Vieux never expresses love for the white women he takes. Instead, their bodies attract a Sade-like glamourization: "My sex celebrates your golden hair, your pink clitoris, your forbidden vagina, your white belly, your bowed neck, your Anglo-Saxon mouth" (61). The unacknowledged inspiration for the rapacious violence of such portraiture is likely the African-American essayist (and confessed ex-rapist) Eldridge Cleaver, whose 1968 poem, "To a White Girl," foresees Laferrière's compulsions:

> I love you
> Because you're white,
> Not because you're charming
> Or bright.
> Your whiteness
> Is a silky thread
> Snaking through my thoughts
> In redhot patterns
> Of lust and desire.
>
> I hate you
> Because you're white.
> Your white meat
> Is nightmare food.
> White is
> The skin of Evil.
> You're my Moby Dick,
> White Witch,

Symbol of the rope and hanging tree,
Of the burning cross.... (Cleaver 25-26)

Vieux declares, "Put black vengeance and white guilt together in the same
bed and you had a night to remember!" (Laferrière, *How to Make Love* 18). His
incessant, sacerdotal citing of "The Glorious Qur'an" highlights his dissident
vision of the caucasian Occident (marked by the sign *America*) as a citadel of
"evil-doers" (104, 115) and "infidels" (24, 99), an empire whose women, as in
any war or crusade, are fair – pale and proper – game. Vieux's penis is a
weapon, one wielded in a manner that knights, even as it skewers, the brand
of sexist racism exemplified by the work of a writer like Michel Cornot:
"L'épée du Noir est une épée. Quand il a passé ta femme à son fil, elle a senti
quelque chose" (quoted in Fanon 139). Sexuality is, for Laferrière, a
continuation of *jihad* by other means.

Homel observes that "One critic went after Laferrière for making all his
white women English-speaking" (8), but the critic was wrong. Vieux lusts
after the British-born, but now *French* actress Jane Birkin (Laferrière, *How to
Make Love* 86) and he lusts after a white Québécoise film star, imagining,
"Carol Laure, slave to a Negro. Why not?" (24). Since Vieux perceives Miz
Literature as his "slave" (35), his dreams of lording it over Laure are likely
rooted in the same race-sex *chiaroscuro* that defines his relationships with
anglophone women. He even exclaims, "I want Carol Laure! I demand Carol
Laure! Bring me Carol Laure!" (89). Plainly, Vieux's attitude towards white
women, whether English or French, iterates the ambivalence that marks the
conclusion of Cleaver's poem:

Loving you thus
And hating you so,
My heart is torn in two.
Crucified. (Cleaver 26)

White women are targets for the settling of scores, but they are also potential
allies in Vieux's attempted conquest of the riches – economic, cultural, sexual
– of the white-majority states of *Amérique du Nord*. As Haitian-Québécois
writer Michel Adam posits in his 1976 poem, "Femme blanche," the white
woman is "[un] cheval de troie / d'hommes noirs / dans les pâles / citadelles"
(26). Miz Literature and Miz Sophisticated Lady serve in precisely this
capacity for Vieux. Yet, they remain pawns in a cold, unholy war of attrition,
one which Vieux means to wage on both sides of Quebec's linguistic divide
and on both sides of the 49th parallel.

Affirming that Laferrière subjects Quebec to glancing criticism in his 1994
text *Chronique de la dérive douce*, nationalist Québécois critic Renaud
Longchamps takes the author to task: "Il serait déplacé aussi de signifier à
Monsieur Laferrière que nous ne l'avons pas invité à cracher dans notre sauce
blanche..., nous lui demanderons bien respecteusement de se la fermer"
(Longchamps 17). Irritated by Laferrière's question, "pourquoi les Blancs ont-

ils toujours la même réaction devant le racisme?" Longchamps answers, with a *soupçon* of ethnocentrism, "Nous aurons la politesse de ne pas lui demander la sienne, ni à son peuple" (*Ibid.*). Longchamps accuses Laferrière of craving "l'universelle gloire américaine et à la vaisselle d'or du couchant" and of seeking to profit "du meilleur des deux mondes [Quebec and the United States], comme le dernier des trafiquants mohawks..." (*Ibid.*). He even draws a line in the snow, so to speak, between "le peuple québécois" who love their "pays" in "tous ses états" and Laferrière, the apparently ungrateful immigrant (*Ibid.*).[15] His tone is acerbic, but the value of Longchamps's forensic critique is that it teases out the collision of nationalisms, Québécois (and white Anglo) versus Black, which lurks within Laferrière's vision of Quebec/North America.

Crucially, references to Black nationalist icons pervade Laferrière's work. Though few Black women appear in *How to Make Love to a Negro*, Vieux catalogues an Afrocentric, religio-historical figure – "the Egyptian princess Taiah" (15) – and vital cultural signifiers – Ella Fitzgerald (69), Bessie Smith (70, 77) and Tina Turner (74). The text is rife with allusions to Black jazz musicians, to Fanon and Cleaver,[16] and to the "Blackest" cult figure of them all, Malcolm X (*Ibid.*).

Despite his nationalist moods, however, Vieux is an avowed individualist. His joust with white society will be won on egocentric and economic grounds. The typewriter through which he seeks to make his fortune is – like his penis – a "terrorist machine" (46). In addition, Vieux avers that "To be a traitor is every writer's destiny" (113). The novel concludes, not with a communal call-to-arms, but with a truly American-style declaration of pragmatic self-interest: "My novel is a handsome hunk of hope. My only chance. *Take it*" (117). At this point, one should imagine a poignant welling up of strings, perhaps laid over a funky, disco beat.

How to Make Love to a Negro rehearses the nationalist-*versus*-liberal dilemma, its narrator assuming, finally, a provisional position on the side of capitalist individualism. Vieux's ideology remains, though, as unstable as his sex-race dichotomies: he ignores the issue of whether he is first or foremost Haitian, Québécois or American, or a tripartite fusion of these identities. And his adoption of a *dépaysé* persona has consequences. His narrative settles "neither into clearly post-colonial counter-discursive subversion nor into neo-colonial submission," to quote Daniel Coleman. Hence, the book both "exposes and ridicules the discursive system that produces the racist stereotypes, which degrade men of African ancestry, and it recycles and recommodifies those very stereotypes in the process" (Coleman 53). Vieux's attempt to mock racism by fucking white women and to live off the proceeds of published accounts of these encounters endorses, ironically, the grotesque, Cornotesque rhetoric that casts Black men as pimps.

Like Laferrière, Seers employs racialized tropes to accent individuality. Unlike Laferrière and Lantagne, though, Seers wields his metaphors with a blithe, unfinessed innocence. In *Fanny*, he ransacks the dark romantic diction of Baudelaire to limn the adoration that a Québécois artist, Sylvain Donat, feels for Fanny Lewis (*née* Johnston), his widowed Black housekeeper: "Her body was a precious jewel-box of mirages and symbols. The color of her skin reflected golden bees, rare orchids, polished wood, ripe chestnuts, fine topaz, delicate coffee, the shimmering brilliance of insects' wings, the down on the breasts of birds" (Dantin, pseud. Seers *Fanny* 141). While Laferrière seems to borrow from Sade to sing his white female characters, Seers turns not only to the Symbolistes, but also, perhaps, to French *Négritude* poets.[17] Unfortunately, however, the tropes of this Québécois author who exiled himself to the United States and married an African-American woman are, in sum, just as confining as those of the Haitian author who exiled himself to North America and married a *pure laine* Québécoise. When Fanny first appears as a tomboy of 12 years of age, Seers explains the vicissitudes of her mixed-race heritage:

> [Her] maternal grandmother had been a slave, the favorite slave, it was said, of the planter Johnston, which no doubt explained why both [Fanny and her older sister, Linda] had delicate brown complexions and thinner, more refined features than are commonly found in their race. (10)

The historical act of rape, of coerced sexual intercourse, has had the happy consequence of infusing in Fanny and her sister enough of the right genetic material to render them more palatable to the Eurocentric eye than their darker-skinned compatriots. It is the memory of exactly such presumedly criminal fornications that motivates Vieux, like some hip, Black Nosferatu, to stalk Montreal's young white *bourgeoises*. Perhaps, too, they are even closer to virtue, which, for the dour Lantagne and the excitable Longchamps, is a decidedly white quality. Fanny is, then, a brand of "tragic mulatto": her Caucasian genes "refine" her features, but her veins tap "the exuberant sap of the jungle" (10). She is torn between two worlds: the white, rarefied sphere of Donat and the black, earthy sphere of her friends and family in Roxbury, a Black section of Boston. Donat is a liberal, deeming Fanny "simply a woman, distinguished solely by the rare qualities that he would have admired in a person of any color" (142); but his antagonist Charlie Ross, a Black crypto nationalist, demands, at the melodramatic climax, that Fanny abandon Donat, "this white man," and "come back with us, with your own kind" (177).

Seers attempts to complicate the racial formula. Donat loves Fanny and he is, consciously, a progressive. Nevertheless, he envisions her as "an *enfant sauvage* fresh from the jungle with the perfume of her virginal nature still around her" (142-43). A New World Carmen, her heart is "primitive" (143). Like Seers's contemporaneous "javanaise," she is "natural," "spontaneous," and an emblem of vitality: "She had taught him how to live again on his own original soil" (*Ibid.*). She is a siren who cancels inhibitions: "He would caress her like a man transported, with the almost sacrilegious headiness of one entering forbidden realms" (142). Clearly Seers markets the standard, Western, romantic *tchotchkes* that assign a "child-like" naturalness, spontaneity and emotion to blackness (and, in a different way, to women).

Contradictorily, though, blackness remains an *imperilled* quality. All the Black male characters are failures. Worse still, after having harboured an unrequited love for Fanny since boyhood, Charlie is the engine of her death. Furthermore, his innate unworthiness is signalled by his "gross lips" (13).[18] The African-American clergyman Father Divine, an historical figure granted a cameo turn in the novel, resembles a spiritual Maurice Duplessis – "a naive and neighborly god who had taken the image of his creatures to move among them, dispensing his gifts in just exchange for their veneration, satisfied with himself and with his universe" (104). Though Black self-expression fills Donat "with increased respect for the mind and the aesthetic sensibilities of Black people" (151), he deems the play *Green Pastures* (1930) "a transformation into popular drama of all of biblical history, as naive black people might conceive it" (150).[19] For her part, Fanny is both strong and weak, an incongruity that I think is intended as metaphoric of her bi-racial status. In addition, she sacrifices her own happiness whenever circumstance requires, and her death is that of a saint: "Emaciated, almost ethereal, even in defeat Fanny's body kept its indestructible youth. Her face had taken on a new, purer beauty, the reflection of her virginal soul" (185). Too, this death scene mirrors the conclusion of Henry Wadsworth Longfellow's narrative poem, *Evangeline: A Tale of Acadie* (1847), a work that Fanny knew in part (128). As Fanny faces her "ultimate trial" (185), she incarnates "devotion and selfless renunciation" (183) and "Patience and tranquil resignation" (185). Likewise, in *Evangeline*, the eponymous heroine exhibits "Patience and abnegation of self, and devotion to others, / ... the lesson that a life of trial and sorrow had taught her" (84). Importantly, the theme of *Evangeline* – defined by Fanny as the separation of two lovers by fate (128), and encapsulated in Seers's "Chanson javanaise" ("J' comprends ton sort, mon p'tit spahi, / T'es comm' moi, la chanç' t'a trahi" [142]) – becomes that of his novel. Fanny is a Black Evangeline separated from her true lover by traitorous fate. Problematically, though, her blackness seems to evaporate as she dies.

Of course, this etherealization of blackness reveals the hard-edged liberalism that composes Seers's racial judgments. Indeed, the omniscient narrator hints that the final solution to racism is assimilation: "Already in certain areas there are more 'blond Africans' than Negroes who hardly show a trace of their ancestry, suggesting for some later date an automatic and highly ironic solution to the 'black problem'" (167). Seers's sentimental liberalism is almost as negative as Lantagne's chequebook ethnocentrism. If blackness is, for her, irremediably Black, for him, it is easily lactified.

Placed against the texts of Lantagne, Laferrière, and Seers, Garneau's 1994 verse-play *Héliotropes* seems unquestionably progressive. Set in a bordello in turn-of-the-century America, the era of ragtime, the play presents a rainbow coalition of prostitutes – Léola ("noire"), Cléopha ("chocolat"), Eugenia ("high yella"), and Blossom ("blanche et blonde"). The women are led by Martha Jane – the fortyish, white madame, and her mature, white, mute, and adopted pianist-daughter, Janey O. When a Black, Scott Joplin-like

"Compositeur" steps into this world, precipitating a moral crisis, the drama becomes a racialized *salon dans le bordel*. Indeed, Martha Jane worries that if she permits the composer to stay, her white male *clientèle* will melt away because "les nègres ça les rend fous" (Garneau 45). Blossom and Cléopha concur, observing, in sequence, that "ils aiment bien les négresses / les hommes blancs / c'est pour ça / qu'ils n'aiment pas les nègres" (46). Here, as in Laferrière and Seers, sexual jealousy is the progenitor of racism.

The Compositeur determines to remain, though, for he is won by the artistry of Janey O, who plays his music with "dignité" (41). Thus, he argues his case, ridiculing, for instance, the cliché that "une musique écrite par un nègre / soit sans profondeur / et que sa joie / soit seulement naïve / une joie pas trop intelligente" (40). He likens himself to great piano composers – Allessandro Scarletti, Ludwig von Beethoven, and Frédéric Chopin, for he has also inherited "un vocabulaire / et j'organise mon héritage [that of the bordello where he learned to play piano] / pour en tirer le plus de beauté possible" (44). By making this claim, the Compositeur disputes Marcuse's racial-romanticist opposition of blackness to European art, the hallucination that "the soul is black ... it is no longer in Beethoven, Schubert, but in the blues, in jazz" (42).

Ultimately, the Compositeur proposes a liberal basis for his induction into this little society, namely, recognition of his talent, his art. Furthermore, as Eugenia sees, he is "un beau nègre" (41). His union with the household would manifest, therefore, a new aesthetic: "Kinship of the beautiful, the divine, the poetic," to quote Marcuse (34). Janey O's performance of the Compositeur's music concretises this integrationist ethic: "elle est blanche / et joue de la musique/noire" (Garneau 59). Furthermore, while the Compositeur has sought "dignité" (41) and "beauté" (44) the women value "intégrité" (14). *Héliotropes* is, then, a liberal manifesto, positing "Beauté, Dignité, Intégrité," against the "yahoo" ideology of the white males who invade the bordello at dusk.

Unswayed by the Compositeur's discourse on art, Martha Jane (a character based on the mid-nineteenth-century American frontierswoman, Calamity Jane) brandishes a revolver and threatens to shoot him (48-9). Eventually, though, she is won over, and allows the Compositeur to join her domicile. She concedes for three reasons: 1) his music does not seem "très nègre" (53), a judgment exalting technique over cultural authenticity; 2) he is as much "un orphélin" and "un bébé" as the prostitutes (79), thus her matriarchy is affirmed; and 3) he is dying of syphillis (79), an argument that obliterates the social liberalism that *Héliotropes* appears to extoll. No serious change must be undertaken to accommodate the Compositeur, for he is not long for this *demi-monde*, anyway. The *dénouement* expresses, as in Seers, an insouciant disrespect for the legitimacy of cultural difference.

While Pellerin manipulates racialized imagery to vandalize the dessicated, unnatural city of *les maudits anglais*, Lantagne uses similar imagery to attack the liberal fantasy that capitalism produces tolerance. Laferrière mouths the credos of individualism, but lobs Black nationalist barbs at North American society. Seers champions a bleached, reified blackness, that is to say, a benign assimilationism. Garneau's gold-hearted matriarchy welcomes an outsider only because he has exploitable skills (the *sine qua non* of any liberal immigration policy). In the end, these writers depict varying levels of anxiety, or discomfort, in regards to the dream of the open society, the *cité libre*. They may strive to be good liberals, but their liberalism possesses, ultimately, a pronounced, ethnocentric tinge.

III

Lantagne, Laferrière, Seers, and Garneau may not offer perfect, political visions, but their works controvert the propaganda that nationalism has ceased to influence Québécois literature. This implicit dissent is important, for several critics have sought to cleanse the literature of its embarrassing poxes of nationalism. In 1970, John Glassco argued that nationalism harmed the work of Québécois poets: they seemed "too often preoccupied by political ... ideas, by the one incandescent ideal of a beleagured Québec – and it is a truism that politics and nationalism have somehow never managed to make really good poetry" (xix). Dorsinville opined, in 1974, that Québécois and Black American writers had jointly moved beyond regressive theories of nationalism. They had attained a stage in their cultural evolution "where the universal is reached through descent into the self, or through overture towards other selves" (210-11), a strategic definition of cultural maturity that rendered *passé* nationalism *per se*. In his introduction to the Fall 1994 *International Poetry Review* "Voices of Quebec" special issue (that includes Pellerin's poem), Roch Smith follows Dorsinville's evolutionary conceit. If, 20 years before, Québécois poets had been slaves to nationalist thinking (a supposition that actually questions Dorsinville's universalist finding of that year), now there are poems that do not betray "specifically Québécois origins" (R. Smith 8), others that represent an "opening to the world" (13), still others that share "the self-reflexive preoccupation with words" that is "a feature of the modern esthetic in much of ... Western literature" (7). Thus, contemporary Quebec poetry has done away with nationalism. In his unpublished paper, "Quebec culture and its American moods," Pierre Nepveu adopts like reasoning. He claims that the "White negroes of America" metaphor adopted by some Québécois in the 1960s to "*assert* our marginality, to claim, in a statement that was both poetic and political, that we belonged to the America of the oppressed, of the unrecognized, of the unnoticed" (15) has "become obsolete" (17). Nepveu speculates that this fate was inevitable, for Québécois "were ... hoping (without always admitting it) to become sort of French-speaking yankees" (18). He finds that this metaphor implied that "our poetry would be, in the French language, a form of jazz, the equivalent of the rythm [sic] and musical idiom practiced by John Coltrane and Miles Davies [sic]" (16). But, he also states that the "white negro" trope carries "some sort of anti-intellectualism" (19), an argument which problematically aligns blackness with intellectual turpitude.

What Dorsinville, Smith, and Nepveu agree upon, however, is their weariness of history, that is to say, of the constant Shakespearianization of liberal versus nationalist tensions. Their solution is to declare, *à la* Fukuyama, the victory of liberalism, to find solace in this brand of arbitrary, Nixonian sorcery. Yet, Dorsinville's hope that nationalism would die out was simply wishful thinking. Smith's thesis is also erroneous, for national feeling persists in Pellerin and Lantagne (and subsists in Garneau). Nepveu's sallies against the "white negro" metaphor are equally meritless. For instance, Yves Préfontaine, a nationalist Québécois poet, hosted a Radio-Canada jazz programme, and has held civil service posts with the *péquiste* Government of Quebec (91-92).[20] He is, arguably, an intellectual "white negro." And what about the author of that Marxist apocalypse, *White Niggers of America*?

Though liberalism prophesies the withering away of history, I think that the texts of Lantagne, Laferrière, Seers, and Garneau demonstrate, amply, that there is simply no escape from its impress. History is, to quote Hardial Bains, "the kind of irresistible force which does not leave anything alone" (19). Rather, one is left only with the eternal, sado-masochistic ecstasy of contradiction. I suspect the existence of just such a dialectic, for, as Mao Zedong maintains, "the struggle of opposites is ceaseless, it goes on both when the opposites are coexisting and when they are transforming themselves into each other" (72). Accordingly, liberal versus nationalist to-ing-and-fro-ing will remain unresolved. Therefore, Québécois writers, like *all* post-colonial writers, will continue to oscillate between nationalism and liberalism, producing, perhaps even frequently, disturbingly perverse racial constructions. To conclude, history ain't history yet....

NOTES

1. By "race," I mean, generally, any combination of conventions – cultural, linguistic, biological – which distinguish or differentiate one group of human beings from another. In this essay, however, I apply the term to cover the indefinite categories of "Black" (connoting Negroid African descent) and "white" (connoting Caucasoid European descent). Though the texts I discuss in this essay invest these words with essentialist or ethnocentric content, I do not presume that they carry such meanings.

2. By "liberalism," I mean an ideology which exalts "liberty," the freedom of the individual, of markets, equality, "small-is-cool" government, experimentation, and the erosion of prejudices. By "nationalism," I mean a conservative ideology that privileges "order," the primacy of communities, regulation of markets, preservation of cultural differences, interventionist (even expansive) government, stability, and the special status of the parochial. I do not, in this essay, engage the fine discriminations proposed by a host of philosophers, from Stephen Toulmin to Charles Taylor. Still, my understanding of these terms has been shaped by George Grant's polemic, *Lament for a Nation*, that argues that "the choice between internationalism and nationalism is the same choice as that between liberalism and conservatism" (86). Grantian conservatism *qua* nationalism seeks essentially "to protect the public good against private freedom" (70). In contrast, liberalism denies "any conception of good that imposes limits on human freedom" (56).

3. My definition of "post-colonial" is informed by Bill Ashcroft, Gareth Griffiths, and Helen Tiffin: "We use the term ... to cover all the culture affected by the imperial process from the moment of colonization to the present day" (2).

4. For a discussion of Haliburton's use of racist caricature, see my article, "White Niggers, Black Slaves: Slavery, Race and Class in T.C. Haliburton's *The Clockmaker*," *Nova Scotia Historical Review* 14.1 (1994): 13-40.

5. In this astonishingly inept book, Fairburn narrates the desires of Montreal graduate student Rhea Northway, who, bored with marriage and dreaming of fame, abandons her repulsive husband, Jeff, and absconds to northern Cape Breton to research the life of an obscure, nineteenth-century writer. There Rhea indulges in an exploitative fling with a fellow student – Abelard Hearn, her "Mi'Kmaq lover" (Fairburn 136). She is a callous manipulatrix: "I toyed with the possibility of using Abelard.... Literary history justified small sins. Abelard might be hurt, I accepted that..."(109). Abelard remains a cypher. His behaviour is senseless, his speech reproduces gangster clichés ("And if you don't change your mind, there are ways of persuading you" [160]), he possesses, puckishly, "the disturbing knack of appearing out of nowhere" (85), and he commits suicide when Rhea betrays his love. *Endless Bay* recycles a rather damnable brew of white paranoia and sexual attraction for the dark Other, a considerable achievement in this time of heightened racial sensitivities.

6. Craig adds that "racism is the theme of many non-fiction works as well..." (139 n.1).

7. Anecdotally, I can state that I know one Africadian who prefers to live in Quebec where she feels that anti-Black racism is less intense that in Nova Scotia.

8. In *Masculine Migrations: Reading the Postcolonial Male in "New Canadian" Narratives* (1998), Daniel Coleman observes that in the English translation of Laferrière's novel, translator David Homel drops the nickname "Vieux" (old man) given the narrator in the original French language version of the novel. Like Coleman, I have decided to use Laferrière's name for the protagonist, rather than Homel's "anonymous." But, I have chosen to draw my citations from Homel's translation.

9. Pellerin's title alludes, perhaps, to Quebec playwright Dominic Champagne's nationalist work *La cité interdite* (1992), which addresses the October Crisis of 1970.

10. It may be objected that the usage ofthe "Negro king" metaphor is not racial, but rather merely an accurate allusion to the manner in which Britain historically conducted it imperial policy in sub-Saharan Africa. I would maintain, though, that the opprobrium, evinced by the phrase is directly related to the innate inferiority implied by "Negro" and its synonyms. In other words, it may not to be imprecise to read "Negro king" as a palimpsest for "nigger."

11. In February 1996, a federal Liberal politician, Stéphane Dion, managed to rankle the editors of *Afrique Tribune*, a Montreal-based, African-Québécois, bi-weekly journal. Scorning Quebec sovereignty, Dion warned, "Si une telle idée devait mener le monde, elle ferait exploser l'Afrique et l'Asie et mettrait à mal l'Europe" (*Afrique Tribune* 16). The journal editorialized, "Curieux tout de même que pour une des rares fois que le continent africain surgit dans le debat, il ait été associé à une explosion alors que l'Europe serait simplement à mal sous la même menace" (16). Happily, in 1996, it is not as easy to hint at the supposed backwardness of Africans as it was in 1968.

12. Lantagne's evocation of this dark, wintry, existential crisis illuminates a similar, much more ludic passage in Québécois author Anne Dandurand's novel *The Cracks* (1992): I'm experiencing the tundra of the soul, much worse than the other, geographic tundra. Readers, I beg you to console me, grant me the Caribbean of kindness, an Africa of goodness, super-nova of human warmth, relieve me of this black hole I'm foundering in, help! (115).

Dandurand's protagonist also utilizes racial *clichés* however. She sums up her one-time Ugandan lover as "the most rigid prick of my entire past, the sexual technique of a pile-driver and a heart whose size was in keeping with my thin little figure" (22).

13. Incidentally, Lantagne's text debuted amid a flurry of ugly statements by Québécois politicos on the status of non-*pure laine* ethnicities in *la belle province*. First published in the autumn 1994 edition of *Nuit blanche*, "Histoire noire" was in Quebec bookstores when then Deputy Premier Bernard Landry charged, on 29 October 1994, that "It's not healthy that democracy in Montreal is completely at the mercy of the ethnic communities' vote." See Julie Barlow (4).

14. Some critics of Laferrière paid fealty to this stereotype. For instance, Étienne recalls that, in response to Laferrière's work, "un grand critique littéraire patenté de *La Presse*, dans son compte rendu, avoue le plus candidement du monde que, dans certains clubs de la ville [Montréal], "les Blanches courent après le sexe des nègres' (citation de mémoire)" (148).

15. While bearing in mind that writers' critiques of their critics are suspect, I must mention that, in a conversation I had with Laferrière in Antigonish, Nova Scotia, on Friday, 8 March 1996, he informed me that Longchamps's comments reflect – I paraphrase – the ignorance of someone who has not travelled widely.

16. Laferrière's sentence, "Look, Mamma, says the Young White Girl, look at the Cut [sic] Negro" (17), echoes Fanon's voicing of white reactions to the presence of a black: "Regarde le nègre!... Maman, un nègre!..." (93). His phrase "Soul on fire" (74) is an ironic reference to Cleaver's *Soul on Ice*.

17. The latter possibility cannot be discounted, for Seers knew Haitian poets. He even planned to publish *Les Enfances de Fanny*, in serial form, in a Haitian newspaper. See R. Dion-Lévesque (1-2).

18. According to Joachim, white authorial depictions of Blacks' supposed "grosses lèvres" connote "animalité, viscosité, mobilité, humidité (rampance), rétractilité, laideur..." (60).

19. Here Donat's sentiments dovetail with those of Mayotte Capécia, the Martiniquaise author who found *Green Pastures* (or *Verts Pâturages*) a nasty shock: "Comment imaginer Dieu sous les traits d'un nègre? Ce n'est pas ainsi que je me représente le paradis" (quoted in Fanon 43). Interestingly, both Seers (white) and Capécia (Black) desired, ultimately, a whitened blackness.

20. Préfontaine has written poetry on the African-American jazz artist John Coltrane: "Coltrane-my-friend-pure-negative-of-my-snow-white-photo / misery of ebony as in the Stravinsky concerto / for petty bourgeois figuring their fractions in guilt / on the Stock Market of horror" (53). His lines enact problematic assessments of blackness, but they cannot be termed anti-intellectual.

ARMAND GARNET RUFFO

Out of the Silence –
The Legacy of E. Pauline Johnson:
An Inquiry into the Lost and Found Work
of Dawendine – Bernice Loft Winslow

Years ago as a student I moved to Ottawa to take up a summer job with the (now-defunct) *Native Perspective Magazine*, published by the National Association of Native Friendship Centres. A relative who knew that I was attending university and that I was interested in writing had called me at my home in Northern Ontario to tell me of an advertisement for a writer he had seen in the magazine. Although I had just got a job changing railway track, I jumped at the opportunity. I called immediately and was asked to come in for an interview. The next day I told my boss that I was quitting and hopped an eastbound train. I was young and prepared to take the gamble.

Two of my first assignments with the magazine were to write an article on E. Pauline Johnson (1861-1913) about whom I really knew very little, and to manage the "literary corner" of the last few pages of the magazine where we would publish poetry and stories as they arrived.

In those days submissions were not plentiful. One poet I chose to publish at the outset was my own Ojibway grandmother. She had always written and recited poetry but had never published, simply because it was quite unheard of when she was growing up in northern Ontario at the turn of the century. To a great extent we are all products of our time and place. Thus I knew that seeing her poetry in print would be a thrill for her, and I set about doing this. The poem that I chose to publish was called "Lost," which ended with the poignant line "Lost am I/ In my native land." Curious about her influences, I asked my grandmother whom she had read as a young woman. Her answer was none other than Pauline Johnson.

I mention my early foray into the world of publishing in the context of two experiences that are distinct yet intimately related. The first has to do with my work as a teacher whose students of Native literature continually ask about the apparent 50-year gap between the writing of Pauline Johnson and modern Native writers such as Harold Cardinal, Maria Campbell, and Howard Adams. The second has to do with the stark realization that the history of Native publishing in Canada, or more precisely the lack of it, attests to a culture of inclusion and, inversely, exclusion. It is with this in mind, then, that I would like to pull together some thoughts about the issue of silence in Native literature during what has been referred to as the "dark days" of the residential school period. In doing so, I will make reference to the lost and found writings of Bernice Loft Winslow, the Mohawk writer Dawendine, a poet profoundly influenced by the work of E. Pauline Johnson.

Not long ago, I was browsing through a shelf-lined wall of books in a cramped second-hand bookstore and came across Desmond Pacey's 1952 publication, *Creative Writing In Canada*. Flipping through the table of contents, I immediately sought out what poems of Pauline Johnson were included in the anthology. I knew full well that at the time of Pacey's text, Johnson was still the sole Native (in her case Mohawk) poet to enjoy publication. In fact, it is not off the mark to claim that hers is the lone voice of Native poetry in Canada until well into the 1960s. To my surprise, I was confronted with Pacey's utter dismissal of the poet. In a single line Pacey sums up Johnson's work: "Pauline Johnson, the daughter of an Indian chief, who won great fame by her native dress and dramatic recitals, but the great bulk of whose work is meretricious" (68). This "great bulk" comprises both poetry and prose, but we do not hear one word about it. Instead, Pacey dedicates six pages to the work of Duncan Campbell Scott, whose poetic career was established through his writing *about* "Indian" people and whose work, I might add, intent on recording a "weird and waning race" (Dragland 192), is regarded today as being of dubious merit. Admittedly, much of Johnson's work, particularly in her second collection, *Canadian Born*, begs the question as to whether Johnson the writer was undermined by Johnson the performer. There is also the related question of her being co-opted into white Canadian society; by this I mean Johnson the Union-Jack-waving poet, extolling the virtues of a fledgling nation. Nevertheless, whatever the meretriciousness of this work, it is by no means all there is to Pauline Johnson.

It is not my intention to focus on the poetry of Pauline Johnson in order to defend her slighted reputation. What I am attempting to do here is illustrate the problem of recognizing and accepting a Native voice as a legitimate literary voice, and the negative ramifications of this failure. The problem, at least in part, is a function of point of view. Certainly Johnson at her best was writing as a Native, specifically as a Mohawk, and it is documented fact that she made no pretence about it. In a now-famous quotation, Johnson states, "There are those who think they pay me a compliment in saying I am just like a white woman. I am Indian, and my aim, my joy, my pride, is to sing the glories of my people" (Johnson ix). It is her Native heritage that provides the foundation for Johnson's best writing in that it is the point of view inherent in the work, evinced thematically in the subjects she chooses to write about. This is most evident in a poem such as "The Cattle Thief," or a story like "As It Was In The Beginning." Johnson's Native perspective is also present in her idyllic nature poetry, such as in her famous "The Song My Paddle Sings." The Canada Johnson writes about is not an urban but rather a rural and Native Canada, where nature is still very present and still non-threatening, where she can still paddle her canoe or gaze out upon an unobstructed mountain and feel connected to the land.

According to a well-known anecdote, Pauline Johnson, dressed in her buckskin attire, attempted to read a poem in the Mohawk language only to be booed off the stage by her white audience. Johnson later wrote that she could swerve very little from the path laid out for her by a white public.

> You thought me more of the true poet, more the child of inspiration than I have proved to be. The reason of my actions in this matter? Well the reason is that the public will not listen to lyrics, will not appreciate real poetry, will in fact not have me as an entertainer if I give them nothing but rhythm, cadence, beauty, thought…. Ye Gods, how I hate their laughter at times, when such laughter is called forth by some of my brainless lines and business. I could do better if they would only let me. (Petrone 82)

In hindsight, it is apparent that in her time Johnson was trapped by both her public, who came to expect an "Indian" performance from the poet, and her critics, who sharply criticized her work. Yet, within this restrictive environment, Johnson still found room to manoeuvre. Long deemed to have little literary merit, Johnson's work has recently begun to be re-evaluated and early judgments are being questioned.[1]

Countering negative assessments of Johnson's work, a poem like "The Cattle Thief" may be read as a Native take on Canadian history, a response to colonial domination well ahead of its time, as well as the poet identifying herself with the female protagonist through the collective pronoun: "You say your cattle are not ours, your meat is not our meat;/ when you pay for the land you live in, *we'll* [her italics] pay for/ the meat we eat" (Johnson 13). This is not the Indian poetry of a Duncan Campbell Scott. I would even go so far as to say that in "The Cattle Thief" Johnson asserts her Native perspective to set the historical record straight, to challenge the "myth" of the heroic pioneer, taming and settling a land empty and ready for the taking. It is a perception of Canada and Canadian history that critics, such as Desmond Pacey some 40 years after Johnson's death in 1913, were still not prepared to hear, let alone accept.

This position is underscored by Pacey's introduction to *Creative Writing in Canada* where he attempts to defend the notion of Canadian culture and literature and, in doing so, severely critiques Native culture. Pacey begins with what might be best described as defiance draped in nationalism. He writes: "In October of 1950 a reviewer in *The Times Literary Supplement* declared that Canada is a country with no indigenous culture. It is difficult to decide what he meant by this declaration. If he used the word 'indigenous' in its strict sense, then his view is a defensible one" (Pacey 1). Evidently, Pacey's idea of what is indigenous to Canadian writing had nothing to do with Canada's "Indigenous" peoples. Had this been the case, then Pauline Johnson could not have been dismissed so readily. In keeping with the nationalistic framework, and in positing thematic commonalities in Canadian literature, Pacey excluded Johnson because she simply did not fit the mould that he and later "thematic" critics cast. I would not hesitate to say that this is due in large part to Johnson's positioning of herself as a Native writer and the focus of her work.

Beth Brant explains that, writing at the turn of the century, Pauline Johnson "had seen ugly change brought to her people. Educated by her white mother in literature and the Classics, she brought a new kind of writing into the world: "fictionalized accounts of the horrors and dangers of colonialism, stories of strong and proud Native women.... While some may think of her language [today] as old-fashioned and dated, her politic remains clear, fresh and beautiful (Brant 37). Yet, with a simple stroke of the pen, Canada's only Native voice of the time was left out of the Canadian "canon," and for all intents and purposes was silenced.

While I have directed my comments to Pacey's 1952 study, having encountered it, as I mentioned, in a recent book browsing expedition, similar observations apply to the work of other critics who also have had a significant influence on the development of Canadian literature. For example, Carl F. Klinck in *The Literary History of Canada*, published some 15 years after Pacey's study, acknowledges Johnson's popularity, considering it "at once surprising and significant," but he is sceptical when it comes to the value of her work: "What value her poems will have when the memory of her vigorous personality has faded it is difficult to say" (Klinck 426). He attributes her continuing popularity to the fact that "Johnson is still what she was at the very beginning, a symbol which satisfied a felt need.... This need to realize topography in terms of life is, of course, the fundamental fact of Canadian experience" (*Ibid*). In her introduction to *The Moccasin Maker*, American critic, A. LaVonne Brown Ruoff, in a brief re-evaluation of Johnson's work and career, remarks that Johnson fulfilled another so-called need as well: "to portray the experiences and emotions of two minority groups, whose voices were little heard in the Canadian literature of Johnson's own day – Indians and women" (34).

These observations return me to Beth Brant, who, in an address to an assembly of Native writers, remarked that "Pauline Johnson is our spiritual grandmother. What we do today as writers must honour her" (37). Certainly there can be no greater value in a writer's work than to influence those who come after. Brant's comment brings me to a central question: If Pauline Johnson is "grandmother" to contemporary Native writers, to whom was she "mother"? Before I can begin to address this question, I must first consider briefly what happened to Native peoples during and following Johnson's career – in particular, the impact of the residential schools.

Johnson untimely death in 1913 is especially tragic for Native peoples. It marks both the loss of Canada's foremost Native poet and the loss of opportunity for new Native voices to develop and build on Johnson's legacy. Ironically, that same year poet Duncan Campbell Scott assumed the position of deputy superintendent general of the Department of Indian Affairs. In this capacity, Scott took it upon himself to employ his astute bureaucratic skills to further the assimilationist policy of the federal government:

> The education of native children in day and residential schools was one of the key elements in Canada's Indian policy from its inception. The destruction of the children's link to their ancestral culture and their assimilation into the dominant society were its main objectives. Although they remained unquestioned during the rise of Duncan Campbell Scott in the Department of Indian Affairs, success continued to elude the policies. When Scott was appointed ... he took measures to render the system more efficient. (Titley 75)

Initiated by the British Colonial Office in the early-nineteenth century for the purpose of civilizing Native peoples and solving the "Indian problem," the policy of residential schools for Native children had dire consequences for Native peoples. It disrupted and alienated them from their own societies and cultures, and resulted in – to use the words of Beth Brant – "ugly change" (37). A report published in the Province of Canada in 1847, which strongly influenced the development of Native educational policy, provides irrefutable evidence of the government's plan to destroy Native culture: "Their education must consist not merely of the training of the mind, but of a weaning from the habits and feelings of their ancestors, and the acquirements of the language, arts and customs of civilized life" (Haig-Brown 29).

Residential schools were first made compulsory in 1894 when the Indian Act was amended (Dickason 334), and they lasted well into the 1960s. In initiating a policy of compulsory education for Native children, the government of Canada had a clear and determined agenda of what it wanted to see happen to Native peoples. "Under the guidance of government agents and evangelical missionaries, the Indians were to be settled in permanent villages and instructed in the English language, Christianity, and agricultural methods. The hoped-for result was self-supporting individuals who were indistinguishable from their fellow citizens" (Titley 3). What this meant was that as many young children as possible were sent to residential missionary-run schools, where they lived in isolation from their families and communities until early adulthood. By then, most could no longer speak their language or participate in the few ceremonies that had gone underground to escape the prying eye of the Indian agents or missionaries. To call such a policy cultural genocide does not seem an exaggeration.

The tragedy of residential schools is twofold. Not only were Native students deprived of their own language and culture (many dying in the process due to disease and neglect), but beyond the rudiments of an industrial education, they learned very little of Euro-Canadian traditions.

According to historian Olive Dickason, "In 1930, three quarters of Native pupils across Canada were in grades one to three; only three in 100 went past grade six.... Such figures could be explained at least partly by the type of curricula Amerindians were subjected to: the emphasis on the 'practical' was such that an Amerindian was lucky to reach grade five by the age of eighteen" (335). Métis writer Lee Maracle draws on family experience to relate how the residential school experience actually undermined the education of Native peoples: "Historically, the difficulty for us in mastering this language [English] was that it was not accessible to us.... My sister spent years praying at convent school, cooking delicious pies and ironing the starched paraphernalia of the nunnery and the priesthood along with dozens of other Native girls. She left school at fifteen, functionally illiterate" (38). It is no wonder that this type of education did not produce many Native poets and writers. It would be a generalization to say that all residential schools subjected their students to intolerable conditions, as there was little standardization among schools. Nevertheless, it is safe to say that children who managed to be educated within their communities were much more likely to retain their Native traditions and language.

It is in this context that we must consider the work of Dawendine, the Mohawk name of Bernice Loft Winslow, who published her first and only book *Iroquois Fires: The Six Nations Lyrics and Lore of Dawendine* at the ripe old age of 93. It is not surprising to discover that, like Pauline Johnson, Dawendine was educated at home, on the Six Nations Reserve, by her parents, and in a small one-room day school (as was my own grandmother) not far from the family farm. Thus, not only did she manage to escape the trauma of residential school, but with her parents' support she went on to attend high school in neighbouring Caledonia. Upon graduation Dawendine followed her brother into the teaching profession (Dawendine 17). Remaining in her community during her formative years allowed her access to her "grandparents and parents [who] provided her with a living link to the past and with role models and precedents for her career as an orator and writer" (Dawendine 14).

As an orator and writer, Dawendine travelled throughout southern Ontario during the 1930s, lecturing at schools and universities, as well as service clubs, church groups, and girls' and women's organizations. She also represented her people at commemorative events, such as the unveiling of historic monuments and plaques (Dawendine 17). It is interesting to note that Dawendine was active, both lecturing and writing, during the so-called "dark days," or what Penny Petrone, in *Native Writing In Canada*, refers to as "the barren period for Native writing in Canada" (95). Significantly, Dawendine's work helps to confirm that Native peoples did manage to express themselves during one of the bleakest periods in Native Canadian history. When Beth Brant speaks of the notion of continuity among Native writers after Pauline Johnson, she refers specifically to contemporary writers, but she could certainly be speaking of Dawendine.

Born on the Six Nations Reserve, the same community that produced Pauline Johnson, and writing a mere 20 years after Johnson's death, Dawendine clearly draws on her predecessor's poetry for inspiration in her own work. It is not surprising, then, that Dawendine's poetry displays a Mohawk perspective similar to that of Johnson. The influence of Johnson's work extends all the way to the very style of Dawendine's writing, their subject matter differing inasmuch as their lives differed. This observation is not lost to Robert Stacey and Donald Smith, the editors of *Iroquois Fires*, who refer to the influence of Pauline Johnson on Dawendine in their introduction:[2]

> When [Dawendine] … posed in Native custom for a publicity photograph in the 1930s, she adopted the profile attitude of perhaps the most famous of Pauline Johnson's platform images. A comparison of titles of individual poems also suggests that the younger writer was influenced by her older mentor in subject matter as well as style. No doubt Bernice drew direct inspiration from the fact that Johnson had written a poem on the legend of "Dawendine, Child of Morning." (Dawendine 16)

Imitating the style and even the themes of another writer is at odds with the concept of individualism developed in the history of Western thought and literature, and may lead to an immediate critical dismissal of a work in question. In Dawendine's case, however, we must consider the purpose of traditional oratory and song, as well as the necessary positioning of both authors as Mohawks. In this context, the following remark by Paula Gunn Allen is illuminating: "American Indian and Western literary traditions differ greatly in the assumed purposes they serve. The purpose of traditional American Indian literature is never simply pure self-expression" (*Sacred Hoop* 55). This is a literature that presents the relationship of the individual to a larger community in which individual voice is seen as being responsible for its well-being. Responsibility to community is a central tenet throughout writing by Native peoples.

> The tribes seek – through song, ceremony, legend, sacred stories (myths), and tales – to embody, articulate, and share reality, to bring the isolated, private self into harmony and balance with this reality, to verbalize the sense of the majesty and reverent mystery of all things, and to actualize, in language, those truths…. (*Ibid.*)

The tradition in which Dawendine's work originates, in continuing in the footsteps of Pauline Johnson, subsumes individual voice within the larger collective voice of her own First Nation. By this I mean that although the "private self" is certainly evident in the writer's work, the latter is rooted in tradition, as is much of Pauline Johnson's. It speaks not only *of* those traditions, but also *from* them. Thus we can say that Dawendine's voice is also the voice of her people. This apparent contradiction is contained and emphasized in the title *Iroquois Fires: The Six Nations Lyrics and Lore of Dawendine*. Dawendine's "voice" and the lyrics and lore of her people are essentially one and the same. It is a concept that is often unrecognized by, and foreign to, Euro-Canadian writers and critics.

In many instances, Dawendine's "lore" is no less than transcriptions of the oral stories she heard growing up in her community. Consider the two opening poems in the collection. Both "Mohawk Prayer" and "Awake America" draw upon a traditional symbol and employ the Mohawk language – the very foundation of culture – to illustrate the cultural integrity and purpose so central to the concept of Native literature. In "Mohawk Prayer," the author offers a culturally coded prayer for her people in which, as the title indicates, Dawendine's individuality is subordinated to the collective identity of her people. Thus, the poem makes no reference to the writer/speaker but addresses the reader/listener directly, offering the benevolence of the Creator under both favourable and adverse conditions: "Yea, in all seasons and weathers/ May the Great Spirit/ Smile kindly upon thee" (Dawendine 48). In doing so, the poem refers to "O-nenh-dah," the white pine, which for the Mohawk people has great spiritual significance as the mythic symbol of peace. Codified in narrative and inextricably bound to the well-being of the Mohawk people themselves, "O-nenh-dah" is featured in the political constitution of the Iroquois Confederacy, known as the Great Law of Peace. The front cover of the *Institutions of Mohawk Government in Kahnawake*, published by the Mohawk Council of Kahnawake, aptly illustrates this. The accompanying text indicates that "the cover drawing symbolizes key elements in Kahnawake's political philosophy ... the pine tree, with its roots and branches, symbolizes the shelter and protection afforded under the Great Law" (Mohawk Council of Kahnawake). This explains in part why "the pines" at Kanesatake held such significance for the Mohawks during the "Oka Crisis."

In "Awake America," which is essentially a call to arms, Dawendine again uses the Mohawk language, this time in the context of preparing for war. Again individuality is subordinated to the collective. Nowhere is there reference to the author as individual; instead the call is addressed outward to "all nations/ From the Atlantic to the Pacific" "Gwan-an! Gwan-an" (Dawendine 49). The poet shouts the cry of the warriors and becomes the voice of the Mohawk warrior. This is not to suggest that Dawendine's personality is totally absent, given over to what I have called a "collective" or "tribal voice." Outrage, despair, love, loss, these too mark the emotional landscape Dawendine inhabits, and it is this landscape that foregrounds individual personality.

The poem "Spirit Fires," subtitled "For Iroquois Dead In World War," emphasizes the collective voice of the Iroquois warrior or soldier and yet, it also reveals something of the poet herself:

For us no Death Songs were sung
No tribal deeds of valour chanted

Beside the rising smoke of mourning camp-fires
We died on alien sod...
And so the Iroquois fought
For honour, truth and justice, right.
And for the freedom of children yet unborn. (Dawendine 67)[3]

While Dawendine readily assumes the voice of the fallen warrior, the emotion evident in the poem arises from the personal response of the poet herself; as a member of the Mohawk nation, she too dies, if not physically, then figuratively, through the decimation of her people after contact.

The personal is even more present in a poem such as "The Moon Of Falling Leaves – Song of the Indian Woman To A Departing Warrior (Interpreted)." While rooted in the language and traditions of the Mohawk people, and their spiritual connection to the land, the poem clearly conveys a personal tone. This may appear contradictory, until it is noted that the text incorporates the voice of both the unknown Indian woman who could be anyone, and the voice of the poet who is a particular "Indian" woman. In a line such as "The Moon of Falling Leaves has come/ And now my love has gone from me" (Dawendine 69), the tone is extremely personal. Although undated (a failing of the collection), "Moon of Falling Leaves...," judging from subject and tone, appears to have been written during the same period as "Spirit Fires."

In some of her most powerful writing, Dawendine addresses "The uselessness, futilities of wars; that hate,/ Greed, and power mis-used can only sear/" (50). Her indignation and scorn find recourse in the integrity and strength of her Mohawk culture: "Again we need moccasined Trails of Peace" (*Ibid*). The poet's plea sounds the depth of the losses both she and her people have suffered. It is this sense of loss that appears in various guises. In "Iroquois Exile," for example, Dawendine tells what her own exile from her people and her land signifies. This, Robert Stacey observes, is "the plight of the diasporic exile living off the reserve" (Dawendine 144):

I live in a city
Flanked by stone
Walls. The sky alone
Glows, and hears the moan
Of the red man's heart.
Lost in the city. (Dawendine 57)

Here the poet's despair rings with clarity. The tone is bleak and unwavering, and we cannot help but feel for the poet and the Native peoples of whom she speaks, "Beloved earth torn/ From me" (*Ibid*). What makes the poem all the more powerful, however, is the note of irony with which it concludes in juxtaposing the gains and losses of her exile. With foresight, the poet tells us that, despite material affluence, the move away from community will have a profound effect on future generations, who may never know their Native traditions:

With maid, discreet
My children go, so neat
Lonely papoose cradles.
Hang, far from a city. (*Ibid.*)

The theme of contemporary Native peoples enduring and adapting to life in a changing world, in which even the "face" of her people is changing, is intimately expressed in a poem where Dawendine addresses her daughter. In the appropriately entitled, "Dawendine Talks to Oh-Wen-Ji-Yoh, 'The Good Earth,' Her Daughter," the author speaks with nostalgia and sorrow of "A line of Chiefs ... drawing to a close" (61). Like much of Dawendine's work, the poem does not dwell on the past simply for the sake of sentimentality but moves outward to address the future. The poet informs her daughter of her dual heritage and the potential to embrace two cultures: "For in you runs the blood of two/ Great races, the red and the white" (63). In doing so, she tells the young girl how she might live her life, "Weigh well the good in both –/ Of Gampa Chief and Grandmother Blue Eyes" (*Ibid*).

The theme of cultural survival and integrity reverberates in the final poems of the collection. "The Cornplanter Tract" is reminiscent of Pauline Johnson's "The Corn Husker":

The wind in the pines remembering
Seems gently to protest at their passing
While far above a hawk, wheeling,
Wheeling, braking on slanted wing
 Looks down on the deserted cabins,
The crumbling corn-cribs.... (Dawendine 83)

A way of life has come to an end; the corn-cribs are no longer in use. In their place stands a school where "The happy sounds of children/ Released from school, at play, Alien sounds of another tongue," make the poet wonder if the children "know their ancient dialects? Do they revere the mighty warriors, as/Chief Cornplanter, of their heritage?" (*Ibid.*). In considering her culture's survival through future generations, the poet turns her attention to the educational system of the dominant society, an issue of concern to Native peoples in general. Is the Euro-Canadian's education effective in maintaining and developing a strong Native culture, or is it merely a tool used to assimilate Native children into Euro-Canadian culture? The question that Dawendine poses turns to "the remembered earth" (Momaday 164). Is it not the land that will always be the cradle of Native culture? This is the final question that Dawendine leaves us with in her poetry:

This only remains, a school!
Or is it only in the sweep of meadow
Grass, and murmuring trees that

One may catch the noble strains
Of music long since past,
Voices of strong and wise warriors
Long since vanished? (83)

Like her "lyrics," Dawendine's "lore" is fundamentally a product of her Mohawk culture, perhaps even more so in that, with the exception of a few pieces, it resides in the oral tradition of her own and other Native communities. In his forward to *The Native Stories From Keepers of the Earth*, Kiowa writer N. Scott Momaday identifies a number of elements common to traditional stories. Among these is "one of the most important of all considerations in human experience: the relationship between man and nature. In the Native American world this relationship is so crucial as to be definitive of the way in which man formulates his own best idea of himself" (Bruchac vii). Dawendine's *The Six Nations Lyrics and Lore* is a literature deeply rooted in an oral tradition. As such, the work exhibits a relationship to language that is inextricably bound to community and nature while serving to "delight and teach" (Bruchac ix).

The stories in the collection range from "One, Two, Three," a personal remembrance of a young girl finding and raising three tiny mice, to traditional Native customs and legends. Whether set in the near or distant past, the stories tell of the intimate relationship between the people and the land. "The Spirit Light," for example, introduces the Mohawk custom of lighting a fire to guide the dead into the spirit world. "The Canoe-Maker's Daughter or Legend of Niagara" tells of the Neutral and the "maiden of the mist," a young woman who sacrifices herself for her independence. In contrast, "The Origin of the Water-Lily" takes place among the Ojibway at "a time when this world was filled with happy people, when all nations were as one" (Dawendine 138) and the star people visited the earth. As mentioned earlier, Dawendine also tells of the Origin of the Pine Tree (O-nenh-dah). Here she provides more details of the significance of this tree to the Mohawk people: "One day the bark of the tree became bruised. The people noticed red blood issuing from the wound.... Then the spirit of the pine tree, the young chief, was heard speaking ... this is my blood" (134). This story highlights Dawendine's people's close relationship to the natural world.

Whether "retelling" a traditional story or presenting a more personalized expression of poetry, Dawendine adheres to a method of communication that traditionally incorporates voice, music, and dance. In drawing upon oral tradition, her work naturally lends itself to performance, reminiscent of the work of Pauline Johnson. And like Johnson's writing, Dawendine's lyrics and lore confront the question of "literary value." What is evident is that stories and songs arising out of Native oral traditions are considered simplistic by dominant literary standards and relegated to the category of "children's literature." Criteria rooted in Western European tradition are applied to a non-Western literature as a means of determining whether the work in question is "literary." Katerie Akiwenzie-Damm refers to this process as "aesthetic colonization." On a practical level, what this determines is no less than publication and dissemination, what gets published and what does not.

Questions of literary value and evaluation, however, have recently come under intense scrutiny in the critical world. Barbara Herrnstein Smith highlights this issue:

> It should also be noted that ... literary authority, like any other normative authority, tends to be vested differentially along lines of general social and cultural dominance (that is, the people whose judgments have institutional power are usually those who have social and cultural power otherwise).... We are also more likely to engage with a text ... if its value has already been marked for us .... As this suggests, our interpretation of a text and our experience of its value are to some extent mutually dependent, and *both* depend upon the particular assumptions, expectations, and interests with which we approach the work." (183-84)

Herrnstein Smith's position implies that to have "literary" value a text must be sanctioned by the authority structure of a society. Members of a society choose a text according to assumptions and expectations based on how their society has judged and hence placed "value" on it. Drawing upon her oral traditions, Dawendine wrote from a position outside of the literary "norm" of the dominant society. As the assumptions and expectations that informed literary judgements were based upon European models, Dawendine's work was judged not for what it was, but for what it was expected to be. Nor was it "valued" as an expression of early Native Canadian writing. We cannot help but ask if Dawendine's long years of silence were a result of her Mohawk heritage and thus her approach to her work.

There is also the fact of Dawendine's lack of institutional power. In the context of culture and empire, Edward Said writes that "the authority of the observer, and of European geographical centrality, is buttressed by a cultural discourse relegating and confining the non-European to a secondary racial, cultural, ontological status" (*Culture and Imperialism* 59). For Dawendine, getting her work published was beyond her control. Centralized in the authority structure of society, Canadian publishers held to their Eurocentricity and showed no interest in her work. Without "real" power, the kind required to effect change, even to have her work published, Dawendine was banished into obscurity. Nevertheless, the poet did have admirers, such as the artist C.W. Jefferys. Jefferys tried to get her work into print, but to no avail. Dawendine's poetry did not appear until some 60 years after she began writing and performing. Half a century is a long time to wait for deserved attention.

In the "Afterword" to *Iroquois Fires* editors Robert Stacey and Donald Smith note that in 1947, when it was thought that the book would be published, writer Paul Wallace, in correspondence with Dawendine, astutely observed that "The handling of this Iroquois form in English will be something new in our language. I am excited about it. You are doing for the Mohawk what William Butler Yeats did for his people in the Irish Literary Renaissance" (Dawendine 149). Such a comment makes me ask how much influence Dawendine's work might have had on Native literature in Canada, and Canadian literature in general, if she had been published as a young woman and encouraged to pursue her writing. I think of my own grandmother who never dared to consider publication, knowing too well the place ascribed to her and her kind of writing in Canadian society. Dawendine's silence is lost potential, and it is to be regretted. Yet, with her re-appearance there is new potential. Native writers now have access to her work and can find inspiration in the knowledge that there was a Native voice struggling to be heard during the "dark days" of the residential school period, and in the knowledge that the "grandchildren" of Pauline Johnson also, albeit unknowingly, follow in the footsteps of Bernice Loft Winslow – Dawendine.

NOTES

I have used the word Mohawk in this essay because it is the term used by both Pauline Johnson and Dawendine to refer to their people. This name is of Algonquin origin; the name they traditionally used to describe themselves is in fact "Kanyen'kehaka – the people of the flint" (Maracle 239).

1. Norman Shrive, in "What Happened to Pauline," *Canadian Literature* 13 (Summer 1962): 25-38, calls for more studies of "this internationally famous versifier and story-teller."
2. I would take issue with Robert Stacey who appears, in the "Afterword," to dismiss Johnson's work outright as "conventional" and "sentimental."
3. The last lines quoted are tinged with irony in that Dawendine's uncle Fredrick Loft, a First World War veteran, had attempted to organize The League of Indians of Canada in order to press Canada to uphold treaty obligations, while the Department of Indian Affairs did everything in its power to oppose and undermine its establishment.

DREW HAYDEN TAYLOR

Alive and Well: Native Theatre in Canada

Native theatre is alive and well in Canada. Today Native theatre is strong, popular, and practically everywhere in the Canadian theatrical community. What once was barren is now bountiful. In 1986 there was one working Native playwright in all of Canada. Today the work of at least two dozen playwrights of aboriginal descent is being produced. If that trend continues, by the year 2020 it is conceivable that everybody in Canada will be a Native playwright!

I have a theory as to why theatre seems to be the medium of choice amongst Native Canadians. We have novelists, we have short-story writers, we have musicians, we have actors, etc., but in terms of artists per capita, theatre has become the predominant vehicle of expression. The reason for this is that theatre is a logical extension of Native storytelling. Traditional storytelling – not just Native storytelling but storytelling in general – is the process of taking your audience on a journey, using your voice, your body, and the spoken word. Moving that journey onto the stage is merely the next logical step. Because of our oral culture Native peoples gravitate towards theatre more than towards the written word where you have to have perfect English or grammatically correct writing. The spotty education offered Native peoples by the government and various societal institutions has not been great. This is one of the reasons I became a playwright: I write as people talk, and the way people talk is not always grammatically correct – therefore I can get away with less than "perfect" English.

At its origins, storytelling was a way of relating the history of the community. It was a way of explaining human nature. A single story could have metaphorical, philosophical or psychological implications. Unfortunately, in today's society, many Native legends have been relegated to the status of quaint children's stories. But legends and stories were never meant to be quaint children's stories. They were told to adults as well as to children, and as you got older, you could tap into a whole new understanding of the story. It was like an onion, you peeled away more and more to get to the core of the story.

Let me give you an example, but please note: I am many things, but a traditional storyteller is not one of them. Telling a good story involves a special talent and years of practice, so please bear with me. The story about the creation of the earth starts with a woman on top of the back of a turtle. The woman has fallen through a hole in the sky and discovers the whole world is flooded. She desperately wants to find land, so she sends animals, one after another, down to the bottom of the water to try to find some earth – a single speck of dirt. The animals keep diving down, some returning empty handed, others dying and floating to the surface without any dirt in their paws. The beaver, the loon, all these different animals try but fail. Finally, the lowly muskrat comes up and says "Please let me try." Now the muskrat is viewed with disdain; he is like a water rat. But he persists and repeats, "Let me try." So the muskrat dives down and he is gone for a long period of time. He goes down, down, down. Everybody thinks he's dead. But finally he surfaces. He is unconscious so he is pulled to shore on the back of the turtle. In his paw there is a tiny bit of dirt. That's all the woman needs to create an earth on the back of a turtle. And that is why North America is referred to by First Nations peoples as Turtle Island.

Now that is a very brief, rough summary of a creation myth, a small segment of the larger myth. How that legend is told for adult understanding was shown to me by the writer and storyteller Basil Johnston. The legend refers to the psychological process of reaching deep inside yourself to find that nugget that is your grounding, your earth, the essence of who you are. The story can be interpreted as the need to survive a dangerous journey with dangerous ramifications. The journey to find that nugget – that is the most important thing – is the story of creation from a different, more philo-sophical or psychological viewpoint. Taking that interpretation – the story as archetypal self-exploration – and then putting it into the theatre, seems like a natural progression. At the same time the story has meaning for children. Take any storyteller, watch him or her work with kids, suspending their disbelief and taking them on a journey, using characters and an interesting plot line – that is the basis of any good theatrical presentation.

There have always been many different forms of theatre in our nations' history. During the onslaught of Christianity, of the government, and the residential school system etc., traditional Native beliefs were deemed offensive and unnecessary. There were numerous attempts to stamp them out and replace them with white North American/European concepts. It is incredibly hard, however, to eradicate the simple act of telling stories. Our culture persevered, and today we are getting our voice back.

Prior to the Second World War, it was illegal for Native peoples to leave the reserve without written permission from the Indian agent. With the advent of the war, many Native peoples enlisted in the armed services. We were exempt from the draft because legally we were not considered citizens of Canada. Because of our warrior traditions, however, and, in some cases, a bizarre loyalty to the King, many Native men enlisted and went to Europe. There they found there were different ways of doing things. They didn't have to just stay on the reserve and do what they were told. After the war, many Native peoples had a more worldly outlook. Also, in 1960, Native peoples finally got the right to vote in Canada. There was a progression of events; it was like a puzzle, each bit falling into place. Native peoples were beginning to understand that there were alternatives. We began to assert ourselves. In 1968 there was a demonstration in Kenora over a park that the Native community wanted back. In 1973 there was Wounded Knee. And so on and so forth.

Each event was a big step towards getting our voice back. There were also little steps in between. In 1967 George Ryga wrote the play *The Ecstasy of Rita Joe*, which became a milestone in Canadian theatre in offering more accurate representations of the urban Indian experience. It was, however, written by a non-Native person and I think most of the cast for the original production in Vancouver was non-Native. Nevertheless it did start people talking about the power of theatre and about the plight of Native peoples. In 1974, an organization was created in Toronto called the Association for Native Development in the Performing and Visual Arts. It set up the Native Theatre School, the first of its kind to teach Native peoples how to act, to teach them theatrical production, and to teach them how to write their own stories. The Theatre School operates during the summer for seven weeks: for four weeks the students train, and for the other three they perform. In addition, they write their own play as a collective, direct it, and then take it on the road for a tour. It has been over 20 years since the Native Theatre School was created, and many well-known Native actors have been a part of the school.

In 1979 the Association for Native Development in the Performing and Visual Arts was invited to perform a play at the International Theatre Festival in Monaco. The members of the troupe found themselves in the awkward position of having no play to perform, so they decided to remedy the situation as best they could. They contacted a Native poet by the name of George Kenny who had written a book of poetry called *Indians Don't Cry*. One of his poems "October Stranger" had good dramatic potential. With the help of an experienced Native actor, they adapted the poem into a play (also called *October Stranger)*, and they took it to Monaco. It was a fiasco. Everybody in Europe seemed to be expecting buckskin, feathers, and beads. Instead these contemporary Native youth came in to do a serious play about a person leaving the reserve to go and live in a city and becoming acculturated. This was not what the people at the Monaco theatre festival wanted to see.

Another important moment in the history of Native theatre was the 1984 creation of a drama company called the De-Ba-Jeh-Mu-Jig Theatre Group. *De-Ba-Jeh-Mu-Jig* is an Ojibway-Cree word meaning storyteller or tattler of tales. The De-Ba-Jeh-Mu-Jig Theatre Group was started by Shirley Cheechoo who is an amazing painter, actress, model, and playwright. Shirley Cheechoo is a person who does whatever intrigues her – if she wants to write a play, she'll write a play; if she wants to do a painting, she'll do a painting. She started De-Ba-Jeh-Mu-Jig as a summer theatre company on the West Bay Reserve on Manitoulin Island. It was created partly to showcase Native legends, both traditional and contemporary, and partly to raise some money by performing for tourists in the summer. Every year the company produced a play.

Although the professionalism of the work was rough to begin with, it developed gradually. The group performed plays such as *Nothing Personal, Nanabush of the 80s,* and a whole series of others that toured communities in and around southern Ontario.

During the 1984-85 season, the De-Ba-Jeh-Mu-Jig Theatre Group was catapulted into the theatrical limelight. The powers-that-be contacted a man they asked to be their artistic director; Shirley was busy and didn't have the time to devote her full attention to the company. The person they approached to go to Manitoulin Island and run the company was a Cree writer by the name of Tomson Highway.

Tomson Highway spent the winter on the island in a portable trailer. The circumstances were not the most enjoyable, but he persevered. He visited a nearby community, about 45 minutes away, called Wikwemikong or Wiki to the local people. It was there he first formulated the idea for a play that would become very important for Native theatre. He noticed all of these women rushing around, going to play a game called ... bingo! He watched and saw people becoming really obsessed. They'd enter the bingo palace, and there would be dead silence, just smoke floating through the room. That is where Tomson first developed the idea for the play *The Rez Sisters*. He wrote the first draft on the island and workshopped it there too. A year later, he came back to Toronto with his script.

In Toronto another Native theatre company, slightly older than the one on Manitoulin, had been formed in 1982 by a group of artistic friends, urban Indians who wanted to act. The Native Earth Performing Arts Company functioned as a collective. Basically people got together saying: "I have an idea for a show, let's go do it." There was no overall structure to the company, no artistic director, no administrator, no core funding, just a room at the Toronto Native Friendship Centre and an occasional show. Then Tomson arrived and became artistic director. He took his play *The Rez Sisters* to a dozen theatre companies in Toronto. Nobody was interested. In my opinion they didn't want to do the play for a very basic reason: the fundamental difference between Native theatre and Western European or Canadian theatre. Every artistic director Tomson showed his play to said, "Nobody cares about a group of seven women wanting to play bingo," and "there's no drama in the story." I've had this experience too with one of my plays. What they were saying, by and large, is that European drama is based on conflict. The story progresses through conflict, information is perceived through conflict. That is the Western dramatic structure, and it is the opposite of Native theatre. To understand this you must remember Native theatre's origins in storytelling. Stories were told in small family groupings. For example, the Ojibway would be in family groupings during the winter living in close quarters. If somebody had a problem, or if somebody was angry and aggressive about making a point about something, it was frowned upon and discouraged because conflict could infringe upon the harmony of the community and thus threaten its survival. Overt or aggressive conflict was actively and urgently discouraged within the family, and this manifested itself within the stories too. A lot of the traditional legends are more narrative than dramatic – the hero goes on a journey, but he doesn't have to fight his way or slay dragons to get to the other end. Again there are exceptions to that rule; I know of many bloody legends within Native storytelling. But on the whole, conflict is discouraged within our community, and our stories reflect that. *The Rez Sisters* is about a group of women going to Toronto to participate in the world's biggest bingo. They do that, then come back. There's no big fight, there's no big car chase, there's no big conflict *per se.* There's squabbling. But it's the squabbling of everyday life – not Shakespearean-style sword-fighting, which is a hell of a way to resolve a story.

Most of the artistic directors didn't know how to handle this different way of telling a story. When I was first trying to interest Morris Podbrey in a Montreal production of my play *Someday,* which is about the "scoop-up" when Native children were taken away for adoption by the Children's Aid Society, he said the structure went against everything he was taught about drama. All the information comes too easily, everybody gets along too well. He liked the story, but felt it was missing something. Larry Lewis, who produced and directed both *Someday* and *The Rez Sisters* in Toronto, had a chat with Morris, explained some things about Native theatre, and the play was mounted in Montreal in 1994.

Lack of conflict is one of the fundamental differences between European and Native drama. For instance, one of the legends I know – again in rough because I'm not a storyteller – is Thunderbird children. Father Thunderbird and Thunderbird children fly around, doing the "Thunderbird thing." The two children see a village of humans and watch what's going on. The male Thunderbird sees the men having these great epic battles, and the female Thunderbird sees the women giving birth and creating life. They become infatuated with human life. Back at Thunderbird camp, the two children, after talking with each other, tell their father, "We would like to become humans." One says, "I would like to become a great warrior," and the other one says, "I would like to create life." Father Thunderbird replies, "Well, I wish you would remain here with me, but if that is your wish I will grant it under one condition. What you have to do is find me the cleanest lodge that exists. You have to go down and find a house, a place to be born that is absolutely immaculate." The two Thunderbird children go from village to village. They find some lodges that are very clean and many that are not very clean, but they can never find an absolutely immaculate and clean lodge.

One day they are travelling by a river and they see a woman heavy with child washing herself in the river. They are curious and follow her back to her camp and watch her enter her lodge. Because they are invisible, they can go in too. She has the cleanest lodge they've ever seen. So they say, "We've found it, father, this is what you've asked, and we've found it." As it happens, the woman gives birth to twins. The boy comes out of the birthing process covered in blood and immediately starts crying, "Oh no, I'm dying, I've been stabbed, I've been pierced, I'm never going to be a great warrior." The mother tells him, "No you're fine, you've just been born, you will grow up to be a great warrior." The same thing happens with the girl. The mother consoles the children who grow up to be a warrior and a great woman elder of the community. They live their lives, they die, and they go back up to the great Father Thunderbird. Now that's a very rough telling of a legend; I'm not doing it justice. But in that legend there's no fight, there's no argument, there's no great conflict. The characters are given an objective, they achieve it, and they go on. This is the structure of a lot of traditional Native legends which, to reiterate, conflicts with the European dramatic process.

Because he couldn't get anybody to produce his play, Tomson Highway decided that he would have to produce it himself. It is a seven-character play and very expensive to mount. Somehow Tomson managed to do it. He raised the money and he co-produced it with his friend Larry Lewis who also directed it. The first week it did abysmally. Part of the reason had to do with another common feature of Native theatre: the play had no central character. *The Rez Sisters* features seven women, all of equal importance, all with an equally important story. Most people are not used to that. They are used to a protagonist – Hamlet for example – at the centre of the story. Each of the Rez sisters has her own story, and each story is of equal weight and equal strength within the context of the play. The same can be said about Tomson's *Dry Lips Oughta Move to Kapuskasing*: all seven men in the play have an equally important story, which is why Tomson will never write for television, which requires protagonists and heroes.

The first week it was performed *The Rez Sisters* almost died. Nobody came to watch it except the reviewers. They had never seen anything like it before! It was like a breath of fresh air, something new, something interesting, something invigorating. It got wonderful reviews. Many times in the first week or so, the director and stage manager literally had to run out to the street and hand out free tickets to people passing by the Native Canadian Centre to come in and see the show. Then the word got out that it was fabulous. By the fourth week there was standing room only. They were turning people away. In the end, the play got such a great response that almost immediately there were offers to produce it in cities all across Canada. They ended up doing a production that toured from British Columbia to Ontario, stopping in all the major cities along the way, doing incredible business. Within the Native community, for the majority of us, *The Rez Sisters* marked the beginning of contemporary Native theatre because that's when people stood up and said, "Hey, what's this? People are telling their own story and they're telling it well."

Because of the success of *The Rez Sisters*, Tomson's next play *Dry Lips Oughta Move to Kapuskasing*, which was a co-production between Theatre Passe-Muraille and Native Earth, did amazing business. It was a three-city production – Winnipeg, Ottawa, and Toronto (at the Royal Alex). It was the first Native play ever to be in any of those three places all at one time. From there, Native playwrights had their own voice.

The second major Native writer to have his plays produced was Daniel David Moses, a well-known poet and short-story writer. Native Earth produced *Cloudy City*, his very first play, which did reasonably well. Around that time I was brought in as artistic director of Native Earth. Playwrights started to come out of the woodwork. We have a festival called "Chuck Begins to Dance." Chuck is another word for the Trickster, Nanabush, or the Raven. It is a festival or workshop of six new Native plays, which are given public readings. For the 1989 festival, Tomson had to beat the bushes to find six plays to workshop – Tomson and Dan were the only ones writing plays. Today I have a stack of Native plays on my desk. I have to make tough decisions and weed out and pick six to produce. In that way it's really quite striking, quite grand, to see how far Native theatre has come.

I was invited to be playwright-in-residence for Native Earth in the 1988-89 season. I had been a journalist, and I had written for television. I had done some documentaries, and I was writing a drama series. I could count the number of plays I had seen on one hand. For me at that time theatre was something done by dead white English people. But I was offered 20 weeks of work – they had got a grant for a playwright residency – 20 weeks of salary just to come in and sit through rehearsals, so I accepted. I went in absolutely disinterested. But I was bitten by the bug, and since 1989, I've had 22 productions of my eight plays. I feel so privileged to sit in the first row of theatre – of Native theatre.

There are many interesting developments in Native theatre. We've been given back our voices to tell our stories. It is fascinating to see what stories are being told and what the voices are saying. I would say that a majority of plays produced in the past, and to a certain extent now, are very, very angry stories. They are basically talking about things that have happened, which have prevented Native peoples from talking in the first place. Tomson likes to quote Lionel Longquash from Saskatchewan who said that before the healing can take place, the poison has to be exposed. This is the reasoning behind *Dry Lips Oughta Move to Kapuskasing*. I became a playwright-in-residence during the original rehearsal period for *Dry Lips*. This play was my introduction to Native theatre. I remember sitting through that rehearsal.

Those who have read or seen *Dry Lips* will know there's a horrific rape scene where a young boy with foetal alcohol syndrome rapes Nanabush, who is in the persona of pregnant Betsy Pegahmagahbow. He rapes her with a crucifix. This image just explodes with metaphoric intent. About the same time, there was a production of Ryga's *The Ecstasy of Rita Joe*. Although it was written by a non-Native person, as I mentioned, it was an important step in the development of Native theatre, and I went to see it. In that play as well, there is a horrible rape. And if we look at other plays, we find more rape scenes. There's mention of a rape in *The Rez Sisters*, there is a rape in *Moonlodge*, there's a homosexual rape in *Fireweed*, there are four or five rapes in *Night of the Trickster,* and I could name more. I'd say in 75 per cent of the Native plays written and produced there is a rape. Why? One theory is that it represents the horrific amount of sexual abuse that exists in Native communities because of the residential school system experiences, because of alcoholism, because of the breakdown of the extended families, because of adoption. Sexual abuse is cyclical in that the abused becomes the abuser. The dramatic version of rape is also the perfect metaphor for what happened to Native culture. In many communities, culture was matrilinear or matriarchal. Another culture comes in, forcing itself on the community, and basically eradicates everything else, subjugating that culture to its will.

I think that this (hi)story is still a large part of what Native playwrights and Native peoples in general are trying to work out through theatre, through art. This is important, but sometimes the work can seem very fixated on that one point. I get a script on my desk, and I wonder what the dysfunction *du jour* will be in *this* play. There are so many different aspects of Native culture waiting to be explored. When I look at all the things that have happened to Native peoples that we're trying to document in our theatre, I think what has got us through those periods is a sense of humour and a tradition of storytelling. Those two things have kept us going. They have helped us grasp who we are. Native peoples have a very special sense of humour. It can be very sarcastic, biting, and almost vicious, or it can be very laid-back. With a lot of my material I try to use humour. I have a series of plays that I refer to as "The Comedies" because I want to celebrate the Native sense of humour, a very important ingredient that has allowed us to survive tragedies. I'm constantly urging people to explore different things about the Native community.

Because Native theatre is so young (barely 10 years old) we're still trying to find the parameters before cultural appropriation occurs – one way or another! People talk about taking our stories, but our stories are taking new forms too. Two years ago we produced a Native opera called *Diva Ojibway.* I do Native comedies (I've been called the Neil Simon of the Native community). We presented a show called *Shame of Oz,* a Native version of the *Wizard of Oz.* The definition of Native theatre is expanding. It is still growing. In the 1970s, Native theatre was either a dramatization of a legend or about a social issue that had to be explained, with no concept of plot or character. Now Native theatre can be practically anything. During the 1980s Native Earth was the only theatre company developing and producing Native theatre. In 1994, there were two different productions of *The Rez Sisters,* one in Hamilton, one in London. In 1995-96 I had six plays being produced across Canada and only one by a Native theatre company. Previously one play might be produced, and then it would disappear. Now, people in other companies are saying, "I hear that's a good play, I'd like to see it, I'd like to produce it." My play *Someday* was produced in Thunder Bay and Vancouver. The momentum is growing and growing, and Native theatre, instead of being the exception, is now an accepted component of contemporary Canadian theatre.

SMARO KAMBOURELI

Staging Cultural Criticism:
Michael Ignatieff's Blood and Belonging
and Myrna Kostash's Bloodlines

"Travel" as a *translation term*. By translation term I mean a word of
apparently general application used for comparison in a strategic and
contingent way. "Travel" has an inextinguishable taint of location by
class, gender, race, and a certain literariness. It offers a good reminder
that all translation terms used in global comparisons – terms like
culture, art, society, peasant, mode of production, man, woman,
modernity, ethnography – get us some distance *and* fall apart.
Tradittore, traduttore. (Clifford, "Traveling Cultures" 110)

Beginning with their publication date, 1993, *Blood and Belonging: Journeys into
the New Nationalism* by Michael Ignatieff and *Bloodlines: A Journey Into Eastern
Europe* by Myrna Kostash have a lot in common. Written by two second-
generation Canadians who foreground their ethnic origins and belong to the
same age group, these travelogues explore more or less the same European
territory and are published under titles that, at least at first reading, have an
uncanny similarity. Yet, Ignatieff and Kostash translate the political, ethnic,
and nationalist issues they confront into two disparate narratives. This
cannot be explained simply by the fact that *Bloodlines*, as the record of 11
years of intermittent travel between 1982 and 1991, ends when *Blood and
Belonging* begins, or that some of the places the two authors visit do not
overlap. Ignatieff's and Kostash's stated agendas might announce a common
objective in their desire to explore the Europe of the late 1980s and early
1990s, but their perspectives and strategies as cultural critics are
diametrically opposed. Or, to put it otherwise, if their narratives might be
translations of the same "original" sites, they also function, I would argue, as
translations of each other, in that they produce radically different discourses.

My interest in *Blood and Belonging* and *Bloodlines* does not lie in the
"original" sites the authors visit or in how faithful or faithless their cultural
translations might be. Rather, I propose to explore why, in the presence of the
same "originals," these two Canadian cultural critics produce such disparate
intercultural translations. My focus, then, will be on how Ignatieff's and
Kostash's texts function as discourses whose "originals" are not exclusively
the troubled European sites they examine but are interwoven with the

authors' self-constructions as cultural critics. How their respective narratives represent these authors' encounters with others has as much to do with the complexity of otherness as with the authors' own narrativization of their methodological practices.

* * *

The discussion that follows is not, strictly speaking, a study in genre, but a few words are in order about these texts' travelogue form, especially by way of explaining how I use the concept of translation. *Bloodlines* and *Blood and Belonging* do not fit neatly into the tradition of travelogues that deal with what Mary Louise Pratt calls "contact zones," "space[s] of colonial encounters" (6), or spaces that "invoke the spatial and temporal copresence of subjects previously separated by geographic and historical disjunctures, and whose trajectories now intersect" (7). *Bloodlines* and *Blood and Belonging* – grounded as they are in the post-colonial or, as Ignatieff would put it, in the postimperial present, a present that has also seen the rise of new nationalistic movements – reverse Pratt's paradigm while reproducing it. They share a number of elements with the large category of writing about cultures defined as ethnography in that there is in them "the inequality inherent to the binary structure of observer/observed" (Chow, *Primitive Passions* 177), but they are not ethnographic studies strictly speaking. In self-consciously strategic moves, both Ignatieff and Kostash locate themselves, with various degrees of success, within sites on which they can make personal claims, claims traceable to their ethnic heritage or to a familiarity constituted by different relations.[1]

Not quite the nativist critics of which Rey Chow is critical, Ignatieff and Kostash embed narratives about others within narratives about themselves.[2] Or, to reverse this figure, they frame their journeys "into" Europe in personal narratives. This is not unusual in the tradition of travelogues: from the narratives of explorers and those of the Victorian and French bourgeois travellers to recent travel accounts such as *Imperium* by Ryszard Kapuscinski and *The European Tribe* by Caryl Phillips, the travelling writer's self-representation is one of the principal tropes of this genre. What is different, however, in *Bloodlines* and *Blood and Belonging*, is that the trope of self-representation is employed in order to authenticate the narrative, as is the case with Ignatieff, or to question authenticity, as is the case with Kostash. The ambivalent use of this embedding or framing strategy points to the relevance these studies of Europe's "others" might have to ethnicity in Canada.[3] This same strategy stresses the value-production of these discourses as intercultural translations.

In the context of what some critics (including Rey Chow) call modernity, namely "the transformation ... of 'national culture' and 'ethnic identity' in and into the newly developed mass media" (Chow, *Primitive Passions* xi), translation reproduces the original source, its origin, at the same time that it dislocates it. My interest here lies in what Chow calls "translation between cultures" (*Ibid.* x). Through her reading of Walter Benjamin, Chow proposes a radical reinterpretation of the function of translation, especially as it applies to ethnography and other modes of writing that involve intercultural interpretation. She begins by reminding us that translation "is actually the traffic between two languages, [but that] we tend to suppress our awareness of this by prioritizing one language over the other, by pretending that the traffic goes in one direction only" (183), a statement that echoes James Clifford's comment that "ethnography is still very much a one-way street" (Clifford, *Writing Culture* 22). "Translation is a unidirectional, one-way process," Chow argues, and this assumes "that translation means a movement from the 'original' to the language of 'translation' but not vice-versa; it is assumed that the value of translation is derived solely from the 'original,' which is the authenticator of itself" (Chow, *Primitive Passions* 184). Instead, as Chow shows, "translation is primarily a process of *putting together*. This process demonstrates that the 'original,' too, is something that has been put together" (185). Translation, then, is a response to the original's "great longing for linguistic complementation" (Benjamin, as quoted in *Ibid.*, 185). Translation supplements the original in the same way that the original asks for its own translation. This "'putting together' is not simply," as Chow remarks, "a deconstructive production of differences. It is *also* a process of 'literalness' that *displays* the way the 'original' itself was put together – that is, in its violence" (*Ibid.*).

This foray into Chow's theory of translation, however brief, is crucial to the staging of my argument. In turning their gazes upon Europe, Ignatieff and Kostash traverse more or less the same geographical terrain, but follow different ideological trajectories. Their texts thus function as double translations in that they *put* the authors' interpretations of the original sites *together* with the ways in which they perform their roles as cultural critics. *Blood and Belonging* and *Bloodlines* are translations of each other not because they reproduce the originals in an iterative manner but precisely because they construct narratives that represent the originals in markedly different ways. The two texts have a supplementary relationship to each other: we can read them as diverse and in many respects contradictory mirror images of the same original. I will attempt to trace their different, if not oppositional trajectories, by focussing on moments early in the texts that are paradigmatic of how the staging and function of self-referentiality are rendered visible through the gazes of these cultural critics, how, in other words, Ignatieff and Kostash perform their stated methodologies.

* * *

Early in the introduction to *Blood and Belonging*, Ignatieff announces that his book was conceived out of the desire "to understand what the new world order actually looks like" (4). Not unlike him, but in a different context, since she "did not know in 1988 that everything was about to change," Kostash states that her study "is not a book about the revolution. This is a book about memory" (*Bloodlines* 1), a book which, "in some still unformulated way ... was also 'about' ethnicity" (*Ibid.* 1-2). Yet, while both of them begin their journeys with a specific "plan" (Kostash, *Bloodlines* 1; Ignatieff 14) that announces their wish to understand the otherness of the cultures they propose to visit, the plans themselves articulate important differences in the positions Ignatieff and Kostash occupy as cultural critics.

Kostash confesses to "los[ing] control of my plan as I met more and more people who took me further and further afield in my inquiries," and that, "between trips, I did a prodigious amount of reading" that "threw into question all the assumptions I had leaned on, on the basis of my limited awareness in Canada" (*Bloodlines* 2). She lets her "plan" be easily displaced in response to the events and people she encounters. She thus fashions[4] her role as cultural critic as one who attempts to suspend her presuppositions: she approaches the sites of her study not as stable historical grounds that will easily fit within the ideological matrix of her values, but as spaces that are inherently fluid and therefore capable of challenging her assumptions about them as well as about her own subjectivity.

Hence her project lacks a thesis that has to be proven true. Instead, it is defined by questions: "Take a second-generation Ukrainian Canadian, a feminist, a writer, an alumna of the 1960s, and put her on a train in Belgrade heading north. What exactly is her business? How does the 'old country' live on in the citizen of the new?" (Kostash, *Bloodlines* 2). Her self-reflexiveness as cultural critic enables her to remain alert to any foundationalist beliefs that might creep into her project. It also warns readers that her narrative is an assemblage of experiences, a construction that yields to the very tentativeness that informs its method.

Calling *Bloodlines* "a book about memory," then, is a gesture that is at once descriptive and methodological: by posing as the protagonist of her narrative – it is a book primarily about *her* memories – she discloses from the start its emplotment, while she enunciates one of the major aspects of her methodology, that of mediation. Thus, at the same time that the subjects about whom she writes are mediated through her representations of them, the narrativization of her memories registers the changes she undergoes as both observer and participant. Memory here functions as an analogue of interpretation, a circumspect sign that declares the sovereignty of the author, as subject, to be contingent on the very object of her study. Accordingly, her cultural criticism is a form of translation that lacks a singular origin. Although *Bloodlines* has a certain narrative continuity, it does not posit the history it examines in the shape of a historical continuum that has an identifiable origin and, by implication, a specific interpretive *telos*.

By contrast, Ignatieff does not seem to waver from his stated purpose. Defining himself as a "cosmopolitan," he sets up an itinerary that is "personal ... but ... not arbitrary": "I chose places I had lived in, cared about, and knew enough about to believe that they could illustrate certain central themes" (14). Like Kostash, Ignatieff announces the personal ties he has with the places he is about to visit, but this autobiographical inscription does not form the core of his narrative. Although Ignatieff's journey has hardly begun at this point, he seems to be privy to the thematic discoveries lying ahead of him;

or, rather, he plans his narrative journey in a way that is certain to "illustrate" what he intends to discover:

> The key narrative of the new world order is the disintegration of nation-states into ethnic civil war; the key architects of that order are warlords; and the key language for our age is ethnic nationalism.
>
> With blithe lightness of mind, we assumed that the world was moving irrevocably beyond nationalism, beyond tribalism, beyond the provincial confines of the identities inscribed in our passports, toward a global market culture that was to be our new home. In retrospect, we were whistling in the dark. The repressed has returned, and its name is nationalism. (5)

These statements of intention do not serve only to reveal the thesis of Ignatieff's narrative; their textuality also embodies the elements that inform Ignatieff's method as cultural critic.

The rhetorical tropes he employs, together with the rapid shift from "I" to "we" in his introduction, make manifest an antagonistic relationship between himself and the sites he plans to visit. Predictably, this antagonism is cast in dialectical terms that speak of a battle whose outcome has already been decided. Identifying with the side that has lost (those whistling in the dark), Ignatieff portrays himself at once as a figure of innocence and experience. Yet his narrative does not originate from within the ambivalence of this epistemological position.

By imaging himself as one of those whistling in the dark, he expresses a certain kind of contrition to mark the end of his innocence: "We soon found out how wrong we were" (Ignatieff 5), he says, referring to how, observing "a new order of free nations beg[inning] to take shape," "we believed that the civic courage which had brought down the last twentieth-century empire might even be strong enough to sustain Russia's transition to democracy" (4-5). Admitting that this assumption was in effect a misreading of the "new world order" does not, however, evoke a position of interpretative discomfort. In fact, Ignatieff offers his narrative as a corrective to that misreading. His admission functions as an epiphanic moment, a moment of reasserted faith in the imperative to fight nationalism: his narrative is nostalgic for a state of affairs that can be only imagined. Yet, even though Ignatieff shows this political imaginary to be a fallacy, he takes on the task of proving the desirability and efficacy of this fallacy. This is, perhaps, the main reason why his introduction, in addition to announcing his plans, offers a compressed analytic account of the history of "Civic and Ethnic Nationalism," "Belonging," and "Cosmopolitanism and Privilege," as the subtitles of its sections suggest. This account has a discernible *telos* in that it advocates "cosmopolitanism," or what he calls "civic nationalism": a state of affairs whereby one "believes in the necessity of nations and in the duty of citizens to defend the capacity of nations to provide the security and the rights we all need in order to live cosmopolitan lives" (14).

There are many puzzling and disturbing elements in Ignatieff's definition of cosmopolitanism, but of particular relevance to my argument here is the "accompanying disdain for the nationalist emotions of others" that Ignatieff sees as being "the last refuge of [a] cosmopolitan" like himself (16). Making the subjects he sets out to encounter the unequivocal object of his disdain exposes the overdetermined nature of Ignatieff's narrative. This is what accounts, partly, for the light and dark imagery he employs as well as for some of the other tropes in his narrative. These elements reinforce Ignatieff's positivistic belief in the evilness of the spectre of nationalism. His role as cultural critic, then, involves his mission partly to expose the danger lurking in the "return of the repressed," and partly to produce meaning for the reading public who might still be "whistling in the dark." His donning a collective persona is thus a strategy of seduction: on the one hand, the "we" refers to a historically specific group – "my generation [that] had almost reconciled itself to growing old in the fearful paralysis of the Cold War" (4) – while, on the other, it is employed to create the impression that his readers are of the same mind as he, agreeing that "a global market culture" is the only means by which to forestall the progress of nationalism.

Ignatieff's authorial intentionality shows his method and position as cultural critic to be almost diametrically opposed to that of Kostash. While she announces her narrative to be a double practice – participation and analysis – Ignatieff expressly establishes an ideological gap between himself and the object of his narrative. Furthermore, he seems to suggest that he holds the "key" to what "we" need to do in order to save the world from the perils of nationalism, thus signaling that he offers his critique of nationalism as the only viable interpretation – a monologic one – and this despite the fact that the surface plurality of his "cosmopolitanism" would suggest otherwise. Against this overdeterminedly expressed ethos, Kostash, in keeping with her own stated intentions and uncertainties, says in her introduction that "each time I travelled I was turned inside out again in what was proving to be the most difficult work of my life as a writer" (*Bloodlines* 2). Both Ignatieff and Kostash sharply articulate how they function as cultural critics, but it is the performativity of their subject-positions that best reveals how the viewpoints from which they travel permeate their respective cultural translations of the sites they visit.

* * *

James Clifford's statement that "every focus excludes; there is no politically innocent methodology for intercultural interpretation" (Clifford, "Traveling Cultures" 97) ought to be, I believe, the basic premise behind every reading of travel literature. My attempt, then, to identify correspondences and disalliances between Ignatieff's and Kostash's scenes of writing and scenes of travelling is not intended to prove that these writers' strategies are not innocent; rather, I wish to explore how the cultural spaces produced by the gazes of these two cultural critics operate differently as modes of signification and are indicative of the extent to which the authors' respective ideological baggage travels along with them.

Both begin their narratives with what is a normative scene in travel writing: the image of a foreigner or a foreign landscape, the kind of encounter that marks the writers' initiation into their journeys of exploration. The ritual function of this initiation is to permit future possibilities, create the atmosphere and pace of the journey, and, as with other modes of writing, seduce the reader into reading.

"Warlords," the first section of Ignatieff's introduction entitled "The Last Refuge," starts with the description of a scene that has, among other things, a very strong narrative and cinematic impact. We are at the "UN checkpoint ... manned by two Canadian infantrymen guarding a road barrier between the Croat- and Serb-held sections of Pakrac, in central Croatia." The van carrying Ignatieff and his travelling crew crosses the checkpoint and passes "two teenage Croatian spotters with their binoculars trained on the Serbian side." When it reaches Serb-held territory it is stopped by 15 armed Serbian paramilitaries, drunk because of wedding festivities in their village. This is how Ignatieff relates what transpires next:

> The drunkest one, with dead eyes and glassy, sweat-beaded skin, forced the van door open and clambered in. "We watching you," he said, making binocular gestures with his hands. "You talk to Ustashe," ... Then he took the pistol out of his belt. "You fucking spies," he said. He ordered the driver out at gunpoint, took the wheel, and began revving the engine. "Why can't I shoot this?" groaned the cameraman in the seat behind. "Because he'll shoot *you*," someone in the back of the van muttered (3).

Why does Ignatieff stage the beginning of his writing at this point and place? Why does he construct such a dramatic scene in the opening of an introduction that is an essay-cum-meditation on "belonging," on the virtues of "civic nationalism," and the perils of what he defines as "ethnic nationalism"? If "kitsch," as he tells us, "is the natural aesthetic of an ethnic 'cleanser'" (Ignatieff 10), what defines the aesthetic of the cosmopolitanism he embodies?

The answer to this question lies in the way he stages interview scenes or arrives at a new site. It is not a coincidence that his narrativized journey starts with crossing borders, a site where violence is imminent. The UN checkpoint signifies not simply his point of entry from Croat- into Serb-held territory but also the mile zero of his journey. At the level of narrative positionality, the UN forces are the third element, at once a prosthetic injunction (Homi Bhabha's expression) and a marker of globalism, where ethnic differences touch conflictually. But the UN's charge to dissolve or mediate tension is undermined here as much by the author's own ironic comment about the UN forces having been stationed there by the "loftily called ... 'international community'" (4) as by the recent tainted history of the UN troops, especially the Canadians and Americans, in Somalia.

In yet another ironic twist, there emerges, from the borderline that the UN occupies, the kind of "modernity" Ignatieff advocates. I quote at some length from his introduction:

Since 1989, we have entered the first era of global cosmopolitanism in which there is no framework of imperial order.

…

The Americans may be the last remaining superpower, but they are not an imperial power: their authority is exercised in the defense of exclusively national interests, not in the maintenance of an imperial system of global order. As a result, large sections of Africa, Eastern Europe, Soviet Asia, Latin America, and the Near East no longer come within any clearly defined sphere of imperial or great-power influence. This means that huge sections of the world's population have won the "right of self-determination" on the cruelest possible terms: they have been simply left to fend for themselves. Not surprisingly, their nation-states are collapsing, as in Somalia and in many other nations of Africa. In crucial zones of the world, once heavily policed by empire – notably the Balkans – populations find themselves without an imperial arbiter to appeal to. Small wonder, then, that unrestrained by stronger hands, they have set upon each other for that final settling of scores so long deferred by the presence of empire. (Ignatieff 12-13)

Empire here has a generic value and a corrective, if not redemptive, function. Ignatieff disorients completely the course of history, for, in the nervousness with which he views ethnic conflicts and postcolonial sites, the causal relationship he sees between the presumed absence of imperial arbiters and the collapse of nation-states becomes a distortion of the process of decolonization. Empire, for him, is configured as a *pharmakon*, but he thinks of *pharmakon* simply as remedy, not as poison. He falls short of calling for the return of imperial order, but the exasperation and melancholy inscribed in his narrative bear the same hysterical signs that he sees stirring the nationalism of "small peoples." The elegiac lyricism of his cultural discourse is ironically and metonymically related to his constructed image of ethnic fanaticism. The cultural projects of both Ignatieff and the ethnic fighters he encounters are equally informed by nostalgia; only the object and means of their nostalgia are different.

In this context, the UN forces are a pale simulacrum of the imperium, a reminder that these "small peoples too weak to establish defensible states of their own" (Ignatieff 13) still have fixed upon them the gaze of the old world order. Ignatieff's own gaze performs exactly the function of the imperial gaze. It is not accidental, then, that the opening scene of *Blood and Belonging* is heavily marked by the technology of visuality. Through naked eyes, binoculars or gestures mimicking binoculars, everyone is watched by everyone else. Ignatieff would have us believe, through the incident involving the frustrated cameraman who cannot shoot the scene because he might be shot at, that he and his travelling crew are the objects of the others' gaze, that they are in fact the "other" on the receiving side of potential violence. And indeed they are, within the schema of political realities that Ignatieff constructs – for they embody the cosmopolitanism of the "West" that threatens and is threatened by such ethnic conflicts.

"Watching," Chow says, "is theoretically defined as the primary agency of violence, an act that pierces the other" (Chow, *Writing Diaspora* 29). I would like to argue, though, that Ignatieff's writing act, his decision to begin his book with this particular scene of border-crossing, changes the surface value of visuality as he inscribes it. The power of the gaze, contrary to the fixity it suggests, lies in its ability to circulate. In its narratively honed version, this scene reveals that the agency of the gaze is located in the violence of Ignatieff's writing act. This violence is constituted not simply in the Derridean sense that writing is a form of displacement but also in the sense that it circulates the image, that it subsumes even the very technology of visuality, the camera. This scene, we are casually invited to notice, is not filmed.

Ignatieff is right, then, when he says that the "itinerary I chose was personal, but, I hoped, not arbitrary" (14). His decision to situate himself in the precarious position of a potential victim/other is a strategic one, for it allows him to appropriate and circulate violence. Violence – be it real, potential or imaginary, physical or intellectual – is used by him to authenticate, on the one hand, the reality of his travel experiences and, on the other, the thesis for which he seeks proof. Another beginning, less carefully chosen, would not have allowed him to deduce the following conclusion from the encounter in this opening scene:

> This was the moment, in my journeys in search of the new nationalism, in which I began to understand what the new world order actually looks like: paramilitaries, drunk on plum brandy and ethnic paranoia, trading shots with each other across a wasteland; a checkpoint between them … and a film crew wondering, for a second or two, whether they were going to get out alive. (Ignatieff 4)

Why he begins a journey seeking simply one kind of nationalism, as the title of his book also stresses, is a question, and one worth exploring, that lies beyond the scope of this study.

What I would like to stress at this point is his second reference, within the first two pages of his introduction, to his film crew. There is nothing strange about this, of course, for it is widely known that *Blood and Belonging* is the writerly other to the BBC film series of the same title. What I find interesting is that, beyond the already mentioned references to Ignatieff's film crew in the introduction (and two references to his translator, Lena, in the chapter focussing on Ukraine), Ignatieff renders his co-travellers invisible throughout the course of the narrative. He appears to function as a lone, self-efficient, and polyglot traveller in no need of mediation, no need of translation. The strategy of concealing these individuals reinforces Ignatieff's authority as a travel/ing writer, as the single enunciating and transmitting agency of the representations we read. Ignatieff narrativizes the cultural sites about which he writes, yet he removes from his narrative its sites of production. Thus Ignatieff dislodges the effect of the spectacle of technology that accompanies him, leaving readers on their own to recognize the author's representation and the apparatuses that inform it. Ignatieff's strategy of elimination brackets the technology of the gaze, a technology that is a direct witness to the market value of the cultural sites he chooses to visit. Ironically, at the same time that he commodifies the violence he encounters and/or constructs, he displaces – more accurately, he hides – the media commodification of ethnic strife.

Not until the "Acknowledgements" section at the very end of the text does Ignatieff share with his readers the information, crucial to a project of this kind, that his journeys and theorizing "depended heavily" on "translators, researchers, and fixers" (255). "I must plead guilty to a deception," he admits coyly in the opening sentence of this section. "The book is written as if I had been traveling alone. In fact, there were never fewer than five people accompanying me at all times" (*Ibid.*). Still, this does not change the fact that he operates in a manner reminiscent of the nineteenth-century European travellers whose companions, servants, translators, carriers or cooks, usually people of colour, never made it into their employers' narratives. As Clifford says, "these individuals have never achieved the status of 'travelers'.... Racism certainly has a great deal to do with this. For in the dominant discourses of travel, a non-white person cannot figure as a heroic explorer, aesthetic interpreter, or scientific authority" (Clifford, "Traveling Cultures" 106). I have no way of knowing if any of Ignatieff's travelling companions were people of colour, but the crucial thing about the absence of his film crew and translators is not so much a matter of race; in their case, class and labour become the structural differential of race. What is significant is Ignatieff's deliberate mistranslation of the contingent factors that must surely have affected his encounters with people, especially those he meets in rural and devastated environments. The intense, if not intrusive presence of a crew complete with cameras and other technological accoutrements (here signs of an imperial order akin to the one whose passage Ignatieff laments), and the mediating presence of a translator, overdetermine Ignatieff's cross-cultural exchanges. His circumvention of these conditions invests his narrative with an immediacy and discreteness that surely are intended to create a semblance that he, as author and cultural critic, is the single purveyor of truth, a truth whose value, as I have tried to demonstrate, is already decided upon before Ignatieff's narrative journey is launched.

In spatial, figural, and historical terms, the opening scene of the book's introduction, then, establishes the *mise en scène* of Ignatieff's entire narrative. It marks the moment when he exits the cosmopolitanism of the West to enter into the "ethnic paranoia" (Ignatieff 4) of the East. With the film camera turned off, ironically signifying his ideological blind spots, he stages a playfield of war, a theatre where viewers and players perform each others' roles. Thus the violence inscribed in the introduction's opening scene is not just the correlative of the heavily armed nationalists on both sides of the border. It is also the result of Ignatieff's own weaponry, the ideological baggage and biases with which he travels – and he doesn't travel light. Only such a scene would allow him to establish in unequivocal terms the *mise en scène* of his travel narrative: that violence is natural to "small peoples too weak to establish defensible states of their own."

The staging strategies Ignatieff employs to construct our first image of ethnic otherness and warfare signify the starting point of his intercultural translation. Thus the crossing point to Pakrac operates as the fleshed-out version of his fantasy about ethnic conflicts, the negative site of the generic realm of his cosmopolitan ideology. We are already deeply enmeshed in his plot at the very moment when he starts his intercultural translation. And it is a plot that holds no surprises, for whether he visits Kurdistan or Ukraine, Germany or Northern Ireland, Quebec or Croatia and Serbia, his fascination with the debris of ethnic conflict remains intact. If kitsch is the aesthetic of ethnic cleansing, as he says, then his aesthetic is a new kind of picturesque art: the battlefield, bombed and burned houses, destroyed farms and gardens – all these, together with the ravaged faces of refugees or fighters, are part of the image repertoire that constitutes the landscape of violence he translates. Significantly, for the purposes of his book, he visits all these places only once. He is the cultural critic as tourist. Or, he is the author of a text in search of characters to flesh out his thesis.

* * *

Ignatieff's introduction is not merely the preamble to his narrative; it is the first act of the drama of ethnic strife that he constructs for his readers. In contrast to Ignatieff's 14-page introduction, Kostash's introduction is barely three pages long. Unlike Ignatieff, who despite his elaborate means of construction does not foreground his act of writing, Kostash immediately draws attention to the fact that her book is "about the territories that exist in the imagination of a Canadian writer, in that of her interlocutors, and in the space between them" (*Bloodlines* 1). The difference between the two writers' methods is apparent. Ignatieff believes, and expects the same of his readers, that the places he visits and about which he writes are transparent, that there is no mediation, in effect no translation. I would even venture to say that he posits his text not as a representation but as an original. Conversely, Kostash acknowledges that the sites we read about in her narrative do not exist as proper loci, but are the products of imagination: hers and that of her interlocutors. More importantly, instead of referring to an "original" site, she points to "the space between" her interlocutors. Contrary to the borderlines we find Ignatieff crossing in order to get to his various destinations, Kostash occupies borderline spaces throughout her narrative.

These in-between spaces enunciate what Kostash does not say in her introduction. To borrow Homi Bhabha's words, Kostash's "access to the image of identity is only ever possible in the *negation* of any sense of originality or plenitude; the process of displacement and differentiation (absence/presence, representation/repetition) renders it a liminal reality" (Bhabha 51). In approaching her subject not from inside a van literally manned with "no fewer than five people" as Ignatieff does (Ignatieff 255), but from a threshold position, Kostash writes from within a liminal relation to the cultural sites she encounters. Thus, while Ignatieff, despite his crossing of geographical borders, inhabits a *terra firma* because of the incalcitrance with which he refuses to budge from his ideological position, Kostash occupies a space that is in effect the consequence of an ongoing suturing process. This liminality is the main reason, I think, why her text lacks a plot that has a definable outline.

Blood and Belonging is offered to the reader as a product: it begins with a thesis about "others" that its author, by means of his passions and various gestures of elision, succeeds in proving for himself. *Bloodlines*, by means of its author's methods, posits itself "by way of an answer" (Kostash, *Bloodlines* 2), an answer, however, which unsettles not only the simplistic polarities that inform the "us" and "them" paradigm of Ignatieff's encounters, but also the hope of ever finding an answer that might become the "origin" of identity. Kostash's passion lies in her drive to ask questions, questions not about "others," but about her own otherness.

> How does the "old country" live on in the citizen of the new? How may I understand these people and their extraordinary history – my blood relations, as it were, from whom I was separated by the accident of being born into the new family line in Canada? How do they imagine the place I come from? Can I trust what I see of theirs? What is the source of my feelings – feelings I didn't even know I had – about their history, their landscape, their languages, their sites of collective memory? What is their claim on me? Mine on them? In other words, what has this part of the world got to do with me? (*Ibid.*)

Although her book is indeed about the state of political affairs in places other than Canada, by positing herself as the central character of her narrative, Kostash displays a keen awareness of the epistemological problems facing ethnographers and political journalists. Her double function as character and author as well as the fact that her narrative is not the result of a series of one-time encounters with her subjects, but rather the representation of a process that includes her subjects' everyday lives, keep her project's contingent circumstances and the values they articulate visible, and therefore vulnerable, at all times.

Kostash's accountability as translator is also fully inscribed in her text. "I set off, sometimes with a companion but usually alone," she says. "Occasionally I had an invitation ... but I was just as happy to make my way as an independent traveller" (*Bloodlines* 1). She learns "to speak Ukrainian" (2), communicates through a "generic Slav speech" (3), and keeps abreast of the changes in Eastern Europe by reading "underground publications" and corresponding with friends (2). As the primary eyewitness and recorder of the events and people she encounters, she knows that she cannot avoid facing up to her responsibilities as cultural translator. Hence the readiness with which she explains "my methods" (2):

> I interviewed without a tape recorder for obvious reasons. My interviews in Czechoslovakia and Poland were done almost exclusively in English. I also conducted interviews two or three times in French and, on my second trip to Ukraine, frequently in Ukrainian....
>
> I have not always used an interviewee's real name in the book, and few of the conversations are reported verbatim, as I always took notes after the interview (2-3).

The act of translation, completely erased in Ignatieff's narrative, is foregrounded in Kostash's introduction and is frequently thematized in the narrative proper. And this is not the only way in which Kostash practises her liminality or problematizes her act of writing.

Laura Mulvey says that in liminality "it is the possibility of change that is celebrated" (171). Kostash does not always celebrate the changes she notices in places and people previously encountered. Quite the contrary, she often laments or critiques those changes (her chapters on Czechoslovakia and the Ukraine would be examples of that); as for the changes she herself undergoes, she can be both celebratory and troubled in acknowledging surprise, awkwardness, guilt or complicity. While the most important change to which Ignatieff accedes concerns the shift from the imperial order to the tribalism of ethnic groups, Kostash, practising as she does a rigorous subjectivity, remains indifferent to monumental discoveries. It is the minutia of life and the particular configurations of such issues as gender, class, and educational differences that grant her narrative its impetus.

This is, I believe, the main reason why her book is structured so differently from Ignatieff's. *Blood and Belonging* has a linear structure; *Bloodlines* is structured in a circuitous fashion. Ignatieff's approach is synchronic in that the narrative of his written record coincides with his one-time visit in each location; despite this, his narrative is presented as a legitimate, all-encompassing representation of the state of affairs he witnesses on individual occasions. By contrast, Kostash's narrative follows a diachronic approach as it incorporates her repeated visits to one place over a period of time in an attempt to rehistoricize and recodify the sites she visits and her position as cultural critic. Moreover, her account of a single visit to a given place is, more often than not, repeated from a different perspective or interrupted by encounters that have taken place in the same location but at a different time or by memories that take her to an entirely different country and period. Thus, while each chapter has a narrative coherence through its focus on an individual country, that coherence is suspended by various devices of fragmentation.

For example "Czechoslovakia," the first chapter of *Bloodlines*, begins, as do all other chapters, with a brief list of landmark events in the history of the country. It is divided into 13 sections bearing titles that are never simply descriptive. They relate ironically and evocatively to Kostash's own perceptual approach to her subjects as well as to the events she narrates. These sections are divided into subsections headed by the name of a city and the year to which the accompanying narrative refers. Thus a single visit to "Prague, 1984" is represented from multiple perspectives. In the first narrative account of "Prague, 1984," the city of Prague figures as the central character, as Kostash attempts to orient herself both physically and historically. In the second occurrence of "Prague, 1984" it is Nikolaj about whom we read. A librarian who has never been able to practise his profession because of the communist regime, Nikolaj shows Kostash "the one place where he may appear in print: a mycological journal. Nikolaj has discovered a mushroom" (*Bloodlines* 12). Before we re-encounter Nikolaj, in "Prague, 1987," we visit "Slovakia, 1984," "Svidnik," and the Jewish cemetery in "Prague, 1984." The succeeding sections of this chapter do not always follow a chronological order. Kostash's accounts of her visits to Prague in 1984, 1987, and 1988 are interrupted by each other and by sections that take the reader to "Prague, 1968" and "Toronto, August 21, 1968."

The effect of this narrative fragmentation is that of time-lag, what Bhabha defines as "the temporal break in representation" through which "emerges the process of agency both as a historical development and as the narrative agency of historical discourse" (191). The many italicized passages that further interrupt this sequence of narratives also achieve a similar time-lag. These passages contain Kostash's remembrances of the past, her belated understanding of a given event, or memories of the people she meets. During the time covered in these passages she is able to recoup her perceptions, reinvent her subjectivity, or mark the alterity of her interlocutors.

Kostash's structural strategies resemble what Clifford calls "the mechanism of collage": "moments are produced in which distinct cultural realities are cut from their contexts and forced into jarring proximity.... [T]his activity ... brings to the work ... elements that continually proclaim their foreignness to the context of presentation" (Clifford, *The Predicament of Culture* 146). The prismatic structure of *Bloodlines* reflects the defamiliarizing process Kostash experiences in the course of her intercultural encounters. By inscribing in her narrative the in-between spaces she and her interlocutors occupy, Kostash discloses the anatomy of intercultural translation. To use Clifford's words, "[t]he cuts and sutures of the research process are left visible; there is no smoothing over or blending of the work's raw data into a homogeneous representation" (*Ibid.*).

The polyphony of Kostash's text echoes the principles followed by Ryszard Kapuscinski in his book *Imperium*. His book, he says, is written polyphonically, meaning that the characters, places, and themes that thread their way through its pages might reappear several times, in different years and contexts. However, in contrast to the principles of polyphony, the whole does not end with a higher and definitive synthesis, but, on the contrary, it disintegrates and falls apart, and the reason for this is that in the course of my writing the book, its main subject and theme fell apart.... (x)

Unbeknownst to Kostash at the time of some of her early journeys, the world she explored was indeed falling apart, but this turn of events does not diminish the impact of her account nor does it undermine the effectiveness of her narrative structure. By composing her book in a discursive fashion that approximates the discursive sites she writes about, Kostash does not practise mimesis, or mimicry for that matter. Instead, she avoids the distinction between subject and object by resisting the object position of her interlocutors. She functions as a cultural critic fully aware of the fact that she cannot help but inhabit an in-between space that might also be a "space of error" (Chow, *Writing Diaspora* 30).

One major aspect of her methodology that renders her book a truly intercultural translation has to do with the kinds of people she decides to meet. "Initially," she says, "my idea was to interview writers of my generation, bred by the events of the 1960s, who were writing from within the opposition in their respective societies. I was most interested in how they coped, as creative people, with the *political* demands of their situation" (*Bloodlines* 1). Although she sticks to her plan to interview writers, she interviews non-writers as well. Often the writers she meets again and again have already become different individuals, in that they cannot write under the regimes in which they live. Her conscious decision to seek out writers is partly related to her left-wing idealism and personal history. As she says, "[i]n 1980 my book about Canadian politics and culture in the sixties had been published, and I was feeling keenly the split in my own country between the creative intelligentsia and the 'men' of action" (*Ibid.*). By meeting writers, no matter how great the ethnic, social, and class distance between them, she is more likely to find a common language between herself and them – more likely, that is, to understand the social and cultural codes through which they construct themselves and speak.

Implicitly, Kostash's choice of objects-as-subjects reflects her awareness that there are gaps to be grappled with between her and her interlocutors. Indeed, these gaps often become the focus of her narrative. Yet the fact that she follows the lives of these people over a span of years, that she sees them becoming dispirited or hopeful, co-opted by political systems or dedicating their lives to a cause they take on, allows her to present these individuals through a complexity that is never present in Ignatieff's one-dimensional and monologic character descriptions. Ignatieff encounters and interviews many people, but the social, cultural, and political range they represent is limited.

His interview subjects include primarily such local authority figures as teachers, priests, mayors of towns, military personnel, anonymous soldiers (Ignatieff calls them paramilitary leaders), and some townspeople. Although Ignatieff often calls the authority figures he interviews untrustworthy, even liars, he continues to seek them out. "Few will talk," he says (37), but nowhere does he acknowledge, as I have suggested above, the presence of his entourage and its impact, or the war conditions under which he approaches his subjects. Although he finds the local authority figures resistant to his project, Ignatieff does not actually address what constitutes authority itself. In a paradoxically strategic fashion, he seeks out the very signs of authority whose inefficiency his project intends to expose. "As you travel through the zones of devastation in central Croatia," he remarks, "you also have the impression that you have fallen through some hole in time and are spinning backward into the past" (37). He, together with his narratively concealed crew, is the only sign of modernity, and this modernity intends to grant authority and authenticity to his narrative.

By positioning himself as the central focalizer of his narrative, Ignatieff remains oblivious to the intersemiotic transformations that inform the kind of translation project he undertakes. I am not, however, suggesting that Kostash gives to her interlocutors an authenticity that I find lacking in Ignatieff's. The point here is not lack of authenticity, but rather the pretext of it. Kostash, by constructing her interlocutors as fully developed and often self-contradictory characters in a narrative that is admittedly focussed on a journey of personal exploration (and not on a journey intent on discovering a preset agenda), inhabits the space defined by what Jean Laplanche calls the third term: "Two terms – the translated and the translator – are either surrendered to a centring on the translator which we've called somewhat narrowly 'ethnocentrism'; or they are surrendered to a centring on what's to be translated, which can in the extreme lead to a refusal to translate." "There must be," he says, "a third term so that translation (and interpretation) exit from ... subjectivity" (as quoted in Chow, *Primitive Passions* 194). Kostash's project, although occasionally hampered by her Left-wing idealism and her construction of the 1960s as the "origin" of a different world order, does not take subjectivity for granted. If anything, its narrative impetus and structure lie in her desire to disassemble the various permutations of subjectivity. Hence she does not fix her gaze on one person captured in a single moment. As an onlooker, as a cultural translator, she resides not within history as product, but within its temporality, thus seeing her interlocutors not as others belonging to another time but as her contemporaries.

* * *

Still, Kostash's narrative is not entirely free of visual technology. Here is how she stages her first visit to Prague in her opening chapter, entitled ironically "Living in the Truth":

PRAGUE, 1984. Prague is the Paris of the East – so said travel guides and
travellers before me. Compared to the unlovely Stalinist renovations of
Kiev and Warsaw and ramshackle Belgrade, Prague is a feast at first
sight. A splendid skyline of Gothic and Baroque towers, domes and
steeples, statuary on the bridges over the Moldau and pretty
cobblestoned mediaeval alleyways – all washed in shades of ochre,
pink and verdigris – have enchanted visitors for centuries. I am
delighted. (*Bloodlines* 6)

Instead of eliding the function of her gaze as that of a tourist, Kostash
celebrates her visual pleasure. Indeed, she does so by overlaying her gaze on
the gazes of others. She sees Prague for the first time, but she knows that the
Prague she sees is not an "original" – for she can look at the city she sees only
by seeing it through the eyes of others. Her gaze, like "the Paris of the East," is
palimpsestic. In this respect, Kostash's cultural translation is already a
rendering of other translations.

A few paragraphs later, Kostash seems to reproduce in her narrative what
Clifford calls "the odd invocation of hotels" (Clifford, "Traveling Cultures"
104), a recurring topos in travel writing:

I look out my hotel window onto Wenceslas Square, which is thick with
the walking wounded of 1984 and the ghosts of the screaming students
and human socialists of 1967. I think of the bare-handed resistance of
'68 and of that same hot summer in the West, where the riot of police
against antiwar protestors in a park in Chicago had been our moral
correlative, we felt, to the students facing down the tanks of Russian
imperialists. *Welcome to Czechago.* Out there are those Czechs who
remember. (*Bloodlines* 8-9)

If the hotel image, according to Clifford, has "nostalgic inclinations" (Clifford,
"Traveling Cultures" 106), clearly, Kostash's gaze upon Wenceslas Square
captures the spectre of history as she remembers it, as she imagines it. She
constructs a liberal vision of intercultural togetherness, but it is a vision
whose nostalgia and romanticism are short-lived. And the time-lag
acknowledged in her narrative here disrupts her fantasy. We have already
read, a page earlier, that "only a hundred metres from my hotel in Wenceslas
Square there are butcher shops with racks of fresh meat, music stores
displaying rock 'n' roll records, a bookshop selling a translation of Joseph
Heller's newest novel, and pleasant wine bars and cafés packed with the
youth of Prague" (*Bloodlines* 6-7). To borrow again from Bhabha, "there is an
agency that seeks revision and reinscription" (191). What Kostash reinscribes,
in her staging of her visit to Prague, is the city's contemporaneity. As Chow
would say, Kostash "allows for a context of cultural translation in which
these 'other' cultures are equally engaged in the contradictions of modernity"
(Chow, *Primitive Passions* 196).

In a corresponding way, the hotel scene in the beginning of "The *Ancien Régime*," the opening section of Ignatieff's first chapter "Croatia and Serbia," best exemplifies the dynamics inherent in the devices he employs to locate himself as cultural critic:

> Wild strawberries were served in a silver cup at breakfast, I remember, followed by hot rolls with apricot jam. The dining room looked over the lake, and when the window was open you could feel the mountain air sweeping across the water, across the white linen tablecloth and then across your face.
>
> The hotel was called the Toplice, on the shores of Lake Bled, in Slovenia. The diplomatic corps spent the summer there, in attendance upon the dictator who took up residence across the lake. My father, like the other diplomats, came to gossip and take the waters. Every morning, he bathed in the heated pools beneath the hotel. I played tennis, ate wild strawberries, rowed on the lake, and conceived a passion for an unapproachable Swedish girl of twelve. Such are my *ancien régime* memories, and they are from Communist Yugoslavia.... (Ignatieff 19).
>
> I had no idea how complicated and ambiguous the division between national and Yugoslav identity actually was. I knew, for example, that Metod, my tennis coach in Bled, always called himself, first and foremost, a Slovenian....
>
> Was that the only time I saw the cracks that were to become fissures? I think so. (Ignatieff 21)

He concludes this brief section with the following words: "I hold on to my *ancien régime* memories. Everyone now says the descent into hell was inevitable. Nothing seemed less likely at the time. My childhood tells me that nothing is inevitable: that is what makes what did happen tragic" (*Ibid.*). Ignatieff implies that there lies in these hotel memories the "original" of his insights about the break-up of Yugoslavia. The romance and privilege of this scene, together with its cosmopolitanism, suggest that the tennis court and the site of his infatuation with a Swedish girl hold the seeds of his aesthetics, the aesthetics of privilege. For whereas this hotel scene includes the markers of a privileged and protected if not an insulated life, the aesthetic category in which the present reality "belongs" is that of a melodrama that Ignatieff, for his part, inscribes as tragedy in that it signifies the loss incurred by what he takes to be the devolution of history.

Whereas Kostash's hotel scene marks the beginning of her meanderings in contemporary Prague, where she will eventually meet – and meet again – Marketa, a woman whose life we follow closely, Ignatieff's scenic hotel description functions as the preamble to the second section in this chapter, entitled "The Narcissism of Minor Difference," an historical essay on Balkan nationalism. When next we enter the present time of his narrative, we are on

"The Highway of Brotherhood and Unity," which gives the title to the third section of this chapter. "I began my journey," he says, "where it used to begin every summer of my Yugoslav childhood.... This was the highway we traveled, in a magnificent black Buick with lots of fins and chrome" (Ignatieff 28). The first people he encounters when he leaves his memories behind are "peasants roll[ing] through the village on hay carts," but their presence is marked by the same value and function that comprise the other elements that constitute the background of the landscape he composes: "The sun was shining. The apple blossom was shimmering in the spring breeze. Peasants rolled through the village on hay carts. Outside the white farmhouse, there was a bronze statue of Tito as partisan hero ... I inspected the maize-filled mattress where he may have slept" (Ignatieff 29). Ignatieff's devices of representation reflect that at this point in his life, having already embarked on a journey into the nationalist strifes of others, he remains unshaken in his faith in the *ancien régime*.

That Ignatieff is still locked within the epistemology exemplified by the hermeneutics of his childhood hotel is evident when, two pages later, we see him back on "The Highway of Brotherhood and Unity":

> I have a superb four-lane motorway all to myself. I stop, get out, cross both lanes and back again. No one. Then I get into the car, take it up to 115 miles an hour, feeling full of adolescent elation. I roar up to a tollbooth only to discover that its windows are smashed and the booths are empty ... I back up and take the tollbooth at full speed.
>
> I have no company [not counting, that is, his travelling crew of no fewer than five men] except for hawks.... (Ignatieff 30)

This narrative moment of abandon signifies at once a lapse in intent and a replication of his memories of a carefree life as a child in former Yugoslavia. Furthermore, it reveals his position as cultural critic to be entirely at odds with the sites he crosses. His is a method of complete disidentification with the object of his study. With Austrian plates on his car, extra petrol in its boot, and a flak jacket to protect him from bullets (Ignatieff 31), Ignatieff appears here as an interloper whose cosmopolitanism is the passport that grants him immunity. That he does not wear his flak jacket – "it is ludicrously cumbersome and in practice useless" (*Ibid.*) – lends his narrative an air of bravado, a kind of naïve heroism that echoes the Hollywood adventures of lone heroes. When, a paragraph later, he "reach[es] the edge of the war zone," Ignatieff is armoured with the confidence ritualistically enacted by his joy ride. With his tropes of disidentification clearly performed – both for the author's own and his readers' benefit – Ignatieff consolidates the legitimacy of the values he represents, and seeks to revalidate them by declaring them absent from the sites he visits.

The complexity of Ignatieff's scenes of cultural translation and self-location clearly contrast with Kostash's desire to sublate otherness. While Kostash is constantly aware of the antagonistic agency informing the cultural sites she translates, she never loses sight of the hybridity of her "originals" and questions the limits of the narrative she constructs. On the other hand, Ignatieff posits himself as a traveller who, paradoxically, doesn't travel. No matter how far he travels or how dangerous the sites he dares himself to visit, he still inhabits the moral fable of his cosmopolitan upbringing.

* * *

Not surprisingly, Ignatieff concludes his study by "end[ing] my journey where I started" (244), that is, summing up the two-pronged theme he announces in the introduction as the focus of his investigation:

> Wherever I went, I found a struggle going on between those who still believe that a nation should be a home to all, and race, color, religion, and creed should be no bar to belonging, and those who want their nation to be home only to their own. It's the battle between the civic and the ethnic nation. I know which side I'm on. I also know which side, right now, happens to be winning. (249)

The circularity of the narrative of Ignatieff's journey dramatizes the ethnic strifes he explores not as interdictions to the worldview he wishes to see upheld, but as a chain of interruptions that will not, he hopes, permanently impede the rise of globalism and cosmopolitanism.

The dialectic of conflict "between the hungry and the sated nations" with which he concludes his study replicates the terms in which he began his journey. What has been gained in transit is the reader's understanding that, for Ignatieff, the ways in which certain nations have come to be "sated" is irrelevant to why other nations remain "hungry." This is apparent in the contradiction that punctuates his summation in the text's penultimate paragraph: "I've lived all my life in sated nation-states," he says, "in places that have no outstanding border disputes, are no longer ruled by foreigners or oppressors, are masters in their own house.... But among the Crimean Tatars, the Kurds, and the Crees, I met the hungry ones, peoples whose very survival will remain at risk until they achieve self-determination" (Ignatieff 248-49). Ignatieff remains oblivious to the antithetical structure that emerges from his division of the world into states like Canada, one of the "sated" nations where he has lived, and "hungry" nations like the Cree people who reside within Canada. Ignatieff slights this image of interpenetration and complicity. This split between "hungry" and "sated" nations, too neat and too facile, confirms Ignatieff's distance as cultural critic from his object. The binary structure of his ideology, then, has an affirmative function, in that it asserts, without contesting, the division of world nations into those that are masters in their own house and those that are oppressed within their masters' domains.

Kostash's narrative concludes without a formal conclusion. It ends with an ensemble of images that at once conclude her chapter on Ukraine and speak of hunger. Instead of providing a neat summation of her journeys' exigencies,

Kostash maintains her storytelling method. Her text leaves the reader with a complex image of a man, the assassin of Vasyl, a "new Soviet man" who delivers the first tractor to his village (*Bloodlines* 248). She describes a scene from a film called *Earth*. The repentant assassin, "circling crazily in the open fields ... flings himself down on this earth.... The place he seeks is the ancient ossuary of the underground, it is the fertilizing black loam, and it is the beginnings of bread" (*Bloodlines* 249). Kostash does not attempt to translate this scene. Ironically, it is her decision not to do so that becomes a subtle interpretative gesture, the presentation of a figure that folds into and remains outside her text in terms of how she and her readers participate in the historical inscriptions that overlay the scene.

One page before her text's last paragraph we read about the "cannibalistic" (*Bloodlines* 247) dream of Gustav Herling while subsisting in the gulag: "'Love and hunger returned to their common biological root, releasing from the depth of my subconsciousness images of women made of fresh dough whom I would bite in fantastic orgies till they streamed with blood and milk, twining their arms which smelt like fresh loaves round my burning head'" (*Bloodlines* 248). This cannibalistic orgy, contained as it is within a nightmarish dream, functions as a metaphor that affirms the imperative not to relinquish the materiality of history while showing how history is *grounded* in the concreteness of experience.

While Ignatieff's cultural translation glosses over the materiality of history, Kostash's cultural translation is decidedly situated within it. This is, I believe, what enables her to conclude her book with "the beginnings of bread" while Ignatieff leaves his readers with images of peoples who are "hungry." Moreover, while Ignatieff employs hunger as a metaphor of deracination, Kostash inscribes hunger in her narrative as a concrete sign of the palpable materiality of history. Even the cannibalism of Herling's nightmare is intended to address the unrelenting focus on the body's drudgery through history.

* * *

Most studies of cultural translation focus on the ways in which ethnographers or cultural critics "deal with problems of interpretation and translating the discourse of alien societies" (Asad 143). For Ignatieff and Kostash, the object of their cultural criticism is not always entirely "alien." Indeed, both of them make a point of stressing their conscious decisions to traverse sites where they might trace their personal or familial histories. But choosing a site that might evoke familiarity does not necessarily mean that such a site rends the veil that constitutes its otherness, that it makes itself transparent, and therefore easily graspable by the cultural critic's gaze. What it means, instead, as I have tried to show in Ignatieff's case, is that there is a danger of cultural malformation whereby cultural criticism translates itself into the very process that veils the other as other. In Kostash's case, the very familiarity that exists or develops between herself and her interlocutors occurs within a liminal space where any direct correspondence between the narrative she creates and the historical struggles she confronts is presented as a site where she draws attention to the production of meaning as a series of affiliations. While Ignatieff elaborates on the distances that separate him from his objects not in order to mediate his interpretation but in order to solidify the valence of the cosmopolitanism he advocates, Kostash seeks to establish affiliations between the conditions she encounters and her own particular historicity. This is the reason why the authors' autobiographical inscriptions are at odds with each other. Ignatieff occupies a filiative position that never becomes the object of his study; instead, this position legitimizes his narrative, enables him to rationalize the differences between the "West" and the "East" as being insurmountable, and assigns to his role as cultural critic the kind of moralizing authority permeating *Blood and Belonging*. Kostash's attempt to locate, if necessary to forge, affiliations, bespeaks her desire to follow not the trajectory of a historical consciousness that pits the "East" against the "West," but rather a route that takes her by the various sites of the historical contingencies – the *Bloodlines*, so to speak – that have produced the very differences Ignatieff assumes to be irreducible.

NOTES
1. This is most apparent in the sections of both texts where the authors write about Ukraine, where they visit familial locations and encounter people with direct ties to their own families. The complexity of what transpires in these scenes demands a study all by itself.
2. As Chow says, "scholarly nativism ... functions squarely within the Orientalist dynamic and ... continues to imprison 'other cultures' within entirely conventional disciplinary boundaries" (*Primitive Passions* 6).
3. I do not have the space to develop this line of argument here, but both *Blood and Belonging* and *Bloodlines* could be read in relation to Canadian multicultural politics in the sense that the two authors' assumptions about the historicity of ethnic constructions derive, partly, from Canadian discourses. Moreover, Ignatieff dedicates an entire chapter to Quebec, while Kostash constantly reminds herself and the reader of the historical contingencies that inform the constructions of ethnicity both in Canada and in European countries.
4. My use of the word fashioning is intended to echo James Clifford's study of "ethnographic subjectivity." "The fashioned, fictional self," he says, "is always located with reference to its culture and coded modes of expression, its language" (Clifford, *Predicament of Culture* 94).

SNEJA GUNEW

Operatic Karaoke and
The Pitfalls of Identity Politics

I wanted to know Helen's body so well I could climb in and zip up her skin around me. (Lau, *Other Women* 184)

The Register of the Visible

The lifestyle magazine *Vancouver* recently ran a lead article by Sam North entitled "Greetings from Asia Town," that was accompanied by a visual consisting of a collage of women's faces, both "Caucasian" and "Asian," in which some faces dissolved into others.[1] The article suggested that Vancouver's population will be half "Asian" in the next century and that the resultant mix will precipitate either tribalism (with its suggestion of serial conflict) or the kind of "morphed" assimilation illustrated by the collage. Although the latter might be perceived as the more benign alternative, it can also be seen as a spectre of miscegenation, the blurring of differences as a result of genealogical contaminations. Indeed, the visibility of "difference" itself is registered via markers of normative racialization. The visible body – what the viewer sees in terms of corporeality – supposedly "explains" these differences. They in turn invoke both the incommensurabilities of post-colonial theory (the untranslatabilities of cultural difference) and the "lifestyle incompatibilities" of "culturalism." The latter is at the core of what Vijay Mishra has dubbed postmodern racism: "What has been dropped from the new racism is race itself. In its place we have cultural difference" (355).[2]

In an attempt to uncouple the visible from mechanisms of naturalized racism such as occur in the article described above, I would like to consider another of the senses, namely the sense of hearing. In so doing, I will suggest that classical opera represents a particularly fertile field for these speculations, as does the "genre" of the conference presentation where they were first aired. In an exploratory effort to investigate these fields, I recently "staged" a performance piece dealing with *Other Women*, the first novel by Canadian poet Evelyn Lau.[3] The attempt to separate the visual from the aural works more clumsily in print, but I will try to reproduce the interpretive strategy of the endeavour in the pages that follow.

Working against the usual aural expectations set up by a conference delivery, the introductory *mise-en-scène* of my presentation excluded my reading voice for the first 15 minutes, as a series of six overhead transparencies were projected. These began with extracts from *Other Women* (184, 189-90) and from *Fresh Girls and Other Stories* (50) followed by an image of the cover of Lau's second collection of poems *Oedipal Dreams* with its iconic portrait of the artist. The fourth transparency featured the following extract from a piece by the Canadian critic Misao Dean:

> Evelyn Lau's picture on the cover of *Oedipal Dreams* is a stark white mask, heavily marked with eyeliner and lipstick in order to evoke the classic female face of Chinese opera. Sold under the sign of the "oriental girl," who is stereotypically both the mincing and modest virgin and the mysterious and sexually skilled courtesan, Lau's books are marketed in a way that evokes both racist and sexist stereotypes.
>
> Lau disclaims responsibility for this public image.... "I like the fact that the photographs don't look like me as a person, because I wouldn't want to be walking down the street and be instantly recognizable. So there's definitely an element of disguise there too." (Dean 24-25)

The fifth transparency presented an excerpt from an interview with the Canadian journalist Jan Wong:

> Evelyn Lau is wearing a baggy oatmeal sweater. So it's not immediately apparent she is one of the few surgically unassisted Chinese women in the world to require a DD-cup bra....
>
> But back to Lau's past. Now, I left my comfortable Montreal home at 19 to voluntarily haul pig manure in China during the Cultural Revolution. But I have trouble understanding why someone so smart would drop out of school and run away from home at 14 and end up as a junkie-whore. Yes, it's hard to be the dutiful daughter of immigrants from China and Hong Kong, the kind who consider friends a frivolity and an 89 per cent exam mark a failure.... But I'm a parent now. Millions of Canadians have overcome such traumas, if that is the word, without self-indulgent melt-downs. ("Evelyn Lau" A11)

The final transparency was accompanied by the first moment of sound in the presentation – a section from the soundtrack of the film based on Lau's text, the autobiographical *Runaway: Diary of a Street Kid*. The extract chosen for the transparency dealt with a heuristic moment in the film when the protagonist experiences an epiphany in the consulting room of her analyst:

> Evelyn: It's like all the stuff about how great you are. It gets to me you know, with Larry, with all of them. And when they come it's like I've done something right for once. Right from the beginning I felt that, that I'm good for something, that I belong.
> Dr Hightower: Go on.
> Evelyn: In prostitution, I mean, I can fulfill someone. Here, right now!

Which I could never do with my parents.

Dr Hightower: Yes.

Evelyn: I could never ... I could never do [anything] with my parents. Does it matter if it's only a john? I mean it's somebody. I mean, at home I could never please them. I could get 95 or do 6 hours of housework and never go out. Always hoping for something, you know. Some sign of love. But nothing was ever good enough. Dad left me and she, she would have a ruler, or her hand, or her mouth. I never had a mouth. She called me lazy, fat, ugly, stupid slut ... every day. And I swallowed it in. And hated myself. O.K., O.K. maybe they do treat me like a piece of meat on the street but at least I'm appreciated there.

Otherwise I'm nobody.

Dr Hightower: You're not nobody Evelyn. That's what they taught you but it's not true.... No!

Evelyn: No. I just wish they could have liked me for who I am. (Dr H. nods). Yeah. Yes....Thanks. (Gunnarson)

At this point my own voice was introduced asking a series of questions. What happens when the visual intervenes, in print or in the mind's eye of the reader, when we join the voice to a body, have the voice issue from what has been coded as a "visible minority" face? How might one circumvent the "disguise" of the stereotype (to echo Lau), the "orientalist" camouflage Lau's persona apparently adopts so that she won't be recognized in the streets? One possible answer is to consider the question of desire in psychoanalysis, as posed, for example, by Slavoj Zizek.

Zizek brings psychoanalytic concepts and interpretative frameworks to bear on questions of the social and the political.[4] He suggests that "The original question of desire is not directly 'What do I want?' but 'What do others want from me? What do they see in me? What am I for others?'" (Zizek, "i Hear You" 117). Zizek's queries lead us to ask how as readers we can avoid the expectation that Lau should "inform" us about what would, in Canada, be termed her visible minority status. How can we acknowledge it in some way and avoid constructing her in terms of a refusal or denial? These are the familiar burdens imposed on the minority writer.

Evelyn Lau represents an enigma in a Canadian and North American west-coast context where Asian-American and Asian-Canadian ethnic or diasporic canons are being hastily assembled with a great deal of relish, given the demographic changes along the west coast over the past decade.[5] The semi-autobiographical work that shot Lau to fame at the precocious age of 18, *Runaway: Diary of a Street Kid*, dealt with a protagonist preferring life on the street to the constraints of family expectations – expectations succinctly outlined in the extract quoted earlier by journalist Jan Wong, herself the author of a recent bestseller *Red China Blues: My Long March from Mao to Now*. That Lau's family is Chinese is, in the written text, almost incidental. In the film version of her novel, however, it is another matter. The demands of the visual medium mean that the ethnic identity of the protagonist and her family inevitably register and have a certain kind of coded presence.

Lau's poetry and short stories explore an overtly heterosexual underworld of sadomasochism, prostitution, and drug addiction and have been seen as deliberately avoiding any hint of a racialized perspective, in relation to which she supposedly has an "insider's" knowledge (Dean; Kamboureli, *Making a Difference* 534). But in all kinds of ways Lau flouts the so-called "empowering" categories with which critics are eager to provide her. Her work rarely appears in anthologies of Asian-Canadian writing, and, by her own account, she refuses to participate in multicultural events (Lau, "Why I Didn't"). This refusal forces those of us who for several decades have attempted to deconstruct totalizing cultural narratives and their attendant regulatory institutional regimes in the name of women, of anti-imperialism, and even multiculturalism (Gunew, *Framing Marginality*), to revisit theories and questions about how to situate the authority to speak and write for those designated as minority cultural players, and how to set up interpretive strategies that move beyond the thematization of cultural difference. These strategies are difficult to develop in an era when the dominant reference points for minoritarian questioning of the hegemonic are a mixture of post-colonial histories with their legacies of scepticism towards totalizing theoretical frameworks; invocations of anti-racism (often in opposition to the perceived "wimpy" liberalism of multiculturalism); and the perceived essentialisms of identity positionings. The slick invocation of terms such as tribalism, ethnic absolutism, and ethnic cleansing in relation to coverage of the war in the former Yugoslavia in particular (Gunew, "Postcolonialism and Multiculturalism") are competing with principled attempts to constitute local pedagogies that incorporate an ethics of recognition in relation to minorities. In the necessary tension between global diasporas, with their networks and coalitions, and localized manifestations and negotiations, how might one locate or construct intellectual and pedagogical interventions that avoid the compromised categories of "ethnic community" and the general reductionism of identity politics? This is where Lau's work becomes so compelling. The next section sketches a possible interpretative strategy for approaching texts such as Lau's. Having attempted to "set the scene" for my argument, I will now link the question of the visible to the acoustic: voice, sound, the aural dimension, all reside within these questions.

The Acoustic Register

In marked contrast to film, opera is one of the cultural areas where there is conventional acceptance of the disjunction between visible bodies and audible voice. Opera demands a suspension of disbelief not only with respect to the "fat tenor/soprano" and the nubile characters they are asked to represent but, as well, in relation to the gender-crossings and racialized or "colour-blind" casting that have always been present in this medium. What the audience "sees" does not get in the way of what they are asked to imagine. Until recently, for example, few of the non-European roles in the standard canonical repertoire were actually sung by those from the requisite categories. There have, however, been flurries of controversy in cases where leading roles were performed by non-European singers.[6] A systematic study of the chequered history of race and opera has still to be written.[7] But generally speaking, opera audiences are accustomed to hearing a voice and imaginatively substituting a very different body from the one that they see on the stage. How might this affect a reading of Lau's work, in relation to the question of desire as posed by Zizek?

In the reviews heralding the reception of Lau's novel, *Other Women*, her critics wondered whether the writer would, or could, ever move beyond the terrain of the underworld of sadomasochism and prostitution (Gunning; Kornreich). My argument is that Lau's work has never been contained by this world, and opera helps us recognize this.

The novel's title *Other Women* – more suggestive of soap opera than opera proper – suggests that the women referred to are those who disrupt the heterosexual couple. Instead, the text is narrated from the point of view of the traditional "mistress," such that the other woman is actually the "wife." Thus, the text as a whole, and most of Lau's work, I would argue, can be interpreted as celebrating the possibilities of the "normal," via the concept of symbolic identification. Slavoj Zizek summarizes the distinction between imaginary and symbolic identification as follows:

> Imaginary identification is identification with the image in which we appear likeable to ourselves, with the image representing "what we would like to be," and symbolic identification, identification with the very place from where we are being observed, *from where* we look at ourselves so that we appear to ourselves likeable, worthy of love. (*The Sublime Object of Ideology* 105)[8]

Symbolic identification is the place of the Other from whence the gaze and interrogation proceed. It is thus more easily identified with the hegemonic codes of the social world. As constituted in Lau's work, it becomes the location of social heteronormativity. The imaginary identification of the adulterous woman is with the wife and the heterosexual couple. She is/they are in the place where she wants to be and from where they observe her. This is seen in the following extracts (which constituted the first transparency of my performance-presentation):

> My fantasies of your wife grew increasingly intimate and violent. I wanted to strip Helen naked, to familiarize myself with her body, her responses; I wanted to put my face against her chest and listen to her heart-beat climb towards orgasm, and then the slowing of her breath and pulse. I wanted to examine between her thighs with the probing interest of a physician, to explore the inches of her skin for marks,

moles, wrinkles, to measure the proportion of muscle to fat, the density and porosity of her skeleton. I wanted to know Helen's body so well I could climb in and zip up her skin around me. (Lau, *Other Women* 184)

* * *

In the months that followed the end of the affair, I thought I saw you, or your wife, everywhere. Your face reflected back at me from the faces of men passing me on the vibrant street at lunch hour. Their eyes flashed like mica, their faces were similarly shaped, and I thought for the first time that in many respects you must be absolutely ordinary, otherwise how could so many strangers bear your resemblance? Yet none of them survived a second look. And so it went for your wife as well. (*Ibid.*)

These sections from Lau's novel, as well as the supposedly "heuristic moment" in the film script (when everything is "explained"), all point to a referential moralistic voice, echoed in the extract from Jan Wong's prescriptive evaluation. Societal standards exist, designated by invisible or spectral scripts, which the protagonist transgresses – visibly and stereotypically. Paradoxically, her excesses of sexual perversion and addiction serve to confirm social standards since the norm as measure is always present as a point of nostalgic invocation. This is demonstrated by the closing pages of *Other Women* from which the above quotations were taken. What is, at one level, a text dealing with obsessive emotional addiction is, at another level, the reconfirmation of the yuppie heterosexual couple as a constitutive norm for sexual-social relations. The fact that the chapters alternate between first-person and third-person functions as a reminder of the mirror-image, the to-and-fro mutually constitutive relationship of the adulterous woman and the wife.

This is one possible reading of Lau's work. It is not the whole story, however, and there are other excesses at work. In opera, there are moments when the point of the music, or aria, functions to exceed meaning, to signify the very disruption of meaning. As Wayne Koestenbaum suggests, in discussing *Madame Butterfly*, "When heterosexuality unveils itself as sumptuous and delusional, the libretto shatters, and shadow-knowledges speak ... by loving Butterfly's entrance more than her death ... by never outgrowing this entrance phrase, I can speak another Butterfly" (200). In *The Angel's Cry*, Michael Poizat admits that "when Callas sings, when she's going to kill herself, maybe it's idiotic, but I snap ... it's hearing the voice, the music, I fall on my knees" (26). The music leaks beyond the container of meaning provided by the libretto, the narrative, and thus permits multiple identifications, including gay ones (Abel 32-34). The resulting exhilaration in turn permits precisely the kinds of disruptive and paradoxical identifications that opera personifies by occluding the visible body and suggesting ventriloquism. In Zizek's formulation, any manifestation of voice is always, to some extent, ventriloquised and exceeds the explanatory parameters of the body it ostensibly occupies. In a recent piece "'I Hear You with My Eyes': or, The Invisible Master," Zizek traces what he calls the homologous mechanisms of gaze and voice in the following manner:

> ... it is as if, when we're talking, whatever we say is an answer to a primordial address by the Other – we're always already addressed, but this address is blank, it cannot be pinpointed to a specific agent, but is a kind of empty a priori, the formal "condition of the possibility" of our speaking.... (90)

This brings me, in a somewhat unusual but pertinent segue, to karaoke and to *Madame Butterfly*, the most obviously orientalist of operas. In the many recent attentions Puccini's opera has received, much has been made of the fact that Cho-Cho San functions as the traditional good woman who sacrifices herself in the name of maternity.[9] She has also figured notoriously as the paradigmatic orientalist fantasy of the ultimate victim and ultimate seductress, both child and *femme fatale*, a combination that informs Misao Dean's essay quoted earlier. David Hwang's play *M. Butterfly*, has explored one kind of gloss on the opera, and Cronenberg's 1993 film of the same name, a slightly different variation. The sustaining fantasy in these two depictions is that "Butterfly" really wants to be the cad Pinkerton and, that vice-versa, Gallimard finally realizes he wants to *be* Butterfly rather than to possess her. Is this not the constant see-sawing or mechanism of vice-versa that has always sustained such binary frameworks? Is this not why one needs to find a way beyond such a paralysing impasse? Therefore I return to the delirium of the aria and of music in general, as documented by Jacques Attali and now many others in the developing field of sound theory, including Zizek who writes: "Voice is that which, in the signifier, resists meaning, it stands for the opaque inertia that cannot be recuperated by meaning ... the moment at which the singing voice cuts loose from its anchoring in meaning and accelerates into a consuming self-enjoyment" ("I Hear You" 103-4). On stage, we see the stereotype of Butterfly just as we see the stereotype of Lau's adulterous woman, and invest it with the withheld "orientalism" of the author. But perhaps it is possible to break this mould by turning from the visual to the acoustic, by situating Lau's text not in the genre of "dirty realism"[10] (suggested by the prevailing themes in her work) but in the lyrical genre of opera and sound.

Kaja Silverman, in her work on the disembodiment of the female voice and desire, has suggested that it is perhaps the mother whom the daughter wishes to seduce.[11] This is a departure from the Freudian scenario of heterosexual seduction between father and daughter. The film script extract of Lau's story presents a classic psychoanalytic example of the Freudian scenario in the sublimated form of male analyst and female analysand. It should be noted, however, that the protagonist recounts her family saga as one where the father is merely absent while the mother remains present and, moreover, has a speaking *mouth*. In *Other Women*, the narrator, speaking of herself in the third-person, repeatedly states that "It seems incredible to her, that at last she is making a sound" (Lau 13) and "she could open her mouth, and with just a few words, enter Helen's life" (Lau 8). In Lau's work the place of symbolic identification appears to reinforce the norm, but the focus on sound rather than sight, and the disjuncture between body and voice, remind us that the heteronormative couple is sustained by the fantasy of its perverse double. What is undeniably all-powerful in Lau's text is the open and speaking (singing) female voice[12] that exceeds the meanings of normativity that have been attached to it. Where that delirium may lead in terms of finding other meanings to Lau's *oeuvre* remains to be seen.

In proposing the at-first-glance odd conjunction of operatic karaoke[13] and Lau's work, I am presenting karaoke as a consummate example of mimicry and ventriloquism. Karaoke is clearly not operatic in the classic sense since its preoccupations, in *Other Women* at least, put the accent on accessories and lifestyles that we have come to associate with soap opera. Operatic karaoke takes bathroom singing to new soap operatic heights.[14] It is both the ultimate accolade and parody of this western musical form, though not necessarily from a race-conscious or post-colonial perspective. Opera has always exceeded and been constituted by its own parodic contradictions (what you see is not what you imagine). In Lau's work, the reader's imagined ventriloquisms of the authorial body are not sustained by the delirium of the textual voice that exceeds the very norms it ostensibly functions to sustain. It might be productive, therefore, to learn to listen for voice outside the traditional narratives of race as currently constituted, with their normative privileging of the visible raced body. These are the possibilities for exceeding the claustrophobic paradigms of identity politics that are so constraining even when benignly situated in the realms of post-colonial and multicultural interrogations. The questions of desire ("What do others want from me? What do they see in me? What am I for others?") continue to be posed by those writers designated "minority writers" to their audiences or readers.[15]

NOTES
1. The popular culture expression for the manipulated faces would probably be that they were "morphing" into each other. The resultant composite invokes the science fiction genre with its twin traditions of utopia and dystopia.
2. Mishra is drawing on the work of Renata Salecl and Etienne Balibar.
3. The piece was presented at the "Transformations: Thinking Through Feminism" conference held at the University of Lancaster, England, 17-19 July 1997.
4. The reason for invoking Zizek's work is that his current popularity is, in part at least, due to the fact that he is managing to bring together those ancient rivals: Marxism and Psychoanalysis. The question of desire in its various manifestations is at the heart of his work and that of his wife, Renata Salecl's, as demonstrated in their recent collaborative text (Salecl and Zizek 1996).
5. Examples from the United States include: King-Kok Cheung ed., *An*

262   SNEJA GUNEW

Interethnic Companion to Asian American Literature (New York: Cambridge University Press, 1997); Shirley Geok-lin Lim & Amy Ling eds., *Reading the Literatures of Asian America* (Philadelphia: Temple University Press, 1992); Sau-ling Cynthia Wong, *Reading Asian American Literature: From Necessity to Extravagance* (Princeton: Princeton University Press, 1993). Canadian examples include: Eva C. Karpinski and Ian Lea eds., *Pens of Many Colours: A Canadian Reader* (Toronto: Harcourt Brace Jovanovich Canada, 1993); Makeda Silvera ed., *The Other Woman: Women of Colour in Contemporary Canadian Literature* (Toronto: Sister Vision Press, 1994); and Bennett Lee and Jim Wong-Chu eds., *Many-Mouthed Birds: Contemporary Writing by Chinese Canadians* (Vancouver/ Toronto: Douglas McIntyre, 1991).

6. Dame Kiri Te Kanawa is a breakthrough case in point though it is interesting to note how much the blonde wig visibly cancels what the name professes to signify in some of her filmed roles.

7. In their recent fascinating study, Linda and Michael Hutcheon (1996) deal with many permutations of illness and opera (including AIDS) but do not deal extensively with race. Matters of race have been mentioned in, for example, Koestenbaum, McClary, and the pioneering work of Catherine Clément, but a systematic study does not as yet to my knowledge exist.

8. The short quotation hardly does justice to this highly complex interaction, and I recommend that interested readers seek out the fuller treatment in chapter three of Zizek's *The Sublime Object of Ideology* and pages 105-110 in particular. To amplify a little further, without overburdening this short essay, Zizek uses the example of "hysterical theatre" in which the hysterical woman identifies with a particular model of the fragile feminine but does so from the vantage point (the place) of the paternal gaze "to which she wants to appear likeable" (106). The underlying question echoes the one quoted earlier: Who sees me in this kind of way?

9. Note that this scenario is repeated even in "modern" versions of the tale such as the musical *Miss Saigon.* See Kondo, chapter two for a recent analysis of the "orientalist" variations and significance of this story.

10. The genre of "dirty realism" as exemplified by the work of Carver, Ford, Mamet etc., appears to be the dominant interpretive framework for the little critical attention Lau's work has received. My thanks to Michael Zeitlin for the information on this genre.

11. "... both to seduce the mother and be seduced by her," Silverman 153.

12. The all-powerful female mouth is also reminiscent, of course, of the castrating vagina dentata.

13. For the colonial history of karaoke as originating in Taiwan see Chen 1996. I am indebted to Rachel Lee for alerting me to this article.

14. In this regard it is interesting to note Lau's poem "My Tragic Opera" (*In the House of Slaves*) that evokes the scenario of an adulterous woman visiting her lover's house while his wife and children are absent. She insinuates herself into the domestic space, particularly the bathroom, as a way of occupying the position of the heterosexual family and its everyday life. The "desiring" moves I have outlined in relation to the novel are clearly visible here as well.

15. At the end of the conference presentation I played the full film extract (starring the incomparable Sandra Oh as Lau) from which the earlier soundtrack had been taken. The hope was that the audience would now see the Chinese-Canadian face as more than merely a "native informant" on ethnicity.

HIROMI GOTO

Alien Texts, Alien Seductions:
The Context of Colour Full Writing[1]

"The question is not whether you believe in aliens. It's whether you believe them."

I have not been abducted by aliens. I have never seen an unidentified flying object. But I am fascinated by the *idea* of aliens. I'm not fanatically fascinated but rather interested in a pseudo-contemporary folklorish way – aliens abducting humans (mostly white folk in Western popular culture), humans abducting aliens, sexy aliens, ugly aliens, nice ones, mean ones. In much the same way I am intrigued by ghost stories, telepathy, and the lovely spinal shiver of *déjà vu*. I don't spend money subscribing to paranormal magazines or surf the Internet for Welcome Aliens clubs. I just like to read about the subject now and then, bring it up at parties, though not in such a way as to *alienate* my friends. I enjoy programmes on TV that have alien content, but only when it is done convincingly. If the programmes are realistic enough, I am there, mouth open in wonder and wanting more. I should specify that I am not interested in mere alien *presence*. For me there must be a hypothetically plausible reason for alien portrayal, some small chance that the story could be *true*. Not simple, this desire, and not necessarily innocent.

So I might say I've been seduced by the concept of aliens, not the aliens themselves.

[Scene 1 or Chapter 1]
When Jim recognized he was lying down on a cool and smooth surface, he understood that he was still alive. The sudden traumatic entry into a new environment had not ended with his death. But the intense sensation of horror would not leave him, and tears seeped from his eyes. Jim was not tied or physically restrained, but he was incapable of any movement. Not a sound, no voices, no mechanical vibrations, but he knew he was not alone. He sensed before he ever saw the alien. Jim's nerve endings screamed, and the hairs on his body stood up in electric denial of what could not be true, could never be true.

The figure was slight, short, could not have been over five feet in height. The head was large, hairless, with flattened facial features. It was the eyes, the alien eyes, black and horribly slanted. On the brink of losing his sanity, Jim realized that it was speaking directly into his mind.

263

I have not been abducted by aliens but I live well aware of race, the alien space I inhabit in a colonized country. If you want out of alien space, you must pretend not to notice daily references to the fact that you are an alien. And it doesn't work. It can never work. Systemic racism dictates that an alien, no matter how genial or easy-going, no matter how self-effacing and self-erasing, will always be recognized as such. Lovable E.T. not only has to phone home but must go home, for the alien's own good. It is a scripted given and an expected and accepted conclusion. Few people will pause to critically interrogate the reasoning behind this. Few people will bother even to pause.

[Seen 1 Or 2]
"Where did you come from?" the alien voice sinister, sibilant. How can a voice be sibilant when it's communicating without a voice? Jim babbled almost hysterically, desperately clinging to the literal.
    "Why are you here?"
    "Huh?" Jim shook his head. Surprised that he could. "What?"
    "Why are you here?"
    "Why am I – ?! Why am I –?! I – I was abducted! You forced me here against my will!"
    "I beg your pardon," the alien politely reprimanded. "But I've just returned to my bedroom and found you sleeping here. Not unlike Goldilocks, no?" The alien managed a slight smile-like motion with its minimal facial features, but Jim couldn't be too sure, the alien's visage was so – inscrutable. Jim looked wildly around for an escape route, for small objects to take home as evidence of his ordeal, to determine if there were more than one of **them.** *But he was compelled by the mesmerizing eyes, the hypnotic pull of something. Or the other.*
    "Do tell me, if you don't mind me asking...."

I have not been abducted by aliens but, in Canada, Aboriginal Peoples and People of Colour face ongoing cultural abduction. There have been large-scale massacres, treaties of deceit, internment, and ongoing institutionalized racism from national to private arenas. If that isn't enough, daily small erosions build over the years, the generations and one day, you're gone.

Oh! Your name is so difficult, I don't know if I can remember it, and where are you from, when are you going back, we're all humans, we're all in this together, at heart we're all the same, the past is the past, you speak English so well, you people are so clever, aren't you lucky you never have to tan to look that way, I haven't offended you have I, I want to be friends so my children will see that I'm not racist....

People have told me that I'm overly sensitive about racism. In itself this is an alien concept to me – how can there be such a thing as being "overly" sensitive about racism? How can racism ever be condoned or excused? My "own kind," even members of my own family, have told me I am overly sensitive about racism. This criticism is even harder to take than the sense of despair and futile anger I face when exposed to "white denial," the systemic disbelief that racism is historically structured and maintained within all aspects of society in a colonized country: its politics, law, education (nothing higher about this institution), administration, mass media, and yes, even its art. "White denial" is the conscious and unconscious perpetration of systemic oppression.

How bleak the future seems, when sisters and brothers have been so racially and culturally colonized that they cannot recognize the oppressive forces of racism changing the slant of their gaze. And yet, I may be too harsh. They may have made choices of survival, the only choice available to them. "I think you're as white as I am," uttered by a white person, is either an intended compliment or a direct insult. It means either acceptance into the oppressive ruling majority or a denigration of attempts at self-affirming cultural identification. The message is still the same. Be white. I'm not surprised when Aboriginal Peoples and People Of Colour are coerced, or choose, to participate with the dominating forces of racial oppression. I am not surprised. But these abductions must end.

[Seen 1 Too Many]
*Sharon sighed, and when the creature, who for some demented reason was lying in her bed (in her very own private space!), twitched at the sound of her breath, Sharon sighed again. What was she to do? Really, she ought to be furious, what with this uninvited presence in her personal space. Then trying to blame **her** for his being there! What nerve! But the creature was quite pathetic, and she didn't want to see any hysteria or melodramatic outburst. Perhaps the creature had been misled. Perhaps lost. Perhaps it was coming down from a particularly bad trip. Well, it wasn't up to her to coddle the pathetic thing.*

"Do you know where you are?" Sharon asked briskly.

"In – In –In –"

"Take a deep breath," Sharon advised. The creature's neck bobbled quite alarmingly, and she rushed to get the wastebasket in case there was spewage. Her bed! She just washed the sheets two days ago!

"W-w-water!"

Now water! Why not just move right in? Sharon stomped out the door to the washroom down the hall. She hadn't brought her own mug, but used the tan-stained plastic tumbler with the slimy bottom. Someone had brought it up from the cafeteria, and no one ever used it unless they were shit-faced. She filled it half full with lukewarm water and grudgingly took it back to the unasked-for visitor. She smirked as she watched the gulps slide down the pale throat.

"Thank you."

"My, my, it has manners. Feeling a little more human now?" Sharon raised her thin eyebrows and didn't at all feel guilty about the slimy cup.

"What strange fluids you drink here."

"What planet are you from?" Sharon rolled her eyes.

I write well aware of race. I cannot imagine writing outside of this context. My subject position and the subject positions of my readers are something that I must be conscious of, incorporate into the integrity of the text. I live in a racialized environment, and the politics of my writing is distinctly Colour Full. In her essay "The Sixth Sensory Organ," Larissa Lai writes of having two writing strategies: to speak with her world at the centre (rather than at the margins) and explain afterwards, if she feels it is necessary and desirable; and to remain open to change and challenge. In this way, she is able to imagine and create new worlds that may not otherwise be written or welcomed.

These are strategies which, in the context of colonized Canada, refuse the nomenclature of "other." They create a context for Colour Full writing, which is a site of strength, possibility, and change. Because of this, Colour Full is subject to attack by a self-perceived, "non-alien" readership, which racializes texts and categorizes them as writing from the margins. The complexity of the work is undercut by a colonizing gaze that compresses diverse experiences into one of simplistic "identity" constructs. Cultural differences are frequently perceived as exotic delicacies meant to be sampled.

There *are* writers, both white and Of Colour, who write purposely to feed the "non-alien's" appetite for the other. After all, this is a consumer world, and "ethnicity" is currently a marketable commodity. "Non-aliens" will let "aliens" seduce them, but only on their own terms, all the while congratulating themselves for their liberal-mindedness. It is unfortunate that Colour Full writing can be read as "alien" because a reader may desire to read it as such.

This became dishearteningly clear when *Ms.*, a feminist, progressive, and politically conscious magazine, approached me for a written contribution. I submitted a fun but biting story about the woes of breastfeeding. The editing process was fine, and the story was almost to publication when they sent me the art work that was to accompany the story. It was a wood-cut type, " highly Oriental," stylized image of a supposed Japanese woman in a kimono with a baby at the breast. Her extremely slanted eyes were crossed and there was nothing funny about it. I had written a story primarily about breastfeeding in which the protagonist was a Japanese Canadian. But *Ms.* had decided to read an alien into the text, had chosen to package it with an alien signifier. I refused the image of course. I told *Ms.* I couldn't possibly have it with my story and heard many distorted excuses of how it wasn't inappropriate, or based on a long-standing "Western" stereotype of the "Oriental Woman." They pulled my story from that issue.

Several months later, the editor at *Ms.* approached me again. We talked a little about how both sides felt extremely disappointed with the earlier interaction. This time *Ms.* suggested a collage-type image and sent me a copy. Instead of an "Oriental" woman, there was a white woman. The image was funky and fun. I went with it. But how sad, I thought, that *Ms.* could only imagine alien or not.

[(Ob)Scene Too]
How horrible, those eyes! Jim almost voided inside his trousers. That such slanted eyes could be capable of rolling. Was it trying to hypnotize him?

The alien appears to have a smooth skin surface, with no noticeable markings, off-white in colour, Jim babbled inside his head. There are four limbs positioned on the body in a humanoid manner. Four fingers on the hands, thumbs opposed. Feet appear to be two-toed in form. There appear to be no identifiable reproductive organs. Gender is indeterminate or unknown....

There are many ways in which "aliens" are constructed in our societies. The prurient horror of an apparently "ungendered" being betrays a homophobic subtext that speaks volumes of a society that continues to assert heterosexist patriarchal primacy. The disabled, the disenfranchised, the deemed "lower" classes, those who are alienated, are all labelled as special interest groups implying that their voices and needs are separate from those of the ruling majority. The "alienated" are many, and my intent is not to silence or override any experience of oppression. It is a strategy of those in power to divert the energies of the oppressed towards fighting among and between themselves. It is in the best interests of a systemically oppressive society to divide people who would be powerful if allied. When I talk about race, I am not talking about race while shutting my eyes to those who are oppressed in different ways. It is critical that there be time and space for all. We will all be heard. We will all make change. Today, I write about race.

[Change Seen]
"Listen, fool!" Sharon hissed. "I don't know what your problem is and I don't really give a shit. Just get out of my room!"

"You mean to say that I don't have to remain here?"

"Get out, I say! Before I call security! God!" Sharon muttered to herself. Freshmen! The first week was the worst, what with the freshies drinking who-knows-what, carousing until all hours. God! She hoped that the jerk got a cold sore, at least stomach cramps, from the dirty bathroom cup.

Jim was relieved, confused, disorientated. There was no immediate physical danger to his person as he had anticipated. But what could the ultimate plan be? Was this the beginning of some sort of experimental psychological study? Perhaps, even now, some hidden monitors watched this bizarre interaction.

Because he was no longer fixated on imagined personal pain, Jim could finally look upon his captor without the filter of fear. And strangely, unwittingly, he found himself becoming aroused. Some small portion of his sensibilities told him it was wrong, heinously wrong, but he couldn't stop his reactions. The alien, perhaps a she?, was so very compelling in her very alien-ness. The large slanted eyes, the pale skin, the lack of bodily hair. Would her body be warm to the touch? Cool? Would she have some special skills, maybe even different body parts, which would take sex into some unknown alien-esque ecstasy? Jim fairly quivered.

"There are –," he gulped, blushed, wished he could surreptitiously slip his hand into his pocket to rearrange himself. "There's not going to be a, uhh, sexual examination?"

How will we go about dismantling our desire to read the alien? How will we disrupt our desire to be seduced by that which does not seek to seduce in the first place? The cultural and language contexts of Colour Full writing do not ask that we read as "site tourists." It demands that we hold ourselves accountable about how we choose to see. When I write from a specific cultural background, I write from a specific site. The reader must contextualize her own location in relation to and in tandem with this site. And are we ready to change? Are we open to challenge? There is no leaving the site after a brief visit. Colour Full writing is home to stay.

[Seen Enough!]
Sharon was beyond anger. She grabbed two fists of sheet and jerked upward, the stupid boy tumbling out of her bed on to the cheap residence carpet. He cowered at her feet, but Sharon nudged him with her thongs out the door as if he were an errant toad. Her friends, Mei and Yukiko, stood in the hallway and watched her last bit of foot prodding, astounded.

"You're not going to believe this!" Sharon rolled her eyes, saw the huddled freshman shudder. "Go away!" she hissed, pulling her friends inside the room and slamming the door on him. The sound of giggling.

Jim scrambled to his feet. My god! He knew there had to be more than one! And the horror! The two new ones looked identical to his first captor! Maybe they were clones! He lurched through metallic doors into a hallway that led to a large open room with bright, unspecific lighting. He heard a faint hum. There were large objects in meaningless colours encircling a flat black monitor. Jim gulped. Perhaps this was the monitor eye that watched all he did, recorded his every action. And the horror! There were other hallways, more doors opening and closing, and the aliens – the aliens were everywhere! They stood in groups chattering, chattering their hideous language. Their horrible unknowable eyes. Jim couldn't stand it, the sheer number of them, their faces indistinguishable from one other, their skin smooth, their obscenely slanted eyes. He fell into a faint in the middle of the lounge with a bulge in the crotch of his trousers. A generous student tossed a baseball cap on top of it, but otherwise, everyone just walked around him.

What of my own desire to hear about aliens? My ongoing fascination with *X-Files,* the cheesie *Encyclopedia of the Unexplained* on my bookshelf; how I ask people I've recently met if they believe in aliens…? Am I projecting my own alienation onto an other? An other who will never talk back to me? Do I imagine that I have the privilege to exoticize aliens without having to negotiate the politics of such an act? Do I imagine myself safe in this space? There are so many questions I must ask myself and struggle to answer. So many questions you must ask yourself and struggle to answer. In my superficial pursuit of alien stories, my love of aliens, I never stopped to ask if the aliens would love me.

NOTES
1. I would like to thank and acknowledge Larissa Lai and Ashok Mathur for the influence of their works, "The Sixth Sensory Organ," *Bringing It Home* (Vancouver: Arsenal Pulp Press, 1996) and "Alien Autopsy, " *Mix magazine* 22.4 (Spring 1997) respectively. And I would like to thank Tamai Kobayashi, Larissa Lai, Aruna Srivastava, and Rita Wong for their support and editorial suggestions. This essay was first performed at the Women and Texts Conference at Leeds University, England, 2-5 July 1997. It has been re-worked for publication.

NOURBESE PHILIP

Taming Our Tomorrows

One of my earliest memories of Canada, having arrived in London, Ontario from the Caribbean, was "discovering" Margaret Laurence through her novel *The Stone Angel*. Laurence was the second Canadian – in all the problematic and ambivalent senses of that word – I had read (the first being Lucy Maud Montgomery). Some years later, after moving to Toronto, I read Laurence's *The Tomorrow Tamer* with delight and a dawning recognition. I had not yet been to Africa, but with one or two exceptions the work rang true. "The Tomorrow Tamer," the title story of Laurence's collection, chronicles the story of the villagers of Owurasu as they struggle with change. Change for the small West African village means a bridge that will span the Owura river and in so doing will destroy the age-old sacred grove beside the river.

> "We do not know whether Owura will suffer his river to be disturbed," Okomfo Ofori said. "If he will not, then I think the fish will die from the river, and the oil palms will wither, and the yams will shrink and dwindle in the planting and the snake will inhabit our huts because the people are dead, and the strangler vine will cover our dwelling places. For our life comes from the river, and if the god's hand is turned against us, what will avail the hands of men?" (Laurence 87)

The changes the new bridge will bring to Owurasu will undoubtedly destroy a way of life some centuries old. When Kofi, one of the young men from the village helping to build the bridge, plunges to his death, the villagers engage in that most human of activities: making sense of catastrophic events that initially appear beyond comprehension. The people of Owurasu understand perfectly well what has happened. The bridge, clearly, has sacrificed Kofi in order to appease the river. The people feel they know the bridge now. The bridge is not as powerful as Owura. The river has been acknowledged as elder. The queenly bridge has paid its homage and is part of Owurasu at last. The villagers understand Kofi to be the sacrifice to tomorrow – the quintessential "tomorrow tamer" – "a man consumed by the gods" who will "live forever."

Many years later, when the debate over issues of appropriation exploded in Canada and lines were being drawn in the sand, I recalled Laurence's book as an example of writers crossing racial, ethnic, and cultural boundaries respectfully. I believed then that you could not effectively prohibit anyone from writing about another culture because you could not enforce such a prohibition. Moreover, a prohibition of this kind would not necessarily guarantee that African, Asian or First Nations writers would be published, or that their works would be reviewed respectfully and their voices heard. And that was the issue – coming to voice. If a writer or artist feels drawn to another culture, the responsible action is for him or her to examine his or her motives. Are you attracted to another culture because you think your own culture is exhausted (as some writers have argued) and you want to spice up your literary imagination with a little exotica? If, upon examination, a writer's motives are not exploitative, then she or he needs to approach the culture with humility and a willingness to learn – not with a sense of entitlement. Finally, she or he needs to accept insightful critique offered by critics from the culture in question. For me the success of *The Tomorrow Tamer* lay in the fact that Laurence did not view the culture of the Other – in this case West African culture – through the eyes of the imperialist or colonizer.

What is it about tomorrows that we need to tame them? Etymologically the word, comprised of two words, "to" and "morrow," means nothing more than towards another morning. But tomorrows have always challenged us, bedeviled us, worried us. The common sentiment in virtually all reflections on "tomorrows" – from the *Corinthians*: "Let us eat and drink for tomorrow we die," to the Tobago proverb: "Every barrow hog got dem Saturday" (Today for me, tomorrow for you) – speaks to a need to manage the haunting mystery that is at the heart of tomorrow. We may ignore tomorrows – *carpe diem* and all that – and live for the present, or we may try and prepare for them. But whatever we do entails attempts to manage, to control, and so to tame our tomorrows.

In the fall of 1995 this country was transfixed by the very real possibility that Quebec would separate. After the referendum, I wrote an article for *Border/lines* entitled "Back to the Future." In a semi-humorous way I was attempting to manage a future or a tomorrow that was unimaginable for many. A Quebec separate from Canada is a vision of tomorrow that frightens many.

For us Africans in the New World tomorrow is a constant problem. We are the only group brought forcibly and unwillingly to the New World, this touted utopia, to help create utopias for others. Cut off from our yesterdays – in fact told that we had no yesterdays, no history – forbidden to live out the promise of the tomorrows of progress of which the New World boasted, we were and still are condemned to a today in which we are intended to be nothing but hewers of wood and drawers of water.

In an odd and disturbing way, time stands still for us Africans. Sometimes it even repeats itself. The promise of tomorrow never comes. Consequently time and its representations present a constant challenge. This is all the more ironic for the fact that African cultures understand in profound ways the fluidity and non-linearity of time. That profound subversion of the idea of past, present, and future that is manifest in the belief in the continuing presence of our ancestors appears in all African cultures. Jazz, the most

272   NOURBESE PHILIP

innovatively challenging music to come out of the New World, the only new music created in the New World, explores the dynamic play of time and timing. It is no accident that this music is fundamentally the expression and product of African aesthetics.

Lest we imagine the past is over, let us think of works like *The Bell Curve,*[1] or those of the so-called scholar, Dinesh D'Souza,[2] who appeared not that long ago on the Canadian Broadcasting Corporation (CBC) (not once but twice) opining that the problem with the Blacks was that they weren't white. These are, indeed, strange times when what is essentially and indisputably hate literature against African people passes as science and is reviewed seriously by newspapers like the *Globe and Mail* without any analysis of the white supremacist and eugenist connections of the authors. Tracts like *The Bell Curve* are nothing but the same old tawdry story of anti-African racism dressed up in new genetic finery. The intent remains the same: to ensure that Africans continue to be deprived of the promise of tomorrow.

How does one begin to respond to a charge that one is inferior and/or cognitively challenged? Silence is sometimes the wisest and best response in the face of such indignity. Silence can also be interpreted as consent. To enter the debate on the terms of those who are disseminating these ideas, who are also powerful and well connected to the media and other institutions that shape opinion is, however, a zero-sum game which one will always lose. Those who make the rules can be counted on to shift and change them when the game demands it.

If one wished one could question why, if Africans are so cognitively challenged, dominant white society exerts (and has always exerted) so much effort to keep them in subservient positions. One could ask why dominant white and European cultures have so unrelentingly stolen the cultural and intellectual products of Africans and then attempted to cover or hide the evidence of this theft. The names Picasso, Brancusi, and Elvis, to mention but three of the most egregious examples, come to mind. If Africans are so cognitively challenged, how did it come to be that world-wide the popular music industry and the fashion industry for youths are driven by African-American aesthetics and style? Why are the cognitively endowed stealing from the cognitively challenged? But then, as I said earlier, to enter this debate is to fall to the debased level of those who would wish to see us return to the status of thing or chattel.

The tomorrows we face today in Canada, and even more so in the province of Ontario, are at best challenging, at worst frightening. Many aspects of life which we hold to be fundamental are being changed before our very eyes. As MBANX, one of the major time shifters, keeps telling us, the times, indeed, are a-changing. What will tomorrow be and bring for our children? Will there be adequate schooling? Will there be jobs? As we see our pensions shrink, and witness the attack on medicare, what do our tomorrows hold in store for us?

The present government in Ontario would have us believe that putting as many publicly owned institutions into the hands of private companies will guarantee a better standard of living. If not today, then tomorrow. In the words of Lewis Carroll, "the rule is jam tomorrow, jam yesterday, but never jam today." To paraphrase, we live in jamless todays on the promise of jamful tomorrows. Many of us know that the profits – the jam – never travel down very far, but just as many are tempted with the promises of jam tomorrow.

Looking to yesterday, however, sometimes helps us to understand the tomorrows our leaders intend for us. In *Black Skins, White Masks*, Frantz Fanon mentions *Prospero and Caliban: Psychology of Colonization* by the colonial writer M. Mannoni, who writes:

> What the colonial in common with Prospero lacks, is awareness of the world of Others, a world in which Others have to be respected. This is the world from which the colonial has fled because he cannot accept men as they are. Rejection of that world is combined with an urge to dominate, an urge which is infantile in origin and which social adaptation has failed to discipline. The reason the colonial himself gives for his flight – whether he says it was the desire to travel, or the desire to escape from the cradle or from the "ancient parapets," or whether he says that he simply wanted a freer life – is of no consequence.... *It was always a question of compromising with the desire for a world without men...."* (Emphasis added)

Fanon comments:

> If one adds that many Europeans go to the colonies because it is possible for them to grow rich quickly there, that with rare exceptions the colonial is a merchant or rather a trafficker, one will have grasped the psychology of the man who arouses in the autochthonous population "the feeling of inferiority."

In the profoundly anti-human policies of our present provincial government, manifest in its attacks on the weakest, the most vulnerable in our society, on children, on the health care system, one has a growing sense that its policies arise from a deep desire for a world without men or women. Without humans. Human beings, with all their messy and oh-so-human needs, are a profound inconvenience to this bottom-line government that generates the feeling that it would be only too happy to see us all become the disappeared. Failing that, we must be reminded regularly of our inferior position. What is happening today in Ontario and in Canada, what has already happened in the United States, the United Kingdom and in New Zealand, is as old as humankind itself: greed, lust for power, and the desire to control others that manifested itself in the colonial and imperial exercises and excesses of yesterday and that returned full blown with the explosive growth and metastasizing of capitalism.

As colonials spread around the world – the Americas, Australia, the Caribbean, Africa – they saw nothing but land for the taking. When Europeans came to Canada, they arrived in a land already peopled by the First Nations peoples, a land not to be owned, but held in trust for tomorrow. This is one of the central beliefs of the First Nations people. The perception of a place as empty can only happen if one is not prepared to listen to the voices of Others, and the colonial has never been prepared to listen to Other voices. That was yesterday, this is today. It must not be tomorrow. That was what the massive demonstration in Toronto – The Days of Action – was about: an attempt to control, to manage, and to tame a vision of tomorrow that horrifies so many of us in Ontario.[3]

A memory: it is winter. I am standing on a frozen lake in Northern Ontario. All around is a stillness, a silence as profound as it is moving. For a brief moment I experience an epiphany, an understanding of the significance of the land to Native peoples and the feeling that until we understand and accept the land in this way, we newcomers will never truly belong.

On the way back from that lake I am listening to the radio and hear the First Nations writer and scholar Georges Sioui discussing the concept of Americity which links the Americas and the Amerindian peoples. In *For An American Autohistory* Sioui writes:

> By studying what is original about Native American culture and therefore about Native history, I shall try to show how modern American societies could benefit from demythologizing their socio-political discourse and becoming aware of their "Americity." That is on this continent where they have just come ashore, they should see spirit, order and thought, instead of a mass of lands and peoples to be removed, displaced, or rearranged.

There is good reason why more recent immigrants to Canada cling to urban areas. They – we – feel more comfortable in the city. We can see others who look like us, despite the fact that many of us are, at most, a generation away from the land in our countries of origin. The town of Minden lies some two hours outside Toronto. For the last few years I have visited there in the summer. Each year I have experienced the overwhelming whiteness of rural Ontario. Walking through the town, I count the number of African, Asian, or First Nations people I see. I have never got past three in any one week. That is a challenge for our tomorrows – to come to an understanding of being able to share in the land – in all aspects of the land and not only in the urban areas with which we are identified. Moreover, we must be able to share the land in the recreational sense, but in a sense of the land as a source of strength and support, as it has been for First Nations people.

The human species today is facing the question of its survival. The way of life known as western civilization is setting out along a path towards death where its culture has no viable responses. The great majority of the world has its roots in the natural world, and it is the natural world, with its traditions, which must prevail if we want to develop societies that are truly free and just. Oddly enough it has been the natural world of Canada that has offered me respite from the prevailing sense of un/belonging that so many African Canadians and people of colour experience.

Journal Entries: June 1996

The only time I feel as if I am of this land is when I leave the city or those times within the city when I interact with the physical land.

Walking through Foxes Den in southwestern Ontario I sense my nervousness as a woman. I see a car parked at the entrance – oops! Who is in the woods? Is there a man down there? I breathe a sigh of relief when I see a couple coming towards me. Am I any safer? I don't know, but the couple nature of it – they're holding hands – reassures me. Two women would have been even more reassuring – two men less so.

I press on. Oh, but it is a beautiful land! The proprietor of the B&B tells me that up above their house, just where one pasture ends and another begins, there is supposed to be an Indian burial ground. There are ghosts who need to haunt us in this land. "It is the duty of the living to heal their ancestors. If these ancestors are not healed, their sick energy will haunt the souls and psyches of those who are responsible for helping them." (Malidome Some)

Oh, but it is a beautiful land! A pale lavender butterfly flutters by. I stop by a pool of stagnant water bordered by bright green scum and filled with the little black bodies. Tadpoles! I poke my stick in the water. They flee. Such power! They don't know who is poking at them. They create a pattern in flight – big heads, little tails – like sperm cells enlarged a thousand times over. That something so small should have muscles! Do they? Their tails wiggling and driving them away in black patterned flight.

The blossoms come in two shades of pink, deep and light, and also white. They brighten the landscape. The ploughed field, the borders of tiny white flowers – all this is oblivious to my ethnicity and race. Rather I am oblivious to my ethnicity and race. For the first time I feel myself think "this is my land" not in the sense of owning it, but of the land possessing me in all its beauty.

And bird sound – ah bird sound …

The naming of things is so important. The urgency or need I feel to name the plants around me, to know them: is this a part of the belonging?

A sprig of cedar in the plastic bottle made into a vase.

Newly formed cones are a beautiful purple colour with soft, green, needle-like leaves – the larch – "an evergreen deciduous." Unbelievable that these tender purple kisses become the stiff brown cones.

On my walks I'm chased by dogs and so I have taken to carrying a big stick which I swing at them with an energy infused by fear. A large, black three-legged dog refuses to give up. I suppose he wants to show that having three legs hasn't slowed him down.

Walking along a back road yesterday – deserted except for the odd car or pick-up stirring up a great deal of dust. As they pass there's always a moment of fear as I wonder: is it going to stop? Will two red-necked crackers à la the American South come out to get me? I'm probably safer along these roads than in Toronto.

As I walk I feel connected with something very old. I plod along with a sense of my smallness in this vast land: me in this vast universe – something about the scale really pleases me. I look up ahead, often worried about whether I have taken on too much or whether I'm going in the right direction, but knowing deep down that just by putting one foot in front of the other I'll get there, and then when I look back and see how far I have come – well!

Golden spears at the side of the road and the hard, prickly thistle. A robin flies along from tree to tree just in front of me as if she wants to see where I'm going. And along the road the scattered sun-bleached bones of trees, the purpled spears of lilac piercing the air with their fragrance.

Some of our so-called leaders have in store for us a vision of a certain kind of tomorrow that we must resist. We must tame those tomorrows that would separate us; that would see us exploit the young and the weak; that would see us exploit the land even further with no thought for the future of tomorrow. The vote that installed Harris was an anti-poor and not-so-subtle racist vote. The code words were welfare cheats and affirmative action abuses. He sweetened the pot further with the promise of a tax break. Those code words triggered many who believed that somehow welfare payments were to blame for the deficit, and unqualified African Canadians and other peoples of colour were taking jobs from properly qualified white Canadians. Consider the fact that one of the first acts of the Harris government was the reinstatement of hollow point bullets for police, which Harris himself said would not please the African Canadian communities. Consider the fact that one of the first tragedies to occur shortly after the election of the Harris government was the killing of the First Nations man, Dudley George, by the provincial police. Little did middle-class Ontario realize that when Harris got through with the weak and the helpless, when he was done putting African Canadians and other peoples of colour in their place, he would come for the middle class and its children. Even doctors and lawyers were not exempt. If they come for your Black brother or sister in the morning and you fail to speak out or support them, then they will undoubtedly come for you in the evening. We are indeed our brothers' and sisters' keepers. That is the lesson that must be taken from Harris's scorched earth policies in Ontario.

Audre Lorde writes that

the true focus of revolutionary change is never merely the oppressive situations which we seek to escape, but that piece of the oppressor which is planted deep within each of us, and which knows only the oppressors' tactics, the oppressors' relationships. Change means growth, and growth can be painful. But we sharpen self-definition by exposing the self in work and struggle together with those whom we define as different from ourselves, although sharing the same goals. (123)

The Owurasu villagers believed that "a man consumed by the gods lives forever." They were then able to live with the "sacrifice" of Kofi. Surely we need not sacrifice our children to have them live forever. We need to tame those tomorrows that envision a world bereft of humans and human values but not through the sacrifice of our children. The Mexican poet Octavio Paz urged that we "imagine our pasts and remember our future – our tomorrows. Those tomorrows – of a better world – are all that we leave our children." That is how our ancestors live on – those who remembered us in their tomorrows and created a better world for us by leaving a legacy of public education, the union movement, a medicare system, a kinder, gentler society. The infrastructure of this legacy is now rapidly being dismantled. It is only in protecting our values that we will tame our tomorrows.

NOTES

1. See Richard J. Herrnstein and Charles Murray, *The Bell Curve: Intelligence and Class Structure in American Life* (New York: Free Press, 1994).
2. Dinesh D'Souza was the senior domestic policy analyst at the White House during the Ronald Reagan administration in the 1980s. He is the author of *The End of Racism* (New York: Free Press, 1995) and *Illiberal Education: The Politics of Race and Sex on Campus* (New York: Free Press 1991).
3. The Metro Days of Action were held 25-26 October 1996 in Toronto, Ontario. They were part of a string of protests against the Harris government held on a rotating basis across the province.

References

Abel, Samuel. *Opera in the Flesh: Sexuality in Operatic Performance.* Boulder, CO: Westview Press, 1996.

Adam, Michel. *Vers-de-terre: (anté-poésie).* Montréal: Les Éditions Dérives, 1976.

Agnant, Marie-Célie. *La dot de Sara.* Montréal: Éditions du Remue-ménage, 1995.

"À L'Horizon." *Afrique Tribune* 2.33 (1-14 mars 1996): 16 .

Alladin, Ibrahim. *Racism in Canadian Schools.* Toronto: Harcourt Brace, 1996.

Allen, Gunn Paula. *The Sacred Hoop: Recovering The Feminine in American Indian Traditions.* Boston: Beacon Press, 1986.

Allen, Lillian. *Women Do This Every Day: Selected Poems of Lillian Allen.* Toronto: Women's Press, 1993.

Alonzo, Anne-Marie. *Écoute, Sultane.* Montréal: L'Hexagone, 1987.

——. *Le Livre des ruptures.* Montréal: NBJ, 1988.

Anderson, Alan B. and James S. Frideres. *Ethnicity in Canada: Theoretical Perspectives.* Toronto: Butterworths, 1981.

Anderson, Benedict. *Imagined Community.* London: Verso, 1991.

Angenot, Marc. "Le discours social: problématique d'ensemble." *Cahiers de recherches sociologiques: Le discours social et ses usages* 2.1 (1984): 19-44.

Angus, Ian. *A Border Within: National Identity, Cultural Plurality, and Wilderness.* Montreal : McGill-Queen's University Press, 1997.

Aquin, Hubert. *Trou de mémoire: roman.* Montréal: Cercle du livre de France, 1968.

Armstrong, Jeannette. "The Disempowerment of First North American Native Peoples and Empowerment Through Their Writing." *An Anthology of Canadian Native Literature in English.* Eds. Daniel David Moses and Terry Goldie. Toronto: Oxford University Press, 1992. 207-11.

—— ed. *Looking at the Words of Our People: First Nations Analysis of Literature.* Penticton, BC: Theytus Books, 1993.

Ashcroft, Bill, Gareth Griffiths and Helen Tiffin. *The Empire Writes Back: Theory and Practice in Post-Colonial Literatures.* London: Routledge, 1989.

Asad, Talal. "The Concept of Cultural Translation in British Social Anthropology." *Writing Culture: The Poetics and Politics of Ethnography.* Eds. James Clifford and George E. Marcus. Berkeley: University of California Press, 1986. 141-64.

Attali, Jacques. *Noise: The Political Economy of Music.* Trans. Brian Massumi. 1985. Minneapolis: University of Minnesota Press, 1989.

Atwood, Margaret. *The Journals of Susanna Moodie.* Toronto: Oxford University Press, 1970.

——. *Surfacing.* Toronto: McClelland & Stewart, 1972.

——. *Survival: A Thematic Guide to Canadian Literature.* Toronto: Anansi, 1972.

Augenbraum, Harold and Ilan Stavans. *Growing up Latino. Memoirs and Stories.* Boston: Houghton Mifflin, 1993.

Bains, Hardial S. *Communism: 1989-1991.* Toronto: Ideological Studies Centre, 1991.

Balzano, Flora. *Soigne ta chute.* Montréal: XYZ, 1991.

Bannerji, Himani. "The Other Family' and Interview with Arun Mukherjee." *Other Solitudes: Canadian Multicultural Fictions*. Eds. Linda Hutcheon and Marion Richmond. Toronto: University of Toronto Press, 1990. 141-52.

—— ed. *Returning the Gaze: Essays on Racism, Feminism and Politics*. Toronto: Sister Vision, 1993.

——. *The Writing on the Wall: Essays on Culture and Politics*. Toronto: TSAR, 1993.

Bannerji, Kaushalya. *A New Remembrance*. Toronto: TSAR, 1993.

Barlow, Julie. "This and That." *This Magazine* 29.5 (December/January 1996): 4.

Barthes, Roland. "The Death of the Author." *Modern Criticism and Theory: A Reader*. Ed. David Lodge. London; New York: Longman, 1988. 167-71.

Bauer, Julien. *Les Minorités au Québec*. Montréal: Boréal, 1994.

Beccarelli Saad, *Tiziana. Vers l'Amérique*. Montréal: Triptyque, 1988.

Behdad, Ali. *Belated Travelers: Orientalism in the Age of Colonial Dissolution*. Durham: Duke University Press, 1994.

Bergland, Betty. "Ideology, Ethnicity, and the Gendered Subject: Reading Immigrant Women's Autobiographies." *Seeking Common Ground: Multi-disciplinary Studies of Immigrant Women in the United States*. Ed. Donna Gabaccia. Westport, CT: Praeger Publishers, 1992. 101-21.

Berrouet-Oriol, R. "L'Effet d'exil." *Vice Versa* 17 (1987): 20-21.

—— et R. Fournier. "L'émergence des écritures migrantes et métisses au Québec." *Québec Studies* 14 (1992): 7-22.

Berry, J.W. and J.A. Laponce eds. *Ethnicity and Culture in Canada: The Research Landscape*. Toronto: University of Toronto Press, 1994.

Bersianik, Louky. *L'Euguélionne*. Montréal: Stanké, 1976.

Bertrand, Pierre. "La langue et l'écriture." *Vice Versa* 28 (mars/avril 1990): 50-52.

Best, Carrie M. *That Lonesome Road: The Autobiography of Carrie M. Best*. New Glasgow, NS: Clarion Publication Company, 1977.

Bhabha, Homi K. *The Location of Culture*. London; New York: Routledge, 1994.

Bhaggiyadatta, Krisantha Sri. *Domestic Bliss*. Toronto: Five Press, 1981.

Bissoondath, Neil. *Selling Illusions: The Cult of Multiculturalism in Canada*. Toronto: Penguin, 1994.

——. *Le marché aux illusions. La méprise du multiculturalisme*. Trans Jean Papineau. Montréal: Boréal, 1995.

Blaeser, Kimberly M. "Native Literature: Seeking a Critical Center." *Looking at the Words of Our People: First Nations Analysis of Literature*. Ed. Jeannette Armstrong. Penticton, BC: Theytus Books, 1993. 51-62.

Blodgett, E.D. "Towards an Ethnic Style." *Canadian Review of Comparative Literature* 22 (1995): 3-4, 623-38.

Bosco, Monique. *Babel-opéra*, Laval: Trois, 1989.

Bouyoucas, Pan. *Une bataille d'Amérique: roman*. Montréal: Quinze, 1976.

——. *Le dernier souffle: roman*. Montréal: Éditions du Jour, 1975.

——. *L'humoriste et l'assassin*. Montréal: Libre expression, 1996.

——. *La vengeance d'un père*. Montréal: Libre Expression, 1997.

Brathwaite, Edward Kamau. *History of the Voice: The Development of Nation Language in Anglophone Caribbean Poetry*. London: New Beacon Books, 1984.

Brand, Dionne. *Bread out of Stone: Recollections, Sex, Recognitions, Race, Dreaming, Politics*. Toronto: Coach House Press, 1994.

——. "Interview with Dagmar Novak." *Other Solitudes: Canadian Multicultural Fictions*. Eds. Linda Hutcheon and Marion Richmond. Toronto: University of Toronto Press, 1990. 271-77.

———. *No Burden To Carry: Narratives of Black Working Women in Ontario 1920s-1950s*. Toronto: Women's Press, 1991.

———. *Sans Souci and Other Stories*. Stratford, ON: Williams-Wallace, 1988.

———. "A Working Paper on Black Women in Toronto: Gender, Race and Class." *Returning the Gaze: Essays on Racism, Feminism and Politics*. Ed. Himani Bannerji. Toronto: Sister Vision, 1993. 220-42.

Brant, Beth. *Writing As Witness: Essay and Talk*. Toronto: Women's Press, 1994.

Brossard, Nicole. *L'amèr: ou Le chapitre effrité*. Montréal: Quinze, 1977.

———. *Le centre blanc: poèmes 1965-1975*. Montréal: Éditions de l'Hexagone, 978.

Brown, Brenda Lea ed. *Bringing it Home: Women Talk About Feminism in Their Lives*. Vancouver: Arsenal Pulp Press, 1996.

Brown, Rosemary. *Being Brown: A Very Public Life*. Toronto: Random House of Canada Ltd., 1989.

Bruchac, Joseph and Michael J. Caduto. *The Native Stories from Keepers of the Earth*. Regina: Fifth House Publishers, 1991.

Brydon, Diana et Helen Tiffin. *Decolonising Fictions*. Sydney: Dangaroo Press, 1993.

Burnet, Jean R. with Howard Palmer. *Coming Canadians: An Introduction to a History of Canada's Peoples*. Toronto: McClelland & Stewart, 1988.

—— et al. eds. *Migration and the Transformation of Cultures*. Toronto: Multicultural History Society of Ontario, 1992.

Buss, Helen M. "Canadian Women's Autobiography: Some Critical Directions." *A Mazing Space: Writing Canadian Women Writing*. Ed. S. Neuman and S. Kamboureli. Edmonton: Longspoon/ NeWest Press, 1986. 154-66.

Caccia, Fulvio et Antonio D'Alfonso. *Quêtes. Textes d'auteurs italo-québécois*. Montréal: Guernica, 1983.

Campbell, Maria. *Halfbreed*. Toronto: McClelland & Stewart, 1973.

Camper, Carol ed. *Miscegenation Blues: Voices of Mixed Race Women*. Toronto: Sister Vision Press, 1994.

Chambers, Iain. *Migrancy, Culture, Identity*. London; New York: Routledge, 1994.

Champagne, Dominic. *La cité interdite: théâtre*. Montréal: VLB Éditeur, 1992.

Charron, François. *La passion d'autonomie: littérature et nationalisme*. Montréal: Les Herbes rouges, 1982.

Charon, Milly. *Between Two Worlds: The Canadian Immigrant Experience*. Revised edition. Montreal: Nu-age Editions, 1988.

———. *Worlds Apart: New Immigrant Voices*. Dunvegan, ON: Cormorant Books, 1989.

Chen, Kuan-Hsing. "Not Yet the Postcolonial Era: The (Super) Nation-State and Transnationalism of Cultural Studies: Responses to Ang and Stratton." *Cultural Studies* 10.1 (1996): 37-70.

Chen, Ying, *La mémoire de l'eau: roman*. Montréal: Leméac, 1992.

———. *L'ingratitude: roman*. Montréal: Leméac, 1995.

Chong, Denise. *The Concubine's Children: Portrait of a Family Divided*. Toronto: Viking, 1994.

Chow, Rey. *Writing Diaspora: Tactics of Intervention in Contemporary Cultural Studies*. Bloomington: Indiana University Press, 1993.

———. *Primitive Passions: Visuality, Sexuality, Ethnography, and Contemporary Chinese Cinema*. New York: Columbia University Press, 1995.

Chung, Ook. *Nouvelles orientales et désorientées*. Montréal: L'Hexagone, 1994.

Clarke, Austin. *In This City*. Toronto: Exile, 1992.

——. *Nine Men Who Laughed*. Markham, ON: Penguin, 1986.

——. *Public Enemies: Police Violence and Black Youth*. Toronto: HarperCollins, 1992.

——. *There Are No Elders*. Toronto: Exile Editions, 1993.

Clarke, George Elliott ed. *Fire on the Water: An Anthology of Black Nova Scotian Writing*. 2 vols. Porter's Lake, NS: Pottersfield, 1991-92.

——. "Towards a Conservative Modernity: Cultural Nationalism in Contemporary Acadian and Africadian Poetry." *Revue Frontenac Review* 9 (1992): 45-63.

——. "White Niggers, Black Slaves: Slavery, Race and Class in T.C. Haliburton's The Clockmaker." *Nova Scotia Historical Review* 14.1 (1994): 13-40.

——. "Must All Blackness be American? Locating Canada in Borden's "Tightrope time," or Nationalizing Gilroy's *The Black Atlantic*." *Canadian Ethnic Studies* 28.3 (1996): 56-71.

Cleaver, Eldridge. *Soul on Ice*. New York: Dell, 1968.

Clément, Catherine. *Opera: or The Undoing of Women*. Trans. Betsy Wing. Minneapolis: University of Minnesota Press, 1988.

Clerc, Jeanne-Marie. "Le renouveau de la parole identitaire." *Le Renouveau de la parole identitaire*. Eds. Mireille Calle-Gruber et Jeanne-Marie Clerc. Montpellier/Kingston: Université Paul-Valéry et Université Queen's, 1993. 7-15.

Cliche, Anne Élaine. *La Pisseuse*. Montréal: Triptyque, 1992.

Clifford, James. *The Predicament of Culture: Twentieth-Century Ethnography, Literature, and Art*. Cambridge, Mass.: Harvard University Press, 1988.

——. "Traveling Cultures." *Cultural Studies*. Eds. Lawrence Grossberg, Cary Nelson and Paula A. Treichler. New York: Routledge, 1992. 96-112.

—— and George E. Marcus eds. *Writing Culture: The Poetics and Politics of Ethnography*. Berkeley: University of California Press, 1986.

Cohen, Matt. "Racial Memories." *Other Solitudes: Canadian Multicultural Fictions*. Eds. Linda Hutcheon and Marion Richmond. Toronto: University of Toronto Press, 1990. 153-72.

Coleman, Daniel. "How to Make Love to a Discursive Genealogy: Dany Laferrière's Metaparody of Racialized Sexuality." Unpublished paper.

——. *Masculine Migrations: Reading the Postcolonial male in "New Canadian" Narratives*. Toronto: University of Toronto Press, 1998.

Conway, Sheelagh. *The Faraway Hills Are Green: Voices of Irish Women in Canada*. Toronto: Women's Press, 1992.

Cooper, Afua. *Memories Have Tongue: Poetry*. Toronto: Sister Vision Press, 1992.

Craig, Terrence. *Racial Attitudes in English-Canadian Fiction, 1905-1980*. Waterloo, ON: Wilfrid Laurier University Press, 1987.

Dabydeen, Cyril. *Goatsong*. Oakville, ON: Mosaic, 1977.

Dahan, Andrée. *Le printemps peut attendre*. Montréal: Quinze, 1985.

D'Alfonso, Antonio. *In Italics: In Defense of Ethnicity*. Toronto: Guernica, 1996.

Damm, Kateri. "Says Who: Colonialism, Identity and Defining Indigenous Literature." *Looking at the Words of Our People: First Nations Analysis of Literature*. Ed. Jeannette Armstrong. Penticton, BC: Theytus Books, 1993. 93-114.

Dandurand, Anne. *The Cracks: A Novel*. Trans. Luise von Flotow. Stratford, ON: Mercury Press, 1992.

Dantin, Louis, pseud. Eugène Seers. "Chanson javanaise." *Louis Dantin: sa vie et son oeuvre*. Gabriel Nadeau. Manchester, NH: Les Éditions Lafayette, 1948. 140-145.

——. *Fanny.* Trans. Raymond Y. Chamberlain. Montreal: Harvest House, 1974. Trans. of *Les Enfances de Fanny.* Montréal: Le cercle du livre de France, 1951.

David, Carole. *L'Endroit où se trouve ton âme.* Montréal: Les Herbes rouges, 1991.

——. *Impala: roman.* Montréal: Les Herbes rouges, 1994.

Dawendine, [Bernice Winslow-Loft]. *Iroquois Fires: The Six Nations Lyrics and Lore of Dawendine.* Ottawa: Penumbra Press, 1995.

Dean, Misao. "Reading Evelyn Right: The Literary Layers of Evelyn Lau." *The Canadian Forum* 73.837 (March 1995): 22-26.

Del Negro, Giovanna. *Looking Through My Mother's Eyes: Life Stories of Nine Italian Immigrant Women in Canada.* Toronto: Guernica, 1997.

Deleuze, Gilles and Félix Guattari. *Kafka: Toward a Minor Literature.* Trans. Dana Polan. Minneapolis: University of Minnesota Press, 1986.

Derrida, Jacques. "Given Time: The Time of the King." Trans. by Peggy Kamuf. *Critical Inquiry.* 18 (Winter 1992):161-87.

Deutsch, Mina. *Mina's Story: A Doctor's Memoir of the Holocaust.* Toronto: ECW Press, 1994.

Dion-Levesque, R. "Louis Dantin." In *Fanny.* By Louis Dantin, pseud Eugène Seers. Trans. Raymond Y. Chamberlain. Montreal: Harvest House, 1971. 1-3.

Dickason, Olive P. *Canada's First Nations: A History of Founding Peoples From Earliest Times.* Toronto: McClelland & Stewart, 1992.

Domaradzki, Théodore F. *Personnalités ethniques au Québec.* Montréal: Institut des civilisations comparées de Montréal, 1990.

Dorsinville, Max. *Caliban Without Prospero: Essay on Quebec and Black Literature.* Erin, ON: Press Porcepic, 1974.

Dragland, Stan. *Floating Voice: Duncan Campbell Scott and the Literature of Treaty 9.* Toronto: Anansi Press. 1994.

Draper, Gary. "The Making of Legends." Review of *Disappearing Moon Cafe* by Sky Lee. *Books in Canada* 19.5 (June/July 1990): 49.

Dupré, Louise. "La Prose métisse du poème: sur Anne-Marie Alonzo." *Québec Studies* 15 (1992/1993): 51-56.

Dybikowski, A. et al. *In the Feminine: Women and Words les femmes et les mots Conference Proceedings.* Edmonton: Longspoon, 1985.

Edwards, Caterina. *The Lion's Mouth.* Edmonton: NeWest Press, 1982.

Edwards, John. *Multilingualism.* London: Routledge, 1994.

Elliott, Emory. ed. *Columbia Literary History of the United States.* New York: Columbia University Press, 1988

Elliott, Jean Leonard and Augie Fleras. *Unequal Relations: An Introduction to Race and Ethnic Dynamics in Canada.* Scarborough: Prentice-Hall, 1992.

Etienne, Gérard. *Le Nègre crucifié: récit.* Montréal: Éditions Balzac, 1994.

——. *La question raciale et raciste dans le roman québécois: Essai d'anthroposémiologie.* Montréal: Éditions Balzac, 1995.

Fairburn, Laura. *Endless Bay: A Novel.* Stratford, ON: Mercury Press, 1994.

Falcón, Angelo. "Puerto Ricans and the Politics of Racial Identity." *Racial and Ethnic Identity: Psychological Development and Creative Expression.* Eds. Herbert W. Harris, Howard C. Blue and Ezra E.H. Griffith. New York: Routledge, 1995. 193-207.

Fanon, Frantz. *Peau noire, masques blancs.* 1952. Paris: Éditions du Seuil, 1971.

Fee, Margery. "What Use Is Ethnicity to Aboriginal Peoples in Canada?" *Canadian Review of Comparative Literature* 22 (1995): 3-4, 683-91.

Fine, Michelle. "Working the Hyphens: Reinventing Self and Other in Qualitative Research." *Handbook of Qualitative Research.* Eds. Norman K. Denizen and Yvonna S. Lincoln. Thousand Oaks: Sage Publications, 1994. 70-82.

Francis, Daniel. *The Imaginary Indian: The Image of the Indian in Canadian Culture.* Vancouver: Arsenal Pulp Press, 1992.

Fraser, Joyce C. *Cry of the Illegal Immigrant.* Toronto: Williams-Wallace 1980.

Fukuyama, Francis. "The End of History?" *The National Interest* (Summer 1989): 3-18.

Fuss, Diana. *Essentially Speaking: Feminism, Nature & Difference.* New York: Routledge, 1989.

Gallop, Jane. *Around 1981: Academic Feminist Literary Theory.* New York: Routledge, 1992.

Garneau, Michel. *Héliotropes: théâtre.* Montréal: VLB Éditeur, 1994.

Glassco, John, ed. Introduction. *The Poetry of French Canada in Translation.* Toronto: Oxford University Press, 1970. xvii-xxvi.

Godard, Barbara. "The Politics of Representation." *Native Writers and Canadian Writing.* Ed. W.H. New. Vancouver: UBC Press, 1990. 183-225.

—— and Coomi S. Vevaina eds. *Intersexions: Issues of Race and Gender in Canadian Women's Writing.* New Delhi: Creative Books, 1996.

Goto, Hiromi. *Chorus of Mushrooms.* Edmonton: NeWest Press, 1994.

Grant, George. *Lament for a Nation: The Defeat of Canadian Nationalism.* Toronto: McClelland & Stewart, 1965.

Gregory, Steven. "We've Been Down This Road Already." *Race.* Eds. Steven Gregory and Roger Sanjek. New Brunswick, NJ: Rutgers University Press, 1994. 18-38.

Grossman, Ibolya Szalai. *An Ordinary Woman in Extraordinary Times.* Toronto: Multicultural History Society of Ontario, 1990.

Grove, Frederick Philip. *A Search for America.* Ottawa: Graphic Publishers, 1927.

Gunnarsson, Sturla (dir). *The Diary of Evelyn Lau.* CBC, 1993.

Gunew, Sneja. "Feminism and the Politics of Irreducible Differences Multiculturalism/ Ethnicity/Race." *Feminism and the Politics of Difference.* Eds. Sneja Gunew and Anna Yeatman. Halifax: Fernwood Publishing, 1993. 1-19.

——. *Framing Marginality: Multicultural Literary Studies.* Carlton, Vic.: Melbourne University Press, 1994.

Gunning, Margaret. "Jury still out on the talents of Evelyn Lau." *Vancouver Sun* [Weekend Sun] 2 September 1995: D13.

Haig-Brown, Celia. *Resistance and Renewal: Surviving the Indian Residential School.* Vancouver: Tillacum Press, 1988.

Harney, Robert F. "'So Great a Heritage as Ours.' Immigration and the Survival of the Canadian Polity." *Daedalus* 117.4 (Fall 1988): 51-97.

Harris, Claire. *The Conception of Winter.* Stratford, ON: Williams-Wallace, 1989.

Harris, Herbert W. "A Conceptual Overview of Race, Ethnicity, and Identity." *Racial and Ethnic Identity: Psychological Development and Creative Expression.* Eds. Herbert W. Harris, Howard C. Blue and Ezra E.H. Griffith. New York: Routledge, 1995. 1-14.

Harvey, Pauline. *Un homme est une valse: roman.* Montréal: Les Herbes rouges, 1992.

Hassoun, Jacques. "Le sentiment d'appartenance." *Discours et mythes de l'ethnicité.* Ed. Nadia Khouri. Montréal: ACFAS, 78 (1992): 37-44.

Hébert, Jacques, and Pierre Elliott Trudeau. *Two Innocents in Red China.* Trans. I.M. Owen. Toronto: Oxford University Press, 1968.

Helly, Denise et Anne Vassal. *Romanciers immigrés: biographies et œuvres publiées au Québec entre 1970 et 1990.* Québec: Institut québécois de recherche sur la culture, 1993.

L'Hérault, Pierre, "Pour une cartographie de l'hétérogène: dérives identitaires des années 1980." *Fictions de l'identitaire au Québec.* Montréal: XYZ, 1991. 53-115.

——. "Les mythologies de Monique Bosco." *Multi-culture, multi-écriture. La voix migrante au féminin en France et au Canada.* Eds. Lucie Lequin et Maïr Verthuy. Paris: L'Harmattan, 1996.

Highway, Tomson. "An Interview with Tomson Highway By Barbara Nahwegahbow." *Beedaudjimowin: A Voice for First Nations* 1.4 (1991): 7-17.

Hill, Lawrence. *Some Great Thing.* Winnipeg: Turnstone Press, 1992.

Hinz, Evelyn J. guest ed. "Idols of Otherness: The Rhetoric and Reality of Multiculturalism." Special issue. *Mosaic* 29.3 (September 1996).

Hoffman, Eva. *Lost in Translation: A Life in a New Language.* New York: Penguin Books, 1989.

Holmes, Boyd. "Dislocations." Review of *Swimming Lessons and Other Stories from Firozsha Baag,* by Rohinton Mistry. *Fiddlehead* 162 (1989): 109-12.

Homel, David. "How to Make Love with the Reader ... Slyly." *Introduction. How to Make Love to a Negro,* by Dany Laferrière. Trans. David Homel. Toronto: Coach House, 1987. 7-10.

Howard, Hilda G. pseud. Hilda Glynn-Ward. *The Writing on the Wall.* Vancouver: *Vancouver Sun,* 1921. Rpt. Toronto: University of Toronto Press, 1974.

Huang, Evelyn (with Lawrence Jeffery) ed. *Chinese Canadians: Voices from a Community.* Vancouver and Toronto: Douglas & McIntyre, 1992.

Hughes, David R. and Evelyn Kallen. *The Anatomy of Racism: Canadian Dimensions.* Montreal: Harvest House, 1974.

Hutcheon, Linda. *The Canadian Postmodern: A Study of Contemporary English-Canadian Fiction.* Toronto: Oxford University Press, 1988.

——. "Crypto-Ethnicity." MLA Conference paper, 1995.

——. *Irony's Edge: The Theory and Politics of Irony.* New York: Routledge, 1994.

—— and Michael Hutcheon. *Opera: Desire, Disease, Death.* Lincoln: University of Nebraska Press, 1996.

—— and Marion Richmond eds. *Other Solitudes: Canadian Multicultural Fictions.* Toronto: Oxford University Press, 1990.

Hwang, David. *M. Butterfly.* New York: Penguin, 1986.

Ignatieff, Michael. *Blood and Belonging: Journeys into the New Nationalism.* Toronto: Penguin, 1993.

Jacobs, Maria. *Precautions Against Death.* Oakville, ON: Mosaic Press, 1983.

Jacoby, Russell. "Marginal Returns, The Trouble with Post-Colonial Theory." *Lingua Franca* 5.6 (1995): 30-37.

Jakubowski, Lisa Marie. *Immigration and the Legalization of Racism.* Halifax: Fernwood Publishing, 1997.

Joachim, Sébastien. *Le Nègre dans le roman blanc: lecture sémiotique et idéologique de romans français et canadiens, 1945-1977.* Montréal: Presses de l'Université de Montréal, 1980.

Johnson, E. Pauline, *Flint and Feather: The Complete Poems of E. Pauline Johnson.* 21st ed. Toronto: The Musson Book Company Ltd., 1931.

Johnston, Basil H. *Indian School Days.* Toronto: Key Porter Books, 1988.

Jonassaint, Jean. "Les Productions littéraires haïtiennes en Amérique du Nord." *Études littéraires* XIII.2 (1980): 313-33.

———. *Le Pouvoir des mots, les maux du pouvoir. Des romanciers haïtiens de l'exil.* Montréal: Presses de l'Université de Montréal, 1986.

———. "De l'autre littérature québécoise, autoportraits." Supplément de *Lettres québécoises* 66 (1992): 16 p.

Kadar, Marlene ed. *Essays on Life Writing: From Genre to Critical Practice.* Toronto: University of Toronto Press, 1992.

———. "The Discourse of Ordinariness and Multicultural History.'" *Essays in Canadian Writing* 60 (Winter 1996): 119-38.

———. "What is Life Writing?" *Reading Life Writing: An Anthology.* Toronto: Oxford University Press, 1993.

Kabamba, Maguy. *La dette coloniale: roman.* Montréal: Humanitas, 1995.

Kamboureli, Smaro. *In the Second Person.* Edmonton: Longspoon, 1985.

——— ed. *Making a Difference: Canadian Multicultural Literature.* Toronto: Oxford University Press, 1996.

———. "The Technology of Ethnicity: Law and Discourse." *Open Letter* 8.5/6 (Winter-Spring 1993): 5-6, 202-17.

Kapuscinski, Ryszard. *Imperium.* Trans. Klara Glowczewska. New York: Knopf, 1994.

Kaup, Monika. "West Indian Canadian Writing: Crossing the Border from Exile to Immigration." *Essays on Canadian Writing* 57 (Winter 1995): 171-93.

Keefer, Janice Kulyk. "Mrs. Mucharski and the Princess." *Other Solitudes: Canadian Multicultural Fictions.* Eds. Linda Hutcheon and Marion Richmond. Toronto: University of Toronto Press, 1990. 278-90.

Kinsella, W.P. *The Moccasin Telegraph and Other Stories.* Markham, ON: Penguin Books, 1983.

Kiriak, Illia. *Sons of the Soil.* 1959. Winnipeg: St. Andrew's College in Winnipeg, 1983.

Kleist, Dorothee V. *Love's Loss, Love's Gain.* Toronto: G.R. Welch Company Ltd., 1979.

Klinck, Carl F. general ed. *Literary History of Canada.* 2nd edition. Toronto: University of Toronto Press, 1976.

Koestenbaum, Wayne. *The Queen's Throat: Opera, Homosexuality and the Mystery of Desire.* New York: Poseidon Press, 1993.

Kojder, Apolonia Maria and Barbara Glogowska. *"Maryina Don't Cry": Memoirs of Two Polish-Canadian Families.* Toronto: Multicultural History Society of Ontario, 1995.

Kondo, Dorinne K. *About Face: Performing Race in Fashion and Theater.* New York: Routledge, 1997.

Kornreich, Jennifer. "Selling Her Soul." *Women's Review of Books* 13.6 (March 1996).

Kostash, Myrna. *All of Baba's Children.* Edmonton, AB: Hurtig Publishers, 1977.

———. *Bloodlines: A Journey into Eastern Europe.* Vancouver: Douglas & McIntyre, 1993.

———. "Eurocentricity: Notes on Metaphors of Place." *Twenty Years of Multiculturalism: Successes and Failures.* Ed. Stella Hryniuk. Winnipeg: St. John's College, 1992. 39-43.

Kreisel, Henry. *The Rich Man: A Novel.* Toronto: McClelland & Stewart, 1948.

Kroetsch, Robert. "The Grammar of Silence: Narrative Patterns in Ethnic Writing." *Canadian Literature* 106 (Fall 1985): 65-74.

———. "Unhiding the Hidden: Recent Canadian Fiction." *Journal of Canadian Fiction* 3 (1974) 43-45.

Kymlicka, Will. "The Impact of Race on Enthocultural Relations in Canada." Paper No. 2 in a series on *Accommodating Ethnocultural Diversity in Canada*. Prepared for the Canadian Heritage Ministry. 11 October 1995.

———. *Multicultural Citizenship: A Liberal Theory of Minority Rights*. Oxford: Clarendon, 1995.

Laferrière, Dany. *Comment faire l'amour avec un Nègre sans se fatiguer*. Montréal: VLB Éditeur, 1985.

———. *How to Make Love to a Negro*. Trans. David Homel. Toronto: Coach House, 1987.

Lalonde, Michèle. *Speak White*. Montréal: L'Héxagone, 1974.

Lamore, Jean, "Transculturation: naissance d'un mot." *Métamorphoses d'une utopie*. Eds. Jean-Michel Lacroix et Fulvio Caccia. Paris, Presses de la Sorbonne nouvelle; Montréal: Triptyque, 1992. 43-47.

Lamy, Suzanne. *La Convention*. Montréal: VLB éditeur/Le Castor astral, 1985.

Lantagne, Suzanne. *Et autres histoires d'amour : nouvelles*. Québec: Éditions de L'instant même, 1995.

Latif Ghattas, Mona. *Le double conte de l'exil*. Montréal: Boréal, 1990.

———. *Quarante voiles pour un exil: récits et fragments poétiques*. Laval: TROIS, 1986.

———. *La triste beauté du monde: poèmes 1981-1991*. Montréal: Editions du Noroît, 1993.

Lau, Evelyn. *Fresh Girls and Other Stories*. Toronto: HarperCollins, 1993.

———. *In the House of Slaves*. Toronto: Coach House, 1994.

———. *Oedipal Dreams*. Victoria: Beach Holme, 1992.

———. *Other Women: A Novel*. Toronto: Random House of Canada, 1995.

———. *Runaway: Diary of a Street Kid*. Toronto: HarperCollins, 1989.

———. "Why I didn't attend the Writing Thru Race Conference." *Globe and Mail* 9 July 1994: D3.

———. *You Are Not Who You Claim*. Victoria, BC: Porcépic Books, 1990.

Lee, Bennett and Jim Wong Chu. *Many Mouthed Birds: Contemporary Writing by Chinese Canadians*. Vancouver; Toronto: Douglas & McIntyre, 1991.

Lee, Dennis. "Cadence, Country, Silence: Writing in Colonial Space." *Boundary* 2.3,I (Fall 1974).

Lee, Sky. *Disappearing Moon Cafe*. Toronto: Douglas & McIntyre, 1990.

Lequin, Lucie. "Elles disent leur dépaysement et bâtissent leur repaysement." *Les Bâtisseuses de la cité*. Ed. Évelyne Tardy et al. ACFAS 29 (1993): 307-19.

—— et Maïr Verthuy. "Nouveaux palimpsestes de la littérature québécoise ou l'écriture migrante au féminin." *Le Renouveau de la parole identitaire*. Eds. Mireille Calle-Gruber et Jeanne-Marie Clerc. Montpellier/Kingston: Université Paul-Valéry et Université Queen's, 1993. 265-75.

———. "Répertoire de l'écriture des femmes migrantes au Québec 1960-1991." *Documentation sur la recherche féministe*. Toronto: Ontario Institute for Studies in Education, 1993.

———. "Sous le signe de la pluralité: l'écriture des femmes migrantes au Québec." *Tessera* 12 (1992): 51-59.

Lentricchia, Frank. *The Edge of Night*. New York: Random House, 1994.

——. "Interview with Imre Salusinszky." *Criticism in Society*. New York: Methuen, 1987. 176- 207.

—— ed. *Introducing Don DeLillo*. Durham: Duke University Press, 1991.

L'Hérault, Pierre. "Pour une cartographie de l'hétérogène: dérives des années 1980." *Fictions de l'identitaire au Québec*. Eds. Sherry Simon et al. Montréal: XYZ Éditeur, 1991. 53-114.

Lim, Shirley Goek-Lin. "Immigration and Diaspora." *An Interethnic Companion to Asian American Literature*. Ed. King-Kok Cheung. New York: Cambridge University Press, 1997. 289-310.

Littleton, James. *Clash of Identities: Essays on Media, Manipulation, and Politics of the Self*. Toronto: Prentice Hall. 1996.

Longchamps, Renaud. "Génies, étonnez-moi!" *Nuit blanche* 58 (décembre 1994). 16-17.

Longfellow, Henry Wadsworth. *Evangeline: A Tale of Acadie*. 1847. Mount Vernon, NY: The Peter Pauper Press, 1947.

Loriggio, Francesco. "The Question of the Corpus: Ethnicity and Canadian Literature." *Future Indicative*. Ed. John Moss. Ottawa: University of Ottawa Press, 1987. 53-70.

—— ed. *Social Pluralism and Literary History: The Literature of the Italian Emigration*. Toronto: Guernica, 1996.

Lorde, Audre. "Age, Race, Class and Sex: Women Redefining Difference." *Sister Outsider: Essays and Speeches*. Trumansburg, NY: Crossing Press, 1984. 114-23.

Ltaif, Nadine. *Entre les fleuves*. Montréal: Guernica, 1991.

——. *Les Métamorphoses d'Ishtar*. Montréal: Guernica, 1987.

Lysenko, Vera. *Yellow Boots: A Novel*. 1952. Edmonton: NeWest Press, 1992.

Mallet, Marilú. *Miami Trip*. Montréal: Québec/Amérique, 1986.

Makabe, Tomoko. *Picture Brides: Japanese Women in Canada*. Trans. Kathleen Chisato Merken. Toronto: Multicultural History Society of Ontario, 1995.

Mandel, Eli. "The Ethnic Voice in Canadian Writing." *Identities: The Impact of Ethnicity on Canadian Society*. Ed. Wsevolod W. Isajiw. Toronto: P. Martin Associates, 1977. 57-68.

Mao Tse-Tung. [Mao Zedong.] *Four Essays on Philosophy*. 1966. Peking [Beijing]: Foreign Languages Press, 1968.

Maracle, Brian. *Back on the Rez: Finding the Way Home*. Toronto: Viking Press, 1996.

Maracle, Lee. *Sojourner's Truth & Other Stories*. Vancouver: Press Gang, 1990.

Marcuse, Herbert. *An Essay on Liberation*. Boston. Beacon Press, 1969.

Mariani, Philip and Jonathan Crory. "In the Shadow of the West: Edward Said." *Discourses: Conversations in Postmodern Art and Culture*. Eds. Russell Ferguson et al. Cambridge, Mass: MIT Press, 1990.

Marlyn, John. *Under the Ribs of Death*. Toronto: McClelland & Stewart, 1957.

Maynard, Fredelle Bruser. *Raisins and Almonds*. 1972. Markham, ON: Penguin Books, 1985.

McClary, Susan. *Feminine Endings: Music, Gender, and Sexuality*. Minneapolis: University of Minnesota Press, 1991.

McFarlane, Scott. "The Haunt of Race: Canada's Multiculturalism Act, The Politics of Incorporation, and Writing Thru Race." *Fuse* 18.3 (Spring 1995): 18-31.

McNaught, Kenneth. *The Penguin History of Canada*. London: Penguin Books, 1988.

Médam, Alain. "Ethnos et polis : à propos du cosmopolitisme montréalais." *Revue internationale d'action communautaire* (printemps 1989): 137-53.

Melnyk, George. "The Indian as Ethnic." *Radical Regionalism.* Edmonton: NeWest Press, 1981.

Micone, Marco. *Gens du silence.* Montréal: Québec/Amérique, 1982.

Miska, John P. *Ethnic and Native Canadian Literature. A Bibliography.* Toronto: University of Toronto Press, 1990.

Mishra, Vijay. "Postmodern Racism." *Meanjin* 55.2 (1996): 346-57.

Mistry, Rohinton. *Tales from Firozsha Baag.* Markham, ON: Penguin, 1987.

Mitic, Trudy D. *Canadian by Choice.* Hantsport, NS: Lancelot Press, 1988.

Momaday, N. Scott. "The Man Made of Words." *The Remembered Earth: An Anthology of Contemporary Native American Literature.* Ed. Geary Hobson. Albuquerque: University of New Mexico Press, 1979. 162-76.

Montero, Gloria. *The Immigrants.* Toronto: James Lorimer and Co., 1977.

Morrell, Carol ed. *Grammar of Dissent: Poetry and Prose.* Fredericton: Goose Lane Editions, 1994.

Morrison, Toni. *Playing in the Dark: Whiteness and the Literary Imagination.* Cambridge, MA: Harvard University Press, 1992.

Moses, Daniel David and Terry Goldie eds. *An Anthology of Canadian Native Literature in English.* Toronto: Oxford University Press, 1992.

Mostow, Joshua S. "Complex Art of the Mosaic." Review of *Disappearing Moon Cafe,* by Sky Lee. *Canadian Literature* 132 (Spring 1992): 174-76.

Mukherjee, Arun. *Oppositional Aesthetics: Readings From a Hyphenated Space.* Toronto, TSAR Publications, 1994.

—— ed. *Sharing Our Experience.* Ottawa: Canadian Advisory Council on the Status of Women, 1993.

——. *Towards an Aesthetic of Opposition: Essays on Literature Criticism & Cultural Imperialism.* Stratford, ON: Williams-Wallace, 1988.

Mukherjee, Bharati. *Darkness.* Markham, ON: Penguin Books, 1985.

Mulvey, Laura. *Visual and Other Pleasures.* Bloomington: Indiana University Press, 1989.

Nelligan, Émile. *Poésies complètes: 1896-1899.* 1952. Montréal: Bibliothèque québécoise, 1989.

Nepveu, Pierre. *L'écologie du réel: mort et naissance de la littérature québécoise contemporaine.* Montréal: Boréal, 1988.

——. "Quebec Culture and its American moods." Unpublished paper presented at Canadian Studies Center, Duke University, Durham, North Carolina, 10 April 1995.

Neuman, Shirley ed. *Autobiography and Questions of Gender.* London: Frank Cass, 1991.

—— and G. Stephenson, eds. *ReImagining Women: Representation of Women in Culture.* Toronto: University of Toronto Press, 1993.

New, W.H. general editor. *Literary History of Canada, Canadian Literature in English.* 2nd ed. Volume 4. Toronto: University of Toronto Press, 1990.

North, Sam. "Asian Town: What will the future hold for a 50-percent-Asian Vancouver?" *Vancouver* 29.7 (November 1996): 46-58.

Pacey, Desmond. *Creative Writing in Canada: A Short History of English-Canadian Literature.* Toronto: The Ryerson Press, 1952.

Paci, Frank. *Black Madonna: A Novel.* Ottawa: Oberon, 1982.

———. "Tasks of the Canadian Novelist Writing on Immigrant Themes." *Contrasts: Comparative Essays on Italian-Canadian Writing.* Ed. J. Pivato. Montreal: Guernica, 1985.

Padolsky, Enoch. "Canadian Ethnic Minority Literature in English." *Ethnicity and Culture in Canada: The Research Landscape.* Eds. J.W. Berry and J.A. Laponce. Toronto: University of Toronto Press, 1994. 361-86.

———. "'Olga in Wonderland': Canadian Ethnic Minority Writing and Post-Colonial Theory." *Canadian Ethnic Studies* 28.3 (1996): 16-28.

———. "The Place of Italian-Canadian Writing." *Journal of Canadian Studies* 21.4 (Winter 1986-7): 138-52.

Palmer, Tamara J. "The Fictionalization of the Vertical Mosaic: The Immigrant, Success and National Mythology." *Canadian Review of Comparative Literature* 16.3-4 (1989): 619-55.

———. "Mythologizing the Journey to and from Otherness: Some Features of the Ethnic Voice in Canadian Literature." *From Melting Pot to Multiculturalism: The Evolution of Ethnic Relations in the United States and Canada.* Ed. Valeria Gennaro Lerda. Rome: Bulzoni, 1990. 91-113.

Parmeswaran, Uma. "How We Won the Olympic Gold." *The Geography of Voice: Canadian Literature of the South Asian Diaspora.* Ed. Diane McGifford. Toronto: TSAR, 1992. 175-82.

Pellerin, Suzanne. "La Cité des interdits." *International Poetry Review* 20.2 (Fall 1994): 44, 46.

Petrone, Penny. *Native Literature in Canada: From the Oral Tradition to the Present.* Toronto: Oxford University Press, 1990.

Philip, Marlene Nourbese. *Frontiers: Essays and Writings on Racism and Culture.* Stratford, ON: Mercury Press, 1992.

Pivato, Joseph. "Constantly Translating: The Challenge for Italian-Canadian Writers." *Canadian Review of Comparative Literature* XIV.1 (1987). 60-76.

——— ed. *Contrasts: Comparative Essays on Italian-Canadian Writing.* Montreal: Guernica, 1991.

———. *Echo: Essays on Other Literatures.* Montréal: Guernica, 1994.

———. "Italian-Canadian Women Writers Recall History." *Canadian Ethnic Studies* 18.1 (1986): 79-88.

———. "Literary Theory and Ethnic Minority Writing."A public lecture presented at Macquarie University, Sydney, Australia, 1991.

———. "Shirt of the Happy Man: Theory and Politics of Ethnic Minority Writing." *Canadian Ethnic Studies.* 28.3 (1996): 29-38.

Poizat, Michel. *The Angel's Cry: Beyond the Pleasure Principle in Opera.* Trans Arthur Denner. Ithaca: Cornell University Press, 1992.

Potrebenko, Helen. *No Streets of Gold: A Social History of Ukrainians in Alberta.* Vancouver: New Star Books, 1977.

Pratt, Mary Louise. *Imperial Eyes: Travel Writing and Transculturation.* London; New York: Routledge, 1992.

Préfontaine, Yves. *This Desert Now.* Trans. Judith Cowan. Montréal: Guernica, 1993.

Raab, Elizabeth. *And Peace Never Came.* Waterloo, ON : Wilfrid Laurier University Press, 1996.

Radwanski, George. *Trudeau.* Toronto: Macmillan, 1978.

Ramirez, Bruno and Paul Tana. *La Sarrasine.* Montréal: Boréal, 1992.

Rasporich, Beverly. "Vera Lysenko's Fictions: Engendering Prairie Spaces." *Prairie Forum* 16.2 (1991): 249-64.

Ravvin, Norman. "Foundational Myths of Multiculturalism and Strategies of Canon Formation." *Mosaic* 29.3 (September 1996): 117-28.

Richler, Mordecai. *The Apprenticeship of Duddy Kravitz.* Toronto: McClelland & Stewart, 1964.

Robin, Régine. *Le naufrage du siècle suivi de Le cheval blanc de Lénine ou l'Histoire autre.* Montréal: XYZ, 1995.

——. "Pour sortir de l'ethnicité." *Métamorphoses d'une utopie.* Eds. Jean-Michel Lacroix et Fulvio Caccia. Paris, Presses de la Sorbonne nouvelle; Montréal: Triptyque, 1992.

——. *La Québecoite.* Montréal: Québec/Amérique, 1983.

Rodríguez, Clara E. "Challenging Racial Hegemony: Puerto Ricans in the United States." *Race.* Eds. Steven Gregory and Roger Sanjek. New Brunswick, NJ: Rutgers University Press, 1994. 131-45.

Rosenberg, Leah. *The Errand Runner: Reflections of a Rabbi's Daughter.* Toronto; New York: John Wiley, 1981.

Roy, Gabrielle. *La Petite Poule d'Eau,* (1950). Montréal: Stanké 10/10, 1980.

Royer, Jean. *Introduction à la poésie québécoise: les poètes et les oeuvres des origines à nos jours.* Montréal: Bibliothèque québécoise, 1989.

Ruoff-Brown, LaVonne. Introduction. *The Mocassin Maker.* Ed. E. Pauline Johnson. Tucson: University of Arizona Press, 1987.

Rychlak, Joseph F. "Morality in a Mediating Mechanism? A Logical Learning Theorist Looks at Social Constructionism." *Social Discourse and Moral Judgement.* Ed. Daniel N. Robinson. San Diego: Academic Press, 1992.

Said, Edward W. *Culture and Imperialism.* New York: Vintage Press, 1994.

——. *Orientalism.* New York: Random House, 1978.

——. *The World, the Text and the Critic.* Cambridge, Mass.: Harvard University Press, 1983.

Salverson, Laura Goodman. *Confessions of an Immigrant's Daughter.* Toronto: University of Toronto Press, 1981.

Sanjek, Roger. "The Enduring Inequalities of Race." *Race.* Eds. Steven Gregory and Roger Sanjek. New Brunswick, NJ: Rutgers University Press, 1994. 1-17.

——. "Intermarriage and the Future of Races in the United States." *Race.* Eds. Steven Gregory and Roger Sanjek. New Brunswick, NJ: Rutgers University Press, 1994. 103-30.

San Juan, E. Jr. "The Cult of Ethnicity and the Fetish of Pluralism: A Counter-hegemonic Critique." *Cultural Critique* 18 (Spring 1991): 215-29.

Schneider, Aili Grönlund. *The Finnish Baker's Daughters.* Toronto: Multicultural History Society of Ontario, 1986.

Scheier, Libby, Sarah Sheard and Eleanor Wachtel. *Language in Her Eye: Views on Writing and Gender by Canadian Women Writing in English.* Toronto: Coach House, 1990.

Seiler, Tamara Palmer. "Mosaic vs. Melting Pot: Images and Realities." *Canada and the United States: Differences That Count.* Ed. David Thomas. Peterborough, ON: Broadview, 1993. 303-25.

Shadd-Evelyn, Karen. *I'd Rather Live in Buxton.* Toronto: Simon and Pierre, 1993.

Sillanpää, Nelma (ed. by edited by Edward W. Laine). *Under the Northern Lights: My Memories of Life in the Finnish Community of Northern Ontario.* Hull, QC: Canadian Museum of Civilization, 1994.

Silvera, Makeda. *The Other Woman: Women of Colour in Contemporary Canadian Literature.* Toronto: Sister Vision Press, 1995.

—— ed. *Piece of My Heart: A Lesbian of Colour Anthology.* Toronto: Sister Vision, 1991.

——. *Silenced: Talks With Working Class West Indian Women About Their Lives and Struggles as Domestic Workers in Canada.* Toronto: Williams-Wallace, 1984.

Silverman, Kaja. *The Acoustic Mirror: The Female Voice in Psychoanalysis and Cinema.* Bloomington: Indiana University Press, 1988.

Simon, Sherry. *Fictions de l'identitaire au Québec.* Montreal: XYZ, 1991.

——. "The Language of Difference: Minority Writers in Quebec." *A/Part: Papers from the 1984 Ottawa Conference on Language, Culture and Literary Identity in Canada.* Ed. J.M. Bumsted. Canadian Literature, Supp. 1 (May 1987): 119-28.

—— et David Leahy. "La recherche au Quebec portant sur l'ecriture ethnique." *Ethnicity and Culture in Canada: The Research Landscape.* Eds. J.W. Berry and J.A. Laponce. Toronto: University of Toronto Press, 1994. 387-409.

——. "Speaking with Authority: The Theatre of Marco Micone." *Canadian Literature* 106 (Fall 1985): 57-64.

Skvorecký, Josef. *The Engineer of Human Souls.* Trans. Paul Wilson. Toronto: Coach House Press, 1984.

Slemon, Stephen. "Monuments of Empire: Allegory/Counter-Discourse/Post-Colonial Writing." *Kunapipi* 9.3 (1987): 1-16.

Smith Herrnstein, Barbara. "Value/Evaluation." *Critical Terms for Literary Study.* Eds. Frank Lentricchia and Thomas McLaughlin. 2nd ed. Chicago: University of Chicago Press, 1995.

Smith, Paul. *Discerning the Subject.* Minneapolis: University of Minnesota Press, 1988.

Smith, Roch. "Voices of Québec Poetry – At Home in a Diverse World." *International Poetry Review: Voix du Québec/Voices of Quebec* 20.2 (Fall 1994): 6-15.

Spivak, Gayatri Chakravorty. "Feminism in Decolonization." *Differences: A Journal of Feminist Cultural Studies* 3.3 (1991): 139-75.

Stummer, Peter O. and Christopher Balme eds. *Fusion of Cultures?* Amsterdam; Atlanta: Rodopi, 1996.

Sullivan, Martin. *Mandate '68.* Toronto; New York: Doubleday, 1968.

Sutherland, Ronald. *The New Hero: Essays in Comparative Quebec/Canadian Literature.* Toronto: Macmillan, 1977.

——. *No Longer a Family Affair: The Foreign-born Writers in French Canada.* Ottawa: Rapport soumis à la direction du Multiculturalisme du Secrétariat d'État, Gouvernement du Canada, 1986.

——. *Second Image: Comparative Studies in Québec/Canadian Literature.* Toronto: New Press, 1971.

Takagi, Dana Y. "Post-Civil Rights Politics and Asian-American Identity: Admissions and Higher Education." *Race.* Eds. Steven Gregory and Roger Sanjek. New Brunswick, NJ: Rutgers University Press, 1994. 229-42.

Talbot, Carol. *Growing Up Black in Canada.* Toronto: Williams-Wallace, 1984.

Taylor, Charles (ed. by Guy Laforest). *Reconciling the Solitudes: Essays on Canadian Federalism and Nationalism.* Montreal: McGill-Queen's University Press, 1993.

Taylor, Drew. "Pretty Like a White Boy: The Adventures of a Blue Eyed Ojibway." *This Magazine* 25.2 (August 1991): 29-30.

The Telling It Book Collective ed. *Telling It: Women and Language Across Cultures. The Transformation of a Conference.* Vancouver: Press Gang, 1990.

The Women's Book Committee, Chinese National Council. *Jin Guo: Voices of Chinese Canadian Women.* Toronto: Women's Press, 1992.

Théoret, France. *Bloody Mary*. Montréal: Les Herbes rouges, 1977.

Titley, Brian. *A Narrow Vision: Duncan Campbell Scott and the Administration of Indian Affairs in Canada*. Vancouver: UBC Press, 1986.

Trudeau, Pierre Elliott. *Federalism and the French Canadians*. Trans. Patricia Claxton. Toronto: Macmillan, 1968.

Tuzi, Marino. *The Power of Allegiances: Identity, Culture, and Representational Strategies*. Toronto: Guernica, 1997.

Tynes, Maxine. *The Door of My Heart*. Lawrencetown Beach, NS: Pottersfield, 1993.

Valgardson, W.D. "The Man From Snaefellsness." *Other Solitudes: Canadian Multicultural Fictions*. Eds. Linda Hutcheon and Marion Richmond. Toronto: University of Toronto Press, 1990. 121-33.

Vallières, Pierre. *Le Devoir de résistance*. Montréal: VLB Éditeur, 1994.

——. *White Niggers of America: The Precocious Autobiography of a Quebec "Terrorist."* Trans. Joan Pinkham. Toronto: McClelland & Stewart, 1971.

Vanderhaeghe, Guy. "What I Learned from Caesar." *Distant Kin, Dutch-Canadian Stories and Poems*. Ed. Hendrika Ruger. Windsor, ON.: Netherlandic Press, 1987.

Vassanji, M.G. *No New Land*. Toronto: McClelland & Stewart, 1991.

Vastel, Michel. *The Outsider: The Life of Pierre Elliott Trudeau*. Trans. Hubert Bauch. Toronto: Macmillan, 1990.

Verdicchio, Pasquale. "Bound by Distance: Italian-Canadian Writing as Decontextualized Subaltern." *VIA: Voices in Italian Americana* 3 (1992): 2.

——. *Devils in Paradise: Writings on Post-Emigrant Cultures*. Toronto: Guernica, 1997.

Verduyn, Christl. "Ecriture et migration au féminin au Québec: de mère en fille." *Multi-culture, multi-écriture : la voix migrante au féminin en France et au Canada*. Ed. Lucie Lequin et Maïr Verthuy. Paris; Montréal: L'Harmattan, 1996. 131-44.

——. "Je: voi (e) s double(s): l'itinéraire littéraire de Nadine Ltaif." *Tessera* 12 (Summer 1992): 98-105.

——. *Lifelines: Marian Engel's Writings*. Montreal: McGill-Queen's University Press, 1995.

——. "Memory Work/Migrant Writing: Mediating Me/Moi." *Intersexions: Issues of Race and Gender in Canadian Women's Writing*. Eds. B. Godard and C.S. Vevaina. New Delhi: Creative Books, 1996. 244-54.

——. "Nouvelles voix/voies: l'écriture de Nadine Ltaif." *Québec Studies* 14 (Spring/Summer 1992): 41-48.

——. "La Voix féminine de l'altérité québécoise littéraire." *Mélanges de littérature canadienne-française et québécoise offerts à Réjean Robidoux*. Eds. Yolande Grisé et Robert Major. Ottawa: Éditions de l'Universite d'Ottawa, 1992. 379-90.

Walcott, D. *The Antilles: Fragments of Epic Memory*. New York: Farrar, Straus and Giroux, 1993.

Walker, James W. St. G. *The Black Loyalists: The Search for a Promised Land in Nova Scotia and Sierra Leone 1783-1870*. Halifax: Longman and Dalhousie University Press, 1976.

Warren, Catherine Elizabeth. *Vignettes of Life: Experiences and Self-Perceptions of New Canadian Women*. Calgary: Detselig, 1986.

Wiebe, Rudy. *Peace Shall Destroy Many*. Toronto: McClelland & Stewart, 1962.

Williamson, Janice. *Sounding Differences: Conversation with Seventeen Canadian Women Writers*. Toronto: University of Toronto Press, 1993.

Wiseman, Adele. *Crackpot*. Toronto: McClelland & Stewart, 1974.

——. *The Old Woman at Play*. Toronto and Vancouver: Clarke, Irwin and Company, 1978.

The Women's Book Committee. *Jin Guo: Voices of Chinese Canadian Women*. Chinese Canadian National Council, Toronto: Women's Press, 1992.

Wong, Jan. "Evelyn Lau gets perfect grades in the school of hard knocks." *Globe & Mail* 3 April 1997 A11.

——. *Red China Blues: My Long March from Mao to Now*. Toronto: Doubleday Press, 1996.

Wong, S. *Asian American Literature: A Brief Introduction and Anthology*. New York: HarperCollins, 1996.

Zack, Naomi. *Race and Mixed Race*. Philadelphia: Temple University Press, 1993.

Zackodnik, Teresa. "'I am Blackening in My Way': Identity and Place in Dionne Brand's *No Language is Neutral*." *Essays on Canadian Writing* 57 (Winter 1995): 194-211.

Zagolin, Bianca. *Une femme à la fenêtre*. Paris, Robert Laffont, 1988.

Zana, Danielle. *Journal d'une homade au pays de Jacques Cartier*. Montreal: Humanistas/Nouvelle optique, 1990.

Zizek, Slavoj. "'I Hear You with my Eyes': or, The Invisible Master." *Gaze and Voice as Love Objects*. Eds. Renata Salecl and Slavoj Zizek. Durham: Duke University Press, 1996.

——. *The Sublime Object of Ideology*. London: Verso, 1989.

Contributors

Himani Bannerji is an Associate Professor in the Department of Sociology at York University. She is the author of *Thinking Through: Essays on Feminism, Marxism and Anti-racism* (1995) and co-editor of *Returning the Gaze: Essays on Racism, Feminism and Politics* (1992).

George Elliott Clarke is an Africadian (Black Nova Scotian) poet and scholar who teaches Canadian, African-Canadian, and African-American literature at Duke University, Durham, North Carolina.

Kateri Akiwenzie-Damm is a "mixed blood" member of the Chippewas of Nawash First Nation. She works as a communications consultant with First Nations groups and also teaches at the En'owkin International School of Writing in Penticton. Her poetry has appeared in many journals, anthologies and audio recordings and her collected work is represented in *heart is a stray bullet* (1993) and *Bloodriver Woman* (1998).

Hiromi Goto is a Japanese-Canadian writer. She is on the Women Of Colour Collective of Calgary and is involved in anti-racist work. Her first novel, *Chorus of Mushrooms*, was the 1995 recipient of The Commonwealth Writers' Prize Best First Book, Canada and Caribbean Region, and the 1995 co-winner of the Canada-Japan Book award. She is currently working on her second novel.

Sneja Gunew is currently Professor of English and Women's Studies at the University of British Columbia. She has edited (with Anna Yeatman) *Feminism and the Politics of Difference* (1993) and (with Fazal Rizvi) *Culture, Difference and the Arts* (1994). Her most recent book is *Framing Marginality: Multicultural Literary Studies* (1994).

Jean Jonassaint fut co-fondateur et directeur de la revue *Dérives* (1975-1987); il a publié entres autres *La Déchirure du (corps) texte et autres brèches* (1982), *Le Pouvoir des mots, les maux du pouvoir,* et *Des romanciers haïtiens de l'exil* (1986). Il enseigne les littératures francophones au Department of Romance Studies de Duke University, Durham, North Carolina.

Smaro Kamboureli is an Associate Professor of Canadian Literature in the Department of English, University of Victoria. She is the editor of *Making a Difference: Canadian Multicultural Literature* (1996).

Eva Karpinski is the co-editor (with Ian Lea) of *Pens of Many Colours: A Canadian Reader*, (1993). Her articles have appeared in the *Journal of Canadian Studies, Canadian Woman Studies*, and *Canadian Ethnic Studies*.

Myrna Kostash has been a freelance writer, instructor in Women's Studies, and an associate film producer at the National Film Board. She is the author of *All of Baba's Children* (1977), *Long Way from Home* (1980), *No Kidding* (1987), and *Bloodlines* (1998). Her most recent book is *The Doomed Bridegroom* (1998).

Janice Kulyk Keefer is Professor of English at the University of Guelph. She is the author of several books of fiction, poetry and literary criticism including *Under Eastern Eyes: A Critical Reading of Maritime Fictions* (1987) and *Travelling Ladies* (1992). Her novel *The Green Library* was short-listed for the 1996 Governor General's Award. Her latest book is *Honey and Ashes: A Story of Family* (1998).

Lucie Lequin est une spécialiste de littérature québécois, auteure de nombreaux articles, et elle enseigne au Département d'études françaises de l'Université Concordia et en assume la direction. Ses recherches actuelles portent sur l'écriture des femmes migrantes au Québec.

Nadine Ltaif est une poète qui a écrit *Les métamorphoses d'Ishtar* (1987), *Entre les fleuves* (1991), et *Élégies du Levant* (1995).

Arun Mukerjee current interests are minority Canadian literatures and Indian literatures. Her latest publication is *Oppositional Aesthetics: Reactions from A Hyphenated Space* (Toronto: TSAR Press, 1995).

Enoch Padolsky teaches Canadian literature in the English Department at Carleton University. Co-editor (with Jean Burnet et al.) of *Migration and the Transformation of Cultures* (Toronto: Multicultural History Society of Ontario, 1992), he has published extensively on interdisciplinary issues in Canadian literary theory and ethnic studies.

Nourbese Philip is a poet, writer, and lawyer. She has published numerous books of poetry including: *Thorns* (1980), *Salmon Courage* (1983), *She Tries Her Tongue; Her Silence Softly Breaks* (1989) (for which she received the prestigious Casa de las Americas prize), and *Looking For Livingstone: An Odyssey of Silence* (1991). Her non-fiction work includes *Showing Grit: Showboating North of the 44th Parallel* (1993) and *A Genealogy of Resistance: And Other Essays* (1997).

Joseph Pivato teaches Comparative Literature at Athabasca University in Alberta. He has written *Echo: Essays on Other Literatures* (1994), edited *Contrasts: Comparative Essays on Italian-Canadian Writing* (1985 and 1991), and co-edited *Literatures of Lesser Diffusion* (1990).

Tamara Palmer Seiler is an Associate Professor in the Canadian Studies Programme in the Faculty of General Studies at the University of Calgary.

Drew Hayden Taylor is an Aboriginal author. He has written nine books of plays, short stories, and essays and is currently finishing an original movie script. His published works include *Bootlegger Blues* (1991), *Someday* (1992), *and Voices* (1992).

Aritha van Herk teaches Creative Writing and Canadian literature at the University of Calgary. She is the author of *Judith* (1978), *The Tent Peg* (1981), *No Fixed Address* (1986), *Places Far From Ellesmere* (1990), and *Restlessness* (1998). She has also published two collections of essays and numerous articles both in scholarly and popular journals.

Christl Verduyn is chair of Canadian Studies at Trent University. She has published numerous articles on women's writing in Quebec and English Canada, and three books: *Margaret Laurence: An Appreciation* (1988), *Dear Marian, Dear Hugh: The MacLennan-Engel Correspondence* (1995), and *Lifelines: Marian Engel's Writings* (1995), which was awarded the 1995 Gabrielle Roy Book Prize (English language).

Maïr Verthuy, professeure titulaire au Département d'études français, ancienne (et première) directrice de l'Institut Simone de Beauvoir, de l'Université Concordia à Montréal, se spécialise dans l'écriture au féminin dans le monde francophone: s'intéressant au multiculturalisme et aux questions identitaires, elle travaille également les auteurs immigrants, hommes et femmes, en France et au Québec.